INVENTING THE NATION

General Editor: Keith Robbins

Ireland

Richard Vincent Comerford
Professor of Modern History,
National University of Ireland, Maynooth

A member of the Hodder Headline Group
LONDON
Co-published in the United States of America by
Oxford University Press Inc., New York

First published in Great Britain in 2003 by
Hodder Arnold, a member of the Hodder Headline Group,
338 Euston Road, London NW1 3BH

http://www.arnoldpublishers.com

Distributed in the United States of America by
Oxford University Press Inc.
198 Madison Avenue, New York, NY10016

The advice and information in this book are believed to be true and
accurate at the date of going to press, but neither the author nor the publisher
can accept any legal responsibility or liability for any errors or omissions.

British Library Cataloguing in Publication Data
A catalogue record for this book is available from the British Library

Library of Congress Cataloging-in-Publication Data
A catalog record for this book is available from the Library of Congress

ISBN 0 340 73111 7 (hb)
ISBN 0 340 73112 5 (pb)

1 2 3 4 5 6 7 8 9 10

Typeset in 10/12 pt Sabon by Phoenix Photosetting, Chatham, Kent
Printed and bound in Malta

What do you think about this book? Or any other Arnold title?
Please send your comments to feedback.arnold@hodder.co.uk

Contents

List of illustrations

General editor's preface

The contemporary world is both repelled and attracted by the existence of the nation. Talk of globalisation sometimes presumes that the nation will fade away as organisations and individuals build for themselves new networks which bypass the commonalities and loyalties expressed in the idea of the nation. Nationalism, too, whenever it is that various writers have supposed it to have 'risen', has been held to have been an unmitigated disaster, at least when it has been accompanied, as it not infrequently has been, by virulent xenophobia and intolerance. In the twentieth century there were significant attempts to restrain or circumvent the influence of nationalism by creating international or supranational structures and agencies.

On the other hand, it is apparent that the nation has not in fact faded away and, despite the surge of new nations, or at least new states, in the second half of that century, there remain across the contemporary world communities which feel themselves to be nations, or are in the process of becoming nations, and who see in the attainment of statehood a legitimate, desirable and beneficial goal. In other contexts, too, old nations reaffirm themselves as necessary carriers of individuality and distinctiveness in a world threatened by homogeneity. It is asserted that the nation remains the essential building block in the structure of the contemporary world. Nationalism need not be vicious. Nations can and do speak peace unto nations.

It becomes clear, however, reading references of 'narrow nationalism' on the one hand or 'national liberation' on the other, that how particular nations come to exist or be defined remains obscure and contentious. This series revisits these issues in the light of extensive debates about national identity which have been conducted over recent decades by historians, anthropologists, political scientists and sociologists in particular. To speak of 'Inventing the Nation' picks up one of the interpretations which has gained favour, or at least excited interest. Influential writers have seen 'invention' taking place in Europe in the 'springtime of the nations' at the dawn of 'modern' history, though their explanations have varied. Others, however, have regarded 'invention' with some suspicion and identify a medieval if not primordial 'nation'. Problems of definition and location clearly abound.

The historian who tackles these issues in relation to the island of Ireland by no means enters virgin territory. The essence of the Irish nation has been contested, sometimes bitterly and violently, over many centuries and, in the context of a politically divided island, remains in certain respects unresolved down to the present. Grand narratives, from one perspective or another, have sought to marginalize or exclude those awkward and unpalatable elements in 'the national story' which interfere with sustaining simplicities. In particular, in the long and complicated relationship between Ireland and the neighbouring structures and peoples of Great Britain, conquest and control, on the one hand, and accommodation and acceptance, on the other, have frequently been given partial and partisan emphasis by contending schools of historians. Professor Comerford needs no reminder of the political uses to which history has been put both in Ireland and in Great Britain. There are, he is well aware, perils which accompany any attempt to transcend orthodoxies which have, at one time or another, buttressed specific constitutional arrangements. It remains the case, with regard to the island of Ireland, unlike any of the other national histories so far considered in this series, that 'inventing the nation' is one thing, 'creating the state' is another. No historian can predict when, if ever, this disjuncture will end.

In adopting his rich thematic approach, however, Professor Comerford has eschewed a linear chronological framework which might presuppose that a fully formed and fixed nation has been 'settled' at a particular point in time. Rather, we witness the involved and ongoing interplay of both harmonious and percussive elements in an evolving 'national story'.

Acknowledgements

The following scholars kindly took time to read and comment on draft chapters: Dr Marie Therese Flanagan (chs 1, 2 and 3); Dr James Kelly (chs 1 and 3); Professor Kim McCone (chs 2 and 4); Dr Barra Ó Donnabháin (ch. 2); Proinsias Uasal Ó Drisceoil (ch. 4); Professor Maurice Harmon (ch. 5); Dr Barra Boydell, Dr Michael Finnegan and Mary Friel (ch. 6); Dr Fearghal McGarry, Dr Terence Dooley and Dr Brian Griffin (ch. 7); Dr Patrick Wallace (ch. 8). Professor Keith Robbins read the entire MS and offered some sage comments. I am indebted to all of them. The responsibility for remaining errors and misconceptions is entirely mine.

I am grateful to all of my academic colleagues in the history department at NUI, Maynooth for fellowship and intellectual stimulation. My debt to Ann Donoghue and Catherine Heslin for their professional office management and their unfailing patience and co-operation is immense. Since 2000 the funding of postdoctoral research fellowships by the Irish Research Council for the Humanities and Social Sciences and the National University of Ireland has enabled the department to act as host to an array of scholars, from each of whom I have learned something new: Colin Barr, Fergus Campbell, Terence Dooley, Charles Flynn, Evi Gkotzaridis, Brian Hanley, Fearghal McGarry, Moira Maguire, Clodagh Tait and David Worthington. Terry, Evi and Fergus have provided particular assistance with this project.

As head of department over a number of years I have had occasion to read the theses, minor and major, of a great many students. I take this opportunity to let the authors, and their research supervisors, know how much I appreciate, and benefit from, the privilege. Thanks to Professor Kim McCone and Dr Fearghal McGarry for the opportunity to read unpublished work. For information generously provided and for other support I thank Dr C.J. Woods, Professor Helen Mulvey, Canon John Crawford, Professor Gerard Gillen, Dr John Gilmartin, Dr Enda Delaney, Dr Louise Fuller, Ann

Matthews, Dr Ekavi Athanassopoulou, Didier Coupaye, Dr Catherine Candy, Theresa Merrigan and Brendan Graham. I have received excellent service from Maynooth library staff, benefiting in particular from the expertise and helpfulness of Mrs Penny Woods. Likewise, Eimear Quinn, Dúchas, the National Museum of Ireland and the National Gallery of Ireland provided illustrations and permissions for reproduction. Fr Gerry O'Hanlon, the Irish Jesuit provincial, generously gave permission to quote extracts from Stephen J. Brown's *Ireland in Fiction*. Jim Keenan kindly produced the map. Leo's assistance at crucial points is appreciated. My greatest debt is owed to Phil for her enduring companionship, understanding and support.

At different times I have enjoyed the hospitality and resources of the National Humanities Center, North Carolina, USA and the Princess Grace Irish Library, Monaco. I take this opportunity to acknowledge the generosity of both institutions.

I am grateful to Professor Keith Robbins, the general editor, for the invitation to contribute to the series and for his patience. At Hodder Arnold, Tiara Misquitta, Christina Wipf Perry and Lesley Riddle have been endlessly helpful.

Finally, thanks to Margaret for allowing me to dedicate this book to her. Out of the generosity of her heart, she instructed me at a tender age in both national languages, and ever since she has been a constant friend to me and mine.

For
Margaret Landy Pritchard
cara buan
sa bhaile is thar lear

A map of Ireland

Introduction

Just as preparing to circumnavigate the globe implies a negation of flat-earth theory, so the no less challenging proposition of writing on the invention of a nation implies a rejection of the essentialist view of nationality. The essentialist assumption incorporates the belief that nations are individually prescribed by nature or by some divine plan, that each has its own personality and a naturally defined (and thus obvious) membership and extent, and that each has about it some kind of informing spirit, reminiscent of the Platonic soul. That this outlook has lost its intellectual purchase is consistent with the demise in Ireland during the 1990s of the old debate, particularly noisy in the 1970s and 1980s, about the 'two nations'. The controversy was premised on the assumption that nations are individually mandated by some natural or divine law, and at issue was whether or not unionists in Northern Ireland participated in British nationhood and were thus entitled to opt out of an all-Ireland polity. Most participants in the debate, not surprisingly, came to conclusions that supported their prior political preferences: unionist sympathisers advocating the case for the presence of two nations on the island and nationalists proclaiming 'one land, one nation'. The well-disposed neutral participant might contrive a one-and-a-half nation theory.

The intellectual escape from the futility of this prescriptive approach is summarised in the title of Benedict Anderson's celebrated book, *Imagined Communities*, with its implication that the nation is a 'construct' and not a 'given'.[1] The philosophical challenge to essentialist nationalism is not new: what has changed is that this challenge is now in tune with the wider intellectual currents of the age. This is separate from the question of the practical and emotional hold of nationalism in the contemporary world: that has

---

[1]   B. Anderson, *Imagined Communities: Reflections on the Origin and Spread of Nationalism* (London and New York, 1983).

been shown in recent decades to be vigorous indeed. Political parties play as effectively as ever on the collective and socio-economic bases of nationalism (and, since we are talking about Ireland, unionism), but ideology, and the terms of political discourse, have changed. Not even the most greenly dyed of nationalist parties goes before the public flourishing the full-blooded rhetoric of old style 'natural law' nationalism, as distinct from aspirations to national unity. The hold of an ideology can be gauged by the amount of invocation of its sainted interpreters. Twenty or thirty years ago, a citation from Wolfe Tone, or Thomas Davis, or Patrick Pearse, or some other giant of the nationalist pantheon, was the most effective weapon for routing an opponent in public debate; now, such invocation is seldom heard.

If the nation cannot be convincingly explained as either a prescribed or inspired phenomenon, that is not to say that it is imagined into existence without rhyme, reason or pattern. To say that it is invented is not to suggest that the nation is for that reason less real or less meaningful. Invention can have overtones of deceit or fraud, but these are not at issue here. Neither should the concept of invention, as applied to a nation, convey a suggestion of creation from nothing, of something drawn on a blank sheet. Rather there are overtones of the Latin *invenire*, meaning 'to find' or 'to discover', for nations are defined and developed largely on the basis of what is already there. That aspect of the essentialist viewpoint has validity. What is no longer defensible in the current state of understanding is the essentialist view that 'what is already there' prescribes or determines what happens next, or what ought to happen next. Rather, what is now generally understood is that choices are continually being made, and initiatives being taken, that discard some of 'what is already there' and draw on the remainder of it in a creative manner, and, moreover, that these choices and initiatives are governed by chance and circumstances as well as by the interests and strategies of various parties. To account for what defines the nation is not, then, a matter of reporting the realisation of some immanent ideal, but of attempting to describe an ongoing process of invention. Putting the case another way, Irishness is not an essence to be identified in various emanations, but a category whose ever-changing contents need to be accounted for. The purpose of this book is to attempt such an account.

This study is indebted to scholarship in the disciplines of sociology, anthropology and political science, but it remains the work of a humanities practitioner, not that of a social scientist. Accordingly, the intention is to explore the particularity and complexity of the subject, and to see what patterns and meanings may be found therein, rather than to test, much less to elaborate, any theory. Generally speaking, historians find more meaning in apposite comparisons, where feasible, than in schematic formulae. That said, this book is also written in the understanding that the attempt to present knowledge in a systematic form is one of the obligations of scholarship. There is no intention here to emulate social scientists by elaborating or reworking definitions of key concepts such as nation, nationalism and nationality.[2] For the purposes of a humanities-style study it would be futile to attempt to deal in terms with strictly defined connotations, for the richness and fluidity of meaning of the key terms as used now and over centuries are such as to render narrow definition impossible or pointless. The challenge, in fact, is to convey changing connotations as they apply in particular sets of circumstances, and above all the changing connotations of Irishness. In an effort to avoid ambiguity and the resort to cliché, only infrequent use is made here of terms such as 'tradition(al)', 'community' and 'identity' that can be invoked all too easily to evade clarification, and that all too frequently perpetuate unexamined assumptions. No doubt, observant readers will quickly spot compensatory lexical behaviour.

Few terms cause more confusion than 'nation' and its derivatives. In the closing decades of the twentieth century the work of a celebrated group of scholars – particularly Kedourie[3], Gellner[4] and Hobsbawm[5] – established a scholarly convention whereby nationalism is deemed to be exclusively a modern phenomenon, that is to say dating no farther back than about 1780. Others, including Adrian Hastings, who points to the existence of nations in the medieval and early modern periods, have challenged this position.[6] It is important not to ignore the insights of either party.

From the late eighteenth century, most notably in the case of France in the 1790s, the nation can be seen assuming a dimension that it had not previously possessed and that has since become its hallmark. What we see, to put it briefly, is the national collectivity taking on a centrality to political life that has it transcend the claims of class, order and private bonds. This meant the mobilisation of the masses of the population, even if this was to be fully achieved only fitfully and over time. Because the ideology of the nation was laid down in the decades before and after 1800, it was deeply marked with the traits of Romanticism. Partly because of a wish to highlight the new dimensions evident from the late eighteenth century, and partly in recognition of the success with which Hobsbawm and the others have imposed their particular definition, it is my intention to use the terms 'nationalism' and 'nationalist' only with reference to the last two and a quarter centuries.

At the same time, with Hastings, I see no adequate reason to proscribe the term 'nation' with respect to the 'imagined communities' of earlier ages. By the twelfth century several populations in western Europe had already been recognised by themselves and by others as possessing a distinctive existence

---

[2] See A. Smith, *Theories of Nationalism* (London, 2nd edn., 1983) for a classic exposition.
[3] E. Kedourie, *Nationalism* (London, 1960).
[4] E. Gellner, *Nations and Nationalism* (Oxford, 1983).
[5] E. Hobsbawm, *Nations and Nationalism since 1780* (Cambridge, 1990).
[6] A. Hastings, *The Construction of Nationhood: Ethnicity, Religion and Nationalism* (Cambridge, 1997).

of enduring character, and it seems reasonable to refer to these as 'nations', always provided that certain precautions are observed. One is the recognition that the Latin word *natio* frequently occurs in medieval sources without having the connotation of 'nation' in any modern sense. Another is that no medieval nation can properly be thought of as either product or occasion of nationalism in its typical modern manifestations. But the principal caveat that has to be entered in respect of the invocation of early nationalities concerns the way in which they are routinely used to create a spurious sense of prescriptive, essential origins for current nationalisms. This is a problem that deserves further reflection.

Historians frequently remind themselves and one another of the hazards of teleology, particularly in the writing of national history. This tendency to assemble historical knowledge in the form of a narrative that leads to an ending or goal (*telos* in Greek) is a well-recognised constrictor of perspective and understanding. The goal is usually either the current state of affairs or one about to be achieved. A teleological interpretation of history is integral to the essentialist outlook, with the nation-state as the achieved or about-to-be-achieved goal. This is thoroughly exemplified in the case of Ireland, not only in nationalist propaganda but also in much scholarly historiography. Closely related but less well recognised, and therefore even more insidious, is the habit of mind which sees modern nations predestined in ancient and medieval societies or cultures. Thus, in most conceptualisations of Ireland, popular and scholarly, there looms an 'ancient Gaelic world' seen as the modern Irish nation in embryo. Recognising that a nation is an 'imagined community' should bring also the recognition that the imagining typically runs wildly forward and backward to create a timeless 'communion of saints', inculcating the notion that the contemporary national collectivity is in moral continuity with earlier national collectivities. Hastings' disavowal of this kind of 'primordialism' is less than decisive and does little to warn against the perils of assuming an organic link between ancient cultures and modern nationalities[7], perils recently highlighted by the medievalist, Patrick J. Geary.[8] By taking Irishness as a category of constantly changing content, as it is proposed to do here, one can allow for the continuities with the past, while at the same time demonstrating the contingent and non-organic character of such continuity.

The same later twentieth-century philosophies that undermined the essentialist understanding of the nation have also shaken the confident, positivist epistemology formerly common to the physical and social sciences and the humanities. The assurance that once permitted the opposing of myth to reality is no longer supportable. Myth is part of reality. 'Myth', as it is used in the following chapters, connotes an account or event, whether factual or fic-

---

[7]   Ibid., pp. 11–12.
[8]   P.J. Geary, *The Myth of Nations: The Medieval Origins of Europe* (Princeton, 2002).

titious, that has been accorded heightened emotional or interpretational significance. In this sense, the Battle of the Boyne in 1690 and the Rebellion of 1798 are both mythic events, while also being of empirically verifiable historical authenticity. One of the main challenges for the historian is to identify and discount the impact of myth-making on the understanding of such episodes. But the whys and wherefores of 1690 and 1798, as of every other aspect of the past, are open to endless revision, and few historians now think in terms of definitive interpretations. Even so, there are interpretations that are downright insupportable, while of the rest some are better founded and more convincing than others. History as a discipline is grounded in the appreciation of specific human experience as recoverable, however partially, through empirical investigation of the past. Like other disciplines, it makes progress by finding new questions to ask of the evidence, whether new or old.

The fact that English imposition on Ireland has included several phases of colonisation, and several variants on domination, might seem to suggest the utility for the Irish case of colonial (and postcolonial) theory, as elaborated for the analysis of the experience of societies outside Europe. In fact, many scholars in other disciplines find it useful (some would scarcely consider formulating the title of an article on any aspect of Irish life, past or present, without the words 'colony' or 'colonial/postcolonial'), but not so many historians do.[9] Colonial theory is an example of a system of archetypal thinking, which can serve with perfect validity the purposes of some social science and literature studies. But archetypes (such as nation, colony, class, empire, exploitation or subordination) are only starting points in that search for delight and meaning in the specificity of human experience that motivates most writers and readers in the discipline of history. The discussion that occasionally flares on the question of whether Ireland has sufficient colonial/postcolonial credentials to qualify it for analysis by colonial theory misses the point and risks a confusion of enterprises. The relevant question is this: Is colonial theory an adequate intellectual tool for the task in hand? For some the answer will be yes, but for most historians of Ireland most of the time the answer is in the negative. This does not mean at all that historians cannot, using their customary methods, explore parallels (and linkages), say, between Ireland and India in the nineteenth and twentieth centuries.

Collectivities imagine nothing as readily as common ancestry, and a study of any nationality has to identify the role of ideas about descent. Common usage is rife with assumptions in this area, as typified by the role of surnames, which have been in general use in Ireland since the tenth century. Presuming that the parentage of individuals is what it appears to be, a sur-

---

[9] See Stephen Howe, *Ireland and Empire: Colonial Legacies in Irish History and Culture* (Oxford, 2000) for an illuminating survey.

name at birth is evidence of descent through the male line. Since most societies have taboos to discourage inbreeding, an individual generally has eight
great-grandparents, and only one of these is represented by the great-grand-
child's surname. Accordingly, to possess an 'Irish' surname (many, though
by no means all, of which in modern Anglicised form begin with 'Mac', 'Mc'
or 'O') is of itself evidence of only limited 'Irish' ancestry, since it represents
only a fraction of the individual's genetic inheritance. But, of course, there
is no such thing as pure Irish (or English or French or Italian) racial descent,
just as there is no more misleading illusion created by the nation than that
of every country possessing a distinct racial 'stock' with no more than a little blurring at the edges.

In fact, the recounting of Irish history is replete with assumptions about
ancestry, and even in most scholarly essays the identification of presumed
ancestry is a paramount consideration. This is justified insofar as presumed
descent is a factor in how historical actors see themselves and are seen by
others, but it can have the effect of inculcating unjustified assumptions
about actual ancestry and widespread misapprehensions about racial origins. Racist ideas ascribing innate qualities (or disqualifications) on the basis
of presumed descent have been a factor in Irish history, but far more prevalent and enduring has been the racialist mindset that assigns people to racial
groupings without necessarily implying innate characterisation. Notions of
Irish origins over the centuries and their relationship to recoverable actual-
ity are dealt with in chapter two.

If most racial categorisation is devoid of racist intent, it much more frequently does have implications of cultural difference. Advocates of essentialist nationality can invoke national culture as if it were an entity with a
life of its own, entitled to command loyalty and allegiance. In such a usage,
culture is synonymous with the prescriptive 'spirit' of the nation, and with
the influential ideas of the late eighteenth century German philosopher,
Herder. Well in advance of the deification of culture by one school of twentieth-century anthropologists, 'Irish culture' was being used as a stick with
which to beat various forms of dissent into submission. Kenan Malik has
highlighted how in the late twentieth century culture had come in some
quarters to be used as a proxy for the disgraced notion of race.[10] Similarly,
some practitioners of Irish studies utilise a Herderian concept of culture to
reintroduce essentialist nationality by the back door. Culture is used
throughout this book in a number of senses, which hopefully will be clear in
each case, but never with overtones of immanence. For the purposes of this
study the most important manifestations of culture are religion and language, which are examined in separate chapters.

In the general usage of social scientists, collectivities, marked out from

---

[10] Kenan Malik, *The Meaning of Race: Race, History and Culture in Western Society*
(London, 1996).

their neighbours by religious or linguistic distinctiveness are referred to as ethnic groups. Acknowledged collective cultural distinctiveness, 'ethnicity' if one wishes to use the term – is one of the components most frequently involved in the concoction of nationality. In the Irish case, an island-wide ethnicity based on language is in evidence from the middle of the first millennium AD. If Ireland was ever mono-ethnic it has not been so since the Scandinavian Vikings began to form settlements at Dublin and elsewhere in the ninth century AD. Since the twelfth century, Ireland has been a theatre of ethnic rivalry. While for much of that period the terms 'Irish' and 'English' might be applied to the rival cultures, it is of the most vital importance to realise that the connotations of each of these descriptors, as well as the issues in contention, have varied enormously over the ages. In the twelfth and thirteenth centuries, language was the signifier of a wide range of differences, including dress and other social customs, agrarian practices and political systems. But, making due allowance for differences of social class, populations living side by side over an extended period can be expected to hybridise their cultures, even if they retain distinguishing marks such as different religions. Indeed, the level of rivalry or animosity between collectivities of any kind is seldom in direct proportion to the amount of difference between them. Down the ages, commentators on Irish matters, as different as the sixteenth-century English poet and adventurer in Ireland, Edmund Spenser,[11] the early twentieth-century Irish revivalist, Daniel Corkery[12] and the later historian, F.S.L. Lyons[13] have on occasion tended to magnify cultural differences in order to rationalise wide political gulfs and conflicting interests. In the hyperbole of such discourse, culture is regularly further magnified into 'civilisation'.

Ethnicity without reference to the structures of power would not go very far in explaining the emergence of any nationality. Thus, the link, such as it is, between modern Irish nationality and early Christian Ireland is provided not by the immanent culture beloved of literary and linguistic revivalists holding forth about ageless traditions, but by political structures. Scholarly discourse on the Irish state is somewhat limited. When Emmet Larkin in 1975 argued that 'Parnell created the modern Irish state'[14] between 1879 and 1886, there was widespread amazement at his temerity in placing the event in advance of independence in the early 1920s, but very little objection on the rather more serious grounds that Ireland had had centuries of experience of the state before the late nineteenth century. Larkin was correct in his own terms, for what he intended by the 'state' was the combination of political forces and economic interests that dominated the Irish Free State

---

11   *A View of the Present State of Ireland* (1596).
12   *The Hidden Ireland* (1924).
13   *Culture and Anarchy in Ireland* (1979).
14   E. Larkin, 'Church, state and nation in modern Ireland' in *American Historical Review*, lxxx, no. 5 (Dec. 1975), p. 1263.

after 1921, namely nationalist politicians, the Catholic clergy and the farmers. But Ireland has had a fully fledged state since early modern times, with
a definite basis in the twelfth century and a significantly distinctive polity for
centuries beforehand. These facts are recognised in at least one relatively
recent study in political science.[15] A pioneering work in the area of science
studies has identified the significance of state-promoted projects in the fashioning of early modern Ireland.[16]

However, the justifiable identification of the state with English domination has discouraged more widespread interest in its analysis. Popular local
resistance to the intrusion of state authority and state-mandated socio-economic order is a widespread feature of early modern societies. However, the
activities of Irish agrarian secret societies, such as the Whiteboys, in the second half of the eighteenth century, have frequently been read as expressions
of nationalist antipathy to English rule. But they may in fact have as much
to do with the history of the state as of the nation: in rural France in the
same era, tax-gathering agents of the *Fermiers Généraux* were regularly left
for dead in ditches by *paysans* who had no nationalist axe to grind but who
resented the impositions of the state. The classic critique of Dublin Castle,
the actual and symbolic locus of state power in Ireland from the twelfth century until 1922, can attribute its iniquities to English domination, so that
the author is freed from the challenge of dealing with the problems of state
power per se.[17] The fact is that much of what characterises Irish national
distinctiveness, from the legal system to local administrative divisions and
the primary education system, is the handiwork of the State over centuries.

Because the homogenisation and standardisation that typify modern society have occurred primarily at national level, these developments are generally attributed to (modern) nationalism. In fact, from medieval times
nationality has implied the adoption of standards, albeit only over limited
areas of life, and particularly the important one of language of administration. One of the principal reasons why the nation is seen to be of so much
greater significance from the 1790s onwards is that the amount of standardising and homogenising of society began to increase dramatically from that
time, most evidently in projects such as national military conscription and
universal primary schooling. The successful functioning of a modern society
depends on the standardisation of everything from the specifications of elec-
trical fuse boxes to the spelling of the national language. Most of this work
of homogenisation and standardisation attributed to the nation and 'nationalism' is in fact the achievement of the state. This elision is well exemplified

[15] G.M. MacMillan, *State, Society and Authority in Ireland: The Foundations of the Modern
      State* (Dublin, 1993).
[16] P.E. Carroll, 'Engineering Ireland: the material constitution of the technoscientific state'
      (Ph.D. dissertation, University of California, San Diego, 1999).
[17] R.B. O'Brien, *Dublin Castle and the Irish People* (London, 1909). Several more recent
      scholarly works are focused on the anticipation of Irish control at the castle.

by Liah Greenfeld's *Nationalism: Five Roads to Modernity,* a book frequently cited as a rehabilitation of nationalism.[18] But Greenfeld's 'nationalism' is, in fact, the supportive ideology of the modernising State, various
examples of which she identifies as nations. What is being celebrated is the
facilitation by certain states of modern commercial and industrial production.

Just as the nationality of individuals in the narrow legal sense represented
by the entry in a passport is a mechanism for controlling movement between
states, so too nationality in the wider sense is deeply concerned with the ideological justification of both the movement and settlement of populations.
Throughout their history, humans have been on the move, whether as entire
migrating populations, or as population segments or assorted individuals
hiving off to new destinations. Numerous nations have myths that acknowledge migratory origins, however inaccurately. The Irish case is examined in
chapter two. Various historic Irish migrations have been heavily mytholo-
gised in the context of nationality, including missionary endeavours in
Europe in the early medieval era, Catholic migration to Europe in the early
modern period, and emigration to the United States of America during and
after the Great Famine of the late 1840s. Participants in each of these movements have contributed significantly to the invention of the Irish nation. A
mythic character also attaches to the eighteenth-century emigration of
Presbyterians from Ulster to the British colonies in North America. Other
episodes of emigration from Ireland are not subject to the same measure of
highlighting, and scholarship has achieved a more balanced coverage than
have the mythmakers.[19]

Much of the rhetoric of nationality is concerned with justifying possession of the land. For this purpose, the migration of the chosen people can be
glorified, or alternatively the relevant mythic motif may be that of native
occupants in immemorial possession. In the Irish case, the myth of migratory origins sits side by side in silent contradiction to that of the indigenous
people, which in turn is explicitly juxtaposed with the myth of the alien settlers. Nationality has provided, in the antinomies of native and newcomer,
the most widely accepted, if not the most informative, of keys to the struggle for control of the land that has been an enduring constant of Irish life for
many centuries past. As with the Magyars, the Poles and the French, so too
in modern Ireland, the lords of the soil were supposed to be of different
stock from the rest of the population. In the 1880s, the Irish nation was re-
imagined so as to exclude them.

Some generations before the emergence of pseudo-scientific racial
theories, certain eighteenth-century philosophers gave much credence to the

---

[18] L. Greenfeld, *Nationalism: Five Roads to Modernity* (Cambridge, MA, 1992).
[19] D.H. Akenson, *The Irish Diaspora: a Primer* (Toronto and Belfast, 1993) provides a geographically comprehensive overview with reference to recent centuries. More racy is T.P.
Coogan, *Wherever Green Is Worn: the Story of the Irish Diaspora* (London, 2000).

concept of national character, linking it to climate and other geographical determinants. By the middle of the following century, moral differences of various kinds were being ascribed not to geography but to race. Irish character came to be discerned as 'Celtic', and the identification remains. So, while popular stereotyping has German trains running on time, Scandinavian taxpayers queuing up to pay their dues and French people universally preoccupied with *la nourriture*, it depicts the Irish as playful, soulful entertainers, who are not overly concerned with the nuts and bolts of ordinary existence. In certain contexts, 'Irish' has some less than complimentary connotations such as 'far-fetched', but in general those Irish people who think of such things are content to exploit the positive aspects of the stereotype. There may indeed be some distinctive national characteristics but, if so, they are based on culture rather than nature, and the weight of national culture, such as it is, can be overestimated. For instance, if, as seems evident, Ireland in many parts is a very litter-strewn country, that does not reflect any innate characteristic, 'Celtic' or other. Some towns, North and South, are spotless. And if the explanation for untidiness does lie in some aspect of 'national culture', it may be nothing more profound than an administrative slackness in the enforcement of certain laws.

The 'Celtic' stereotyping of the Irish finds concrete expression in the Irish pub. The last two decades of the twentieth century witnessed the mushrooming of this invention around the globe, wherever international commercialism had a foothold. The Irish pub is an astute variation on the English pub that had been marketed abroad earlier with less success, adding the attractive element of 'Celticity', which amounts in effect to the promise of music, singing and general drollery conveyed by the Gaelic word *craic*. In fact, many of the earnest young men and women of the Irish revolution at the beginning of the twentieth century perceived drink and public houses as a menace to the welfare and morale of the nation. Two decades of campaigning by such people bore fruit in 1924 when the Intoxicating Liquor Act passed by the parliament of the newly independent state decreed that all public houses remain closed on the national holiday, St Patrick's Day. The apotheosis of the pub as the shrine of Irishness half a century later serves as a reminder that nationality is invented not only by those politically motivated or those creatively inspired, but also by commercial interests exploiting the market place.

Commercialised entertainment, rather than politics, literature or public service, has provided the two Irish celebrities best known around the world at the dawn of the twenty-first century. Although the two in question, the footballer Roy Keane and the rock-band leader Bono, are known as Irish, what they do is scarcely distinctively Irish, even if they are thought of as bringing something 'Irish' to it. In the same way, Pope John Paul II, the greatest Polish celebrity of the age, may be thought of as bringing some supposedly Polish attitudes to the papacy, but there is nothing distinctively

Polish about being pope. In discussing Irishness as a category, it is useful and interesting to recognise that some of the contents are nation-specific while others are localised portions of cosmopolitan things. This distinction is used particularly in the chapters 'Music, song and dance', 'Sport' and 'Artefacts', and it is also of relevance to the chapters on language and literature.

Nothing in this book is likely to satisfy a reader anticipating proof of Irish exceptionalism, unless an invitation to convert gives satisfaction. Likely to be disappointed are not only those expecting evidence of 'Paddy's' incorrigibility, but also Irish people searching for marks of inherent distinctive quality on the basis of which to preen themselves. (The two groups may partially overlap.) A distinction is to be drawn, however, between exceptionalism and uniqueness. Every nation is unique, and this book attempts to provide an account of a unique, long-established and ever-changing nationality that is the basis of a vibrant modern nationalism and that has provided the imaginative and ideological title deeds of one of the almost two hundred members of the United Nations organisation.

The combination of myth and ideology that goes into the imagining of a nation is not a coherent totality. Consequently, while this book strives for systematic exposition, what it attempts to describe is very far from being a consistent or coherent system of ideas. The concepts, thoughts and emotions that sustain political stances are seldom coherent for individuals and never for collectivities, even at any one time. For instance, the notion of an Irish race has for long co-existed, frequently within the same heads, with the idea of a nation formed without reference to race. Similarly, in respect of religion, language and many less central factors, the posited relationship to nationality is frequently inconsistent even in the thought of a single individual.

In any event, political life in the past, as in the present, was driven not by ideas but by interests, not excluding, of course, interest groups ostensibly cemented by ideology. Collectivities guided by elites and individuals contend for hegemony in a complex power game in which ideology is only one weapon among many. One of the principal functions of the nation is to provide a defined arena for political contention, and by this criterion, as by others, Ireland is indeed an ancient nation. Chapter one ('Polities') provides a framework within which the matters in subsequent chapters can be located, but a study such as this cannot attempt to deal in any detail with the fascinating complexity of Irish political history, much of it propounded in terms of nationality, that is the subject matter of so many books.

A book like this, while it may attempt to be systematic, cannot aspire to anything remotely resembling completeness of coverage of the subject. A circumnavigation, by following one route, misses out on others. Another author, or the same author at another time, would doubtless choose to call at different ports. The most important thing is to complete the journey. Even in respect of the limited list of sites visited, disclaimers are in order. Most areas of the history of Ireland have benefited from several generations of intensive scholarly attention in the course of the twentieth century, so that only specialists can hope to have access to all the nuances and details of the current state of knowledge. Accordingly, an overview such as is attempted here runs a very high risk – despite the author's best efforts – of not doing justice to the achievements of experts in various fields. I can only beg the indulgence of those whose insights I may have missed or misunderstood.

Ireland is not alone in having some enduring anomalies of nomenclature. The Government of Ireland Act of 1920 divided the country into two polities, Northern Ireland and Southern Ireland. In 1922, the latter became the Irish Free State. Under the 1937 Constitution, the name of the independent state, in English, is Ireland, which is also the common name for the entire island and could, before the constitutional changes arising from the Belfast Agreement, be interpreted as implying a territorial claim on Northern Ireland. By an act of 1948, the state may also be described as the 'Republic of Ireland'. The name of the state in Irish is 'Éire' according to the constitution, a usage reflected on coins and stamps and other official items. However, the use of 'Éire' in an English-language context – for instance by English tabloid newspapers – was for long resented, as amounting to a refusal to employ the term 'Ireland'. To use a name for the southern state when writing in English other than 'Ireland' or 'the Republic of Ireland' (such as the 'Twenty Six Counties', or the 'Free State', or 'Éire'), is a refusal of respect. There is a similar refusal of respect involved in using any name other than 'Northern Ireland' for the northern polity, except that unionists would not be offended by 'Ulster', the use of which, however, has no basis in law and is not justified geographically, since the province of Ulster consists of nine counties. Nationalists for a long time used the term 'six counties' as a device to avoid the official name. The much reduced number who still refuse to use the name 'Northern Ireland' now sometimes resort to 'North of Ireland' or ' the north of Ireland'. Besides involving a refusal of respect and having no legal or constitutional basis, these are geographically inaccurate, since the most northerly part of Ireland, the Inishowen peninsula, is in County Donegal and so is part of the Republic. Informally, terms such as 'the North', 'the South' and 'the Republic' provide inoffensive synonyms for the more formal terms.

Although the term 'British Isles' has a basis of considerable antiquity, it has long posed a problem for many Irish nationalists as implying a concession of political and/or cultural unity of the archipelago. At the same time, the desirability of a geographical term for the islands is pressing, and proposed value-free alternatives, such as the 'Atlantic Archipelago' or the 'Islands of the North Atlantic' have not attracted much support. In recent years, the term 'British Isles' has come to be used ever more freely by Irish people, a sure sign of the shedding of hegemonic overtones.

In respect of personal names, Irish historiography has particular problems arising from the country's linguistic history. Should the eighth Earl of Kildare be referred to by his English name, Gerald; the Gaelic version of that, Gearóid; or, the Anglicised version of the latter, Garrett? Issues about the standardisation of Gaelic orthography add a further layer of difficulty. The series, A New History of Ireland,[20] has endeavoured to establish standard usages, which are also to be found in the *Oxford Companion to Irish History*.[21] In respect of the twentieth century, there is the added complication of individuals who adopt Gaelic versions of originally English or Anglicised names. Thus, John MacNeill became Eoin Mac Néill, but is generally known as Eoin MacNeill. In this book I have generally used the versions best known to the reading public, thus, Brian Boru rather than Brian Bóruma or Brian Boirimhe, Dermot MacMurrough rather than Diarmait Mac Murchada, and Patrick Pearse rather than Pádraig Mac Piarais.[22]

---

[20] See the section entitled 'Further reading', p. 268.

[21] Ed. by Sean Connolly (2nd edn., 2002).

[22] The many works relating to Ireland that discuss issues raised here include R.F. Foster, *The Irish Story: Telling Tales and Making it up in Ireland* (London, 2001); P. Maume, *The Long Gestation: Irish Nationalist Life, 1891–1918* (Dublin, 1999); D. Pringle, *One Island, Two Nations? A Political Geographical Analysis of the National Conflict in Ireland* (New York, 1985); P. O'Farrell, *England and Ireland Since 1800* (Oxford, 1975); C.C. O'Brien, *States of Ireland* (London, 1972); D. Cairns and S. Richards, *Writing Ireland: Colonialism, Nationalism and Culture* (Manchester, 1988); H. Kearney, *The British Isles: a History of Four Nations* (Cambridge, 1989); E. Malcolm, *Ireland Sober, Ireland Free: Drink and Temperance in Nineteenth-Century Ireland* (Dublin, 1986).

1

Polities

The concept of Ireland as a distinct political entity – a 'country' in what is perhaps the principal meaning of that word – is fundamental to Irish nationality. The instinct that longs for territorial integrity can be a powerful element in national self-awareness, particularly when the territory has the clear definition of an island. However, not every island is one country: Hispaniola, New Guinea, Borneo and Timor are not, and, if Britain is one, that has been the case only since 1707. So, the fact that the island of Ireland has been recognised as a single political entity through most of its recorded history should not be seen as an inevitability. By the same token, Ireland with Britain constitutes an archipelago which, as in the cases of Japan, the Philippines, Indonesia and New Zealand, might have come to constitute the single home country of all its inhabitants. The emergence within the archipelago of four recognised countries, three of them on the island of Britain (England, Wales and Scotland), had come to pass by the middle of the twelfth century, although the English-Scottish and English-Welsh boundaries would not be finally decided for centuries. This outcome reflected a combination of factors, including physical geography, culture, power and ideology. A different conjuncture of these factors might have produced a different outcome. For instance, while culture was a major factor in the definition of Irish identity (as discussed in more detail in chapter four), if it had been the only determinant, the Irish polity would have extended beyond the island to include much of the west of Scotland. Part of what became Wales might have been included if Irish settlements there in the wake of the fifth-century collapse of Roman power in Britain had endured.

Geographically, Ireland enjoyed a level of cohesiveness significantly greater than that of Britain, yet conquest or invasion at particular times might have led to the division of the island or its incorporation into a larger entity. As it happened, Ireland, unlike most of the larger island, had not been part of the Roman Empire. Throughout the historical period and down to the middle of the twelfth century the only major intrusion of outside power had been that of the Scandinavian Vikings, which had culminated in the creation of coastal trading towns – Dublin, Wexford, Waterford, Cork, Limerick – rather than large-scale territorial occupation. And political conflict within Ireland, though highly factious, was driven largely by ambitions of achieving unified control of the island. In fact, the idea of the island of Ireland as a distinct political entity was well established by the twelfth century, and the central medieval mental map of an archipelago of four countries has proved to be enduring.

We are not considering four national essences with an ineluctable claim to an enduring place in the unfolding of history, but four polities, produced by a particular conjuncture of circumstances, that gained sufficient acceptance to become established as permanent structures. The fact that they have survived does not prove that their survival was inevitable. But, in surviving, each provided a focus for a distinctive and ever-changing nationality. Culture, mainly as associated with language, was an element in the distinctiveness of each of the four countries in the twelfth century, and political distinction would facilitate distinctive cultural developments. The belief that the nation lives through the ages, informed by the same indefeasible, characteristic culture is a fundamental tenet of modern essentialist nationalism, assiduously propagated and widely imbided. This powerful myth employs a static concept of culture that is at variance with observable data: culture is in constant flux and what survives over time is a matter of contingency, and that which survives is transformed. While culture contributed to the definition of these nationalities, at all stages the cultures have been in constant flux. Far from being expressions of some enduring essence, modern Irish, Scottish and Welsh nationalities are, above all, products of the circumstances of the political entities within which they have developed.

The identification of four emergent polities in the mid-twelfth century needs to be balanced by two caveats in particular. Firstly, inter-country boundaries had next to no impact on daily life and commerce, nor on popular awareness, nor indeed on the exercise of local power, such as would apply in later ages. For centuries to come, the north of Ireland and the west of Scotland would continue to have more in common with each other than either had with Dublin or Edinburgh. There were no post boxes and no national colours in which they might be painted.

Secondly, while the fourfold division of the islands reflected the balance of factors already referred to, this balance was under threat from the beginning because of the unequal strength of the four polities. From the tenth century much of England had enjoyed many of the advantages of a unitary state, and this situation was, if anything, enhanced when, in 1066, a Norman elite under William the Conqueror established itself at the apex of

Figure 1.1 Newgrange tumulus, County Meath (photograph courtesy of Dúchas: the Heritage Service). The mound with passageway and tomb is estimated to date from shortly before 3000 BC. The passageway, leading from the central opening, is aligned to the rising sun at the winter solstice. The white quartz façade is a twentieth-century conjectural reconstruction using fallen stones uncovered on the site.

English ruling structures.[1] The desire for security and the other attractions of expanded power drove the English state and some of its population to a centuries-long policy of subordination of its neighbours, both in the archipelago and on the continent. Ultimately this led to a remarkable exercise in territorial, economic and cultural expansion on the world stage – the British Empire – in which considerable numbers of Scots, Welsh and Irish would participate. In addition to its head start in terms of political organisation, England benefited, by comparison with its three neighbours on the archipelago, from a larger share of factors favouring economic prosperity, such as productive land, mineral wealth and proximity to the European mainland. England had an urban infrastructure going back to Roman times that would always be denser than the urban systems of the other three. The dominance in terms of population enjoyed by England in our own times – with about eighty per cent of the population of the archipelago on just over forty per cent of the land surface area – was not always so pronounced. And the island of Ireland with just over one quarter of the land surface area of the two islands combined, and currently with less than ten per cent of the population, was not always so relatively low in numbers: indeed around 1800 the population of Ireland is reckoned to have been half that of Britain. Nevertheless, throughout the past millennium, England was at all times both the most populous and the wealthiest of the four nations.

English expansionism, based as it was on superior resources, was never devoid of theoretical justification. Kings of England from the tenth century, or so it would be alleged on behalf of some of their successors, claimed to possess an imperial crown, meaning that their remit extended to the entire island of Britain and possibly also to Ireland. The particular ambiguity of 'Britain' is in evidence from quite early in the second millennium: politically neutral geographical expression or hegemonic 'England' writ large? That English power would not have engaged with Ireland is scarcely conceivable, but the character of that engagement was largely dependent on the fortuitous circumstances in which it occurred, and chief among these was the internal disposition of power in Ireland.

By and large, English imposition on Ireland and Scotland has not involved serious attempts to abolish them as polities. One of the concerns of this chapter will be to identify those phases of history in which English policy attempted to assimilate Ireland to England. But such aspirations usually referred to cultural matters: in general, English rulers intended not to assimilate Ireland into an English polity but to integrate it safely into a congeries of polities dominated by England.

The main sources for the history of early medieval Ireland are the

---

[1] J. Campbell, 'The United Kingdom of England: the Anglo-Saxon achievement' in A. Grant and K.J. Stringer (eds), *Uniting the Kingdom? The Enigma of British History* (London, 1995), pp. 31–47.

unwieldy but voluminous fragments of a literary culture in Latin and the vernacular. Few European societies are so well documented for the centuries after the fall of the Roman Empire. Little of this material dates from earlier than the seventh century and much of it survived only as transcribed and redacted, and sometimes reworked to a purpose, in later centuries down to the twelfth and even beyond. The evidence thus available is rich but exceptionally challenging. Interpreting it in modern times has been the task of a group of distinguished, but numerically few, scholars, beginning with Eoin MacNeill (1867–1945). They are limited in number by a formidable linguistic barrier: a working knowledge of Old Irish is not easily acquired. The twentieth century saw knowledge of early Irish history placed on a scholarly footing, but examination of the evidence has not always yielded easy and generally agreed answers about the structures and deployment of power. The result has been that some basic issues are still subjects of contention and are likely so to remain at least until a large body of under-utilised material has been more fully explored.[2]

As it came into the light of documented history just after the middle of the first millennium AD, political power in Ireland was divided between scores of dominant dynasties whose heads (each called a *rí*, or king) ruled over more or less diminutive territories (each called a *tuath*), the boundaries of which were subject to considerable change over time. While these petty rulers may have enjoyed the trappings of an archaic sacral kingship, it was losing its significance. Just as elsewhere in Europe at the time, succession was not by primogeniture but was notionally a matter of election from among members of the ruling dynasty. In practice, 'succession was determined by family power politics: the strong succeeded, the weak went to the wall'.[3] Similarly, differential power affected the relationship between rulers. At no time known to history were all these kings equal and independent. The political map of Ireland was constantly being altered with the fragmentation of dynasties, the contraction of the old and the arrival of the new. Within the *tuath*, the dynasts ruled over a socially and economically stratified and genetically diverse population of agriculturalists. That ruler and ruled were bound by a blood relationship is a misapprehension sometimes caused by the use of the term 'tribe' to translate *tuath*. ('Clan' is an alternative, but it has the disadvantage of suggesting the imaginative world of the novelist Walter Scott.) An established pattern of a small number of powerful kings exercising a wide suzerainty over other kings (who themselves might hold still weaker kings in tribute) was reflected in the concept of provinces. The Irish word for province literally means a fifth, but the division of the island was neither comprehensive nor stable, and not too much substance should be accorded to the canonical fivefold division into Leinster, Munster,

---

[2]   See C. Etchingham, 'Early Irish history' in K. McCone and K. Simms (eds), *Progress in Medieval Irish Studies* (Maynooth, 1996), pp. 123–53.

[3]   D. Ó Corráin, *Ireland before the Normans* (Dublin, 1972), p. 39.

Connacht, Ulster and Meath, the first four of which provide the names of the modern provincial divisions.

Customary norms of Irish society, covering everything from the rights of kings to the rules governing the division of property, were written down in the seventh and eighth centuries.[4] Thus was created a corpus of fascinating, if formidable, content referred to in later times as the Brehon laws (from *brethem*, the word for a judge). In the caste-like social organisation of the time the judges, as guardians and interpreters of the laws, became a hereditary privileged group. Analogies with later legal practice may not hold up. A *brethem* was more like an arbitrator bringing authority and precedent to bear on the resolution of disputes than the agent of a system of royal justice. His laws were customary, not the products of a definite act of authority by a ruler.

Contrary to a belief held widely and over many centuries, there is no basis for thinking that ancient Ireland was a realm ruled over from time immemorial by 'high-kings' seated at Tara, or anywhere else. Indeed the Brehon laws barely presumed a king of Ireland to exist.[5] Yet, even as they were being set down, the beginnings of kingship of Ireland were emerging. The impetus came from the Uí Néill, a dynasty associated with the northern and western provinces, various branches of which controlled much of the northern half of the country from the seventh to the eleventh centuries. They purported to justify their expansionism by laying claim to an island-wide kingship for which the term *rí Érenn* ('king of Ireland') came into use. This institution is referred to in the conventions of modern scholarship as the high kingship. From early on, the Uí Néill had scholarly, which is to say clerical, collaborators. The Christianised learned classes had interests and perspectives that transcended the petty kingdoms and the provinces. In the Old Testament they had the model of a people of several tribes with a central kingship. If Israel had a king, why not Ireland? But there was more involved than emulation of the chosen people, for the church of Armagh saw in an alliance with the rising Uí Néill the opportunity to establish its own primacy over other churches throughout the land. In due course, propagandist scholars projected the origins of the high-kingship into a remote past and conjured up a succession list, given colour by names such as Conn of the Hundred Battles, Niall of the Nine Hostages and Cormac Mac Airt.

At the heart of this myth was Tara (see illustration p. 20). Here on a ridge (which becomes a hill in popular and patriotic usage) set in the richest of land, with an extensive view in all directions over the flat midlands of Ireland, is a site with a mound and earthworks, most of which were already

---

[4]   F. Kelly, *A Guide to Early Irish Law* (Dublin, 1988); L. Breathnach, 'Law' in McCone and Simms (eds), *Progress in Medieval Studies*, pp. 107–21.
[5]   Kelly, *Guide*, p. 18; see F.J. Byrne, *Irish Kings and High Kings* (London, 1973), p. 254 and Etchingham, as above, pp. 131–2.

Figure 1.2 Hill of Tara, County Meath from the air (photograph courtesy of Dúchas: the Heritage Service). The remains date from various periods. Tara was never the site of the medieval royal halls imagined by some in modern times.

abandoned ancient monuments by the seventh century AD. Given the mystique of the remains and the majesty of the location it is not surprising that Tara featured prominently in legend as a place with sacral associations. Such was its status that from the seventh century the propagandists of the high-kings identified Tara as the seat of the imaginary ancient kingship of Ireland, and the high-kings accordingly described themselves as the kings of Tara. This did not mean that they ruled from there, much less that they made it the location of banqueting halls, thrones, royal chambers and the other legendary accoutrements of monarchy in imaginative modern depictions. Tara was the symbol, but not the seat, of the kingship of Ireland. The closest historically attested approximation to the exercise of royal authority there was an annual week-long assembly presided over by the king of Tara at nearby Tailtiu (the *oenach Tailten*) that was accompanied by games and athletic contests and had a fitful existence over centuries.

In the course of the ninth and tenth centuries, a succession of Uí Néill leaders vindicated the claims of the high-kingship by displaying the capacity to exercise coercive power throughout the island. The institution entered a new phase around AD 1000 when Brian Boru of the Dál Cais, king of Cashel, having established himself as the dominant power in the southern half of the country, advanced his influence northwards and reduced the Uí Néill and others to submission. Brian's emergence as High-king was sealed with an endorsement by the church of Armagh, which he visited in 1005 bearing a gift of twenty ounces of gold. A solemn record of his visit describes him not simply as king of Ireland but as *imperator Scottorum* ('emperor of the Irish').[6]

When the king of Leinster and the Scandinavian town of Dublin, lynchpins in his system of alliances, sought to renege on their commitments to Brian, he engaged them and allies of theirs from the Isle of Man and other foreign parts in battle outside the city of Clontarf in 1014. While his forces were victorious, Brian himself was killed. The Battle of Clontarf assumed symbolic status in subsequent Irish history as effecting the expulsion of the invader from the soil of Ireland. This purposeful exaggeration (Brian had no interest in expelling the Scandinavians of Dublin, he simply wished to dominate them) was invented just a century later in a propagandist historical work, *Cogadh Gaedhel re Gallaibh* ('The war of the Gael against the foreigner'), produced for the benefit of Brian Boru's great-grandson. This is of particular interest as evidence for the development by the early twelfth century of a consciousness of Ireland as a distinct political entity to be defended against outsiders, in other words of a sense of nationality. Several instances have been cited from the Gaelic annals (another genre practised by the learned classes and a source of great importance for medieval Irish history) of the use in the twelfth century of the term *fir Érenn* ('the men of Ireland')

---

6   A. Gwynn, 'Brian in Armagh, 1005' in *Seanchas Ardmhacha*, vol. 9 (1978–9), pp. 35–50.

with reference to the followers of prominent kings.[7] There is of course no reason to infer that the outlook of political and scholarly elites extended to the consciousness of the populace at large.

The purpose of *Cogadh Gaedhel re Gallaibh* was to assist Brian Boru's descendant in his own quest for power. For centuries, the Uí Néill had fought among themselves for the title of high-king, and some of them had gained it: the career of Brian Boru had revealed that anyone with a sufficient power base might aspire to that achievement. Over the following century and a half, the leaders of a handful of powerful kingdoms contended for supremacy throughout the land. At the same time, Irish kingship followed the trends of its contemporary equivalents on the continent. Irish kings imposed laws, raised taxes, made grants of land, recognised the strategic importance of towns and of the Church, appointed royal officials and developed the latest methods of warfare by land and sea.[8] But these exponents of monarchy were provincial kings vying with one another for the high-kingship of Ireland, which, having been won, could not be conveyed in an orderly fashion to a successor, but had to be fought for all over again on the death or military decline of the holder. All the appropriate concepts for an Irish monarchy were in place and many of the practices, but nobody could gain a sufficient dominance over other contenders to establish the necessary institutional stability. Meanwhile, Scotland, with a more culturally diverse population than that of Ireland, had acquired an effective and durable monarchy in the eleventh century, ironically at the initiative of a Gaelic-speaking dynasty. England had been a kingdom of an even higher order of coherence since the tenth century. The example of other lands pointed inexorably to the patterns of the age, and the learned and ruling elites of Ireland in the twelfth century were not collectively caught in any attitudinal time-warp. The fact that provincial kings did not attempt to consolidate their local power by establishing independent monarchies set off against the rest of the island is consistent with the understanding that the concept of Ireland as an integral polity carried considerable force.

The place of Ireland in the wider world of recognised polities was authenticated by the seal of the papacy. On an initiative originating in Ireland itself, the diocesan structure was rationalised and brought into line with the norms of contemporary continental reform, the process culminating with the Synod of Kells in AD 1152. Four archbishoprics were instituted, the business being transacted under the supervision of a papal legate, whose journey to Ireland King Stephen of England had endeavoured to impede. The territorial integrity of the island as an ecclesiastical unit was sealed with the former Viking towns, Christianised for some generations, being firmly

---

[7]   D. Ó Corráin, 'Nationality and kingship in pre-Norman Ireland' in T.W. Moody (ed.), *Nationality and the Pursuit of National Independence* (Belfast, 1978), p. 8.
[8]   Ibid., pp. 21–35.

encompassed within the papally endorsed scheme. In earlier decades, bishops of Dublin and of Waterford had turned to the Archbishop of Canterbury for consecration, and even the O'Briens of Dál Cais had looked in the same direction for a worthy ecclesiastical collaborator. By the Synod of Kells, piecemeal English interloping in the affairs of the Church in Ireland was precluded and the ambitions of Canterbury in respect of Ireland were thwarted. For comparative purposes, it is interesting to note that a nearly contemporaneous effort from Wales to fend off Canterbury was unsuccessful, while the Scottish Church escaped a similar fate only at the price of a form of direct rule from Rome.[9]

The papacy was highly influential as the legitimator of emerging monarchies in medieval western Europe, laying claim to authority derived from the ancient Roman Empire, a claim supported by the 'Donation of Constantine', ostensibly a legal instrument of the first Christian emperor but actually an eighth- or ninth-century forgery. Ireland might have a reorganised system of Church government, but to support this Rome sought everywhere a reliable secular arm, and Ireland did not have the stable monarchy that could provide it. Besides, Gaelic marriage customs had never been brought into line with the law of the Church, and prominent rulers were themselves among the worst offenders in the eyes of reformers, regularly divorcing and remarrying. When in 1155 the Pope was requested at the behest of Canterbury to authorise an invasion of Ireland by Henry II the outcome was a papal document, *Laudabiliter*, which did indeed authorise such an invasion for the purpose of promoting religious reform, but did not revoke the Irish Church's independence of Canterbury. In later times, nationalists, if they admitted the authenticity of the document at all, would point out that the pope in question, Adrian IV, was an Englishman, without adverting to the service that *Laudabiliter* and the mid-twelfth century papacy had done to the cause of securing a distinct Irish polity. In the event, Henry made no immediate response.

Henry II was drawn into Irish affairs as a consequence of the country's want of centralised power, after Dermot MacMurrough, recently deposed King of Leinster, sought his aid in a conflict rooted in competition for the high-kingship. With Henry's permission, MacMurrough recruited knights and soldiers from among the Anglo-Normans of Wales, some of whom returned with him in 1167. Others, including Robert FitzStephen and Maurice FitzGerald, followed in 1169: their landing at Bannow Bay in 1169 is conventionally regarded as the beginning of the 'Norman invasion'. Richard de Clare, alias Strongbow, landed near Waterford in 1170. He quickly captured the city and there married MacMurrough's daughter, Aoife, whose hand he had been promised, with the succession of Leinster as

9   M.T. Flanagan, *Irish Society, Anglo-Norman Settlers, Angevin Kingship: Interactions in Ireland in the Late Twelfth Century* (Oxford, 1989), pp. 7–55.

her dowry. The need to control his over-successful and unreliable vassals drew Henry II to Ireland for the winter of 1171–72. A great many Irish kings offered their submission. A synod at Cashel adopting continental discipline, and subsequent communications from Pope Alexander III, confirmed the theory that the invasion was a papally approved intervention in the interest of religious reform.

Henry was disposed to find a compromise with Irish leaders that would secure his interests and theirs. The Treaty of Windsor (1175) was an attempt by Henry II to involve Rory O'Connor, King of Connacht and High-king of Ireland (the last one with any meaningful claim on that title), in the governance of the country. Good intentions were stymied by the endemic divisiveness of the country's power structures, the expansionist thrust of Anglo-Norman society in that age of greedy and ruthless crusaders, and the English King's preoccupations elsewhere. Soon, in violation of undertakings given to Gaelic dynasts who had proffered their loyalty, much of the country had been divided among grantees – de Lacy, de Courcy, Cogan, de Burgo, Theobald Walter and others – who proceeded to make good their claims by the sword. The relatively smooth accession of the Normans to control of England after the Battle of Hastings in 1066 was not to be replicated in Ireland a century later, because the latter country was not a unified polity controlled from any central point. Instead of quickly forming a ruling elite throughout the country, the Anglo-Normans in Ireland had an impact that varied greatly across the land. They introduced through east Ulster, most of Leinster and much of Munster, without any central planning, substantial colonies of farmers and artisans from England and elsewhere that transformed landholding and agriculture and promoted urban development. Elsewhere in Munster and Connacht, they established lordships over the pre-existing population, introducing their accustomed system of land tenure more or less completely, but not a large body of colonists. In the south-west of Munster, in the territory of the O'Briens beyond the lower Shannon, and over central and western Ulster they failed to establish any foothold.

The subsequent confusion of power and authority was encompassed in a polity known for three and a half centuries as the lordship of Ireland. Henry II had designated his youngest son John as Lord of Ireland in 1177 and John had assumed this title in 1185. However, he unexpectedly succeeded to the throne of England in 1199, with the result that the lordship of Ireland instead of being autocephalous, as Henry II had intended, came to adhere in the English Crown, so that henceforth the king of England was *ipso facto* lord of Ireland.[10] The new regime put on a formal basis the foundations of what would become the Irish state. Permanent offices of authority were

---

[10]   J. Lydon, 'Ireland and the English Crown, 1171–1541' in *Irish Historical Studies*, xxix, no. 115 (May 1995), pp. 281–94.

instituted, a centre of royal power was established at Dublin Castle and the beginnings of the process of shiring introduced at least the forms of local government and local justice on the English model. Mirroring developments in England and Europe generally, an Irish parliament emerged in the thirteenth century.

Allegiance to this regime was limited to those who came to describe themselves as the English of Ireland, primarily the heirs of the colonists and the inhabitants of the towns and, of course, more recent arrivals from England. Those of Gaelic language and inheritance, seen as the Irish of Ireland (the 'pure' or 'meere' Irish), generally did not give such loyalty, and it came not to be expected of them, so that they were deemed not to be subjects of the law and were, in fact, excluded from its protection of life and property. Concomitantly, the efficacy of the king's government in Ireland was confined to areas where its adherents were dominant. From about 1300 onwards, this was shrinking territory. A military campaign in Ireland from 1315 to 1318 by Edward Bruce, brother of the King of Scotland, seriously disrupted government control within the lordship and contributed to a general upsurge of confidence on the part of the Gaelic power structures which had survived, more fragmented than ever, over much of the west and north and in the southern midlands and, in pockets, even within Leinster itself. The Black Death in 1348–49 hit the colony and the towns disproportionately hard, and led to a drain of agricultural labour to a similarly depopulated England.

The ebb and flow of territorial advantage in the fourteenth and fifteenth centuries is marked by one phenomenon that has assumed mythic status, namely the English Pale. The 'Pale' has come to stand as a metaphor for an alien element in the national body, politic and cultural, a metropolis materially comfortable but spiritually barren, drawing from foreign rather than native wellsprings. The basis of this in historical reality is that from the early fifteenth century it was government policy to provide for an in-depth defensive frontier for a territory stretching from the coast between Dundalk and the Wicklow Mountains and deep into Meath at the farthest point. Perfected by the end of the century, it allowed the protected population to enjoy relative freedom from the need for constant vigilance against predatory bands that was required in less favoured parts of the lordship.[11]

From the mid-fifteenth century onwards, royal authority was at such a discount in Ireland that the office of lord deputy, the English king's chief administrator in Ireland, was conferred over an extended period on the most powerful magnates in the country, the eighth and ninth Earls of Kildare, both named Garrett FitzGerald. Based at Maynooth, and so on the edge of the Pale, and connected by marriage alliances and multifarious

---

[11] S.G. Ellis, *Ireland in the Age of the Tudors, 1447–1603: English Expansion and the End of Gaelic Rule* (London, 1998), pp. 70–4.

forms of mutual obligation with a host of local power brokers, English and Gaelic, throughout the country, the FitzGeralds, when allowed as lords deputy to combine the authority of the Crown with their territorial influence, could provide stability. On several occasions, when removed from office by the King, they were able to instigate enough trouble to make their restoration seem necessary for the preservation of order. The position of the FitzGeralds around the turn of the sixteenth century was reminiscent, in many respects, of a high-king of earlier times. In each case, the ability to strike directly or by proxy against an enemy anywhere throughout the land was the acid test. This was also a cardinal mark of the early modern prince, and the intimations of national monarchy surrounding the eighth and ninth Earls of Kildare are unmistakable.[12] But unlike their contemporaries elsewhere, and like the medieval Gaelic dynasts, the Earls of Kildare had no structures to provide for continuity. Their position was dependent on relentless opportunism and perpetual vigilance. They stood not on a platform, but on a logpile that would sooner or later roll from beneath their feet.

The character of the English state changed significantly in the early decades of the sixteenth century, following the trend of the period towards enhanced central control, the elimination of seigniorial jurisdiction and other anomalies and the assertion of sovereignty. The development is epitomised by Henry VIII's break with the papacy and also by his destruction of the power of the marcher lords of the north of England. Especially among its beneficiaries – clerks, bureaucrats and courtiers – the new order was justified by an ideology that has led recently in one school of political science to the identification of Tudor England as the first instance of a nation in the modern sense.[13] There was no intention of incorporating Ireland into this nation, but the development of a new concept of the State in England had implications for the lordship of Ireland. An act of rebellion in 1534 by the son and heir of the ninth Earl of Kildare ('Silken' Thomas, Earl of Offaly) was followed, not by the customary round of concession and reconciliation, but by the despatch of an army from England and the decisive crushing of the FitzGeralds: six of them, including Thomas, were sent to the Tower of London and subsequently executed. In Ireland henceforth, only the state could hold the ring, a consideration that pointed towards the imposition of central authority over the entire island. In Ireland, as in England, the new ideology of the state had its adherents and they helped to shepherd through dramatic changes in the framework of law and administration, culminating in an Act of 1541 that transformed the lordship of Ireland into the kingdom of Ireland, to inhere in Henry VIII and his successors as kings of England.[14]

---

12 O.D. Edwards, 'Ireland' in *idem* (ed.), *Celtic Nationalism* (London, 1968), pp. 16–17.
13 L. Greenfeld, *Nationalism: Five Roads to Modernity* (Cambridge, MA, 1992).
14 B. Bradshaw, *The Irish Constitutional Revolution of the Sixteenth Century* (Cambridge, 1979).

The papacy no longer held the theoretical title deeds of the Irish polity. All the inhabitants would henceforth be under the law, an aspiration expressed by the participation of Gaelic dynastic leaders (now 'chieftains' or 'lords' rather than 'kings') in the proclamation of the new monarchy.[15]

Making the writ of the monarch run throughout the new kingdom was to take another sixty years and to involve the plantation of colonies, subjugation by military force, and the expenditure of vast amounts of treasure, particularly in the closing decades of the reign of Queen Elizabeth I (who ruled from 1559 to 1603). There was no master plan and the process was complicated, especially in its later phases, by the issue of religion (see chapter three). In an early, optimistic phase it was hoped to recruit the Gaelic lords to the new order by offering them royal titles to their lands in return for a formal submission, but the complexities of the interests at stake proved too much for this formula, and piecemeal suppression ensued. The stakes were raised to new heights for Elizabeth when the papacy and the Spanish Habsburgs began to see Ireland as an arena in which English power and security could be challenged. The Desmond Rebellion of 1579 was supported directly by the papacy. In the final phase of military resistance to Elizabeth, in which Hugh O'Neill, Earl of Tyrone, emerged as her most serious opponent, a Spanish army landed in his support at Kinsale, he and his allies having offered the Spanish King the disposal of the kingship of Ireland. The defeat of this expedition in December 1601 marked the conclusion of the Tudor conquest of Ireland.

The consequences, beneficial and otherwise, would be reaped by the Stuart dynasty that acceded to the English throne in 1603 in the person of James I, otherwise James VI of Scotland. The following decades constituted a period of major development in the structures of the Irish state. The exemplar was that of England, so that in many ways the resulting product was more like the English model than was the Scottish equivalent. On the other hand, circumstances were so different that the Irish state in many respects took on a character of its own.[16] And, in any case, the intention was that the Irish and English states, however alike, would be distinct. The creation and durability of an Irish state on an English model is epitomised by the completion of the process of shiring, with its standardisation of local government and administration, begun in the late twelfth century and extended to the entire country by 1606. Thus was Ireland endowed with the thirty-two counties that have become the bulwark of local identities and part of the mystique of the nation. The Irish counties provide a striking example of how the mundane structures of the state can be clothed in glory by nationality.

---

[15] C. Lennon, *Sixteenth-century Ireland: the Incomplete Conquest* (Dublin, 1994), p. 144.
[16] J.M. McLaughlin, 'The making of the Irish Leviathan, 1603–25: state-building in Ireland during the reign of James VI and I' (Ph.D. dissertation, NUI Galway, 1999).

The state-building thrust behind the institution of the kingdom of Ireland had implications for homogenisation not only of power but of culture. An Act of 1537 lamented that the differences of language, dress and manners within the island gave the impression that the people were 'as it were of sundry sorts, or rather of sundry countries, where indeed they be wholly together one body'.[17] The aspiration towards cultural uniformity, seen as a co-requisite of civil government, was not always expressed in such eirenic terms but, however it was expressed, the assumption was that the common civilisation would be English, whether that of the English of Ireland or of the English of England. The latter distinction was crucial because its political meaning was the difference between a new Ireland dominated by Palesmen and one dominated by new arrivals from England. The task was beyond the human resources of the Pale and, as it happened, England in the second half of the sixteenth century, as four centuries earlier, had a surplus population, ripe for expansion abroad. The closing decades of the century were marked by a great influx into Ireland of soldiers, colonists, government officials, clerics and adventurers that continued into the new century. They included such personalities as the poet Edmund Spenser, Sir Walter Raleigh, Sir John Davies and Richard Boyle, and are generally referred to collectively by historians as the 'New English', in contradistinction to the 'Old English', the established English of Ireland. The latter found the government of Ireland being taken out of their hands and soon developed a sense of collective resentment.

This influx was justified by those of its participants who thought beyond personal gain as a crusade not only to subdue Ireland politically but also to transform it socially and economically and to sweep aside both the 'barbarity' of the Old Irish, that is the Gaelic population, and the 'degeneracy' of the Old English. The logical corollary in the eyes of idealists among these 'civilisers' was constitutional assimilation with England, but that did not become the objective of official policy except for a brief period in the 1650s. The concept of multiple polities is helpful for an appreciation of the status of Ireland *vis-à-vis* England at this time and for a long time to come. In the early modern period it was normal over much of central and western Europe for monarchs to inherit and rule different parts of their dominions under different titles. This was the case in the Low Countries, in Spain, and in the territories of the Austrian emperor. From 1171 to 1800, with a short break in the middle of the seventeenth century, Ireland was one of a number of polities sharing a common ruler on the model of multiple monarchy, and from 1800 to 1921 the substance was the same, even if the formal situation was different.

The defeat of O'Neill (followed by his departure with remaining allies

---

[17] Cited by G.A. Hayes McCoy, in T.W. Moody et al. (ed.), *Early Modern Ireland, 1534–1691* (Oxford, 1986), p. 51.

from Ireland in 1607 in 'the flight of the earls'), rightly seen as marking the end of the political infrastructure of Gaelic culture, is one of the prime occasions of nostalgia in nationalist historiography, there being an implicit assumption that the alternative to defeat was the reversion to a Gaelic idyll. However, the only question in 1600 was which completely new and probably difficult future Ireland would have. One historian has put the matter in perspective with the comment that the defeat of O'Neill:

> probably prevented Ireland as a whole developing on similar lines to Poland: a land controlled by territorial magnates, justified by a militant Counter-Reformation ideology and worked by an enserfed peasantry.[18]

The government of Ireland in the early seventeenth century posed many problems for James I, and for Charles I who succeeded him in 1625. James had dealt with instability in middle and west Ulster, the last area to come under the secure authority of the Crown, by means of an extensive plantation scheme inaugurated in 1608 which placed there a large colony of Scots and English. This supplemented extensive informal settlement by Scots in Antrim and Down. Elsewhere in the country, the thrusting New English interest threatened the interests of the Old English, while the Old Irish were thoroughly marginalised. The attachment of the two latter groups to Roman Catholicism was a source of serious discontent. As Lord Deputy in the 1630s, Thomas Wentworth, later Earl of Strafford, displaying absolutist disdain for sectional interests, managed to alienate almost everyone. In the early 1640s, Irish problems became enmeshed in a crisis affecting Charles's other kingdoms that led on to the English Civil War and a conflict that was to have dramatic consequences for all three countries.

Opposition to his religious policy in Scotland drew Charles into a war with his Scottish subjects that led to them invading the north of England in August 1640. In order to raise an army to oppose them, Charles had to have recourse to the summoning of the English Parliament, which he had managed to do without since 1629. The Puritan interest, intensely disenchanted with the King's High Church ecclesiastical policy and much else besides, found in Parliament their opportunity to make a stand. In Ireland, intelligence of this newly gained advantage of the Puritans gave rise to the gravest apprehension among the Catholics. Against this background, Catholics in Ulster came out in rebellion in October 1641, attacking the Scots and English settlers and claiming to be acting at the King's behest. News of this, and especially accounts, grossly exaggerated for propaganda purposes, of the outrages perpetrated against the colonists, were used to fuel feeling in England against the King and against the Irish Catholics, by association with whom

---

[18] H. Morgan, 'The end of Gaelic Ulster: a thematic interpretation of events between 1534 and 1610' in *Irish Historical Studies*, xxvi, no. 101 (May 1988), p. 30.

the King's cause could be vilified. Under the circumstances, Catholics else-where in Ireland, Old English and Old Irish, felt that they had no choice but to throw in their lot with the Ulster rebels, since all could expect to suffer the wrath of the Puritans if it were to be unleashed in Ireland. These devel-opments further strengthened the determination of the English Parliament to send an army to Ireland. In March 1642, Charles II gave his consent to the Act of Adventurers, under which money contributed to the raising of an army for Ireland would be repaid in the form of confiscated Irish land. Before this could happen, King and Parliament had gone to war in England.

In early 1642, representatives of the Irish Catholics met at Kilkenny and formed an assembly to protect their interests. They declared for the King, if only because of the implications his defeat would have for themselves, and they styled themselves the Confederate Catholics of Ireland. The Confederation created administrative structures, at least on paper, and replicated the atmosphere of a Counter-Reformation polity, at least in Kilkenny and some other towns. Armies were maintained in the field, the leadership being supplied by Owen Roe O'Neill and Thomas Preston, two returned generals of the Spanish armies in the Netherlands. They operated in an extremely complicated field of forces. The Earl of Ormonde main-tained the King's army in Ireland. There was also a mainly New English army giving allegiance to the English Parliament. A Scottish army landed in County Antrim in April 1642. The Confederates sought foreign assistance, but without offering the kingship of Ireland as an incentive, since they were professedly loyal to Charles I. Support came from the papacy, especially in the person of a papal nuncio, Archbishop Rinuccini. The Confederates fell into serious internal disputes about tactics and policy that demoralised their supporters, and they had but very debilitated forces in place to oppose the arrival of Oliver Cromwell with a powerful, fully equipped army in August 1649.[19] Nine months later, after a forceful campaign mainly of siege war-fare, Cromwell was able to return to England knowing that Ireland had been secured for Parliament, although the war continued until 1652. Tens of thousands of Confederate soldiers who surrendered on terms were allowed to go into foreign service, but there was no general peace agree-ment. By 1652, Ireland was in the same devastated and depopulated condi-tion as parts of central Europe at the conclusion of the Thirty Years War in 1648, and for the same reasons. Armies on all sides had had recourse to scorched earth tactics and had otherwise drained the land of resources. A weakened population was easy prey for plague and disease.

The campaign, and the years of 'Cromwellian' government that followed, have given Cromwell a notorious name in Irish nationalist and Catholic dis-course, something undoubtedly reinforced by the demonisation of the regi-

---

[19] M. Ó Siochrú, *Confederate Ireland, 1642–49: A Constitutional and Political Analysis* (Dublin, 1999).

cide in England in later times. Thus, in both countries it became customary in popular lore to attribute to Cromwell the destruction of almost every old ruin in the landscape. In Ireland, the most emotive Cromwellian trope concerns the massacre of defenders and inhabitants of Drogheda and Wexford after the capture of those towns in September and October 1649. Drogheda and Wexford provided Catholics with a myth to counter that of October 1641.[20] In any case, Cromwell came to Ireland full of righteous indignation about the massacres of 1641 and with a presumption about the blood-guilt of all Irish Catholics in the matter. Also there were large debts that could only be redeemed by the confiscation of land. Under the Commonwealth regime, most of the Catholic landowners of Ireland, Old Irish and Old English alike, were dispossessed by law, many of them receiving smaller holdings in Connacht by way of compensation. (Hence the commonplace attribution to Cromwell of the dictum 'to hell or to Connacht'.) Some did move west of the Shannon, while others remained on their old holdings, now as tenants of new landlords. The inequity of the confiscation was compounded by the chaotic manner of its execution.

In January 1649, coincident with the execution of Charles I, Parliament had abolished the monarchy in England and Ireland, and as Cromwell arrived in Ireland later that year he believed that he was mandated to impose English laws. The new order was given constitutional shape in 1653 with the establishment of the Commonwealth, the only attempt in history to govern the two islands as a single unitary state. Cromwell as Lord Protector ruled with a single council of state.[21] As in England and Scotland, recalcitrants and displaced persons – and there were many more of these in Ireland – were liable to be rounded up by the self-righteous republican regime and shipped off to the West Indies or Virginia. In Ireland, as in Britain, the creation of military-administrative districts provided a hint of revolutionary innovation. Innovative, too, if not very successful for its immediate purposes, was the government's promotion, in connection with the confiscation and transfer of Irish property, of a series of land surveys conducted by William Petty. With the restoration of the monarchy in 1660, revolutionary experiments and the unitary state were abandoned and Ireland became a kingdom once again. By comparison with the situation in 1641, the Old Irish and Old English had lost heavily and the gainers were the New English who were now sometimes called the 'old Protestants' to distinguish them from the small but not insignificant group of 'new' Protestants that had arrived under the auspices of the Commonwealth.

---

[20] For a fresh viewpoint, see Tom Reilly, *An Honourable Enemy: The Untold Story of the Cromwellian Invasion of Ireland* (Dingle, 1999).

[21] J. Morrill, 'Three kingdoms and one commonwealth?: the enigma of mid-seventeenth-century Britain and Ireland' in A. Grant and K.J. Stringer (eds), *Uniting the Kingdom? The Enigma of British History* (London, 1995).

When Charles II was succeeded in 1685 by his brother, James II, the fact that the new King was a Roman Catholic created an atmosphere of crisis throughout his kingdoms. The arrival of a son and heir, and with him the prospect of a Catholic dynasty, brought matters to a head. The dominant representatives of Protestant England, motivated by fear not only of popery but also of the absolutist tendencies with which they associated it, effectively deposed the King, bestowing the throne jointly on the Stadholder of the United Provinces of the Netherlands, William of Orange, and on his wife Mary, who was the Protestant daughter of James. This 'glorious revolution' was a serious disappointment to the Catholic interest in Ireland. James had made several provisions favourable to his co-religionists, holding out for them the prospect of access to public office and the reversal of the Cromwellian land settlement. He had even appointed a Catholic viceroy of Ireland, Richard Talbot, Earl of Tyrconnell. Thus when James, ousted from England, declared his intention of fighting to recover his position, he had in Ireland a firm base from which to launch his campaign. James had the backing of Louis XIV of France, who was then encircled by an alliance of European powers, under the leadership of William of Orange, intent on curbing his expansionism. The restoration of James II would be a major strategic blow to Louis's enemies. Thus, in the years 1690–91 Ireland became host to two large European armies and came to be, as never before or since, the pivot of an international war. It was also a civil war. The Protestant interest in Ireland generally rallied to William of Orange with happy consequences for them. The 'war of the two kings' provided a series of victories that would form the stuff of a myth of salvation: the Siege of Derry; the Battle of the Boyne; the Battle of Aughrim.

Although defeated, James II, with the support of the French monarchy and eventually the papacy, maintained in exile his claims to the thrones he had lost, and after his death these claims were continued by his son under the title of James III. The Jacobite cause ('Jacobus' is Latin for James) drew support from Catholics, from many Scots and also from a not insignificant number of Protestants in Britain and Ireland who, for one reason or another, including attachment to the idea of the divine right of kings, were disenchanted with William and Mary and their successors. The accession following Mary's death in 1714 of the Elector of Hanover (as George I) on the principle of Protestant succession hardened the divide. While there was a widespread cult of the Jacobite cause in Ireland precisely as an Irish cause, this did not involve any questioning of the assumption that Ireland would remain joined with England and Scotland through the Crown.

Yet, changes in the character of the monarchy, heralded by the revolution of 1688, were undermining the workability of the multiple monarchy. Irish Catholic leaders had surrendered at Limerick in October 1691 on terms negotiated with William's representatives, yet in the years that followed, the King had difficulty in having his side of the bargain honoured because of the opposition of Protestants in the Irish Parliament to the passage of the required measures. This epitomised the decline of the royal prerogative, a trend that in this instance was to the benefit of the Protestants of Ireland, but that was simultaneously placing them at a disadvantage in relation to England. English rulers had generally given priority to the interests of England in their dealings with Ireland, but that need not be invariably the case while the royal prerogative permitted freedom of action to the monarch. The growing answerability of the Crown to parliament at Westminster (eventually formalised by the development of cabinet government in the course of the eighteenth century) institutionalised the controlling position of English interests and the subordination of other polities. In the case of Scotland, this problem was short-circuited in 1707 by a union of parliaments in the newly proclaimed Kingdom of Great Britain. Ireland was not deemed to be ready for such a union in the early eighteenth century, and the stage was thus set for generations of dispute about the standing of the kingdom and parliament of Ireland vis-à-vis the parliament at Westminster.

Debate about the relative status of the Irish parliament went back at least to the fifteenth century. An act of 1494, Poynings' Law, intended to ensure that a lord deputy such as the earl of Kildare could not use parliament to ends not approved by the king, was employed in later times to give the privy council in London control over the initiation and wording of legislation. In the late 1630s, Old English and New English had developed arguments for the rights of the Irish kingdom that were specifically designed to counter the claims, not of the English parliament, but of the Lord Deputy, Thomas Wentworth. Even more contentious from the 1690s onwards was the question of the right of Parliament at Westminster to legislate for Ireland. By the terms of the Declaratory Act of 1720, Westminster reasserted its right to do so. A notable exercise of this right had been seen in 1699 with the passage at Westminster of the Woollen Act, prohibiting the export of woollen goods from Ireland to any destination other than England. In fact, this was but another in a series of measures designed to subordinate Irish to English economic interests. The mercantilist economic system established by the English Navigation Acts of the 1660s provided the framework for successful English commercial exploitation of the overseas colonies, and English legislation, reflecting the interests of English business, constrained Irish participation in that system, and in several ways subordinated Irish exports to English advantage. Constitutional and commercial restrictions together were perceived as grievances by the Protestants who made up the body politic of Ireland after 1692. The consequence was rhetoric of national self-assertion that made an indelible mark on the connotation of Irishness. Building on earlier foundations, William Molyneux issued in 1699 his *Case against Ireland being bound by acts of the English parliament stated*. Intense and successful resistance to a royal patent of 1722 for the introduction of copper coinage ('Wood's halfpence') was fuelled by resentment against perceived English exploitation of Ireland. The episode was the occasion of Jonathan Swift's celebrated *Drapier's Letters*.

Those who asserted the claims of the Irish interest came to be known as 'patriots', in a borrowing from contemporary European usage. With the arrival on the scene of the Dublin radical Charles Lucas (1713–71), it is possible to see the emergence of patriotism as a cause with a popular following. Dissatisfaction among Irish Protestants about the subordination of their commercial interests and national status was a constant of the politics of the eighteenth century. British Governments managed it on an ad hoc basis and did so without major upheaval until the outbreak of rebellion in the North American colonies in the mid-1770s changed the balance of forces in Ireland. The withdrawal of soldiers from Ireland provided the occasion for the institution of an armed volunteering movement. The effective use of the Volunteers and of the crisis by the patriot movement forced the British Government into concessions under the two long-standing headings of grievance. In 1780, Ireland was granted 'free trade', meaning equality with Britain within the mercantilist system, and in 1782 the Declaratory Act was repealed at Westminster and Poynings' Law amended, with the effect that the Irish Parliament was allowed to assume all the trappings of equality. The ensuing epoch is usually associated with the name of Henry Grattan, the central parliamentary figure in its realisation and also the supreme patriot orator, who declared before the House of Commons on 16 April 1782: 'I am now to address a free people . . . Ireland is now a nation'.[22] The assertion of national rights by Irish patriots in the eighteenth century has been identified as nationalism by some historians, while others withhold the term on the basis that patriotism did not comprehend those social and mental transformations, particularly the ideal of separatism, released by the French Revolution in the 1790s. At stake is the definition of nationalism one cares to use, rather than any matter of fact.

The architectural glories of eighteenth-century Ireland, symbols of a dominant elite of landowners augmented by a prosperous commercial and legal establishment, reached their apogee in the final decades of the century in the shape of Dublin's Custom House and the great Parliament House itself, the first such structure in Europe built to accommodate a bi-cameral legislature. The architecture was a fair reflection of contemporary economic conditions, but it belied the political prospects. While Britain and Ireland were now in principle two independent kingdoms with the same monarch, that monarch, even in respect of his Irish crown, functioned through a cabinet that was answerable to the British Parliament. Accordingly, the British Government continued to appoint the Irish executive and to control its policies. National

---

[22]   D.O. Madden, *Speeches of Grattan* (Dublin, 1862), p. 70.

self-esteem had been enhanced by the advent of an independent parliament, but the Irish Government was not answerable to the Irish Parliament.

At the same time, Grattan's parliament proved incapable of securing its power base in the country either by extending the franchise or by admitting Roman Catholics to the political system on an equal footing. Such matters were put in a drastically new setting in the years after the outbreak of the French Revolution in 1789. In the blissful dawn of expectation that lit up most of Europe in the early 1790s, radicals in Ireland, as elsewhere, glimpsed the hope of a new order founded on liberty and equality. Then, in 1793, Britain went to war with revolutionary France, Ireland automatically following as a realm of George III. With those in power in Britain and Ireland now dedicated to perpetuating the status quo, the advocates of reform, especially as gathered together in the Society of United Irishmen (founded 1791), turned to conspiracy and revolution, and to nationalism. Their most inspirational figure, Theobald Wolfe Tone (1763–98), formulated a policy of complete separation from Britain, to be achieved by rebellion with French support. Like all the French-sponsored revolutionary regimes of the 1790s, whether in Italy, the Rhineland, or the Low Countries, Tone's new Ireland would be a republic. Thus Irish nationalism in the modern sense, and Irish republican separatism as a doctrine, both date from the same era. But, though contemporaneous and related, they are not the same thing.

French aid for the United Irishmen was ill-fated and their grand plans resulted not in irresistible revolution but in a series of uncoordinated rebellions in different parts of the country in the summer of 1798, most notably in Wexford. All were suppressed, but the scale of death in the course of insurrection and repression, running to tens of thousands, signified the demise of the former power system in Ireland. For several decades, British ministers had contemplated union as the ultimate answer to the problem of Anglo-Irish relations, few having faith in the durability of the 'constitution of 1782'.[23] The discrediting of existing arrangements in 1798, and the continuing threat of strategic intervention in Ireland by the French enemy, made the option of union irresistible for the Prime Minister, William Pitt. The Irish Parliament was persuaded to vote itself out of existence with the Act of Union of 1800, not ultimately because many MPs received material inducements to support the measure (which they did), but because a significant section of Irish Protestant opinion calculated on a more secure future in a polity with a Protestant majority. On 1 January 1801 the United Kingdom of Great Britain and Ireland came into being, with one parliament at Westminster, comprising a hundred seats in the House of Commons for members from Irish constituencies.

After 1707, Scotland had retained its own separate and frequently dis-

---

[23] J. Kelly, *Prelude to Union: Anglo-Irish Politics in the 1780s* (Cork, 1992).

tinctive institutions, parliament excepted. With its own Church and its own laws and legal system, Scotland clearly had not been assimilated into the new polity of Great Britain. Despite the legal fiction of union, Scotland had been integrated into what was still in practice a multiple state rather than being assimilated into a unitary state. Despite, or perhaps because of, anomalies, the Scottish union had been a success. The Irish union was similarly anomalous, but the anomalies were not the same as in the Scottish case. The Established Church in Ireland was united with the Church of England; Ireland retained its own body of laws, but had a legal system in common with England; and Ireland retained the office of lord lieutenant, the holder presiding over a bureaucracy in Dublin Castle that had developed over the centuries to serve a distinct polity. In Ireland, as in Scotland, union did not involve any serious attempt to obliterate the distinctive administrative structures inherited from the past. Through the nineteenth century, Westminster would pass laws that applied to the United Kingdom as a whole, laws that applied only to Great Britain, laws that applied only to England and Wales (eventually laws that applied to Wales only), laws that applied only to Scotland and laws that applied only to Ireland.

While the Act of Union legislated for integration rather than assimilation, there were those in the early nineteenth century, in and out of government, who dreamed of reforming Ireland culturally, socially and morally to the point of assimilation. Not since the middle of the seventeenth century had hopes of a recasting of Irish society to an English standard been entertained by so many. The best-known manifestation of this was the evangelical campaign to convert Irish Catholics to Protestantism, known as the 'second Reformation' (see chapters three and four). After it had become clear that this was more productive of disturbance than 'civility' in public life, the Government acted decisively in 1831 to direct its own influence away from the religious sphere and into what it intended to be a non-denominational system of state-supported primary schooling, the 'national school' scheme. The exact meaning of 'national' here requires some consideration. The system was certainly 'national' insofar as it was connected with the state. But it was also intended to promote nationality – a British nationality – as illustrated in statements such as the following in a prescribed textbook:

> On the east of Ireland is England where the queen lives. Many people who live in Ireland were born in England, and we speak the same language and are called one nation.[24]

But whatever the intentions of its creators, the system was confined to Ireland and it became one of the most characteristic institutions of Irish public life in every corner of the land, as to a large extent it still remains in

---

[24] Commissioners of national education, *Second Book of Lessons* (Dublin, 1847), p. 135.

the South. In other words, a distinct state promoted a distinct nationality, however unintentionally.

In Ireland under the Union, state-driven homogenisation occurred at the Irish level in respect of some aspects of life, such as schooling, and at United Kingdom level in respect of other areas, such as the postal service. In other words, while the state in Ireland was to some extent part of the wider British system, it was for the most part a distinct entity. By comparison with the remainder of the United Kingdom, the state in nineteenth-century Ireland was interventionist and centralising to a precocious degree, as is illustrated by the national schools (1831), the dispensary system (1805 and 1851), a country-wide constabulary (1836), the standardisation of place names (Ordnance Survey, 1825–41) and a uniform cadastral survey (Griffith's valuation, 1848–60) such as would have been rejected in England as evidence of an intolerable, paternalistic 'Prussianism'. Thus, Westminster legislation and government policy served in many ways to create institutions that extended, enhanced and defined the content of Irishness.

The nationalisation of mindsets in the early nineteenth century was advanced significantly in Ireland by the campaign for political equality for Catholics, usually referred to as Catholic Emancipation, culminating (successfully) as it did in the late 1820s with a mass mobilisation that had scarcely any contemporary European equivalent. The controller of this campaign, Daniel O'Connell (1775–1847), took advantage of his status as popular tribune to follow up with a demand for repeal of the Act of Union, and in the early 1840s he launched another (this time unsuccessful) mass campaign to that end. O'Connell's stated objective was that of the eighteenth-century patriots, that Ireland should be governed by the king (or queen), lords and commons of Ireland, and he had himself little sense of the Romantic take on nationality. Nevertheless, the movement that he led – and he may have harnessed it as much as creating it – has the unmistakable socio-political features of a modern nationalism. Fully developed nationalist ideology arrived in the 1840s with the emergence among O'Connell's supporters of a youthful intelligentsia, eventually known as Young Ireland, which was keenly attuned to recent currents of thought in Europe. From 1842 onwards, their weekly, the *Nation*, espoused an idealised nationality given potent expression by their principal ideologue, Thomas Davis (1814–45).

In drumming up support for his campaigns, O'Connell was able to make much of the economic troubles afflicting the country, which he blamed on the Union. The Union may not have been the cause of these problems, but it certainly had not proved to be any kind of panacea for an economy with a rapidly expanding population, a high proportion of which by the 1820s lived in dire poverty. The virtual disappearance of the domestic textile industry in the face of imported manufactures and the serious downturn in agriculture after 1815 provided a popular orator with much rhetorical

ammunition. At the same time, some of O'Connell's most important supporters came from among those who were prospering as distributors of
imported goods, particularly retail shopkeepers.

Much worse was to come at the end of O'Connell's career when after an
extensive failure of the potato crop in 1845, blight resulted in the total failure of the crop in 1846. This convinced all concerned that what was the sole
sustenance of perhaps one third of a population of over eight million, was
no longer dependable. Even if they could survive in the short term, the cottiers and renters of potato ground and their families clearly had no future on
their minuscule plots, for no alternative crop could sustain them on the
same acreage. The response of Lord John Russell's government was nig-
gardly, out of the needs of party politics, out of economic ideology, out of
incompetence, and also out of fear that assistance might delay the acceptance of the need for change. At base, change meant mass migration from
rural Ireland. Well over a million appear to have emigrated in the period
1846–50. Those who died of hunger, malnutrition and associated diseases
in the same period may have numbered up to a million: there is no certainty
about the figures. Nothing that the Government could have done would
have averted widespread excess mortality, but that the judicious expenditure of more public money, or even the more efficient application of what
was spent, could have saved numerous lives seems certain. Certain, too, is
the fact that in the eyes of laissez-faire ideologues in and out of government,
given to fretting over the problem of Irish rural backwardness, the sudden
loss of popular faith in the subsistence potato economy was like a deliverance. None of this amounts to any kind of evidence in support of allegations, which sometimes occur in nationalist rhetoric and colonial studies
speculations, to the effect that the Government caused the famine or
behaved with genocidal intent.

Emigration in the course of the famine brought to light what would be an
enduring ambivalence in Irish national thinking. By and large, their neighbours seem to have been as reconciled as the British Government to seeing
cottiers and impoverished smallholders abandon their holdings and thus
facilitate consolidation of farms for those remaining behind. On the other
hand, the more intense concept of nationality then developing induced a
sense of alarm at the loss of numbers to the nation. Thomas Davis had spoken in terms of a self-governing Ireland supporting a population of tens of
millions. Those who had imbibed his ideas felt a suspicion that the British
approved of emigration because it sapped the strength of the Irish nation.
There would be for generations to come a contradiction between attachment to an economy that required the emigration of many of the sons and
daughters of the land, and a nationalist ideology that viewed emigration as
almost tantamount to treason. It was in truth a one-sided struggle, with
economy prevailing over ideology at every turn.

In the aftermath of the famine, Irish society was altered. Almost everyone was now participating in a cash economy, as 'Indian meal' (ground American corn) on sale in shops became an accepted supplement to the unreliable potato. The former confusion of landholding was much clarified and tenant farmers were clearly visible as a socio-economic class, and agriculture (meaning both landlords and tenants) as the dominant interest over most of the island. A railway network was laid across the land. While industry languished over much of the country, the north-east became home to state-of-the-art linen manufacturing, engineering and shipbuilding enterprises. Rather like south Wales, Belfast together with some of its hinterland was, arguably, assimilated into the industrial economy of Britain, into which the economy of the remainder of the country was merely integrated – as a source of agricultural produce. As it happened, the region of intensive industrial development approximated with the area of Protestant demographic dominance. Whether based on industry or agriculture, a modernising economy throughout the island supported cultural change in the direction of conformity to the ways of the commercialised world. The more uniform and disciplined lifestyle desired for the Irish by evangelicals and reformers in the early nineteenth century did indeed come to pass, to a very great extent, but without the changes of allegiance in respect of nations and denominations that had once seemed to some to be prerequisite.

The sense of the nation as the source of meaning and point of reference of collective life flourished in Ireland as elsewhere in Europe in the decades after 1848, even though the Irish contribution to the year of revolutions – a hopeless, localised attempt at rebellion instigated by the Young Irelanders – was the subject of much derision and, like the famine, seriously dented confidence in the capacity of Ireland to function as an independent polity. In the 1850s and 1860s much of the expanding newspaper business, especially Dublin-based and provincial weeklies, was in the editorial hands of an able intelligentsia for whom nationality was their key inspiration.[25] While they seldom advanced specific programmes of political action they were prime disseminators of the nationalist outlook.

A particular case was the *Irish People* (1863–65), the mouthpiece of the Fenian movement led by James Stephens that had as its core the Irish Republican Brotherhood (IRB), an armed conspiracy founded in 1858 with a view to taking advantage of a (mistakenly) anticipated Anglo-French war to strike for Irish independence.[26] Their ill-fated attempt at a rising in March 1867 suggested that, until the day of England's difficulty with a major foreign foe arrived, the Fenians, even with their extensive Irish-American alliance, would not pose a serious military threat to British power. However, their success in recruiting the enthusiasm of tens of thousands of

---

[25] M.-L. Legg, *Newspapers and Nationalism: The Irish Provincial Press, 1850–92* (Dublin, 1999), pp. 29–50.

[26] R.V. Comerford, *The Fenians in Context: Irish Politics and Society, 1848–82* (Dublin, 2nd edn., 1998), pp. 43–66.

young men demonstrated the existence of disaffection that could readily be channelled into rebelliousness. Majority nationalist opinion, fearful of revolution and hopeless bloodshed, was antagonistic to the Fenians until it became clear that they would not be able to foment a rebellion. Thereafter, imprisoned Fenians came to symbolise the public purposes of nationalists in general, and three of them executed in England in November 1867, Allen, Larkin and O'Brien, became the 'Manchester martyrs' of song, story and annual commemoration.

From the early 1870s, to be a sworn Fenian or IRB man was the normative mode of expression of individual identification with the national cause. The extent to which this implied involvement in organisational activity varied enormously with time and place and individual inclination. To attempt to define Fenians in terms of political objectives without also referring to personal and social factors is misleading, but it is clear that the political idea they predominantly had in common was that of separatism. This put them at odds with the position of the great majority of Irish nationalists who throughout the nineteenth century were content to think of an accommodation with Britain. And many Fenians displayed a willingness to join in the politics of the majority, either because they did not feel very strongly about Fenian ideology or were seeking to achieve Fenian ends through constitutional means.

Fenians were in the background when in 1870 the Conservative Protestant lawyer Isaac Butt launched the Home Government Association, a body whose stated aim was the inauguration of self-government in local matters for Ireland, Scotland and England, with the imperial parliament retaining control of common concerns, including defence and foreign policy. Three years later, as Butt revamped his organisation, Fenians were again deeply implicated. The new Home Rule League provided the umbrella under which sixty MPs won seats at the general election of 1874. Home Rule, as devised by Butt, was a formula for acknowledging Ireland's distinctiveness while keeping the country integrated within the United Kingdom, and it was calculated to promote conciliation within Ireland and between Irish needs and British interests. The headline set by the British North America Act of 1867 in providing for a federal arrangement in Canada to balance competing interests was an obvious model.

In a classic instance of the political coup, known as the 'new departure', the Home Rule movement became the object of a takeover in the late 1870s. The occasion of the coup was a severe deterioration in the rural economy that left tenant farmers facing debt and the less favoured of them facing hunger. The perpetrators of the coup were Charles Stewart Parnell, Michael Davitt and John Devoy. Parnell was a Wicklow landlord sitting in parliament for Meath. The other two were Fenians based respectively in Ireland and in the USA, but they were making use of the different Fenian organisations in which they were prominent, rather than carrying out Fenian policy.

The chosen vehicle was the Land League, and the dominant strategy was that of persuading tenant farmers to withhold rents. The consequences included a sharp polarisation of society throughout much of the country, that isolated the landed classes and gentry. The outcomes of the 'new departure' included the 1881 Land Act, which effectively gave the farmers co-ownership of the soil, the permanent economic and political disablement of the landlords as a class, and the emergence of Parnell as a national hero and, following the general election of 1880, as leader of a more forceful Home Rule Party which came to be called the Nationalist Party. In the mid-1880s a redistribution of parliamentary seats, together with an extension of the franchise, made parliamentary elections more reflective of popular opinion, so that at the general election of 1885, Parnell and his party secured eighty-five of the Irish seats on the strength of a now pervasive nationalism. The other eighteen seats (located mainly in the north-east) went to candidates explicitly opposed to Home Rule.

For all its changed ethos from the days of Isaac Butt, Home Rule as demanded by Parnell was still a matter of a parliament for Ireland at a level below Westminster. Parnell had on occasion hinted at something beyond this, as in his remark in 1885 that 'no man has the right to fix the boundary to the march of a nation'.[27] Such talk had the effect of disarming the reservations of separatists. Parnell's greatest triumph came when, in the light of the outcome of the 1885 general election, the Prime Minister, W.E. Gladstone, declared himself in favour of Home Rule for Ireland and, in 1886, introduced a bill to that end in the House of Commons. This was the culmination of twenty years of at least notional commitment by the Liberal statesman to the principle that Ireland should be governed by 'Irish ideas': his Irish Church Act of 1869 had disestablished the Protestant State Church. In the event, a revolt among Gladstone's own MPs saw his Home Rule bill of 1886 defeated in the House of Commons. In 1893 a second Home Rule bill passed the Commons but was defeated in the Lords. By then, the opponents of Home Rule had formed a cohesive unionist movement exhibiting all the features associated with a nationalist mobilisation and linked with the Conservative Party at Westminster. For nearly twenty years afterwards, the constitutional future of Ireland was a question in deadlock until political and constitutional changes at Westminster – and particularly the abolition in 1911 of the absolute veto of the House of Lords – again favoured the nationalists. In 1913, with the enactment of Home Rule the following year a political certainty, the conflict between nationalists and unionists found expression in two newly formed paramilitary volunteer forces, the Ulster Volunteer Force and the Irish (National) Volunteers and, for the first time in more than a century, the capacity of the British government to impose its will in Ireland was placed in serious doubt. Home Rule for Ireland was on

---

[27] P. Bew, *C.S. Parnell* (Dublin, 1980), p. 70.

the statute book at the outbreak of the Great War in 1914, only to be suspended until the war's end, or so it was intended.

Measured by most criteria, nationalism was vibrant in Ireland in the
decades before 1914. Nevertheless, the great majority of nationalists were
prepared to accept a constitutional accommodation with Britain as provided for in each of the three Home Rule proposals. This was in line with a
widespread, if by no means universal, acceptance in Europe that burgeoning
nationalities should continue to exist within the composite polities. Even
Arthur Griffith (1871–1922), founder of Sinn Féin, the most radical Irish
nationalist ideologue of the period and advocate of an extreme form of economic autarky, proposed the maintenance of the imperial nexus: he promoted the idea of a dual monarchy along the lines of the post-1867
Austro-Hungarian Empire, as he understood it. In Autumn 1914, encouraged by the nationalist leader, John Redmond (1856–1918), putative Prime
Minister of a Home Rule Ireland, tens of thousands of his followers flocked
to enlist in the British army, happy that this was an act of Irish patriotism.

Throughout Europe, the Great War overturned the presumption in
favour of composite polities and led to the triumph of the principle of self-
determination and the break-up of the Austro-Hungarian, Russian, German
and Ottoman Empires. In Irish nationalist perceptions, the mystique of
British power that had rendered Ireland's continuation within the United
Kingdom, albeit in a Home Rule arrangement, seem a natural inevitability
was severely shaken by the evidence of the war in France. The point was
made close to home at Easter 1916 when an army of less than two thousand
rebels, having declared an Irish Republic, was able to hold much of the centre of Dublin in defiance of Crown forces for the best part of a week. The
execution of Patrick Pearse, James Connolly and the other leaders created
separatist martyrs. Soon, public opinion among nationalists was ready for
the separatist message, delivered by a younger generation of leaders under
the banner of a revived Sinn Féin, and dominated by the survivors of the
1916 Rising, among whom Eamon de Valera was pre-eminent. The swing
was enhanced by the introduction, in time for the post-war election in
December 1918, of the Representation of the People Act, giving the vote to
all males at twenty-one and to women at thirty. Sinn Féin, having won sev-
enty-three of one hundred and five Irish seats, proceeded in January 1919 to
establish a parliament in Dublin (Dáil Éireann), and a government, and to
declare Irish independence. The subsequent attempt to obtain a hearing at
the Paris Peace Conference was rebuffed (defeated empires only were having
their subordinate nationalities liberated), but the logic of the Irish case was
inescapable.

There ensued a struggle between the Dáil Éireann government and the
British administration for control of the country. The creation of alternative
structures by Sinn Féin – especially in the areas of courts and local government – was a significant part of the contest. It is better remembered, how-

ever, in nationalist mythology as the War of Independence in which the Irish Volunteers (otherwise the Irish Republican Army), a body not under the control of Dáil Éireann, nor indeed in full control of its own members at local level, destroyed the policing power and intelligence gathering of Dublin Castle throughout much of the country by means of attacks on police stations, ambushes of Crown forces and individual assassinations. The British response of reprisals and repression compounded the terror and ensured the heroic status of the rebels. If they did not exactly drive out the British, they made the price of a continued British effort to control the country highly unattractive, not least in terms of public opinion in Britain and the USA.

By 1914, the exclusion of the unionist heartland from the control of a Dublin administration had already been seen in London as the only way of resolving the Home Rule crisis. Subsequent events had further diminished the likelihood that unionists in the north-east could be prevailed upon to accept rule from Dublin. Partition was formally introduced by means of the Government of Ireland Act of 1920. Two entities were thereby created, Northern Ireland (six counties in the north-east) and Southern Ireland, each to have a form of Home Rule. The unionist majority in the north-east readily accepted the arrangement, leaving the British Government free to negotiate the fate of Southern Ireland with Sinn Féin. The Articles of Agreement (otherwise the Anglo-Irish Treaty) of December 1921, going far beyond Home Rule, provided for effective independence for a twenty-six-county Irish Free State. Substance was one thing, form was another. The British insisted that the concession be made within the framework of British constitutional convention and so the new state was to have the form of a dominion, the status enjoyed by Canada, Australia, New Zealand and South Africa within the British Empire, or the British Commonwealth as it was now called. This arrangement, involving as it did the reservation of certain formal functions to the king and of an ultimate authority to the Crown, was rejected by those on the Irish side, including de Valera, for whom any concession to monarchy was unacceptable. The republic became the catch-cry of the opponents of the treaty in the subsequent civil war (1922–23) that blighted the launching of the Irish Free State and cost the life of its most forceful agent and army commander-in-chief, Michael Collins.

Whereas, a mere decade before, Home Rule within the United Kingdom had been acceptable as an acknowledgement of Irish nationality, by the early 1920s the vastly greater independence conferred by dominion status was perceived as a shackle on the nation. Thus had Ireland partaken in the Europe-wide triumph of the concept of national self-determination. Even those who had accepted the Treaty and fought to have it enforced were eager to remove the constraints that it imposed.[28] Thus, the ministers of the

[28] D.W. Harkness, *The Restless Dominion* (London, 1969).

Irish Free State were to the forefront in promoting the evolution of the Empire into the Commonwealth, leading to the enactment in 1931 of the Statute of Westminster, whereby Westminster relinquished its claim to legislate for the dominions. This opened the way to the dismantling of the dominion status of the Irish Free State, which was achieved by De Valera following his accession to power as leader of Fianna Fáil in 1932.

The 1937 Constitution was designed to legitimise the Irish state as an expression of the nation and of the national will. Implicitly repudiating the monarchical framework of British constitutional law, article 1 declares:

> The Irish nation hereby affirms its inalienable, indefeasible, and sovereign right to choose its own form of government, to determine its relations with other nations, and to develop its life, political, economic and cultural, in accordance with its own genius and traditions.

While technically the new constitution could have been adopted by the ordinary legislative process, de Valera invoked the principle of popular sovereignty by putting it to a plebiscite and enshrining within it the principle of the referendum. If its theoretical foundations were thus radically altered, there was little substantial change in the inherited structures of the state, developed over centuries or put in place since 1922, other than the introduction of a figurehead presidency. If there was no mention of British monarch or Commonwealth in the constitution, de Valera had left an opening for both in the External Relations Act of 1936. Under its terms, the king was authorised to act in certain diplomatic matters for Ireland as for other members of the Commonwealth, subject to the advice of the Irish government. In this way ambassadors to Ireland continued to present their credentials in London. The External Relations Act was repealed and the final links with Crown and Commonwealth severed by an act of 1948 that also provided for the declaration the following year of the Republic of Ireland. In response, Westminster passed the Ireland Act of 1949 under which the position of Northern Ireland within the United Kingdom was reaffirmed.

Partition hung heavily over all constitutional politics in the South. Maintaining the link with the British Commonwealth had been the only eirenic gesture towards the unionists that de Valera's nationalist ideology would allow him to make, and it did nothing to counteract the impact of the irredentist language of the 1937 Constitution. Articles 2 and 3 asserted the right of the Dublin Government to rule over 'the whole island of Ireland, its islands and the territorial seas', while foregoing the exercise of that right 'pending the reintegration of the national territory'. The outcome of the constitutional initiatives of the years 1920–22 had not been so much to divide Ireland into two comparable successor polities as to cut off one corner of the island and name it Northern Ireland, with the southern state inheriting the mantle of the integral Ireland but now shorn of its 'fourth green field'.

Northern Ireland had been given legal and political existence but it still had to a large extent to be invented, and much would depend on the success of that exercise. The Orange myth provided unionists with a foundation legend, and it scarcely mattered for this purpose that Aughrim and the Boyne lay in the South and that the majority of the population of Derry was nationalist. Although three of the counties of Ulster were not included in Northern Ireland, the new polity took unto itself the identity of the ancient province, a development facilitated by the fact that pre-1920 unionist organisation was on a provincial basis. Thus the ruling party was named the Ulster Unionist Party, rather than the Northern Ireland Unionist Party. With friend and foe disinclined, for different reasons, to talk of Northern Ireland as a state, 'the province' became a common alternative usage for unionists. Meanwhile, the work of the state was creating its own realities. While Northern Ireland was subject to legislation made at Westminster for the United Kingdom, its domestic law – building on the existing Irish corpus – was now made by its own parliament.

The monumental new building constructed at Stormont to house the parliament, and opened in 1932, is a classic statement of civil power. The development of a new Belfast-based administration with its own distinctive configuration of ministries, the reorganisation of local government in the 'province', and the local impact of the economic and fiscal regime of the United Kingdom, meant that the state in Northern Ireland came to diverge in structure from that in the South to the point where even anti-partitionists would not seriously envisage its undoing in detail. The vulnerability of Northern Ireland lay not in a failure to invent a distinctive polity but in the failure to win the support of the large nationalist/Catholic minority of the population. This was in turn due, either partially or entirely, to politically motivated discrimination (in matters such as employment, public housing and local government franchises) that was not unparalleled by the standards of the Western world before World War Two, but that had become intolerable by the 1960s. Inability to respond adequately to the consequent civil rights demands led to the suspension of the Stormont regime in 1972 and the resumption of direct rule from London. The civil disturbances, paramilitary terror campaigns and Crown force activities that delineate the 'Troubles' of the period from the late 1960s to the late 1990s cost more than three thousand lives.

The Belfast Agreement signed on Good Friday 1998 documents the internal configuration of Irish polities at the close of the twentieth century. What it shows is that Northern Ireland, in less than eighty years, has established itself as an enduring entity but has not succeeded in winning exclusive status within its territory at the expense of the ancient country of Ireland. Nationalist parties have agreed to legitimise and participate in a Northern

Ireland regime located at Stormont. In return, they have secured the creation of a North/South ministerial council, under the auspices of which bodies have been established that have power to administer island-wide policies and structures in designated areas such as languages, tourism and waterways. This is an obvious gesture towards all-Ireland government, but not unitary Irish government, for in the constitution of these bodies both administrations have equal representation, a clear concession of some form of parity between the two regimes, carrying overtones of federalism. Even more strikingly, the electorate of the Republic voted in May 1998 by an overwhelming majority to delete the claim of the Dublin government on the entire island contained in articles 2 and 3 of the 1937 constitution and to concede the right of a majority in Northern Ireland either to maintain membership of the United Kingdom or to opt for a united Ireland. It is not unprecedented for governments to make territorial concessions, but there can be very few instances of an irredentist claim being abandoned by plebiscite. Arguably, Irish nationalists are being generous because of an easy expectation that there is something inevitable about Irish unity. But their leaders also seem to accept, at least tacitly, that a unitary Ireland, as distinct from a united Ireland, is no longer feasible and that the distinctiveness of the six-county polity is assured, whichever 'sovereign' state it decides to adhere to.

While aspects of Irishness had been shaped for centuries in an Irish polity, it was only from 1922 that nationalists had control of one. In the following fifteen years they succeeded impressively with the politics of national self-assertion and they promoted (and exploited) nationalist ideology and culture in various guises. On the other hand, their record then and later was less than impressive in the development of state institutions. There was no great architectural expression of national self-assertion on the lines of Stormont. Instead, the former Dublin town house of the dukes of Leinster was adapted as a parliament building. There was no conservationist thrust behind this: it could be utilised when necessary, but architecture from earlier times – particularly in the form of the stately home or big house – was for long regarded as a relic of oppression and some kind of affront to the nation.[29] The same attitude applied to written records. The Public Record Office of Ireland with contents going back to the Middle Ages suffered collateral destruction in the civil warfare of June 1922. While the building was restored, official attitudes to the preservation of archives were lacking in the civic enthusiasm that is the norm for nation states, and compared unfavourably with policy in Northern Ireland, where the Public Record Office of Northern Ireland was established by an Act of 1923. Not until 1986 was comparable legislation enacted in the South, leading to the for-

---

[29] T.M. Dooley, *The Decline of the Big House in Ireland: A Study of Irish Landed Families, 1860–1960* (Dublin, 2001).

mation of the National Archives. Significantly, de Valera bequeathed his personal papers not to any state repository but to the Franciscan convent at Killiney.

National pageantry was never developed in a systematic way. There were impressive displays by the forces of the state on occasions, but no equivalent of France's Bastille Day or 4 July in the USA emerged. A Garden of Remembrance was created in Dublin, but not until the 1960s. The National Day of Commemoration, eventually inaugurated in the 1980s, embodies a sensitivity to diversity of allegiances that is far removed from the triumphalism of its equivalents elsewhere. Displays of triumphalism and chauvinism have not been lacking, but they tend to be unstructured, casual, one-off or left to private initiative.

The truth is that most of the leadership elite, particularly in the early decades of independence, while they idolised the nation, had an ideological suspicion of the state, and thought of themselves not as having achieved control of it but as having escaped from it. The sources of this attitude lay in one particular stream of contemporary political thought, with strong Catholic affinities. Many factors, not least the influence of British norms, went to ensure the survival of parliamentary democracy on the Westminster model in the Irish Free State in the 1920s and 1930s when it was being subverted elsewhere in Europe, and the weakness of 'nation-state' ideology may have been one of those factors.

The history of the currency in independent Ireland might be taken as paradigmatic. There was no question of the new state causing the upheaval to vested interests that an independent currency would have implied, and sterling continued in use as previously. When a separate Irish currency was eventually established by an Act of 1927, it was embellished by a set of handsome and distinctive new coins that were recognisably Irish and bore no royal head, but it was fixed securely at one hundred per cent parity with sterling, and backed by bullion and British government securities. Parity with sterling was broken only in 1979 when Ireland joined the European Monetary System, which in turn proved to be the preliminary to the formation of a European currency that the republic readily embraced.

The ideal of economic self-sufficiency was promoted as a plank in the Fianna Fáil election platform in 1932, and it had considerable attractions in the era of increased protectionism that accompanied the depression of the early 1930s. From 1932, the new Government's policy of promoting manufacturing industry in Ireland through a system of tariffs, quotas and other controls produced results in terms of increased industrial employment and the fostering of a protected manufacturing sector.[30] The simultaneous attempt to establish more people securely on the land in labour-intensive agriculture was less successful. Britain remained the dominant foreign

---

[30] M.E. Daly, *Industrial Development and Irish National Identity, 1922–39* (Syracuse, 1992).

market and the Anglo-Irish Trade Agreement of 1938 secured terms that ensured substantial protection of Irish industry and limited access to British markets for agricultural produce. Bargaining with the British about the terms of trade, rather than having matters decided by market forces, was a significant form of national self-assertion. From the 1930s, the doctrine of economic self-sufficiency became part of the rhetoric of Irish nationalism and this proved to be a handicap when, in the wake of World War Two, the adoption of free trade and foreign investment were called for if the country was to participate in the new prosperity. Sean Lemass (1899–1971), who as minister in the 1930s had been an apostle of self-sufficiency, is one of the icons of modern Ireland because of his leading role in the escape from this straitjacket during his time as taoiseach (prime minister) from 1959 to 1966.

The Anglo-Irish Free Trade Agreement of 1965 marked the abandonment of a core value of the dominant nationalist ideology. Joining the European Economic Community in 1973 involved a pooling of sovereignty that subverted the doctrines of generations of those nationalist ideologues that post-independence politicians were accustomed to invoke as infallible guides to orthodoxy. In the enabling referendum, eighty-three per cent of those voting expressed support: nationalism like everything else about nationality is adjustable, flexible, renegotiable, as circumstances dictate. The most compelling circumstance in the EEC referendum was that the United Kingdom was about to join, and Ireland could not contemplate disruption of access to British markets. Having joined the EEC (subsequently renamed the European Community and later the European Union), Ireland achieved a level of independence of the British market such as the policy of self-sufficiency never provided, but the dependence remains significant.

With many of the landmarks of national distinctiveness disappearing all around, the principle of military neutrality has taken hold in Ireland as a symbolic assertion of independence. A policy adopted of necessity at the beginning of World War Two because any other course would almost certainly have led to the destabilisation of the state, it was justified afterwards, when membership of NATO was first an option, on the ground that partition made such collaboration with Britain impossible. Then, following accession to the United Nations in 1955, neutrality, as between the two cold war blocks, allowed Ireland to make a worthwhile impression on that stage. Old-style nationalist chauvinism is an element in the currently strong sentiment on the subject of neutrality, but on its own it would tend towards armed neutrality rather than the unarmed (and inexpensive) variety that is Ireland's. Other contributory attitudes include sublimated social radicalism, reservations about the global might of the USA, moral aversion to militarism, a morally inspired wish to make the world a better place, and the belief that neutrality allows Ireland to have a distinctive role on the world stage.

The European movement has amounted from the beginning to an admission that the apotheosis of the nation state after the Great War was not the answer to the need for stability and security. To that extent, it is an attempt to find an acceptable alternative way of providing some of the functions of the pre-1914 empires. For the member countries, the European Union has taken its place alongside the state as a field of legislated homogenisation. This transcending of the national polities tends to be under-noticed because in most member countries, including Ireland, national elites are disinclined to draw attention to it. There is no myth of Europe capable of competing with the myths of the nations. Benedict Anderson has argued that the emergence of nationalism in colonial empires owed more than a little to the frustration of officials trapped in the provinces and denied the possibility of advancement to the positions of higher authority in the metropolitan country.[31] This kind of problem does not arise in the EU. On the contrary, one of the outstanding attractions of the Union, especially for the citizens of a smaller country, is that its positions of influence and power up to the highest level are not subject to any restriction concerning origins. Irish people have reached the top strata in the civil service and the European parliament. Less happily, the EU has not fully overcome another critical weakness of the old empires: the inability to be the arena of democracy, the place where the citizens vote their rulers into or out of office on the basis of general consensus, and thereby legitimise authority. That is still largely the function of the nation state, and has been exercised in independent Ireland over a period of eighty years. The Unionist regime in Northern Ireland collapsed after fifty years through want of legitimacy owing to lack of general consensus. The Belfast Agreement has put in place a system designed to ensure consensus and legitimacy but that may not greatly facilitate change of government.

For the purposes of understanding the evolution of Irish nationality, two points stand out from a review of the Irish polity over the ages. Firstly, the concept or reality of Ireland as a distinct polity has served through much of recorded history to secure Irishness as a category with substantial content. As well as giving the student of things Irish much to examine over a period of nearly one and a half millennia this (as will be seen in the next chapter) has provided the inventors of Irish nationality, and particularly nationalists of the early twentieth century, with an opportunity to present a nationalism that was largely of their own construction as the essential, divinely ordained manifestation of an ancient nation.

Secondly, the study of Irish polities brings home the extent to which the Irish state, and as a consequence the definition of Irishness, have been informed by English influence. Two things follow from this. One is an overlap between the cultures of modern Ireland and those of England, and

---

31 B. Anderson, *Imagined Communities: Reflections on the Origin and Spread of Nationalism* (London, revised edn., 1991), pp. 60–5.

Britain at large, to an extent that has few parallels as between separate states: this is epitomised by the presence in Britain of a large population with strong current connections with Ireland. The other is a tendency of Irish nationalist discourse to focus attention on those areas that can be represented as owing nothing to English influence and either to ignore the overlap or, at times of particular stress, to crusade against selected aspects of it under the banner of de-Anglicisation.[32]

---

[32] Wide-ranging discussion of issues arising in this chapter can be found in D.G. Boyce, *Nationalism in Ireland* (London, 3rd edn., 1995); M. Hechter, *Internal Colonialism: the Celtic Fringe in British National Development, 1536–1966* (London, 1975); N. Mansergh, *The Irish Question, 1840–1921* (London, rev. edn., 1965); K. Jeffery (ed.), *'An Irish Empire?': Aspects of Ireland and the British Empire* (Manchester, 1996).

|2|

Origins

Nowhere is nation-invention more in evidence than in the matter of origins. The collective ideology of nations, as of families, tribes and ethnic groups, almost invariably centres on a myth of group origins. Thus, modern Italians see themselves as descendants of the ancient Romans, while French citizens of every creed and colour have the Gauls as putative ancestors. Such assumptions may be congruent with historical facts or they may be patent fictions, or something in between. And these myths are seldom simple and unchanging. Different understandings of American origins have placed centre stage the landings of Columbus, of the Pilgrim Fathers, of the 'huddled masses' on Ellis Island and of enslaved Africans. At various times and in various combinations, English origin myths have invoked Ancient Britons, Romans, Angles, Saxons, Danes and Normans.

The seminal Irish origin myth is found in the *Lebor Gabála Érenn* (literally 'Book of the Taking of Ireland', usually referred to in English as the 'Book of Invasions' and in modern Irish as *Leabhar Gabhála*), an eleventh-century compilation of earlier (probably eighth- and ninth-century) material, and itself subsequently the subject of several further recensions. The milieu of this composition was that of a learned ecclesiastical culture informed by the Bible and by Latin literature. In this setting, a story was invented which depicted the origins of Irish ruling families in terms of the biblical and classical worlds, and in particular as paralleling the experiences of the Hebrews depicted in the Old Testament. Pharaoh's Egypt, Scythia (the modern Ukraine), Crete and Spain all feature in this account of a wandering people. The saga culminates with the arrival in Ireland of the sons of Míl Espáne (Míl of Spain). To complete the biblical parallel, the promised land had to be won by force from earlier occupiers. And in line with the chronology of the renowned ecclesiastical historian Eusebius, a cyclical scheme had to be employed. Accordingly, accounts were constructed of

earlier successive invasions by Parthalonians, Nemedians, Fir Bolg and
Tuatha Dé Danann. The subordinate or unfree contemporary peoples were
identified as descendants of the Fir Bolg. To be a Milesian, a descendant of
Míl, was to belong to the tribes of the elect. Over time, and in response to
changes in the configuration of power, details of the legend were modified
so as to admit ever more lineages and families to the privilege of descent
from Míl. It is important to appreciate that the Milesian myth was invented
to justify the status of ruling dynasties.[1]

By the eighth century the supposed Milesians had already come to
describe themselves by the term *Goídel* (latterly *Gael*), derived originally
from an uncomplimentary Welsh epithet. Not for another thousand years or
more would the idea take hold that Welsh and Irish were both 'Celts' and
thus of a common stock. The Welsh and other Britons possessed an origin
myth focused on descent from a fictional Brutus, or Britto, great-grandson
of Aeneas, the legendary founder of Rome. With similar inventiveness, the
learned men of the Gaels placed among the ancestors of Míl a certain
Gaedel Glas, supposed grandson of Noah, thereby glorifying their collective
name with a pseudo-biblical derivation.

The Gaels called their island country Ériu (later Éire), and a dozen names
besides, including Banba, Fotla and Fál. In some versions of the myth, Ériu
was a goddess identified with the land itself and had borne the heirs of the
sons of Míl from whom all subsequent Milesian lineages claimed descent.
Julius Caesar, who conquered Gaul, and in 55–54 BC invaded Britain,
referred to the neighbouring island as Hibernia in his *De bello Gallico*. The
subsequent usage of *Hiberni* (or *Hibernici*) to designate the inhabitants in
Latin was supplemented from the fourth century by the new term *Scotti* (or
Scoti, plural of *Scotus*), assigned in the context of warlike raiding against
Roman Britain. By this time, the Gaels had extended their influence to the
western part of what they called Alba and the Romans called Caledonia,
and what in later centuries came to be called Scotland. The original homeland of the *Scoti* would acquire the designation of Ireland, the first part of
the word deriving from Ériu. (In later centuries, the attribution to Scotland
of the medieval *Scoti* and their achievements would cause confusion and
resentment.) Meanwhile, the myth-makers of the *Leabhar Gabhála* had
devised an exalted derivation for *Scotus* by inserting a Pharaoh's daughter
named Scota into the ancestry of the Milesians. Indeed, the prominent place
of Scythia in the origin myth is due largely to another approach to explaining the derivation of *Scotus*: for some medieval scholars – and the mindset
survives – the similarity between Scythia and Scotia was sufficient to justify

---

[1]   The standard (and much criticised) edition is R.A.S. Macalister (ed. and trans.), *Lebor
      Gabála Érenn: the Book of the Taking of Ireland* (London, 5 vols, 1938–56). John Carey's
      translation of one recension is available in John T. Koch (ed.), *The Celtic Heroic Age:
      Literary Sources for Ancient Celtic Europe and Early Ireland and Wales* (3rd edn.,
      Andover, MA and Aberystwyth, 2000), pp. 226–71.

predication of a link. In the same way, the prominence of Spain in the story is probably due to the superficial resemblance of 'Iberia' and 'Hibernia'. In similar vein, Míl Espáne turns out to have no more basis in scholarship than a rendition of the Latin 'miles Hispaniae', literally 'soldier of Spain'.[2]

Scholars are now generally agreed that the *Leabhar Gabhála*, while revealing much about the society that generated it, has no reliability as a source for its ostensible subject, the early peopling of the country. Archaeologists identify occupation by hunter-gatherers from about 7000 BC. Agriculture was established with the early Neolithic Age, about 4000 BC, and in time supported a culture immortalised by a series of monumental passage tombs of which Newgrange (*c.*3000 BC) is the most celebrated. From the Bronze Age (*c.*2000 BC–*c.*500 BC) there is a rich legacy of ornamental gold work and bronze instruments. The use of iron arrived about the middle of the first millennium BC, and a few generations of scholars in the twentieth century linked this with linguistic change that led to the eventual dominance of a new language throughout the island – 'Goidelic' or 'Gaelic'.

The extent to which all or any of these cultural changes, extending over many millennia, were consequential on population replacement is a key question in Irish pre-history, and indeed the issue retains its interest in respect of the period of documented history that begins in the fifth century. At one extreme, every significant change can be put down to the arrival of a new set of conquerors (the 'invasionist' model), while at the other end stand advocates of 'immobilism', who see no need to postulate any outside influence after a first settlement, other than those of peaceful commercial exchange. A recent authoritative survey suggests that the way ahead may lie in the invocation of a sophisticated appreciation of migration as a vector of cultural and population change.[3] But in any event, it is vital to banish mental links between that population movement, whatever form (or, more probably, forms) it took, and the incursion of the legendary sons of Míl Espáne in the *Leabhar Gabhála*.

The first invasion of Ireland recorded in contemporary documents was that of the Vikings, whose language provided the original of the Teutonic second element in the name 'Ireland'. The assaults of these Scandinavian freebooters in the ninth and tenth centuries gave the term Gall, with the meaning of foreigner, i.e. foreigner, a menacing resonance, particularly for the monastic communities who were their principal victims – and who also controlled the writing of the records. After the Vikings had settled down and intermarried with Gaelic inhabitants, and – through the trade of the towns they had themselves founded – had become an integral part of the

2   John Carey, *The Irish National Origin-Legend: Synthetic Pseudohistory* (Cambridge, 1994), p. 8.
3   J.P. Mallory and B. Ó Donnabháin, 'The origins of the population of Ireland: a survey of putative immigrations in Irish prehistory and history' in *Emania 17* (1998), pp. 47–71.

economy and politics of the country, the polar opposition of *Gael* and *Gall*
still retained a heavy charge.

The invading Anglo-Normans (so called) of the late twelfth century were
followed by their own chronicler in the person of the Pembrokeshire-born
cleric Giraldus Cambrensis (Gerald of Wales) (1146–1223), whose summary of the settlement history of Ireland followed the general model of the
Leabhar Gabhála.[4] That material was available to him because a Latin version of it was in circulation, and had been for centuries. For his own purposes, Giraldus interpolated into the pseudo-history of Irish origins an
element of the pseudo-history of British origins as recounted by Geoffrey of
Monmouth, with the tale of how Gurguintius, King of the Britons, assigned
Ireland to the Basclenses, a wandering people he happened to encounter.[5] By
this precedent and by other accretions, Giraldus purported to establish a
precedent for the right of his King, Henry II, to dispose of the island in his
turn. However, the adoption by Giraldus of the *Leabhar Gabhála* framework helped to secure a long future for the Irish myth.

Giraldus's desire to justify external intervention in Ireland led him on to
a denigration of Irish character and mores in a catalogue that runs from customs which he may genuinely have seen as backward (such as bareback
horse-riding), through stereotypical allegations about laziness and lack of
industry, to obviously far-fetched and malicious intimations of treachery,
debauchery and bestiality. While his comments on the clergy were judi-
ciously ambivalent, he asserted that in parts of the country the people were
neither evangelised nor baptised, and threw in the gratuitous observation
that all the country's saints were confessors and none of them martyrs,
nobody having been found willing 'to cement the foundation of the growing
church with the shedding of his blood'.[6] Apart from its specific political
function, this diatribe reflected the contemporary reforming western
Church's prejudices and concerns about the state of religion in Ireland. In
any event, Cambrensis became the chosen authority of those who, down to
early modern times and beyond, have sought evidence for the barbarity of
Irish ways. And this attitude, invariably associated with Cambrensis, introduced a new and subsequently recurrent element into consideration of Irish
origins, namely, the issue of whether Irish society before the arrival of the
Anglo-Normans was civilised or barbaric.

Concerted expression of indignation against Cambrensis was not to come
until the early modern period. Before that, the origins that mattered most
were not those of an imagined community but of lineages, families and
dynastic rulers. So, while the *Leabhar Gabhála* posited a common origin for

---

[4] Gerald of Wales, *The History and Topography of Ireland* (London, 1983), ed. by John
    O'Meara, pp. 92–100.
[5] Ibid.
[6] Gerald of Wales, *History and Topography*, pp. 100–20.

the Gaels, it simultaneously provided the basis for distinctions between different lines of descent among them. Genealogy (*seanchas*) was one of the major fields of study in the ecclesiastical schools of early Christian Ireland, the wealth even of what has survived the depredation of the ages bearing witness to the importance of (perceived) ancestry in the contemporary political and social system. Powerful families justified their status by reference to the branches of a numerously ramified genealogical tree. The standing of a king was inseparable from his place on a chain of paternity reaching upwards to Noah and Adam (the male line only was considered). If all lines led back to Adam they were not all equal: whether in terms of individuals or lineages, the family tree established a hierarchy of worth. And to have any kind of genealogical tree was to belong to the aristocracy and to be set apart from the common people. Genealogy continued to be a central concern of Gaelic culture in the later medieval period, and the praise poetry of the bard, in flattering the chieftain, made as much as possible of his ancestry. It was a preoccupation shared with other European elites, including the Anglo-Norman aristocracy, and, in due course, Gaelic bards would minister to the genealogical vanity of barons who had adopted Gaelic language and ways. Collections of *seanchas* compiled in the seventeenth century include many families with non-Gaelic names and pedigrees. By then, following the collapse of the Gaelic political system, one of the grievances of the bards was that, while their former patrons had tumbled down, some of the people without pedigree were rising in the world.

Meanwhile, Milesians had followed the Anglo-Normans in adopting coats of arms, seals and other appurtenances of heraldry. Irishmen seeking employment in Europe in the seventeenth and eighteenth centuries had much to gain by way of advancement under the *ancien régime* through establishing their noble status. They were frequently assisted in this – for suitable fees – by the office of the Ulster King at Arms established in Dublin Castle since 1552, whose main business was with the more recent noble creations of the Crown.[7]

Although they had ceased to be of much practical use by the end of the eighteenth century, Anglo-Norman and Milesian genealogies continued to command interest. When General Patrice de MacMahon burst on the European scene as leader of the triumphant French campaign in northern Italy in the summer of 1859, the Irish nationalist newspaper press carried genealogies linking him to Brian Boru, Míl, Noah and Adam. In 1943 Eamon de Valera saw to the suppression of the post of Ulster King at Arms and its replacement by that of Chief Herald of Ireland in the Genealogical Office. Subsequently, procedures were put in place to recognise the 'rightful' claimants to the chieftancy of Gaelic families, and by the end of 1944,

---

[7] Susan Hood, *Royal Roots, Republican Inheritance: the Survival of the Office of Arms* (Dublin, 2002).

fifteen had been so recognised on the basis of direct descent from former chiefs.[8] This was a travesty of Gaelic succession practices, but it serves as a reminder of what is the dominant origin myth of modern Ireland, namely that in which the Gael is the legitimate proprietor, to be restored to his own (there was no question of female succession) by political independence. Evident, too, is the precedence in de Valera's thinking of origin myth over any egalitarian or republican principles. Here, as in other fields, gestures came easily to the independent state, provided that they cost little in the world of making and spending: the newly recognised chieftains were not about to be granted any resumption of presumed ancestral properties. These, of course, were by now in the hands of a class whose claims had also on occasion been advanced on the basis of descent from the dispossessed Gaels – the Irish farmers.

'Clan' gatherings supported by commercial interests constitute a niche segment of the Irish tourism market that has been identified for promotion. However, it is likely that most of those who gather to celebrate the family surname are more interested in tracing their own immediate forebears than in admiring the pedigree of the chieftain. The twentieth century has democratised genealogy as so much else, a development well illustrated by the large numbers of visitors from abroad who annually spend portions of their precious vacation time in the facilities of the National Library of Ireland, reconstructing the family tree.

If the desire to trace ancestors is stronger among the descendants of exiles, this is not to say that the Irish at home are more knowledgeable on the subject. Few people in modern society retain orally transmitted knowledge, including names and identities of progenitors, beyond the second or third generation. De Valera's deference to Gaelic chieftains notwithstanding, in a society transformed by nationalism, individual and family descent pales into insignificance alongside assumptions about national origins. The Gaelic term *mórtas cine* (pride of ancestry), originally referring to the self-regard of ruling families (a conceit shared with the high-born of all pre-modern societies), transfers easily to the popular chauvinism of later times. Analogously, assumptions about family genealogy meld into notions of collective origins that feed the myths of race. While it is easy to decry the credulousness of those who constructed detailed genealogies stretching back to Adam, many historians and others, in Ireland and elsewhere, continue to be mesmerised by the concept of descent.

While the Anglo-Normans have entered the perceived story of Irish origins as a single racial entity, theirs is a case that illustrates the limitations of such racial categorisation. Gaelic sources referred to them initially as *Sacsain* (literally 'Saxons', but in practice a usage for 'English') and, after

---

8   Press statement on behalf of the minister of Arts and Heritage: http://www.ireland.com/
     newspaper/breaking/2001/0128/breaking24.htm [28 Jan. 2001].

they had settled, by the epithet *Gaill*, reserving the term *Sacsain* for the residents of England. The knights speaking Norman-French who came to Ireland in the second half of the twelfth century were from families that had been settled for a century in England and Wales and had intermarried with the prior inhabitants. The footsoldiers and other followers were of Welsh, English, Flemish and Breton backgrounds. To describe the invaders as Normans, Anglo-Normans, Cambro-Normans or Anglo-French, as various scholars have done, is to focus on their ruling elite, but no single term for them is beyond criticism. They referred to themselves, before and after coming to Ireland, as 'Anglais', and in writing Latin as 'Angli', thereby identifying with the kingdom of England conquered by their recent progenitors.

However they are named, the invaders, having failed to gain control of the entire country, created a polity beholden to the English monarchy that encompassed only portions of the population. Throughout the remainder of the medieval period, a legal distinction was maintained between the two 'nations', English and Irish. In the later Middle Ages, as the distinctive culture of the English in Ireland – language, dress, laws and customs – was melding with its Gaelic counterpart, the legal distinction was upheld all the more fervently. Concomitantly, the Gaelic poets maintained as an axiom the Gael v Gall dichotomy. However effective the divisions may have been in legal or cultural terms (and that could be seriously questioned), what needs to be emphasised is that they represent no watertight separation along racial lines.[9] Intermarriage alone would have seen to that, but it is also clear that considerable numbers of Gaelic inhabitants were admitted by purchase or otherwise to the privileges of being English. In other words, the distinction between the two 'nations' in medieval Ireland, like many distinctions between nations, was supported by a myth and rhetoric of origins that concealed as much as it revealed. Such illusions are greatly helped by the conventions of patrilineal genealogy which conceal over half of the genetic inheritance of the produce of a 'mixed' union.

In the early modern period, the definition of origins acquired fresh vigour. The rich and varied preoccupations of humanist scholars and writers included, where politics so required, the justification of confessional ecclesiastical systems and the elaboration of honourable 'national' pasts for newly burgeoning states. In some countries, Ireland included, the two functions could be combined. The Tudor conquest had established the Irish state on an entirely new footing with a Protestant state religion. James Ussher (1581–1656), born in Dublin, an early student at Trinity College, and ultimately Archbishop of Armagh, was a towering figure in the scholarship of the age. On the basis of his prodigious learning, he delved deeply into the early history of Christianity in Ireland, and discerned there and in subsequent developments the foundations of a national Protestant Church. For

---

[9]   K. Nicholls, *Gaelic and Gaelicised Ireland in the Later Middle Ages* (Dublin, 1972), p. 4.

good measure, he made the case also for the originally Protestant character of Christianity in Britain, though carefully maintaining the separateness of Ireland, in his *Discourse on the Religion Anciently Professed by the Irish and English* (1623). Ussher defended the name and fame of Ireland in combating attempts, especially by Thomas Dempster, to appropriate as adornments of the history of Scotland those *Scoti* of the early medieval period famed for learning and piety, and he made a major contribution in both ideological and strategic terms to the fashioning of the Protestant Church of Ireland as a distinctive institution.

Protestantism excepted, scholarly ideologues on the other side of the confessional divide shared Ussher's general concerns. They, too, deployed the scholarship of the age to explore the Irish Christian past, in which they descried the foundations of a Catholic nation. But the Catholics had additional concerns. Living, as so many of them were, in exile in Europe and dependent on the goodwill of others, they were required to justify themselves, and the basis of their importunacy, to foreigners by turn curious, supportive and resentful.[10] Their biggest challenge was how to present a united front: the Catholic exiles were drawn from both medieval 'nations', from Gaelic Ireland and the English culture of the Pale and the towns. For them to postulate a single Irish Catholic nation was a notable feat of invention and an exercise fraught with tension.

Most of the émigrés from Ireland, in the closing decades of the sixteenth century, resided in the Low Countries, where Ortelius and Mercator were just then perfecting the arts of cartography, leading to the publication of reliable and widely available atlases.[11] So they had early experience of the nation-making impact of the national map – the familiar icon of one's country – that continues to have so much impact on the inculcation of nationality. A pioneer among them was Richard Stanihurst (1547–1618), son of a Dublin notable, uncle of James Ussher and an Oxford graduate. His 1570s' contribution to Holinshed's *Chronicles* shows him attuned to the hopes for the cultural reform and unification of Ireland set out by the previous generation of Pale reformers. He asserted that Gaelic society, while undoubtedly in need of civilisation, should be reached not through coercion but by means of 'humane and persuasive methods'.[12] By the early 1580s, Stanihurst had embraced Counter-Reformation Catholicism, going to live in the Low Countries where it was being advanced by the strong arm of Philip II of Spain. At Antwerp, he published his *De rebus in Hibernia gestis* (1584), intending to provide an international audience with an introduction to the island and its history. While the certainty of the superiority of his own people is again evident, the treatment of the Gaelic Irish is noticeably more cir-

---

[10]   See Gráinne Henry, *The Irish Military Community in Spanish Flanders* (Dublin, 1992).
[11]   C. Lennon, *Sixteenth-century Ireland: The Incomplete Conquest* (Dublin, 1994), pp. 2–3.
[12]   C. Lennon, *Richard Stanihurst, the Dubliner, 1547–1618* (Dublin, 1981), p. 39.

cumspect and tolerant than in his earlier work. Practical politics meant that in the invention of an Irish Catholic nation, the Gaelic Irish, whatever their perceived faults, could not be excluded and so could not be disowned.

Neither could the English of Ireland be written out of such a history. In the early seventeenth century, Philip O'Sullivan Beare (*c*.1590–*c*.1634) rejected and denounced what he saw as Stanihurst's denigration of the culture, customs and history of the Gaels. At the same time he felt constrained to postulate – without producing any substantiating evidence – that, in old age, Stanihurst had come to repent of his allegedly defamatory published opinions. The Palesman had once used the term 'Anglo-Hiberni' ('Anglo-Irish') instead of the customary 'Anglici' (English) to describe those of his own background, as an expression of their distinctiveness from the English of England. He was castigated by O'Sullivan Beare, not for assuming the 'Irish' part of the epithet but for retaining the 'Anglo' part. Henceforth, O'Sullivan declared, all the Catholics of Ireland, irrespective of background, should be called Irish.[13]

In fact, they were to retain separate designations for the better part of a century, as the Old Irish and the Old English, the latter now severely distinguished from the New English, the recently arrived and predominantly Protestant place seekers and planters who were securing and benefiting from the advance of Crown control. But the accommodation between the two Catholic groups that strategy demanded was pressing the exiled literati towards the invention of a single national identity.[14] Richard Creagh (1523–86), scion of a Limerick merchant family of English culture, papally appointed Archbishop of Armagh from 1564, was apparently thinking, at least by the early 1580s, in terms of a national history founded on the *Leabhar Gabhála* myth.[15] Following along these lines, a priest of the next generation who had studied at Rheims and Bordeaux, Geoffrey Keating (*c*.1580–*c*.1644), was to compose the most successful formulation of an origin myth for the Irish Catholic nation. Like Stanihurst, Keating was identified by his surname as one of the Old English, but the ethos of the minor landowning and culturally mixed society of south Tipperary to which he belonged was at a far remove from that of the Dublin merchant class, particularly in the matter of language. Not only did Keating have a fluent knowledge of Irish, but he also possessed a thorough command of Gaelic learning. In his *Foras feasa ar Éirinn* ('Compendium of knowledge about Ireland'), completed in 1634, he reformulated the contents of the *Leabhar Gabhála*, the *seanchas* and other inherited material in contemporary prose

---

[13] C. Lennon, *Stanihurst*, pp. 117–19.

[14] See Thomas O'Connor, 'Towards the invention of the Irish Catholic *natio*: Thomas Messingham's *Florilegium*' in *Irish Theological Quarterly*, vol. 64, no. 2 (1999), pp. 157–78.

[15] Colm Lennon, *An Irish Prisoner of Conscience of the Tudor Era: Archbishop Richard Creagh of Armagh, 1523–86* (Dublin, 2000), p. 138.

form to produce a coherent and engaging story. It concludes with the arrival of the Normans, the last of a series of invasions, and as close to the time of writing as one might care to come in setting out the history of an ancient and Christian civilisation. The main concern of the work is a celebration of the legends and history of the Gaels. In his prologue, Keating listed and denounced historians, from Giraldus Cambrensis to Stanihurst, who had found fault with the civilisation of the Gaelic Irish, making much of the fact that he himself was of Old English stock and therefore a witness from the other side. Keating deployed his sources and arguments using the techniques of humanist scholarship, as did so many contemporary authors of national histories, and he used the weapons of scholarly disputation to attack with great effect the arguments of opponents. But, in an unashamed exercise in double standards, he scarcely ever applied critical methods to test the credibility of his own sources and interpretations.

He fits his own people in at the end in an obviously secondary place. Nonetheless, theirs is an honourable role. Strongbow, Hugh de Lacy and others from among the first set of Anglo-Norman arrivals are admitted to have behaved disgracefully, as a punishment for which they are allegedly without descendants. Others, he protests, behaved honourably and their numerous progeny have been agents of beneficence, worldly and spiritual. The legitimacy of the settlement is carefully demonstrated, specifically in terms of Gaelic consent. In 1092, Keating asserts, the nobles of Ireland, unable to agree among themselves on any other arrangement, had unanimously ceded the sovereignty of Ireland to the Pope. Accordingly, Pope Adrian IV was enabled to grant lordship of Ireland to the King of England, Henry II, which he did in 1155. It followed that the King was entirely within his rights in authorising the descent of his barons on the island, and in conferring fiefdoms upon them, a point underscored by the submission of the Irish lords to Henry during his visit to Ireland in 1171–72. The weakest part of this argument was its first premise – no such cession had occurred in 1092 – but, as throughout his work, Keating's concern is with constructing a myth, not with establishing veracity for its own sake. Keating's point was that Henry II, and therefore in his own time Charles I, was rightful king of Ireland, not by conquest but following free submission. Within a decade, the Old English lawyer, Patrick Darcy (1598–1668), a pioneering constitutional thinker, was arguing on the same basis for the legislative independence of the Irish Parliament.

If by choosing to write his work in Irish, Keating made a salient point about the centrality of things Gaelic to his view of the country, it is one that has to be taken in conjunction with his adoption of the previously little used term *Éireannach* for 'Irishman'. This was an inclusive usage in place of the old dichotomy of *Gael* v. *Gall*, and fitted with O'Sullivan Beare's call for a common name for the members of a newly forged nation. *Foras feasa ar Éirinn* was not to appear in print until long after Keating's death but, circulating widely in manuscript form in the original Irish and in English and Latin translations, it became the dominant account of Irish origins, establishing the enduring myth of Ireland as a Gaelic nation into which the Old English had been honourably integrated (see illustration p. 132).[16]

Keating was a priest imbued with Tridentine theology who wrote several works of Catholic piety. Under the banner of Protestantism, a newly forming elite was menacing the interests of his society and his religion. Given the circumstances of the times, Keating certainly did not envisage that anyone but Catholics could have membership of the national community adumbrated in *Foras feasa ar Éirinn*. Like contemporaries such as Thomas Messingham (*c.*1575–*c.*1638), another Old English priest, Keating presented an Irish nationality defined by adherence to the Catholic faith,[17] and like Messingham, or O'Sullivan Beare, Keating would not have considered the possibility that a Protestant, of whatever birth or ancestry, might be part of the nation he was celebrating. But his formulation, unlike others, had an openness that he scarcely contemplated and that would enhance its viability in future times. Thus, in the first published English translation of *Foras feasa*, that of Dermod O'Connor in 1723, 'Christian' is used systematically where Keating had written 'Catholic', without destroying the coherence of the argument: this would be impossible with the works of his Catholic contemporaries. Implicit in the twelfth-century conclusion of *Foras feasa* and in its entire thrust is a repudiation of the legitimacy of the New English incursion of Keating's own day, but his invasionist model had a logic of its own which might be used again.

The extended prologue to *Foras feasa* is devoted to rebuttal of Giraldus Cambrensis and other authors such as Spenser, Camden, Moryson and Davies, whom Keating deems to have denigrated the Irish people or things Irish. The point ultimately at issue was whether Ireland had been in a state of barbarism or civility before the arrival of the Normans. From early in the twelfth century, if not before, there is record of some of the English elites describing in disparaging terms the culture and customs of all those in Britain and Ireland who lay outside of England's politically and economically advanced polity. The terms in which Cambrensis described the Irish are strongly reminiscent of William of Malmesbury's unflattering depiction of the Welsh a few decades earlier.[18]

In respect of Ireland, the motif of backwardness would serve to justify the Anglo-Norman incursion, the Tudor conquest and, to a greater or lesser

---

[16] Bernadette Cunningham, *The World of Geoffrey Keating: History, Myth and Religion in Seventeenth-Century Ireland* (Dublin, 2002), pp. 173–225. The standard edition is *Foras feasa ar Éirinn: the History of Ireland*, eds David Comyn and P.S. Dinneen (London, 4 vols, 1902–14); the 1987 reprint has an introduction by Breandán Ó Buachalla.

[17] See T. O'Connor, above.

[18] John Gillingham, 'Foundations of a disunited kingdom' in A. Grant and K.J. Stringer (eds), *Uniting the Kingdom?: The Enigma of British History* (London, 1995), pp. 55–61.

extent, other 'civilising' missions extending down to the nineteenth century. Wilful ignorance of pre-Anglo-Norman achievement in Ireland became a much-utilised gambit on the English side. In response, Irish propagandists resorted to the invention of Gaelic golden ages, cultural or political, depending on need. Thus Keating conjured up, on the basis of very insubstantial evidence, a pre-Norman political system that was a model of harmonious monarchy linking ruler and ruled in a way that would be the envy of any early seventeenth-century polity. The kingdom of Ireland, complete with basic constitution and representative functions, is depicted as a Gaelic institution and one that was conveyed to Henry II by the free consent of the native princes.[19]

Rebuttal of Cambrensis, and assertion of ancient greatness, characterised the work of a sequence of Catholic historians following Keating, including John Lynch (*c.*1599–*c.*1673), Roderick O'Flaherty (1629–1718), Abbé James MacGeoghegan (1702–63) and Charles O'Conor (1710–91). The location of the Golden Age might alternate between the pre-Christian and Christian eras, depending on the needs of the moment. Conversely, New English authors from Edmund Spenser (1552–99) to Richard Cox (1650–1733), taking their cues from Cambrensis, presented pre-Anglo-Norman Ireland in an unflattering light, if indeed there was any light at all; and alleged that, the earlier colony having grown degenerate and succumbed to native barbarism, a new settlement was needed.

Repudiation of the Gaelic past was not an attitude that could be maintained unreservedly after taking up residence in Ireland. For one thing, the ideological underpinnings of the Established Church were firmly placed in the middle of the first millennium, so that the pulpit message of native barbarism had to be diluted with acknowledgement of an early, pre-Anglo-Norman Church blessedly free of the Roman yoke. Even before Ussher set the standard in the early seventeenth century, several late sixteenth-century churchmen newly arrived from England had made a beginning.[20] There is evidence that in the early eighteenth century several bishops of the Established Church were very well acquainted with, and well disposed towards, favourable accounts of Gaelic civilisation both before and after the arrival of Christianity.[21] Such accounts were available in print in Roderick O'Flaherty's *Ogygia, seu rerum Hibernicorum chronologia* (London, 1685) and Dermod O'Connor's English-language version of *Foras feasa* published

[19] See Brendan Bradshaw, 'Geoffrey Keating: apologist of Irish Ireland' in B. Bradshaw, A. Hadfield and W. Maley (eds), *Representing Ireland: Literature and the Origins of Conflict, 1534–1660* (Cambridge, 1993), p. 170.

[20] A. Ford, 'James Ussher and the formation of an Irish identity' in B. Bradshaw and P. Roberts (eds), *British Consciousness and Identity: The Making of Britain, 1533–1707* (Cambridge, 1998), p. 191.

[21] J.R. Hill, 'Popery and Protestantism, civil and religious liberty: the disputed lessons of Irish history, 1690–1812' in *Past & Present*, no. 118 (1988), p. 103.

in London and Dublin in 1723 and 1724 respectively. The appearance of the latter stymied the plans of the Kèrry-born Church of Ireland Dean of Trim, Anthony Raymond (1675–1726), a student of Irish, to publish his own history of Ireland, which would probably have been based very closely on Keating. Raymond had hoped to contradict 'the common notion that the Irish nation before the English came among them were a rude uncivilised people and governed by barbarous laws and customs'.[22]

By this time, political considerations were even more compelling than religious ones for, in its search for formulae to maximise its advantages, the ruling Protestant interest, on occasion, found the Irish past useful. As residents of Ireland they automatically had new concerns, dictated by geography and politics. With Westminster legislation in the 1690s putting Irish trade at a disadvantage against that of England, William Molyneux issued his *Case of Ireland's being Bound by Acts of Parliament in England Stated* (1698), harbinger of a series of assertions of the constitutional rights of Ireland, to which the most celebrated contribution would be Jonathan Swift's *Drapier's Letters* (1724–25). One of Molyneux's arguments was based on the premise that the Crown had acquired Ireland in the time of Henry II by consent and not by conquest. As with the Old English Keating and Darcy, this was a significant gesture towards identification with Gaelic origins, even if other arguments used by Molyneux and later advocates of his cause were based on asserting the entitlements of Protestants in Ireland as people of English descent. Indeed, following Sir John Davies, Molyneux and others toyed on occasion with an origin myth in which people of English stock (Old and New) formed the great majority of the population of Ireland. The Irish House of Commons of 1640, in which the Old English were prominent, had referred purposefully to the 'loyal and dutiful people of Ireland, being now for the most part derived from British ancestors'.[23] Statistics and ancestry both being such malleable subjects, it was not 'facts' about numbers or origins that rendered this embryonic myth non-viable. Rather, confessional division would rule out the possibility of elite unity around any myth of neighbouring-island ancestry for the population of Ireland, firstly because the Old English, as Catholics, would seldom again after 1640 be allowed to hold counsel as equals with the New English, and secondly because the New English came to see the Scottish-derived Presbyterians of Ulster as a greater menace than the Catholics. The alternative Keatingite myth of an indigenous population absorbing invaders would have a longer lease of life.

The Irish-born Abbé James MacGeoghegan who wrote his *History of Ireland* (Paris, 1758–62) in the France of the philosophes, acknowledged the

---

[22] Alan Harrison, *The Dean's Friend: Anthony Raymond (1675–1726), Jonathan Swift, and the Irish Language* (Dublin, 1999), p. 100.
[23] Quoted in E. Curtis and R.B. McDowell (eds), *Irish Historical Documents, 1172–1922* (London, 1943), p. 142.

implausibility of the suggestion that alone among the origin-tales of European nations, that of the Gaels might stand up to rational scrutiny. Yet he felt impelled to retell it:[24] obviously it had become a shibboleth. Charles O'Conor of Belnagare (1710–91), self-conscious descendant of the last high-king, Gaelic scholar and Catholic gentleman, was preoccupied with proving within the Milesian framework that pre-Christian Ireland had been home to a cultivated society. Finding the Scythian connection to be a serious propaganda disadvantage in this regard (Edmund Spenser, for example, had invoked Scythian origins as a probable explanation for Irish barbarism) O'Conor postulated that during their sojourn in Spain the Milesians had acquired the arts of civilisation brought there by the Phoenicians.[25] This conceit was taken up enthusiastically by Colonel Charles Vallancey (1721–1812), an English army officer stationed in Ireland, who became infatuated with the antiquities of the country and ventured to write about them on the basis of very limited competence.

Vallancey's fantasies drew down upon him and upon the entire Milesian myth the sharp criticism of Edward Ledwich (1738–1823), a Church of Ireland clergyman. Ledwich, who made liberal and apparently confident use of Gaelic sources, complimented Keating's literary style but dismissed the *Leabhar Gabhála* as comprising 'idle tales' and traced a critique of the story of Spanish origins back to Camden's *Britannia* (1586).[26] Ledwich – who uses footnotes to identify his sources – is possibly the first writer on Irish history with whose methodology a modern academic historian can identify, which, of course, is no guarantee that he is always reliable in his conclusions. Remarkably, having dismissed Keating, Ledwich proceeded to draw up his own list of invasions, including Fir Bolg and Fomorians, that drew on wider scholarship that had been influenced by the *Foras feasa* in a way that Ledwich obviously did not recognise. Down to the middle of the nineteenth century, reaction against Ledwich and sympathy with Vallancey's point of view inspired resistance to some of the de-mythologising conclusions of evidence-based archaeology, such as George Petrie's conclusion that Ireland's unique round towers were of medieval Christian provenance rather than products of a pre-Christian civilisation of oriental derivation.[27] Ledwich was resented not simply for repudiation of Keating but for another novelty which we will consider presently.

Whatever its implications for politics and identity, and they were various, there is no mistaking the fact that there was antagonism to the metropolitan

---

[24] 1869 edn., New York, p. 34ff.
[25] See C. O'Halloran, 'Ownership of the past: antiquarian debate and ethnic identity in Scotland and Ireland' in S.J. Connolly et al., *Conflict, Identity and Economic Development: Ireland and Scotland, 1600–1939* (Preston, 1999), p. 145.
[26] E. Ledwich, *Antiquities of Ireland* (Dublin, 1790).
[27] Joop Leerssen, *Remembrance and Imagination: Patterns in the Historical and Literary Representation of Ireland in the Nineteenth Century* (Cork, 1996), pp. 126–43.

English on the part of Protestants in eighteenth-century Ireland, who nonetheless considered themselves to be of English nationality.[28] Following a fitful career over three-quarters of a century, the assertiveness of the Protestant elite in Ireland was fully mobilised in the Volunteer movement of the 1770s, and was subsequently given institutional expression in the shape of Grattan's parliament, all under the banner of 'patriotism' and the 'Irish nation'. By this time, a small but not insignificant number of the Protestant elite had taken to the study of Irish language and antiquities, and some had even come to identify the ancient Gaels as their ancestors. In its pursuit and exercise of parliamentary independence, the Protestant elite had envisaged itself as the Irish nation. Along the way, a significant element of that elite saw the advantage and the attraction of the Gaelic myth as the basis for that nation. The ensuing pursuit of Gaelic antiquarianism by Protestants is typified by the founding of the Royal Irish Academy in the mid-1780s, the attempt of the patriot politician Henry Flood (1732–91) to bequeath funds for the establishment of a chair of Irish at Trinity College, and the publications of Charles Vallancey, Joseph Cooper Walker (1761–1810) and Charlotte Brooke (*c.*1740–1793) (see chapters four and five).

All of this happened in the context of an awareness of Keating, something well illustrated by the iconography of the Milesian crown. The frontispiece of O'Connor's translation of the *Foras feasa* was a highly imaginative depiction of Brian Boru wearing a peculiar crown with points around the rim. Later in the century, this version of the crown, which in fact has no serious historical credentials, appears in various political and literary contexts, including the iconography of the Royal Irish Academy.[29] When in 1785 the Belfast Presbyterian, William Drennan, wrote of the Volunteers as being 'all native Irish under the control of an English pale'[30] he was embracing the Keating myth, but it did not prove to serve the perceived needs of a sufficient number of the Volunteers to describe a realisable convergence of interests.

Most of the patriots did not see their assertion of Irish nationality as a repudiation of their English origins. In more recent times there has developed the expectation that everyone will have a clear-cut national or ethnic label ready for classification by census takers, political commentators and cultural analysts. If, even under pressure of this expectation, many of our contemporaries still fail to categorise themselves neatly, it is clearly futile to presume upon conformity in earlier times. Just as many inhabitants of Scotland and Wales did (and do) see themselves as both British and Scottish or Welsh, typical Protestants in Ireland in the eighteenth century and later

---

28 S.J. Connolly, *Religion, Law and Power: The Making of Protestant Ireland, 1660–70* (Oxford, 1992), p. 121.
29 J.R. Hill, 'Irish identities before and after the act of union' in *Radharc: The Chronicles of Glucksman Ireland House at New York University*, vol. 2 (Nov. 2001), pp. 57–8.
30 Cited by I. McBride in T. Claydon and I. McBride (eds), *Protestantism and National Identity in Britain and Ireland, c.1650–c.1850* (Cambridge, 1998), p. 257.

saw themselves both as English (or Scottish if they were Presbyterian) and as being of Ireland. The inexactness of usage is well illustrated, to select one of numerous possible examples, in the case of Archbishop William King (1650–1729), who in 1708 referred almost simultaneously to the Catholics as 'the Irish' and to the Protestants as 'the people of Ireland'.[31] Many who were proud of the Irish nation as manifested in the Volunteers and the Parliament of 1782 might yet have qualms about applying the epithet 'Irish' to themselves: that term never quite lost connotations of popery and incivility.[32] But weightier than any such prejudices was the fact that 'Irish' never quite ceased to have overtones of a politicised Catholic collectivity, a consideration that was to be reinforced by popular mobilisations from the 1790s onwards.

In the eighteenth century, unwillingness to promote a common identification with the Presbyterians of the north-east discouraged members of the Established Church in Ireland from embracing the term 'British'.[33] That inhibition was removed by the nineteenth-century rapprochement of Anglicans and Presbyterians, combining to face the threat of Catholic mobilisation and repeal of the Union. However, numerous Protestants in the nineteenth century, including supporters of the Union, saw themselves as Irish. William Lecky, as a student in Trinity College in the 1850s, indulged with fellow students in Young Ireland-type celebrations of nationality.[34] It would appear that only in the Troubles of the later twentieth century did the preponderance of unionists opt decisively for the self-designation of 'British and not Irish' as against 'British and Irish'.

The term 'Anglo-Irish', used occasionally over centuries, came to be applied regularly to groups and individuals in the later nineteenth century, with connotations that included 'Protestant', 'unionist' and 'upper class'. At this stage it began to be applied by historians to those of the 'English nation' in medieval Ireland and to the New English and all subsequent Protestant elites in Ireland. J.C. Beckett (1912–96) was one historian who used it, and a particularly distinguished and dispassionate one. But, while Beckett used the term 'Anglo-Irish' freely in his writings, he eventually entered a protest against it, claiming, with good reason, that it had been promulgated in the late nineteenth century with a view to classifying one set of Irish people as less 'truly' Irish than others, and so was a racialist gambit. (We will see in later chapters how the same epithet was used around the same time and with the same intent in the fields of literature and music.) Beckett might have strengthened his case by challenging the simplistic notions of ancestry

---

[31]   Cited in S.J. Connolly, *Religion, Law and Power*, p. 119.

[32]   D.W. Hayton, 'Anglo-Irish attitudes: changing perceptions of national identity among the Protestant ascendancy in Ireland, *c*.1690–1750' in *Studies in Eighteenth-century Culture*, no. 17 (1987), pp. 145–57.

[33]   Ibid., p. 151.

[34]   Donal McCartney, *W.E.H. Lecky: Historian and Politician, 1838–1903* (Dublin, 1994).

that lay behind the usage, but in fact he himself seems to have accepted these notions while (justifiably) deploring the conclusions drawn from them by others.[35] Moreover, Beckett depicted the contribution of ruling-class Protestants (the 'Anglo-Irish') to Irish life over the centuries as one of two major Irish 'traditions'. This was a very valuable corrective to the exclusivist rhetoric of Catholic nationalists, but the invocation of tradition in this sense can easily lead back to racialist assumptions.

In fact, designation as 'Anglo-Irish' was willingly adopted in the later nineteenth century by upper-middle-class and landed Protestants, who readily accepted the (dubious) suggestion of racial distinctiveness. The hyphenated epithet has provided a starting point for assumptions about the dilemma of people stranded between two countries. Both before and after independence, a significant proportion of the 'Anglo-Irish' left a country in which their political status had been undermined. However, many others from all social and religious categories also left under duress, including victimised and frightened Protestant farmers from the South not encompassed by the 'Anglo-Irish'. Since the seventeenth century, if not earlier, there have been those of all religious and political persuasions and of innumerable occupations – actors and lawyers, clergy and medics, farm labourers and tinsmiths, merchants and landowners – whose world has comprehended both islands. Except by invocation of dubious assumptions about race, how much justification is there for designating one group rather than another as Anglo-Irish?

In any case, the expression is simply inefficient, even by its own terms. While it is used by historians with reference to the entire membership of the colony in the Middle Ages (probably its most defensible usage) it is, as we have just seen, limited by class as well as religion when applied to later periods. Nobody talks of Belfast shipworkers or Protestant shop assistants in the South as Anglo-Irish. Of course, like 'Norman' or 'Anglo-Norman', the term 'Anglo-Irish' has an established place in the historiographical vocabulary and cannot be dis-invented, but the cautious reader will be wary of its connotations.

The rhetoric of the United Irishmen in the 1790s had offered the prospect of a nation built from scratch without reference to particular origins. The invocation by Theobald Wolfe Tone (1763–98) of 'the common name of Irishman' reflected the revolutionary dawn in which the shadow of inherited differences would vanish.[36] But this 'end of history' was not to be, either in Ireland or Europe. By the 1830s, the intellectuals of the age had come around to viewing nationality as an inspired entity rooted in soil, blood and race. Daniel O'Connell, whose sensibilities, like Tone's, had been formed in

---

[35] J.C. Beckett, *The Anglo-Irish Tradition* (London, 1976), pp. 10–11, 148–9.
[36] Marianne Elliott, *Wolfe Tone: Prophet of Irish Independence* (New Haven and London, 1989), p. 126.

the age of reason, had little appreciation of this. The new sensibility came to Ireland largely in the guise of Celticity.

In 1707, a Welsh-born Oxford scholar, Edward Lhuyd, published a book, *Archaeologia Britannica*, that was to have a major impact on the scholarly study of the origins of languages.[37] It substantiated the claim that Gaelic (spoken in Ireland, Scotland and the Isle of Man) was related to Welsh, Cornish and Breton, which were recognisably related to one another and also to ancient Gaulish, once spoken in the territory of modern France. Although these linkages had been adumbrated by a few other scholars, it was Lhuyd's painstaking research that provided the clinching evidence. The name applied by Lhuyd to this newly defined family of languages was 'Celtic'. In his comprehensive deconstruction of Celticity, the anthropologist Malcolm Chapman argues that Lhuyd might with equal justification have named his newly discovered linguistic clutch 'Gaulish' or even 'British'.[38]

The Gauls ('Galli') had featured as a northern menace to ancient Rome before their conquest by Caesar in the first century BC. They were identified with the Celts ('Keltoi'), who from the sixth century BC were the subject of Greek accounts (to us frustratingly sparse) of a warlike people from north of the Alps and extending into the Iberian peninsula, northern Italy and, later, Asia Minor, where they have been identified with the Galatians. The pre-Roman inhabitants of Britain, and hence the Welsh, had been occasionally linked with the Celts by the early modern *savants* of classical literature, but nobody had made a similar connection in respect of the Gaels. The historian Eoin MacNeill was to note ironically that of 'the three great populations of northern and western Europe' known to the learned of ancient Ireland from classical Latin authors – the Iberians, the Celts and the Scythians – 'they excluded the Celts and included the other two, some selecting the Iberians and others the Scythians as the ancestral people from which the Gaels were descended'.[39]

The work of philologists of the eighteenth and nineteenth centuries developed the 'Indo-European' or 'Aryan' hypothesis, which links most of the surviving languages of Europe, together with Persian and the languages of Northern India, notably Sanskrit, to a single family tree. The root language, Indo-European or Aryan, and several others on the stem, are conjectures whose general characteristics can be plotted as those of pieces missing from an otherwise complete jigsaw puzzle. That the Celtic languages belong to the Indo-European system, being linked through a conjectural common

---

[37] Edward Lhuyd, *Archaeologia Britannica: An Account of the Languages, Histories and Customs of the Original Inhabitants of Great Britain: vol 1: glossography* (Shannon, 1971) provides a facsimile of the 1707 original and an introduction by Anne and William O'Sullivan.

[38] Malcolm Chapman, *The Celts: The Construction of a Myth* (London, 1992), p. 207.

[39] Eoin MacNeill, *Phases of Irish History* (Dublin, 1919), p. 11.

Celtic, was established with finality only in the 1830s. At the same period, nationalist ideology in Europe was developing an essentialist, *Volk*-oriented character, giving a new potency to the age-old habit of drawing racial inferences from language. In other words, languages provided convenient building blocks for simplistic racial constructs just as the concept of race was about to take hold of the way in which many intellectuals viewed the world.

Before Lhuyd, only a handful of scholars suspected that Irish history or language had anything to do with Welsh or Breton, and they had no hard evidence. Keating, writing in the early seventeenth century, knew nothing of 'Celtic' connections: it was because of their presumed Gaelic/Milesian ancestry that he and other Gaelic scholars hailed James I and Charles II. Keating rejected the thesis of the Scotsman George Buchanan, who in 1582 had opined, without any evidence of the kind later produced by Lhuyd, that the Gaels were related to the Welsh. If the Celtic hypothesis was sustained, then Irish origins were shared with the pre-Roman-invasion British, and that supposition would threaten the thousand-year-old story of the more than two-thousand-year-old independent Irish monarchy. Ledwich was reviled most of all because of the way in which he took account of Lhuyd and the Celts, and because he drew the plausible but unproven inference that the Celts had conquered Britain first and that some of them had then invaded Ireland. To make matters worse he (mistakenly) supposed that, because the Gaelic language was found historically in both Scotland and Ireland, it had been brought to the latter in the first instance from the former, thus undermining the Irish case in a long-standing feud with the Scots.

From 1833, the *Dublin University Magazine* brought to light a coterie of young Protestant intellectuals devoted to an Irish nationhood within the union, under Protestant leadership, and enthusiastic for the promotion of a cultural nationality that would be 'racy of the soil'.[40] Coming from a similar background, Thomas Davis (1814–45) went a step further, and in 1841 joined O'Connell's Repeal Association. Having founded the *Nation* in 1842 together with Charles Gavan Duffy and John Blake Dillon, Davis set about promoting a new brand of Irish nationality.[41] It is doubtful if anyone before or since has captured more compellingly the potential of patriotic endeavour for the transformation of Ireland. And it was Davis as leader-writer at the *Nation* who banished any remaining reservations about the Celts.

Davis was intensely attracted to the principles of the United Irishmen. As the Protestant son of a British army surgeon, Davis had every reason to appreciate a national ideal that made the individual's background irrele-

---

[40] See J. Spence, 'Isaac Butt, Irish nationality and the conditional defence of the union, 1833–70' in D.G. Boyce and A. O'Day (eds), *Defenders of the Union: A Survey of British and Irish Unionism since 1801* (London and New York, 2001), pp. 65–89.

[41] Helen F. Mulvey, *Thomas Davis and Ireland: A Biographical Survey* (Washington, 2003).

vant, but he was in any case sufficiently practical in his outlook to see the great advantages of such an approach for forwarding the cause of Irish nationality. Nevertheless, he was also an enthusiast for the emergent racialising nationalism on the continent. In particular, he discovered in French historical writing of the 1830s, especially the work of Jules Michelet and Augustin Thierry, the glorification of the Celts as the racial basis of French and Irish nationality. For Wolfe Tone and for O'Connell, race had not been a matter of interest: the term 'Celt' is scarcely to be found in their lexicons. By contrast, the Celt was the leitmotif of Davis's writings, and the pen-name over which most of his contributions to the *Nation* appeared. Thus he was constantly caught between, on the one hand, celebrating the Celt and so inculcating the cult of race and, on the other hand, offering reassurance to the descendants of Danes (the term he used for the Vikings), Normans and Saxons that their place in the Irish nation was secure because race did not matter. The paradoxes do not end there. Davis was from one point of view the stereotypical Romantic nationalist and detractor of modernisation, but he was also a realist with an eye to the scientific, and would not have been one to deny the scholarly evidence, such as it appeared to be, about Ireland and the Celts.

In the scheme of racial divisions tendentiously linked to language that took hold of nineteenth-century thought, some races were superior to others. In this context, the Celts, particularly as represented by the Irish, came to be depicted as less worthy, less able and less deserving than the Teutonic category to which Angles, Saxons and therefore the modern English were thought to belong. It was nothing new to have conflicts related to the subordinate role of Ireland in the United Kingdom, or the clash of religious and class interests, or economic crisis, depicted in the implicitly essentialist terms of English *versus* Irish, but, expressed as Teuton/Saxon against Celt, such differences assumed an even more ineluctable aspect. In any event, by the late 1840s, friend and foe were using Celt as a synonym for Gaelic Irish.

Twelve years after Davis's untimely death, several associates of his were behind the launching in 1857 of what proved to be a short-lived 'periodical of Irish national literature', predictably entitled the *Celt*. Not too precipitately, the question of 'the Celtic race' and its place in the order of things was addressed. Over five issues, the theories and fancies of ethnologists and archaeologists, philologists and physiognomists were mixed and matched, producing little to command interest apart from a hypothesis that 'the Irish' were originally dark-haired but had been rendered red-haired by centuries of oppression. An attempted escape from the maze by recourse to a theory of geographical determinism having proved unsuccessful, the eventual resolution was a two-way bet: on the one hand, a reversion to the principles of Geoffrey Keating and Wolfe Tone ('We wish to be *Irishmen*, let those who will be Celts or Saxons'), and on the other hand, a daring assertion in respect of contemporary preoccupations ('. . . in reality there is but the one race in these countries, and that is the Celtic.').[42]

This fabrication of race was not wholly unfavourable to Celts, who were part of the reputedly superior Aryan race, whatever their lowly position within it.[43] The supposed superiority was a scientific-sounding reformulation of long-established prejudices; it justified contemporary imperialisms, and would provide an intellectual rationalisation for genocidal policy in the twentieth century. Innocent as he was of complicity in past, present or future unsavouriness, Canon Ulick J. Bourke, in his publication of 1875, *The Aryan Origin of the Gaelic Race and Language*, rejoiced that:

> Science shows that [Irishmen] are with Englishmen and Scotchmen brethren of the one great Aryan family, who, thousands of years ago, emigrated from Persia in the East to the most western portion of Europe and made island homes of Erin and Britain.[44]

From the linguistic point of view Gaelic was the prime exhibit in the Celtic display, and the interest shown by continental scholars in the language was a source of considerable pride for the small number of Irish people paying heed to such matters. Their good feelings were underpinned in 1865 with the appearance in the *Cornhill Magazine* of the series of articles by Matthew Arnold, Professor of Poetry at Oxford, subsequently published as *On the Study of Celtic Literature* (1867). Wallowing unquestioningly in assumptions about racial character, Arnold depicted the Celt as the source of creativity, imagination and femininity, without whose contribution industrialising society would be rendered soulless. By the 1870s, archaeological excavations on the continent were providing evidence of high achievement in artistic creation – especially associated with the La Tène epoch – that could be attributed to the ancient Celts.

The explicit corollary of Arnold's compliments about a penchant for things of the spirit was that the Celt lacked the stolid qualities required for political self-government. Thomas Davis had implied as much two decades earlier when, writing in a context in which he used Celt and Gael interchangably, he declared that an Irish national government would have need of 'the Brehon law and the maxims of Westminster, the cloudy and lightening genius of the Gael, the placid strength of the Sassenach and the marshalling might of the Norman'.[45] The rise of the Home Rule movement in the 1870s and 1880s can be explained as convincingly as anything else in

---

42   *Celt*, 19 and 26 Sept. 1857, 28 Nov. 1857, 5 and 12 Dec. 1857.
43   See C. Morash, 'Celticism: between race and culture' in *Irish Review*, no. 20 (Winter/Spring 1997), pp. 29–36.
44   pp. 3–4.
45   T.O. Davis, *Prose Writings of Thomas Davis*, edited by T.W. Rolleston (London, 1890), p. 194.

history by reference to political, economic and confessional considerations, and without reference to the impact of Celticism. And when eventually, in the early twentieth century, cadres influenced by a later wave of Celticism achieved prominence in nationalist politics, they predictably ignored the politically disabling aspect of the myth. Race theory like most forms of ideology is more frequently the servant than the source of power. Thus, to suggest that racialist ideology was a major causal factor in the denial of Home Rule to Ireland in the decades before 1914 may be a case of putting the cart before the horse. Nevertheless, it is clear that British-based opponents of Home Rule could draw much self-justification from notions of the unfitness of the Celt for self-government.[46] From the 1840s to the 1890s, historians of England such as Macaulay and Froude, and their counterparts in Germany and the USA, promoted enthusiastically an understanding of the past and of the present in which race, and specifically the inherited advantages of the Teuton and the Anglo-Saxon, was the key interpreter.

Meanwhile, politically motivated division had blunted the impact of scholarship on the study of Irish history. In mid-eighteenth century Scotland, enlightenment historiography put party disputes about history at a discount. Near-contemporary attempts to achieve a similar consensus in respect of Ireland were to fail. The cause of the failure lay not with the inventive shortcomings of the historians but with the political divisions that precluded consensus or unconcern about the past. While the main stumbling block was not pre-history or early history but the events of the seventeenth century, especially 1641,[47] the treatment of all periods was affected.

Despite the scholarly unveiling of a Celtic past and the progress of archaeology and philology, the legends transmitted by Keating retained their place in history books through the nineteenth century and into the twentieth. Canon Bourke may have adjusted his understanding of ancient history to allow for the light shed by linguistics, but many others did not. More commonly, the Celts were identified with the Milesians and the resulting ambiguity about the links with Britons, ancient and modern, might or might not be addressed. Such syncretism was completely in line with a practice going back by way of Keating to the compilers of the *Leabhar Gabhála*. A textbook from 1905 intended for Irish-American classrooms opens a section on 'early inhabitants' as follows:

> There are various controversies regarding the origin of the Celtic race; but, whatever their origin may have been the people whom St Patrick found upon his

---

[46] See L.P. Curtis, Jr, *Anglo-Saxons and Celts: A Study of Anglo-Irish Prejudice in Victorian England* (Bridgeport, 1968), pp. 64–104.

[47] See J. Liechty, 'Testing the depth of Catholic/Protestant conflict: the case of Thomas Leland's "History of Ireland", 1773' in *Archivium. Hibernicum*, no. 40 (1987), pp. 13–28.

advent to Ireland were of three distinct types, the Firbolgs, the Tuatha Dé Danaans [sic] and the Milesians.[48]

The next few pages are a distillation, at whatever remove, from the *Foras feasa*. Eleanor Hull (1860–1935) in *Pagan Ireland* (1904) provides a summary of the Celtic invasion of Britain and Ireland as then hypothesised, but still feels constrained to regale the reader with a succinct version of the old invasion myth, complete with conjectural chronology.[49]

With Eoin MacNeill (1867–1945), cultural nationalist, professor at University College, Dublin and political activist, the application of modern standards of scholarship to the early history of Ireland was fully achieved. In the foreword to *Phases of Irish History* (1919), MacNeill specifies just one piece of required reading for those who wish to follow his arguments, namely Keating's account of the pre-Christian period. Much of the book is an implicit rejection of the historicity of Keating's *corpus* and of the *Leabhar Gabhála*. MacNeill was one of the most prominent political nationalists of his generation and, not surprisingly, he found grist for his own mill in early and medieval history. In maximising, as he does, the case for a country-wide sense of Ireland and its cultural institutions from the sixth to the twelfth centuries, he is patently seeking historical justification for the nationality that he was so devoted to in his own life. This is Keating without the incredible legends and the unsubstantiated stories. Playing Giraldus Cambrensis to MacNeill's Keating is G.H. Orpen (1852–1932), author of the formidable four volumes of *Ireland under the Normans* (1911–20) who, from his unionist perspective, was accustomed to minimise the evidence of developed native institutions and national consciousness that his critic maximised. MacNeill had re-founded, on the basis of twentieth-century learning, the myth of the contemporary nation as necessary continuation of an ancient inheritance. Essential to the arguments of both MacNeill and Orpen was the assumption that circumstances observable in the far distant past – a culturally coherent nation in the eyes of one, anarchy and barbarism in the eyes of the other – had contemporary implications, prescribing respectively Irish independence and the maintenance of the Union. While he brought the Celtic dimension firmly within the realms of historical scholarship, MacNeill never allowed the Gaelic to be subsumed in the Celtic. In this he was not only observing scholarly caution: like other advocates of Irish political independence, he was eager to avoid the trammels of the pan-Celtic movement that had no advanced nationalist agenda.

MacNeill was forthright on the subject of race, dismissing out of hand the concept of Celtic racial purity:

---

[48] A.M. Nolan, *A History of Ireland for Schools, Academies and Colleges* (Chicago, reprint edn., 1911), p. 15.
[49] pp. 1ff.

> There is no existing Latin race, no Teutonic race, no Anglo-Saxon race, no Celtic
> race. Each of the groups to whom these names are popularly applied is a mixture
> of various races which can be distinguished, and for the most part they are a mix-
> ture of the same races, though not in every case in the same proportions . . . The
> term Celtic is indicative of language, not of race.[50]

While this leaves open the theoretical possibility of a pure race, it disposes
very firmly of race as an issue in current and historical discourses about
Ireland. Others were not so clear-minded, and assertions by his contemporaries about the exceptionalism of the Celt covered multitudinous pages of
newspapers, periodicals and monographs. In this discourse, Celts were usually synonymous with the Irish: the Welsh, the Scots and, less frequently, the
Bretons, could be included when convenient. Irish Protestants could be
counted in as Celts or near-Celts or non-Celts, or simply ignored, as the case
required.

The work of Dr Sophie Bryant (1850–1922) may be taken as an example.
Born in Dublin, brought up in County Fermanagh, and in her own terms
Anglo-Irish, she was a distinguished mathematician and educationalist. For
much of her adult life she was a London-based campaigner for Home Rule.
Writing *Celtic Ireland* (1889) and then *The Genius of the Gael: A Study in
Celtic Psychology* (1915), with chapter headings such as 'The psychology of
the Celt', 'The social genius of the Gael' and 'The Gael in respect of spiritual
insight', she was well read in contemporary Irish scholarship and literature
and was certainly one of the better informed practitioners of the genre. In
discussing 'The composite Irish nation of today', Bryant asserted that 'the
mutual intelligibility of Sir Edward Carson [Unionist leader] and Mr
Timothy Healy [Nationalist MP] is a thing of which one feels assured as a
psychological necessity' (p. 19) and that 'for centuries past the Irish of each
generation have fostered the new-comers and added them in spirit to the
Gaelic race' (p. 20). The first proposition may be incapable of either proof
or disproof, but Sir Edward must surely be seen as the living refutation of
the second. Throughout the book, the author displays reason, sense and
taste in her general political, aesthetic and educational views, while at the
same time engaging in trite generalisations about Irish/Celtic/Gaelic (and
occasionally other) national character:

> Sociable to strangers, loyal to comrades, affectionate and faithful to family and
> friends – such all the world over the Irishman is admitted to be. (p.104) . . .
> Irishmen have a great capacity for differing, but when they agree there is no stop-
> ping them. (p.142) . . . His emphatic personality makes the Irishman fiery in dis-
> pute, his sociability disposes him, during the intervals of warfare, to expand in
> friendly sympathy towards his enemies. (pp. 154–5)

---

[50] E. MacNeill, *Phases of Irish History*, pp. 2, 3.

Even when they are critical, the judgements are worthless generalisations, as for example: 'In Celtic uncultured nature the instinct to give pleasure perhaps has the upper hand of the instinct to tell truth.' (p. 95)

For most purposes, Celt and Gael were regarded as synonymous and coterminous, but Celticity was the guise under which Irish nationality was racialised in the second half of the nineteenth century. Matthew Arnold's intervention on its own would scarcely have brought this about if the circumstances had not been already propitious. Archbishop Thomas W. Croke (1824–1902) of Cashel was echoing Sir Walter Scott and Thomas Davis as well as Arnold when he declared in 1875 that 'the Irish Celt is from nature ardent and excitable, highly sympathetic, daring, devoted and generous'.[51] This was said by way of a tribute to Daniel O'Connell for his adroit handling of this potentially explosive package in the shape of the Irish masses. In the course of distancing himself from the Phoenix Park murders of May 1882, the Fenian John Devoy declared that 'the Celtic nature revolts at the bare idea of assassination while it welcomes the thought of conflict in the open field'.[52] Patrick Pearse was scarcely eighteen when he pronounced that 'the Gael is not like other men: the spade and the loom and the sword are not for him'.[53] Contradiction, inconsistency and nonsense typify the compilation of characteristics ascribed by priests, poets and politicians to the 'Irish Celt' over several generations. The same tendentious and frequently self-contradictory 'essentialising' process was being applied or had been applied to other nationalities, so that by the early twentieth century, Europe was awash with rhetoric implying that each nationality had its own distinctive 'nature', a condition generally conveyed by the term 'race'.

Daniel O'Connell had been a radical opponent of black slavery and of Jewish disabilities. John Mitchel (1815–75), who succeeded Davis as principal leader-writer at the *Nation* in 1845, had set a less happy headline for Irish nationalists' approach to race by his outspoken defence of black slavery: he became a leading propagandist for the Confederates in the US Civil War. In the event, formulated Irish attitudes to Jews and black people have been variable. In the preface to the 1913 edition of Mitchel's *Jail Journal*, Arthur Griffith stoutly defended not only the former's Anglophobia but also, in sometimes brutal language, his support for slavery. Eoin MacNeill, with reference to his firm objection to the description of early historic Irish society as 'tribal', conceded that he was influenced by the desire to fend off comparisons with modern 'Australian or Central African aboriginies'.[54] When guardians of Irish musical taste were campaigning against jazz in the 1920s and 1930s, many of them did not hesitate to use crude racial argu-

---

[51] *O'Connell Centenary Record, 1875* (Dublin, 1878), p. 101.
[52] *Irish Nation* (New York), 29 July 1882.
[53] *Collected Works of Pádraic H. Pearse* (Dublin, 1924), vol. 4, p. 221.
[54] Eoin MacNeill, *Phases of Irish History* (Dublin, 1919), p. 290.

ments in citing its supposed African origins as damning evidence. However, by the early 1970s, MacNeill's successor as professor of Early Irish History at University College, Dublin could signal changed sensibility with the remark that 'the modern student in a world very different to that of MacNeill and his contemporaries, need not scorn to turn to Africa for parallels to early Irish society'.[55] In the same decade, a black Irishman, Phil Lynott, achieved celebrity status and widespread respect at home and abroad on the basis of his success as a rock singer. Hamburg-born Sir Otto Jaffé (1846–1929), a linen exporter, was lord mayor of Belfast in 1899 and 1904.

Less favoured in socio-economic terms was the Jewish population of several thousands produced by migration from eastern Europe in the closing decades of the century. Attitudes and responses to this presence and to the wider Jewish question were mixed. The campaign of ostracisation against the Jews in Limerick in 1904 is the country's most notorious incidence of anti-Semitism. No life was lost and the episode may be seen as an incautious manifestation, sparked by the pulpit oratory of an over-zealous priest, of normally discreet bigotry, against a distinctive minority, a bigotry fuelled by prejudices concerning race, religion and economics. Popular edginess about the Jew gives the point to Leopold Bloom's role as a central character in James Joyce's *Ulysses*. The 'Jewish congregations' were among the religious groups given explicit recognition in article 44 of the 1937 constitution, but like most other countries, independent Ireland was callous and tight-fisted in its response to the plight of the Jews of Europe from 1933 to 1945.[56] An anthology of anti-Semitic sentiments recorded in Ireland from the 1890s to the 1940s would make distasteful and depressing reading, but it would probably look tame and derivative by international standards. Robert Briscoe (1894–1969), a founder member of Fianna Fáil and Lord Mayor of Dublin in 1956 and 1961, set a headline for Jewish involvement in Irish politics which flourished until the late 1990s.

If notions of race as a mechanism for exclusion had little purchase in Ireland by the later twentieth century, that is not to say that thinking in terms of race had ceased to matter. In fact, the major division in Irish political life has been widely understood and explained in terms of origins and, at least by implication and often explicitly, by race. The great polarisation between nationalists and unionists crystallised in the 1880s around the issue of Home Rule, and more than a century later it endures as the core of the Northern Ireland dilemma. The issue was regularly interpreted in the decades before and after 1900 in terms of Anglo-Saxon against Celt, these

[55] F.J. Byrne, 'MacNeill the historian' in F.X. Martin and F.J. Byrne (eds), *The Scholar Revolutionary: Eoin MacNeill, 1867–1945, and the Making of the New Ireland* (Shannon, 1973), p. 27.
[56] See Dermot Keogh, *Jews in Twentieth-century Ireland: Refugees, Anti-Semitism and the Holocaust* (Cork, 1998).

being deemed identical with settler and native. Whether the racial referents are explicit or not, the formula is stable. Thus nationalists appear in the role of indigenous inhabitants while unionists are British settlers who refuse to be absorbed. This conceptualisation is shared by both sides and by the generality of outside observers. Here is an agreed conceptual framework within which Home Rule, independence, partition and the governance and future of Northern Ireland have been contended. For those on both sides, the nub of the matter has been whether or not the settlers will be absorbed by the natives. The corollary was that the very presence of unionists in the country could be problematic. Sinn Féin activist and future Free State minister, Kevin O'Higgins, declared in 1919 that:

> If those who were planted in Ireland three centuries ago on the confiscated territory of the native Irish are not prepared to live in loyalty and obedience to the government of Ireland then they can leave the country and the Irish government will be prepared to acquire their interest not by confiscation but by purchase.[57]

Eamon de Valera wondered aloud at the Fianna Fáil party's Ard Fheis (annual convention) in 1939 about the possibility of a solution to partition encompassing the transfer (presumably to England or Scotland) of 'those who do not want to be Irish'.[58] This has overtones of the exchange of ethnic populations between Greece and Turkey in the 1920s, even if de Valera, when it suited his purposes, could assert that there was no racial distinction on the island to justify partition.

The native/settler model is a myth insofar as it simplifies and highlights selective elements of an explanation. It certainly has sufficient verisimilitude to make it serviceable. There is more than enough on the historical record to sustain the rhetoric and imagery of dispossession, grievance and persecution on the one hand, and of settlement, cultivation and siege on the other. But there is not enough substance to render satisfactory at the level of scholarly analysis the native/settler archetype that is so satisfying at the mythic level. The definition of unionists as the descendants of the planters and settlers of earlier centuries collapses in the face of even a moderately sophisticated examination of the question of ancestry. The representation of nationalists as heirs by pure descent of a 'native' population is, if anything, even more problematic. It is not possible on any intellectually supportable basis to dichotomise the population of Ireland between indigenous inhabitants and descendants of settlers. And it must be remembered that, in common with most notions surrounding nationality, the settler/native motif can co-exist with the invocation, when it suits, of an apparently contradictory line, such as the denial that differences of origin have anything to do with the case.

---

57 Quoted in M. Laffan, *The Resurrection of Ireland: The Sinn Féin Party, 1916–23* (Cambridge, 1999), p. 227.
58 *Irish Times*, 14 Dec. 1939.

For some, the native/settler dichotomy has an essential cultural dimension, the nationalists being the bearers of the ancient Gaelic civilisation set against an encroaching Anglicisation. This is a conceit. Since the middle of the eighteenth century, Gaelic-speaking society has been making a transition towards assimilation into a wider western and specifically English-speaking culture, and the process was far advanced by the time of the first Home Rule Bill in 1886. At that point a high proportion of those seeking to preserve the linguistic inheritance of the old culture were unionists. Only subsequently did the Irish language come to be identified with nationalist politics (see chapter four).

Admirable attempts have been made in Northern Ireland since the early 1980s to promote mutual respect between the two antagonistic collectivities by encouraging appreciation of one another's cultural activities. Invocation of 'the two traditions' has become a commonplace euphemism. True indeed, the *camán* (hurling stick) and the Lambeg drum are icons of nationalism and unionism respectively, but as such they are emblems, not causes. Toleration of cultural difference is, of course, vital to peaceful co-existence. Such difference is undeniable: many nationalists cultivate Gaelic games and many unionists participate in or turn out to support Orange marches on 12 July. However, most of what can be described as culture is common to almost all the inhabitants of the island and the neighbouring island, and if the search for cultural difference is pushed to its conclusions the end result is the identification not of two but of many cultures. The only aspect of culture that comes near to coinciding with political division in pre-independence Ireland or in Northern Ireland is religion. The explanatory value of that close coincidence will be explored in chapter three.

Originally the native/settler myth was wonderfully self-serving for both sides. Long-downtrodden natives have an unanswerable case for liberation and independence and the sympathy of the world. Settlers under threat have a persuasive case for not being cut off and abandoned to the mercy of their enemies. Unfortunately for unionists, the myth has become counter-productive for them. Settlers as a category have gone down seriously in the estimation of international public opinion since the middle of the twentieth century and every presumption is against them. When Northern Ireland entered an era of instability in the late 1960s, unionists found themselves at a considerable disadvantage in terms of public relations and international sympathy, and the settler image had much to do with this.

As the examples of MacNeill and Orpen demonstrate, a change from popular to scholarly history-writing does not necessarily imply a conversion to non-partisanship. In Ireland in the nineteenth century, as elsewhere, the writing of history was tied up with invention of the nation. The case of W.E.H. Lecky (1838–1903), perhaps the most celebrated of all Irish historians, deserves attention here. While some patriotic Protestant intellectuals, such as those at the *Dublin University Magazine*, looked to the Gaelic past, others, including Lecky, found their golden age in the era of Grattan's parliament. Although Lecky's publications in European history reach back in coverage to the Roman Empire, his work on the history of Ireland is centred on the Grattan era, which he viewed through the glow of his own mid-nineteenth-century Liberalism. The first of five volumes of his great *History of Ireland in the Eighteenth Century* (London, 1892–96) brings the coverage down to 1760, leaving four volumes for the subsequent four decades. Lecky's verbal attack on the penalisation of Irish Catholics in the eighteenth century, together with his lionisation of Grattan's parliament and his excoriation of the passage of the Act of Union, provided tons of historical ballast for advocates of Home Rule and more, ranging from W.E. Gladstone to Patrick Pearse. As it happened, Lecky himself was opposed to Home Rule in the circumstances of the late nineteenth century: the socio-economic dimension of the Parnellite movement, with its assault on landlord property, appeared to him to be the manifestation of a democracy incompatible with liberty. But neither this, nor his election to parliament as member for Trinity College, Dublin in the Unionist interest (1896–1902), diminished the usefulness or impact of his publications as nationalist propaganda.[59] Thus, a nationalism that was already supplied with a plethora of supportive and justificatory history books found its most useful texts in the work of a Unionist MP.

Just as nationalism had its formidable historiographical arsenal, so the emergence of partition as a possibility and then as a reality prompted the development of a historiography, scholarly and non-scholarly, that would justify the apartness of Ulster. A significant foundation was in place in the literature on the Scotch-Irish that had flourished in the later nineteenth century both in Ulster and in the USA. The post-partition period saw the appearance of substantial works such as D.A. Chart, *A History of Northern Ireland* (Belfast, 1927) and Cyril Falls, *The Birth of Ulster* (London, 1936).[60] By the 1930s, the cultural geographer and archaeologist at Queen's University, Belfast, E. Estyn Evans, was finding in the postulated distinctiveness of Ulster megaliths a prehistoric adumbration of Northern Ireland.[61] This occurred in a context in which, in the south, prehistoric archaeology was treated by some of its chief practitioners as a celebration, or even worship, of nationality.

There has been a more recent unionist challenge to the nationalist claim on the inheritance of ancient Ireland, and Ulster in particular. Ian

[59] Donal McCartney, *W.E.H. Lecky: Historian and Politician, 1838–1903* (Dublin, 1994).
[60] A. Jackson, 'Unionist myths, 1912–85' in *Past & Present*, no. 136 (Aug. 1992) pp. 164–85; I. McBride, 'Ulster and the British problem' in R. English and G. Walker (eds), *Unionism in Modern Ireland: New Perspectives in Politics and Culture* (London, 1996), pp. 1–18.
[61] M. Stout, 'Emyr Estyn Evans and Northern Ireland: the archaeology and geography of a new state' in J.A. Atkinson et al. (ed.), *Nationalism and Archaeology* (Glasgow, 1996), pp. 19–20.

Adamson's *The Cruithin: The Ancient Kindred,* first published in 1974 and frequently reprinted, works through assorted primary and secondary sources in the endeavour to show that the population of Ulster has ancient non-Gaelic antecedents. His work is at least a salutary reminder that the myth of a common Milesian descent stands on insubstantial foundations, on which different myths, equally credible or incredible, might have been built. As substantial portions of the body of early medieval Irish literature were made accessible in English in the later nineteenth century, the saga of the *Táin Bó Cuailgne,* first recorded in the eighth century, attracted particular attention. Its hero, Cuchulain, became an icon of revolutionary nationalism. In the saga, however, his heroics culminate in a single-handed defence of the gap of the North against an army from the South, and on this basis he has been cited at various times in the twentieth century as an exemplar of Ulster's separateness.

From early in the twentieth century, academic historians, internationally, had begun to wean the discipline away from subservience to national myth-making. This was one of the impulses behind the organisational developments generally associated with the names of R. Dudley Edwards and T.W. Moody that culminated in the appearance in 1938 of the journal *Irish Historical Studies,* self-consciously designed to cater for scholars from throughout the island and from all backgrounds. While calculated to keep nationalism (and unionism) at arm's length from the academic study of history, this initiative was itself a classic exercise in the promotion of nationality. Prior to this, there had been individual professional historians of Ireland, several of them outstanding, but without any formal collective existence. Now there would be a nationally organised profession with a journal and other basics of standardisation such as annual bibliographies and a style sheet. As with all standardisation there may have been some loss of individual colour, but the outcome was the flourishing of research on Irish history in Irish universities in subsequent decades and international respect for the Irish branch of the profession. The reference and ancillary volumes of A New History of Ireland which Moody masterminded in subsequent decades are essential (and frequently cribbed) tools for the historian of Ireland, while Edwards' campaigning on the archives issue has had a profound if delayed impact, particularly in respect of the survival of twentieth-century material. The depth of the service to Irish nationality rendered by Moody, Edwards and those who worked with them in the launching of *Irish Historical Studies* is illustrated by the sophistication of the mechanisms which they devised in order to achieve a federal-style all-Ireland arrangement that allowed nationalists and unionists to co-operate without loss of political face by either side. In the acrid atmosphere of the 1930s they anticipated by sixty years what political leaders eventually found their way to in the Belfast Agreement of 1998. To have achieved this with history, of all disciplines, was a remarkable success.

Meanwhile, in the schools, less eirenic governmental purposes were at work. In the North, the study of British history was prescribed to the substantial exclusion of Irish history, while in the South, teachers were encouraged to tell the history of Ireland as a story of seven centuries of militant struggle against English domination. But school history books used in the Free State continued to retell the Milesian legend, albeit with more or less effective disclaimers about its veracity, and it was still being taught in some schools in the 1960s. Only a little ingenuity was required in order to syncretise Milesians and republicans into a narrative that linked the legendary King Cormac Mac Airt with the High-king Brian Boru and the heroic revolutionary Patrick Pearse. Noteworthy is the fact that this endurance of a twelve-hundred-year-old Gaelic myth owed nothing to the turn-of-the-century linguistic, literary or political revival movements. This sin against the scientific light should be put in international context before it is judged too harshly: an Irish historian pointed out in the 1970s that most modern textbooks on Roman history continued to list early kings for whose existence there is no documentation.[62] The paradigm of the *Leabhar Gabhála* has been taken as justification of an understanding of Irish origins that rests on the pure racial inheritance of the ultimately victorious Milesians. It can also be represented as setting the headline for the repeated absorption of newcomers of different origins. But it is an anachronism to read concern with either racial exclusiveness or racial toleration into an early medieval document that is concerned not with either of these but with the genealogy of ruling families.

In the latter decades of the twentieth century, the Celtic theme returned with renewed vigour to suffuse the meaning of Irishness. As before, it could be extended when convenient to cover things Scottish, Welsh, Manx, Cornish, Breton and sometimes even Galician. Indeed, the Celtic label serves as an occasion for various worthwhile cultural events that bring together, for example, musicians and film-makers from the north-western periphery of the European Union. Since the Celtic languages are not mutually comprehensible, the lingua franca is inevitably English. One of the better-established uses of the term 'Celtic' is as a collective identifier for the three less powerful, less populous and geographically less favoured countries that share the archipelago with England. The point was hammered home with the emergence in the last quarter of the twentieth century of the phrase 'the Celtic fringe' (allegedly first coined in 1907 by the Conservative leader Arthur Balfour) as a term of scholarly description. The three countries may fit several of the same paradigms in terms of historical and contemporary experience, and they have a common link with an ancient family of languages, but if the suggestion conveyed in describing them as Celtic is that they or their inhabitants have something 'essential' in common not shared

---

[62] F.J. Byrne, *Irish Kings and High-kings* (Dublin, 1973), pp. 52–3.

with England, that is a delusion. Despite evocations of a common Celticity, and notwithstanding the historical and current strength of the links between Scotland and the northern part of Ireland (including Donegal), Ireland generally continues to have less contact and less familiarity with Scotland and Wales than with England.

It is, however, in respect of things Irish that the Celtic epithet is mainly applied. 'The Celtic tiger' was coined to suggest a comparison between the spectacularly burgeoning economy of the South in the 1990s and the earlier flourishing of small nation 'tiger' economies in South East Asia. However, this association with mammon has not quite destroyed the impression of Celtic as a synonym for things of the spirit. There is nonetheless an undoubted coarsening of the usage, so that Celtic crosses, Celtic soul, Celtic mind and Celtic spirit have been joined by Celtic rock, Celtic rhythm, Celtic chocolates, Celtic needlepoint, Celtic helicopters and, even, in the title of a TV series, the Celtic fist ('An dorn Ceilteach'). The latter, dealing with the feats of boxers of Irish, Scottish and Welsh origin, was screened on an Irish channel in 1998, replete with unquestioning commentary to the effect that 'the Celts were born to fight'. And it typifies current use of the concept. The connotations of 'Celtic' in day-to-day usage range from assumptions based on unexamined racialist thinking to a more or less pretentious way of saying 'Irish'. The term is granted indulgence not generally accorded to its counterparts: invocation of, say, the Anglo-Saxon mind, or the Teutonic fist, would evoke derision or even outrage. Arnoldian condescension lives on, and continues to be gratefully accepted and even openly courted. Almost every interview on Irish radio or television with a visitor from abroad incorporates an invitation, explicit or implicit, to say what exceptional, friendly and wonderful people the Irish are. Thus, while the 'disabling' aspect of the Celtic racial myth has had little or no impact on the structures of Irish politics, as exemplified by the emergence of a self-assertive nation state, it has had a significant impact on the perception and self-perception of Irish people.

With reference to any modern society, to ancestry, or to race, 'Celtic' has no substantial meaning. It is most safely used as a linguistic term covering a clearly defined family of languages, and may also be applied with circumspection to aspects of the cultures of certain ancient and medieval societies. There is no certainty that behind the name 'Keltoi', as used by the Greeks, there lay a single ethnic group, self-conscious or otherwise. And until the eighteenth century it is unlikely that anyone, anywhere, thought of themselves as being Celtic. On the continent, the residues identified with the ancient Celts are mainly settlement remains, placenames, and a wealth of artefacts, especially those in the styles named after the sites of Hallstat and La Tène; the continental Celtic languages are attested only by rare and fragmentary inscriptions. Imposing meaningful patterns on this evidence, extending as it does over many centuries and a large part of Europe, is an elaborate, challenging and inevitably inconclusive business.[63] The archaeologist Simon James has taken a lead in advocating caution about the ascription of ancient Celtic ethnicity, especially in respect of Britain and Ireland. In the mid-twentieth century, scholars tended to assume that the arrival and triumph of the Celtic languages in the islands was the consequence of an overpowering military invasion by a branch of the Celtic family and that at least substantial replacement of population was involved. A currently prominent view holds that archaeological evidence does not support such a thesis: there is no proof of an overwhelming invasion, and material relics of the kind associated with the continental Celts, specifically La Tène artefacts, are unevenly distributed, largely confined to the northern half of the island, and could, in any case, have been spread by a process of diffusion among ruling elites.[64]

The linguistic evidence has to be given its due weight. It was in Britain and Ireland that Celtic languages survived, supporting medieval and modern literatures that are extant. In any event, influential population movement, even if not the only factor, would seem to be a prerequisite for the elimination in Ireland of earlier tongues and their replacement at a relatively late date by a language (Gaelic) having its antecedents on the continent. Could the triumph of Gaelic throughout the land have been as complex a business as the change to English, which took much of the second half of the second millennium AD to effect, and involved not only population movement but everything from military conquest through the calculation of economic advantage to the following of elite example? It is surely something of a contradiction to hold that the modern English-speaking Ireland is still 'essentially' Irish, while at the same time assuming that Celtic-speaking early historical Ireland must have been 'essentially' Celtic.

The spectacular progress in recent years of the science of genetics offers to shed new and previously unimaginable light on past population movements and settlement patterns, using both the examination of DNA traces retrieved from skeletal remains and the analysis of aspects of DNA in living populations.[65] With the complexity of genetics likely to be a problem for historians, and the complexity of history a challenge to geneticists, the achievement and dissemination of worthwhile insights will be a demanding task for all concerned. Additional information brings limited additional enlightenment unless it prompts the posing of new and better questions. To

---

[63] See B. Cunliffe, *The Ancient Celts* (London, 1997).

[64] S. James, *The Atlantic Celts: Ancient People or Modern Invention?* (London, 1999); see also B. Raftery, *Pagan Celtic Ireland: The Enigma of the Irish Iron Age* (London, 1994), p. 228; B. Ó Donnabháin, 'An appalling vista? The Celts and the archaeology of later prehistoric Ireland' in A. Desmond et al., *New Agendas in Irish Prehistory: Papers in Commemoration of Liz Anderson* (Bray, 2000), pp. 189–96.

[65] See Daniel Bradley, 'Y-chromosome variations and Irish origins' in *Nature*, 23 Mar. 2000, p. 351.

ask of this new evidence the old questions such as 'Who are the Irish?' or 'Where did the Irish people come from?' could be to re-enforce preconceptions that feed the voracious appetite for myths of national origins.[66]

Even a summary review such as this would scarcely be complete without some reference to the origin myths of Americans with Irish ancestry. Down to and including the first quarter of the nineteenth century, those in North America who were nominally or consciously of Irish origin were predominantly Presbyterians who had emigrated in large numbers from Ulster. Under the terms of a 'Scotch-Irish' myth invented in the nineteenth century, all Protestants in the USA identified as of Irish ancestry were deemed to be descendants of Scots who had spent a few years or decades in Ulster before moving on to America and playing a leading role in the settlement of the land and in the making of the United States. One of the many distortions in this particular myth is the ignoring of the numerical contribution to the group in question provided by Catholics from other parts of Ireland having no known links with Scotland who were assimilated to the dominant religious ethos. The point of the Scotch-Irish myth was to set its subjects apart from the waves of Irish Catholics arriving as the nineteenth century progressed who preserved a Catholic identity and were becoming a large, sometimes menacing, and lowly regarded element in American society. These, in turn, provided the basis for the Irish-American myth, within whose folds so many millions were to find comfort and meaning. The dramatic increase in the influx occasioned by the Great Famine is at the heart of the myth. While there has always been ambivalence about the attitude of nationalists in Ireland to the famine (some using it freely in anti-English rhetoric, others not inclined to identify the nation with a calamitous failure), for Irish-Americans the 'potato famine' has become the basis of their origin myth. The coffin ship is to them as the *Mayflower* and Columbus's caravels have been to others.[67] But explanation of Irish origins, as distinct from Irish-American origins, seems to have displayed in America, as in Ireland, an extended fascination with the Milesians.[68]

---

[66] See B. Ó Donnabháin, 'aDNA and Archaeology' in *Archaeology Ireland* (Summer 2001), pp. 34–5; G. Cooney and E. Grogan, 'An archaeological solution to the "Irish" problem?' in *Emania* 9 (1991), pp. 33–43.

[67] K.A. Miller, *Emigrants and Exiles: Ireland and the Irish Exodus to North America* (New York, 1985); L.J. McCaffrey, *The Irish Catholic Diaspora in America* (Washington, D.C., revised edn., 1997); K. Kenny, *The American Irish: A History* (London, 2000).

[68] Future discussion of the issues in this chapter will be informed by H.F. Mulvey, *Thomas Davis and Ireland: A Biographical Study* (Washington, 2003).

3

Religion

Few countries can have their nationality described without some reference to religion, even if in many cases the reference is now largely historical. In many instances religious affiliation is still virtually synonymous with membership of the nation, but even where this situation is most apparently straightforward, complexity abounds. The relationship of religion to the state and, therefore, its place in the definition of the nation depends on many considerations, not least the organisational form taken by a particular religion in a specific place and time. For instance, it matters greatly whether or not a religion sustains its own power structures, and whether or not it supports a learned class that dominates public culture. Christianity in various forms has been singularly enduring and influential in the invention and reinvention of nationality in Ireland.

Numerous peoples in Europe and beyond have been defined by religion or in terms of a world-view drawn from religious sources. The Gaelic culture emerging into historical view in the seventh century was already deeply marked by Christianity and, as we have seen in chapter two, it was busily developing an origin myth set in the framework of the Old Testament and inspired by headlines derived from Church fathers such as Eusebius and Isidore of Seville. We have seen also how, in the central medieval period, the papacy set the seal of its approval on the separate identity of the Irish polity. Religion, both as ideology and power complex, would continue to be central to Irish nationality.

Through the various reiterations of Irish nationality, the figure of Patrick, apostle and patron saint of Ireland, has been a constant presence. Little is known with certainty of him except that he lived in the fifth century, was a native of Roman Britain carried into slavery in Ireland, and that, having escaped, he subsequently returned to preach Christianity to the Irish. The sources for this information are his own writings, the *Confession* and the

Letter to Coroticus, the earliest documents of Irish history. Patrick was not the only or even the first evangeliser of the Irish. Pope Celestius in 431 despatched a bishop named Palladius to Ireland to minister to Christians already living there. The consensus among scholars is that the Christianisation of Ireland was a piecemeal process that began before Patrick's mission, to which Patrick contributed substantially, and which was far from complete at the time of his death. Memory of him appears to have been lost for a century or more, not even his place of burial being recorded. Only his two short pieces in idiosyncratic Latin saved him from oblivion. The invention of Patrick as apostle of Ireland began in the seventh century. The purpose of this myth making was to advance the claims to primacy of the see of Armagh, which had appropriated Patrick as its founder, although there is no proof of any link in the apostle's lifetime. The campaign of the church of Armagh for ecclesiastical primacy went hand in hand with the attempts of its patrons, the Uí Néill, to establish the high-kingship.

By the ninth century, an elaborate hagiography was in place, in Latin and in the vernacular. Legendary journeys through the length and breadth of the land were attributed to the saint, and a list had been elaborated of churches supposedly founded by Patrick, and so chargeable for tribute to the see of Armagh. The simple Christian pastor revealed in his own writings, strug-

Figure 3.1 Ardagh chalice (National Museum of Ireland). Rediscovered as part of a large hoard in the nineteenth century, the chalice dates from the middle of the eighth century.

Figure 3.2 Shrine of St Patrick's Bell (National Museum of Ireland). This container, dating from about AD 1100, was made for an unadorned bell of much earlier date.

gling to defend his flock and his reputation, was now depicted as a triumphant miracle-worker stalking the land and brooking no opposition. It was as thaumaturge and supernatural power-broker that Patrick entered popular folklore. The story of his banishment of the snakes from Irish soil, first attested in the twelfth century, is one of the best-known legends, not just of Ireland but of the western world. At least from the ninth century, the Patrician legends imply something like elect status for the people of Ireland, insofar as they have a heavenly champion in the national saint. Most reassuringly, Patrick in, as it were, a kind of Palatine jurisdiction, had acquired the right to replace Christ as the judge of the Irish on the Day of General Judgement. Early legends identified the holy mountain of the former pagan dispensation with the Christian apostle, under the name of Croagh Patrick. The most renowned place of pilgrimage in late medieval Ireland, a cave situated on Lough Derg in Co. Donegal, achieved European fame as St Patrick's Purgatory.

A set-piece legend in the hagiography dating from the seventh century depicts Patrick lighting the Paschal fire on the hill of Slane in defiance of the high-king at nearby Tara. In the dénouement, the king and his court submit to the new religion. This was an unmistakable lesson concerning the link between religion and power. So successful was the promotion of the legend of Patrick that the primacy of Armagh came to be accepted not only throughout Gaelic society but also in due course by the papacy, which endorsed the primacy at the Synod of Kells, 1152. The first Anglo-Norman adventurer to obtain a foothold in Ulster, John de Courcy, took pains to identify himself as a mentor of the see of Armagh and of the Patrician inheritance at Downpatrick, his supposed resting place. The collegiate church founded by the Anglo-Normans immediately outside the walls of Dublin in 1192 and raised to cathedral status in 1213 is named St Patrick's in honour of the national patron. In 1872, the Church of Ireland declared it a national cathedral.

In the era of the Reformation, Patrick loomed large in the contentions of the confessional scholars. Was he a man of the Bible, free of papal influence and Romish corruptions, and so an exemplar of the true religion that the Protestant Reformation was dedicated to recovering? Or was he a dedicated son of Rome and so a witness to the faith of the Counter-Reformation? The evidence could, of course, be interpreted either way, depending on the prior convictions of the scholars. Ultimately, Catholics would draw more on him, but that was only because saints had a more exalted place in the Catholic scheme of things. In the Church of Ireland, with its lesser but nonetheless definite function for saints, Patrick would continue to be a source of distinctiveness and inspiration to be drawn upon more or less strongly as changing circumstances dictated. Patrick's British birth provided an ambivalence that was useful for all who felt it necessary to represent the impact of the neighbouring island on Ireland as a boon in religious and other terms. Faced as they were with intractable pastoral problems in dealing with their own situation, eighteenth-century Church of Ireland ecclesiastics, many of them translated from England, could identify with Patrick.

Counter-Reformation ideologues found Patrick particularly useful as an Irish saint who was the object of particular devotion on the part of both Old English and Old Irish, for the division between English and Gaelic nations in the later medieval period had carried over into the Church and religious life. The dominant modern iconography of Patrick is exemplified in the frontispiece of Thomas Messingham's *Florilegium insulae sanctorum* (1624), where the be-mitred apostle, every inch a resplendent seventeenth-century prelate, crushes snakes underfoot. From this period onwards, 'Patrick' becomes much utilised as a given name, although it was not until more recent centuries that 'Paddy' would replace 'Tadhg' (or 'Téig') as the stock name for an Irishman.

The use of Patrick for Catholic purposes took a fresh turn in the mid-eighteenth century. With the stature of the papacy in decline throughout Catholic Europe, and the age of enlightenment challenging the basis of confessional intolerance, Catholic apologists such as Charles O'Conor and Sylvester O'Halloran sought to convince Protestants that the religious affiliation of Catholics did not imply any political subservience to Rome. To this end, they presented a version of St Patrick's career more akin to that espoused by Protestants than by Catholics of preceding generations. O'Conor and O'Halloran were at one with Protestants such as Henry Brooke and Joseph C. Walker in highlighting claims concerning the advanced state of civilisation in Ireland before the advent of Christianity. From this perspective, the supposedly smooth and instantaneous conversion of Ireland was a function of the predisposition of a highly cultivated society, rather than a tribute to the genius of the evangeliser. Protestants with more philosophical concerns noted the prevalence of miracles in accounts of Patrick's mission and suspected the intrusion of credulous minds. But the place of Patrick as the trans-secular representative of Ireland remained beyond question. When in 1783 a royal order was founded to provide Ireland with its own equivalent of the Orders of the Garter and Thistle, it was named the Order of St Patrick. And when in the 1790s the Order's place of formal assembly, St Patrick's Hall in Dublin Castle, was decorated, one of the key panels was devoted to a depiction of the legend of Patrick lighting the Paschal fire at Slane.[1] By the 1830s, the administration in Dublin Castle was identifying the state with the celebration of St Patrick's Day rather than with any date in the Williamite calendar beloved of conservative Protestants.[2]

---

[1]   See Bridget McCormack, *Perceptions of St Patrick in Eighteenth-century Ireland* (Dublin, 2000).

[2]   J.R. Hill, 'National festivals, the state and "protestant ascendancy" in Ireland' in *Irish Historical Studies*, xxiv, no. 93 (May 1984), pp. 30–51.

From the earliest emergence of the cult of Patrick, 17 March, as the credited date of his death, had been adopted as his feast day. By the late seventeenth century it was well established as a day of popular celebration and
holidaymaking, marked by the wearing of crosses or of shamrock, once an
item of Irish diet and now hailed as an emblem of the national patron and,
by extension, of the nation. The apostle of Ireland was supposed to have
used the green trefoil in his catechetical labours to illustrate the doctrine of
the triune God. With the flourishing of associational life in the eighteenth
century among the middle classes and aristocracy, St Patrick was commonly
invoked as a token of their fellowship by Irish (and predominantly
Protestant) groupings on both sides of the Atlantic. This 'fraternal' type of
celebration, centring on banquets, died only slowly: in the early years of the
nineteenth century, Belfast Presbyterians were accustomed to hold banquets
to mark 17 March. But as the century progressed, the feast was primarily
marked by informal popular celebrations associated preponderantly with
Catholics.

In the early years of the twentieth century, the serious young men and
women of the Gaelic League, who would set the moral tone of independent
Ireland, endeavoured to cleanse 17 March of its spiritous and less spiritual
aspect so that it would be an appropriate national day for a decent and self-
consciously respectable people.[3] Their campaign of street demonstrations
and letter writing was an episode in a war for moral leadership waged
against the Irish Parliamentary Party and its publican supporters.[4] The outcome included an Act of Parliament of 1903 declaring St Patrick's Day a
bank holiday and, following independence, imposing nearly forty years of
official 'drought' on 17 March. The Gaelic League and the guardians of
national propriety had succeeded in turning a rumbustuous popular holiday
and fair day into a puritan Sunday, lightened, admittedly, by Gaelic games
and other wholesome entertainment. This outcome undoubtedly made some
people feel good about the self-respect of the newly independent state, but it
had significant consequences for the national day. Henceforth, the Irish
abroad, and especially in the United States, set the celebratory pace. The
practice of parading on St Patrick's Day is believed to have begun with Irish
soldiers in British service in New York in the 1760s, and by the nineteenth
century Irish Americans had come to celebrate the day in a variety of ways.[5]
The availability of American attention on 17 March was to do much to
drive the marking of the national festival at home. De Valera's St Patrick's
Day radio broadcasts of the 1930s are a case in point. More recently, commercially driven interests have seized on American parading practices to

---

[3]   Pauline Mooney, 'A symbol for the nation: the national holiday campaign, 1901–03' (M.A.
      thesis, N.U.I. (Maynooth), 1992).
[4]   Bank Holiday (Ireland) Act (3 Edw. VII, c. 1).
[5]   M. Cronin and D. Adair, *The Wearing of the Green: A History of St Patrick's Day* (London
      and New York, 2002), pp. 10–11.

enliven and formalise celebrations in Ireland for 17 March. One of the objectives is to prevail upon Irish Americans to have the Irish American experience of the day in Ireland. The parades in Ireland, however, are generally presided over by politicians of the third rank, almost all ministers and junior ministers being engaged to do the honours at various venues in America and around the globe. There can scarcely be any comparable case of a country's leadership annually departing en masse to celebrate the national festival abroad. It is as if the Brazilian ministers were to travel to other countries to preside over Mardi Gras. It is, indeed, tempting to look for at least part of the explanation in a felt need for the approval of outsiders. This would be consonant with subservience to imperatives of Celticity.

While the popular celebration of St Patrick's Day had become largely a Catholic phenomenon, the nineteenth and twentieth centuries witnessed the consolidation of the place of Patrick in the liturgies and practices of various denominations, exemplified by such developments as the naming in his honour of countless churches and educational establishments in Ireland and on the overseas missions of various denominations, and the celebrations in 1932 and 1961 to mark the 1500th anniversaries of widely received dates for, respectively, his arrival in Ireland and his death. Like the study of Scripture, Patrician scholarship in the second half of the twentieth century has been largely removed from the arena of inter-confessional controversy, an achievement best represented by the scholarship of R.P.C. Hanson, subsequently Church of Ireland Bishop of Clogher.[6] This does not prevent various denominations from making their own of the national apostle, albeit more discreetly than in former times. For a common acceptance of Patrick, or of the gospel whose transmission to Ireland he personifies, never precluded the most serious confessional divisions.

Patrick as patron of Ireland has been linked over centuries in a trio of holy persons with Brigid and Colmcille. The cult of St Brigid as monastic foundress and miracle-worker was the doing of the church of Kildare, and it was prompted by the same expansionist ambitions, ecclesiastical and secular, that lay behind Armagh's contemporaneous but ultimately more successful cult of Patrick. There is no contemporary evidence for Brigid's existence and she may be entirely a figure of legend: Patrick's authenticity would be similarly in question if his two texts had not survived. Much of what has been written about her is consonant with the possibility that Brigid is a Christianised version of a pagan deity. Whatever its basis, the presence of Brigid in the pantheon is a fortuitous acknowledgement of womanhood within a discourse that is generally male dominated.

St Colmcille (alias Columba) (521–597), closely linked by birth to the northern Uí Néill, was a famous founder of monasteries in Ireland (at Derry

---

6   *St Patrick: His Origins and Career* (Oxford, 1968).

and Durrow) and a pioneer of the practice of going into self-imposed exile in Ireland or abroad for the sake of Christ, either as a form of asceticism or to spread the gospel. In 563 he founded the monastery of Iona in an area of Gaelic influence in the inner Hebrides. From here a mission was directed to the pagan Picts of eastern Scotland, and Irish ecclesiastics acquired access to Northumbria where they had a not inconsiderable impact. Columbanus (died 615), founder of monasteries at Luxeuil and Bobbio, is the outstanding representative of the medieval clerics who went by way of Christian exile from Ireland to continental Europe. They contributed significantly, especially in the seventh century, to the Christianisation of rural Gaul and other parts of western Europe and they came with an impressive level of learning derived from the flourishing ecclesiastical schools of Ireland. Both their missionary impact and their learning are incorporated into a myth of long standing in which, having firstly provided a refuge for religion and learning overrun in dark-age Europe, golden-age Ireland subsequently re-implanted faith and scholarship on the continent. The more exaggerated versions depict the Irish as the saviours of western civilisation.[7] The belief that Europe owes a historical debt to Ireland is part of the national self-image.

A myth of more recent vintage concerning early Christian Ireland is summed up in the term 'Celtic Christianity'. From the seventh century onwards, the Church in England, especially southern England, reflecting political and social conditions and the recent conversion of the Anglo-Saxons by a mission from Rome, was more highly structured and more in line with the norms prevailing in western Europe than was the case elsewhere in the archipelago. This state of affairs is exemplified by a delay on the part of some Irish and Welsh churchmen of the seventh century in adopting the Roman method for the calculation of the date of Easter. Over a thousand years later, after the common origins of the Irish and Welsh languages had been uncovered, the non-English churches were given a retrospective common identity as 'the Celtic Church'. Many present-day historians of the early modern period continue to compound this impression by appearing to convey the idea that churchmen and controversialists in the aftermath of the sixteenth-century Reformation were accustomed to refer to the medieval religion, and the churches, of Ireland, Scotland and Wales as 'Celtic'.[8] Building on this mistaken identity and on the Arnoldian connotations of Celticity, an attempt has been made in more recent times to find in 'Celtic Christianity' a validating antecedent for 'new age' religion. But there is no sustainable basis for postulating that speakers of Celtic languages

---

[7]   For an authoritative survey of the issues see M.T. Flanagan, 'The contribution of Irish missionaries and scholars to medieval Christianity' in B. Bradshaw and D. Keogh (eds), *Christianity in Ireland: Revisiting the Story* (Dublin, 2002), pp. 30–43.

[8]   See, for example, N. Canny, *Making Ireland British, 1580–1650* (Oxford, 2001), pp. 423, 425.

shared any further common characteristics from which others were excluded, and there is no sound basis for believing that they were collectively more spiritual, more attuned to nature, or kinder to animals, than were their contemporaries. The illusion that the 'Celts' subscribed to a gentle religion of the spirit, untrammelled by legalism, is particularly unfortunate in the light of the fact that medieval Irish monks bequeathed to the western Church, in the form of the penitentials, a system (analogous with the Brehon laws) that reduced Christian atonement for sin to a tariff system of exhaustively graduated punishments.[9]

With the possible exception of competition for land, nothing has had a more momentous impact on the history of Ireland – and of Irish nationality – in the past five hundred years than the divisions arising from the failure of either the Protestant or Catholic Reformation to prevail throughout the land. In early modern states, divided religious allegiance was much more serious than a mere source of potential strife within the body politic. Political collectivities were defined in terms of religious affiliation, so that religious division implied rival definitions of the polity and a threat to the sovereignty of princes. The conditions that linked religion to the definition of nationality survived exceptionally late in Ireland and their decline coincided with the emergence of a political democratisation that nurtured old animosities on a renewed basis.

In Ireland, as in England, the Reformation began, in the 1530s, as an assertion by Henry VIII of the standing of the monarchy as against that of the papacy in the matter of authority over the Church, its discipline and its revenues. Protestant doctrine was introduced in the reign of Edward VI (1547–43), to be suppressed in the reign of Queen Mary (1553–58) and reinstated in a particular form at the beginning of the reign of Elizabeth I (1558–1603). While the state advanced in efficiency in sixteenth-century Ireland, its remit was nonetheless impaired both in terms of extent and depth, and this weakness is central to an understanding of the failure to gather the entire population into the Protestant fold. It is a crucial point that the weakness of the state was a matter not only of extent of territorial reach but of depth of structural penetration.

That a choice had to be made between the religion of Rome and that of the state was a realisation that emerged only over decades. There was no significant opposition when in 1536 the parliament in Dublin proclaimed Henry Supreme Head of the Church, nor when in 1539–40 monastic houses within the areas of effective royal jurisdiction were suppressed. The beneficiaries of the consequent distribution of spoils – the lands, properties and privileges of the religious houses – included many Old English notables whose families a generation or two later would be bastions of the Catholic

---

[9]   Ibid.; D.E. Meek, 'Modern Celtic Christianity' in T. Brown (ed.), *Celticism* (Amsterdam, 1996), pp. 143–57; Ludwig Bieler (ed.), *The Irish Penitentials* (Dublin, 1963).

Reformation. The parliament of 1560 readily approved the Elizabethan religious settlement. The papal excommunication of the Queen in 1570 signalled the drawing of a clear distinction between Catholic and Protestant, such as would prevail within a generation. Almost all of the New English – there were a few exceptions – rallied to the official religion: their interests and prospects were dependent on the state, and the ideology that supported their venturing into Ireland was in the circumstances of the Elizabethan age inseparable from Protestantism. They were joined by small but not insignificant numbers of Old English and Old Irish, but together they did not constitute a sufficient base for an effective country-wide marshalling of the state Church. If we take it that in Ireland, as in England and elsewhere, popular attachment to accustomed rituals and ways was such as to require decisive intervention if it was to be overcome, then the failure to deploy adequate ecclesiastical resources in the service of the Irish Reformation in the second half of the sixteenth century assumes high significance. The resources that mattered were largely controlled on a local basis by Old English and Old Irish elites, the majority of whom were secured for the Counter-Reformation while the Government was still in the process of establishing its political and military writ throughout the land. Material support for the latter endeavour was raised partially by fiscal impositions on the population of the Old English territories, thus creating disaffection among the customarily loyal.

Richard Stanihurst, an exemplar of Old English alienation from the new order, was twenty-six in 1573 at the death of his father, one of a long line of office holders under the Crown in the Dublin administration. The resulting vacancy in the general escheatorship was filled not by a Stanihurst but by 'one John Crofton, a staunch Protestant, newly arrived from England'.[10] While this one episode in itself does not explain Stanihurst's subsequent self-exile, it typifies the exclusion that goes some of the way towards making sense of the majority elite Old English option for Counter-Reformation Catholicism. If there was push, there was also pull: by the 1590s the social networks of Old English and Old Irish had been largely tapped into a vigorous stream of Tridentine evangelisation transmitted by priests trained in continental seminaries. And, as we have seen in chapter two, an ideology was being put in place that identified Roman Catholicism as the essence of Irishness.

Disaffection in religious matters had political implications that would be difficult to avoid. The excommunication of the Queen amounted to papal encouragement to overthrow Elizabeth. The massacre of French Protestants on St Bartholomew's Day in August 1572, together with the revolt in the Netherlands against the Government of Philip II of Spain, looked set by the mid-1570s to create an international maelstrom of dynastic and religious

---

[10]   C. Lennon, *Richard Stanihurst, the Dubliner 1547–1618*, p. 34.

conflicts. Against this background, James Fitzmaurice Fitzgerald of the partially Gaelicised Munster house of Desmond, left for the continent in 1575, returning in 1579 with a papal commission and a small military force. The holy war proclaimed by Fitzmaurice quickly degenerated into an episode of his family's drawn-out and losing campaign of resistance to the extension of state power and the encroachment of land-hungry New English, but he had launched the concept of a militant union of faith and fatherland.

Hugh O'Neill (*c.*1550–1616), Earl of Tyrone, utilised this formula when in the 1590s his long-running chess game with Elizabethan government in Ulster led him to stake everything on open rebellion against the Crown. O'Neill had Spanish support, eventually embodied in the ill-fated expeditionary force that landed at Kinsale in 1601, and he had put together a widespread confederacy among the Old Irish. In Rome, the Old English ecclesiastic, Peter Lombard, argued O'Neill's case, but not even an appeal to the Catholicism with which they now so warmly identified could tempt the Old English as a body to discard their civil allegiance. When in 1603 James VI of Scotland succeeded as James I of England and of Ireland, he had no more loyal subjects than the Catholic Old English, who were determined to combine papal religion with loyalty to their Protestant monarch. They maintained this stance even when the early hope that he would not enforce his predecessor's restrictions on Catholicism proved to be unfounded. Among the Old Irish, the high but very vague notion of an alternative to the English monarch had largely dissolved by 1603 and they too could accept James, finding in his Scottish birth the route to a Gaelic ancestry that made of him a descendant of Míl. Geoffrey Keating, writing in the 1630s, took particular care to identify James, however tendentiously, with Gaelic kingship.[11] For a decade or more after the accession of Charles I in 1625 it seemed as if collective bargaining with the monarch could produce a modus vivendi in religion as in other areas. The overweening, absolutist style of Thomas Wentworth as Lord Deputy in the 1630s and the assault on the royal prerogative in the English parliament from 1640 put paid to hopes of a negotiated compromise.

Caught up in the crisis embracing England, Scotland and Ireland that was to eventuate in the English Civil War of 1642–49, and motivated by local tensions and economic insecurity, gentry-led Catholics in Ulster in October 1641 seized control of much of the province, in which their co-religionists constituted a very substantial majority. The rebels had no plans for a general massacre of their neighbours but, in conditions of anarchy, Protestant settlers under the Ulster plantation who had been in peaceful possession for thirty years, were subjected to attacks that included dispossession, ritual humiliation and killing by sword, drowning and burning. There can be no certainty about the scale of casualties, but deaths of Protestant men, women

---

[11] *Foras Feasa,* i, pp. 208–9.

and children by violence and exposure certainly numbered many thousands. English Puritans exploited the attack on the settlers for propaganda purposes, representing the personal violence as planned and premeditated on the part of the organisers of rebellion and grossly exaggerating the number of victims. Lurid pamphlet accounts of the massacre of Protestants by Irish Catholics proved invaluable to Puritans in the struggle with the King for English hearts and minds. These accounts found enduring shape in a classic of propaganda literature.[12] Thus was created one of the most salient myths in Irish history. As is the way with myth, its appeal was not diminished in the minds of adherents by considerations such as the retaliatory massacres of Catholics in Ulster in the following year or the earlier headlines in the use of massacre set by the government side during the Elizabethan conquest.

Awareness that the Puritans would not distinguish between Irish Catholics if and when it came to wreaking vengeance for the massacre of Protestants helped, with other considerations, to propel the leadership elites of Old English and Old Irish Catholics together in late 1641. The motto of their confederacy, which came to have its headquarters in Kilkenny, bound them in support not only of God and country but also of the King, although in fact they were in rebellion against him. The tensions created by the dual loyalty were to give rise to serious disputes within the ranks of the Catholic clergy for the remainder of the century and beyond. During the period of the Confederation, political disputes about relations with the lord lieutenant, the Earl (later Duke) of Ormond, *de jure* and de facto the king's right-hand man in Ireland, became identified with questions of principle concerning the rival claims of king and pope on the Catholic subject's conscience. Archbishop Rinuccini, who arrived from Italy in 1645 as papal nuncio to the Confederation, was a proponent of uncompromising Counter-Reformation policies that would require a full restoration of the rights and property of the Catholic Church. He was opposed by a politique interest, heir to several generations of endeavour to secure a compromise that would allow Catholics to enjoy toleration under a Protestant monarch.

The needs of most early modern political and religious systems demanded conformity to the state religion. As early as 1555, in the Peace of Augsburg, the principle of *cuius regio, eius religio*, whereby the religion of those in power would prevail in any given territory, had been adopted in the politically fragmented and religiously divided German lands. The Low Countries to which so many Irish Catholics had recourse in the 1580s were at that time a theatre of conflict, in which religious affiliation had become a pre-eminent consideration. During that decade, the Protestant-controlled towns of Flanders were one after another reduced by siege to the obedience of the King of Spain, the inhabitants then being accorded a period of some months

---

[12] J. Temple, *The Irish Rebellion: or, the history of the beginning and first progress of the general rebellion raised within the kingdom of Ireland upon the three and twentieth day of October 1641* (London, 1646).

in which they should conform to the Catholic religion or leave the jurisdiction, taking with them only whatever they could carry. The Low Countries were quickly settling into two separate polities, the Habsburg south, in which Catholic uniformity was imposed by the civil power, and a Protestant-dominated north, the United Provinces, in which Catholics were initially severely pressed but ultimately tolerated, though not however on terms of civil or religious equality. From the passing of the Edict of Nantes in 1598 until its revocation by Louis XIV in 1685, the kingdom of France had a version of the latter model in which the minority was formally tolerated, except that the roles of Catholics and Protestants were reversed. From 1685, France followed the model of Catholic absolutism, giving hundreds of thousands of Protestants the option of conformity to Catholicism or exile. Under the *ancien régime*, the concept of an official state religion was central to political systems, and where the population was not uniformly of the official persuasion those dissenting were legally disadvantaged and to a greater or lesser extent excluded from civil life. Ireland was no exception to this general principle.

No ruler had been more aware of the political attractions of uniformity in religion than Elizabeth I. Her ecclesiastical settlement was designed to be acceptable to the greatest number, rather than to promote any particular theological dogma, and she looked for no more than outward conformity. By the 1590s it was abundantly clear that the plan was working in England and had failed as far as Ireland was concerned, and that the latter country would have competing ecclesiastical systems. For over four centuries, with an interruption from 1649 to 1660, the Church of Ireland would be the Established Church, and for most of that time conformity to it would be the touchstone of loyalty and a requirement for the enjoyment of the full benefits of citizenship, in particular eligibility for public office. In the 1590s, the State Church had one durable competitor, a Catholicism newly reinvigorated from continental sources; another would arise in the 1640s in the form of Presbyterianism.

The many Scottish settlers in Ulster had generally taken their religious formation from the Scottish Reformation but on Irish soil had accommodated their convictions and disciplines to the forms of the Established Church. Such compromise became more difficult to endure following the increase in fervour associated with the Covenanting movement in Scotland in the 1630s, coinciding as it did with pressure to conform to the Laudian model of state Church. The arrival of a Scottish army at Carrickfergus in April 1642 was soon followed by the institution of formal Presbyterian structures. Like other forms of dissenting religion, Presbyterianism flourished under the Commonwealth, and in the decades that followed it alone among them possessed the necessary toughness to thrive amid the restoration of monarchy and state Church. While religious and social life would continue to be enriched by Quaker and Baptist communities, they had contracted so much by the end of the century that 'for practical purposes . . . Irish Protestant Dissent meant Ulster Presbyterianism'.[13]

Cromwell was committed to the principle of freedom of conscience, but this did not extend to the practice of the Catholic religion, which his theological prejudices stigmatised as idolatry. The early 1650s was the period of the most thoroughgoing persecution of Catholicism, and particularly the priesthood, in Ireland. Additionally, Cromwell had a deep prejudice about the collective complicity of Irish Catholics in the mythic massacre of 1641, which he saw as having been compounded by the Catholic confederacy and its wars. The fact that Irish Catholics faced collective retribution had been signalled as early as 1642 by the English Parliament's 'Act of Adventurers'. This provided for the despatch of an army to Ireland funded by money that would be repaid in land to be forfeited from Irish 'rebels'. The threat became reality in the 1650s with a wholesale confiscation of land that was intended to remunerate the soldiers of Cromwell's army and refund those who had financed it. No distinction was made between Old English Catholics and Old Irish Catholics, as those landowners who could not prove 'constant good affection' to the cause of parliament were expropriated and assigned in return much smaller holdings in Connacht. Catholic townspeople were similarly deprived of their properties and expelled. The 1650s was the decisive decade in the struggle between Catholics and Protestants for control of the land of Ireland. Protestants henceforth enjoyed an advantage that only another cataclysm could overthrow. Nonetheless, and while the Restoration settlement did little by way of reversal, there was still a substantial Catholic interest. (And it was the proprietors of land who had been banished to Connacht, not the population who worked the land; indeed, many dispossessed proprietors remained on as tenants.) Ireland would be, like the United Provinces and France, one of the polities with a denominationally divided population. The Irish case, however, was different in two important respects.

Firstly, the religious divide in Ireland came to be equated with assumed racial or national origins. Thus Catholic was identified with Irish, Church of Ireland with English (albeit English of Ireland, as in 'the people of Ireland') and Presbyterian with Scotch (albeit Ulster-Scots or Scotch-Irish). These equations are open to the same fundamental objection as other simplifications of ancestry, but even on their own terms they are not sustainable. It was, of course, true that most members of the Church of Ireland in the early seventeenth century were New English, but it was also the case that the Church of Ireland from the beginning included among its members bearers of such old Irish surnames as O'Brien, Brady, O'Hara and McGrath, not to mention a host of Old English names. In Ulster, various Gaelic families gave

[13] S. Connolly, *Religion, Law and Power: The Making of Protestant Ireland, 1660–1760* (Oxford, 1992), p. 161.

adherence to Presbyterianism. On the other hand, there are several instances of New English families who adhered to Catholicism and of the descendants of New English or of Cromwellians becoming Catholic: Nicholas Madgett, the grandson of a Cromwellian officer, became Roman Catholic Bishop of Kerry in 1753. Needless to say, the Bishop had three other grandparents, but by the conventions of ancestor invention they are invisible. By the late seventeenth century, a significant proportion of the population of Ireland was descended from various combinations of Old Irish, Old English, New English and New Protestants, but the individuals involved were each taken to have only one such ancestry; and, of course, it is a gross misconception to think of these four ethnicities as possessing any racial distinctiveness in the first place.

By this juncture Ireland had witnessed the crystallisation of three broad political collectivities which coincided as fully as these things ever do with the threefold religious division into Catholic, Church of Ireland and Presbyterian. This is not to deny that an enormous gulf in terms of status and wealth separated the upper and lower echelons of each grouping and that such considerations mattered more than religious affiliation in the day-to-day lives of most people. Neither is it being denied that for many, particularly among the poor, affiliations of any kind, apart from those of family and kindred, mattered very little. And, as with all schematic classifications of society, there were those who could not be definitively assigned to any of the categories. Yet it is clear that in the eyes of the law and for the purposes of the elites, the threefold division by religion was definitive. In contemporary usage, the term 'Protestant' referred only to the Church of Ireland and its members, and did not include Presbyterians. Only in the nineteenth century did 'Protestant' come to cover all the denominations that acknowledged the Reformation.

The clarity of the basis of the threefold division in the eighteenth century was obscured by the superimposition on the denominations in both Irish language and English language usage of the racially derived designations of Irish (*Gael*), English (*Sasanach*) and Scottish (*Albanach*). As the eighteenth century progressed, the rigidity of this usage in English slackened, with the term 'popish' rather than 'Irish' being applied to Catholics, and with Protestants who wished to distance themselves from a metropolitan power whose interference in their affairs they resented, seeking various circumlocutions to describe themselves. However, politico-religious difference on the island continued to be conceptualised not as division within a nation but as difference between nationalities. French Protestants or Dutch Catholics might be seen as standing apart from the true Catholic or Calvinist nation, but there was no suggestion that they constituted or appertained to a different nation. In Ireland, the situation was otherwise.

The second distinguishing feature of religious difference in early modern Ireland from the perspective of European norms was that the politically dominant religion was not, and never became, numerically dominant. As we have seen, the shallowness of state control, together with the effectiveness of the Tridentine mission, ensured that the bulk of the population became partisans of reformed Catholicism by the end of the sixteenth century, even when they may have had little appreciation of the doctrinal differences between the Churches. However, that was not necessarily the end of the matter. Lutheran Sweden and Catholic Spain had shown that a strong monarchy could secure something close to total confessional uniformity. The Spanish Netherlands in the 1580s and Bohemia in the 1620s and 1630s (where the Austrian Habsburgs anticipated Cromwell in confessional reverse, with a little help from some Irish Catholic exiles) demonstrated that a sufficiently determined regime could change drastically the religious complexion of a polity. In Ireland, the Cromwellians displayed in the early 1650s the kind of ruthlessness that might indeed have uprooted Catholicism if it had been persisted in, and if it had been accompanied by an effective Protestant mission.[14] The strength within English and Irish Protestantism of Calvinist conviction about predestination to salvation (and damnation) would be an enduring damper on the drive to convert Catholics in the following century and a half. Furthermore, an all-out drive for conversion would have given the clergy a much more central place in the polity than the ruling lay interests were prepared to concede. Conversion efforts were but fitful, and it would appear that the Catholic proportion of the population was never much lower than seventy-five per cent. For ruling Protestants in early modern Ireland, superiority in numbers was a less important consideration than superiority in landownership and *ancien régime* privilege.

Plantation and confiscation, most notably under the Commonwealth, left the greater part of the land of Ireland in Protestant hands. The centrality of land ownership to the conflicts of the seventeenth century was well illustrated when the Catholic James II, deposed in England and replaced by the Dutchman, William of Orange, made his stand in Ireland in 1689 and agreed to summon a parliament dominated by his Irish Catholic supporters. The most momentous measure adopted was for a return to the landholding situation of 1641, at which time Catholics owned about sixty per cent of the land. This would have left the beneficiaries of the Cromwellian plantations losing out to the heirs of dispossessed Catholics. The Catholic gentry assembled in the Jacobite parliament coerced the King in to this drastic measure that would galvanise Protestant property holders against him. Interestingly, the Catholic gentry were much easier to satisfy in the realm of religion. They did not press for any interference with the Church establishment, apart from the release of those outside the Established Church from the obligation to pay tithes and a declaration of freedom of conscience.

---

[14] T.C. Barnard, *Cromwellian Ireland. English Government and Reform in Ireland, 1649–60* (Oxford, 1975), pp. 172–82.

The war of 1690–91 between James and William had major international and dynastic implications, but it was also a war that polarised Catholics and Protestants in a contest for the government and land of Ireland.[15] The Siege of Derry and the Battles of the Boyne and Aughrim that together turned the struggle decisively in William's favour determined the aspect of power in Ireland at least for a century to come. Together with the massacres of 1641, these victories over the forces of popish tyranny provided Irish Protestants with a myth of deliverance.

In the aftermath of Aughrim came another round of confiscation, this time of the lands of James's Catholic supporters. By 1703 only fourteen per cent of Irish land is estimated to have remained in Catholic ownership. But with the Jacobite claim on the throne still supported by the French monarchy, by the papacy, and by most of the Catholics of Ireland at home and in military service on the continent, and possibly by some of their own Tory notables in Church and state, Irish Protestants felt they had reason to fear for the future. Herein lies part of the explanation for the congeries of laws drastically affecting the rights and status of Catholics passed by the Irish Parliament between 1695 and 1745, generally known to history as the penal laws.

These laws were not the products of a single coherent scheme, each in fact arising out of an individual set of political circumstances. However, a number of objectives may be discerned, among the clearest and most effectively realised being the disarming of Catholics and the diminution of the amount of land owned by them. Faced with draconian restrictions on their rights to acquire or bequeath property in land, most of the remaining Catholic landlords conformed to the Established Church. Catholics were excluded from the franchise, from parliament and corporations, from holding public office, and from the law and all other professions except medicine. By these measures, the public life of the country was made the exclusive reserve of adherents of the state religion, who also controlled most of the land, and therefore the wealth and influence of the country.

The penal laws affecting the Catholic Church were as draconian as those in respect of the Catholic elites, but they were not enforced with anything like the same consistency and rigour: the desire to bring the entire population into the Anglican fold was in the eighteenth century confined to a small number of ecclesiastics and had little or no appeal to the wielders of political power in Ireland. Besides, moves against individual Catholic clergymen tended to antagonise the populace at a local level and so to make life difficult for the magistrates. By 1704, legislation was in place that made illegal the presence in Ireland of Catholic bishops or religious, or of any category of 'popish' minister other than about one thousand parish priests registered

---

[15] R. Gillespie, 'The Irish Protestants and James II, 1688–90' in *Irish Historical Studies*, xvii, no. 110 (Nov. 1992), pp. 124–33.

with the authorities. As these individuals died they would not be replaced, if the laws were successfully enforced, and their ministry would die with them. An Act of 1709 required the registered priests to take an oath abjuring allegiance to the Stuarts on pain of banishment. Only a few complied, but no general banishment followed. In defiance of the law, priests, religious and bishops did enter the country and in effect were allowed to conduct their ministry provided that they did so in a discreet fashion and, in particular, that they did not cause any open offence to Protestantism. But the law could be invoked in arbitrary fashion against individuals or more generally. On a number of occasions of perceived crisis, the last of them in 1744, the Government ordered the temporary closure of all places of Catholic worship. Penal laws apart, the fact that the Catholic Church in Ireland did not have access to the ecclesiastical buildings and endowments of the country set it apart from the normal conditions of Catholicism in continental Europe. Among the features of Catholic culture prohibited by law were the creation of religious endowments and the conducting of schools. There was no law prohibiting the practice of their religion by the Catholic laity, although individuals could be required to reveal to a magistrate the identity of a priest whose mass they had attended.[16]

Just as the main measures of the penal code were partly a response to continuing Catholic allegiance to the Jacobite cause, so in turn they had the effect of deepening that loyalty. The popes continued until the death of James III in 1766 to recognise the Stuarts and, consistently with this policy, they conceded to the Jacobite court in exile, as to other Catholic monarchies, the right of nomination of bishops. Where the hierarchy led others followed. At a time when the Protestants of four countries and beyond were being offered an umbrella British identity focused on the Protestant monarchy, Irish Catholic elites, from emigré clerical place-seekers in the Theology Faculty of the Sorbonne in Paris to the localised literati of the Gaelic scribal inheritance, were participants in another, if smaller, transnational politico-religious cult, that of Jacobitism, focused on 'the king over the water'.[17] It was a measure of the success of the political aspects of the penal laws that widespread Jacobite feeling found no active expression in Ireland during the rising fomented in Scotland and England in 1745–46 by the landing of Prince Charles Edward. His final defeat at Culloden in 1746 marked the end of any credible possibility of a Stuart restoration, and by the 1750s prominent Catholics can be seen endeavouring to find a formal accommodation with the Protestant monarchy. To this end, the Catholic Association was formed in Dublin in 1756 and the Catholic Committee in 1760. By the mid-century, a Catholic commercial urban elite, many of its members very

---

[16] M. Wall, 'The penal laws, 1681–1760' in *Catholic Ireland in the Eighteenth Century: Collected Essays of Maureen Wall* (Dublin, 1989), pp. 1–60.

[17] The Irish language sources are extensively explored and contextualised in Breandán Ó Buachalla, *Aisling ghéar: na Stíobhartaigh agus an tAos Léinn 1603–1788* (Dublin, 1996).

wealthy, had emerged. The growing commercial wealth of Catholics and the security needs of the British Empire, especially the demand for military manpower, would make the continued exclusion of the largest politico-religious body in Ireland unsustainable. In 1759, with the Seven Years' War at its height, the recruitment of Irish Catholic soldiers into the British army was officially countenanced.

The position of Presbyterians was also in line for change. The Established Church saw in the Presbyterians a highly motivated body under disciplined direction, inimical to the episcopal system that their co-religionists had overthrown in Scotland. For sixty years or so after the restoration of the monarchy in 1660, the freedom of Presbyterians to act as a religious body was subject to legal interference by Established Church interests. Their position is well epitomised by the *regium donum*, a government grant designated for the support of the clergy, first made in 1672, that served both as a form of official recognition and also as a controlling mechanism in the hands of civil authority. The grant was increased as a reward for staunch support of the Williamite cause in 1690–91, but not until 1719 was the freedom of worship of Presbyterians guaranteed, by the Toleration Act of that year. But they still suffered legal disabilities, as legislation of 1704 stipulated that holders of paid public office in central, local and urban government should be communicants of the Church of Ireland. Thus, like Roman Catholics, but not to anything like the same degree, Presbyterians were excluded from the establishment, something that they resented greatly. Presbyterians were particularly affected by internal doctrinal divisions, with the issue of whether or not ministers at installation should be required to subscribe to the test of faith elaborated in the Westminster Confession at the centre of the problem. The anti-subscribing New Light Party achieved dominance of the Ulster Synod in the eighteenth century but at the cost of defections to the subscribing Seceders. The abolition of the sacramental test in 1780 ended formal restrictions on the political rights of Presbyterians and signified a weakening of confessional exclusivity as an acceptable basis for the exercise of political power.

The extension of a similar level of civil and political rights to Catholics would be a much greater challenge. Between 1778 and 1793 a series of measures passed into law, in some cases after bitter debate in the Irish Parliament and following considerable pressure from the British Government, that greatly eased the disabilities of Catholics and of their Church, but still left them excluded from various public offices and from taking seats in parliament. The patriot movement that asserted the constitutional claims of the kingdom of Ireland, that inspired the mobilisation of the Volunteers in 1778–79, and that found its ultimate expression in Grattan's parliament, had started out with the idea of a Protestant nation, and only a section of it ever came around to embracing the non-confessional concept of nationality that the circumstances and ideas of the age promoted in some

Figure 3.3 Francis Wheatley, *A view of College Green with a meeting of the Volunteers on 4 November 1779*, oil on canvas (National Gallery of Ireland). The centrepiece is the famous equestrian statue of William III that stood from 1701 until 1929 (see chapter eight).

quarters. Anticipating changes of a kind more usually associated with the Revolution of 1789, Louis XVI had restored political rights to French Protestants in 1787. Grattan's Parliament followed not French example but that of the several states of the USA that maintained restrictions on the political rights of Catholics, and would continue to do so far into the nineteenth century. Nevertheless, the closing decades of the century were marked by a major change in the dominant view of the place of religious collectivities in the Irish nation. Admission to the professions, to full property rights, to certain public offices, and to the vote, signified that instead of being excluded as formerly, Catholics were now being admitted to the body politic, albeit on a subordinate basis. Exclusion from parliament remained.

The term 'Protestant ascendancy', which has been traced to the 1780s, came later to denote a group of people, the politically privileged Protestants of the eighteenth and nineteenth centuries. Originally it referred to the presumed right of Protestants to rule the country in a context in which Catholics would be admitted to public life, but only on a second-class basis. In this sense, Protestant ascendancy was a change from the Protestant exclusiveness and Catholic exclusion that marked the stand-off of the generations after 1691. Whatever chance such a formula might have had as an acceptable compromise pending future developments was undermined in the flood of expectations and apprehensions released by the French Revolution. After the fall of the Bastille, no politicised interest, such as Irish Catholics were increasingly coming to be, was likely to rest content indefinitely with subordinate status. And similarly, no privileged ruling elite, such as the Protestant placeholders and landowners of Ireland, would be inclined to relax its grip. 'Protestant ascendancy' became the slogan of reaction.[18] The Williamite myth represented an evocation of liberty, originally as the antithesis of popery. In a remarkable transformation, it appeared to many in the 1780s as if Roman Catholics might be admitted to the liberty of the children of William. In 1789, the local Catholic bishop and priests participated with the corporation and Protestant and Presbyterian dignitaries in the centenary commemoration of the relief of the siege of Derry.[19] Six years later all had changed again, and the foundation of the Orange Order marked the appropriation in the cause of reaction and Protestant ascendancy of the cult of 'Enniskillen, Derry, Aughrim and the Boyne', to the dismay over the following centuries of Catholics and liberal Protestants alike.

In the revolutionary dawn of the 1790s, the Society of United Irishmen was formed by Catholics, Protestants and Presbyterians who envisaged a new era of liberty and equality. Their formula, at least on the surface, represented the reinvention of Irish nationality on the basis of the abandon-

---

[18] J.R. Hill, 'The meaning and significance of Protestant ascendancy, 1787–1840' in *Ireland after the Union: Proceedings of the Second Joint Meeting of the Royal Irish Academy and the British Academy, London, 1986* (Oxford, 1989), pp. 1–22.

[19] B. Walker, *Past and Present: History, Identity and Politics in Ireland* (Belfast, 2000), p. 5.

ment of confessional divisions. In the intention of their most effective spokesman and strategist, Theobald Wolfe Tone, there would henceforth be a union of 'Catholic, Protestant and Dissenter'. The extent to which this ideological transition was achieved, particularly by rank and file supporters, is a matter of some question. With politicised Irish Catholics going out of their way to disavow any allegiance to the pope in civil matters, and with the new regime in France humbling the Catholic Church, it seemed to radical Presbyterians that the long-desired demise of popery was at hand. Those of them who joined the United Irishmen were under the illusion – sustainable for a few years in the 1790s – that Catholicism as they had known it was a thing of the past and that the Revolution initiated in France in 1789 was the realisation of their apocalyptic hopes.[20] In this respect, as in others, the United Irishmen's rebellion of 1798 proved to be a disappointment, serving as it did to herald not the dissolution of confessional animosities but their intensification.

One element in the rationale for the union of Ireland with Great Britain was the provision of a wider arena for the accommodation of Irish differences. As it turned out this advantage was not realised, as both the archaic and progressive aspects of the unwritten British constitution served in different ways to exacerbate religious tensions in nineteenth-century Ireland. The refusal of 'Catholic emancipation' down to 1829 was not only a consequence of endemic British suspicion of popery, but was of a piece with the maintenance of a range of *ancien régime* features, some of which have survived in the British constitution into the twenty-first century. Thus, while the Relief Act of 1829 made Catholics in Britain and Ireland eligible to sit in parliament and hold most offices of state, it debarred them from the very highest public offices. After 1829, the emancipated Catholics of Ireland found themselves still paying tithes to the Established Church; the government of most of the main cities and towns was in the control of closed and predominantly Protestant corporations until 1840; and the Anglican Church, with a following of about ten per cent of the population, retained established status until 1870.

Gladstone's first term of office (1868–74) saw not only to disestablishment but also to the abolition of various oaths and tests disadvantageous or distasteful to Catholics. But disinclination to invoke first principles meant that not until 1920 for Ireland (and not yet for Britain) was there legislation rendering void, as a category, all enactments imposing disadvantage in respect of religious belief.[21] This conservatism in the matter of constitutional forms was part of the exceptional formula that worked so well for modern Britain, but it had adverse consequences in Ireland, especially because it

---

[20] I.R. McBride, *Scripture Politics: Ulster Presbyterians and Irish Radicalism in the Late Eighteenth Century* (Oxford, 1998), pp. 186–206.

[21] Clause 5 (2) of Government of Ireland Act, 1920 (10 & 11 Geo. V, cap. 67).

involved tardiness in acknowledging the civil rights of Catholics. At the same time, the liberalising aspects of the British system facilitated the expression and promotion of the resentment that its backward-looking aspects fomented. Thus the mobilisations of the Catholic populace by O'Connell's Catholic Association in the 1820s and his Repeal Association in the 1840s were manifestations such as would have been permitted in very few places in Europe before 1848. In Ireland there was sufficient freedom of association and freedom of the press to facilitate impressive agitation of grievances.

Catholics had naturally always resented the penal laws, but the rhetoric which expressed that resentment in terms that would endure was fashioned in the period 1790–1820, when most of the offensive code had been repealed but full equality was being denied. Denouncers included the Protestant statesman, Edmund Burke (1729–97), the revolutionary, Theobald Wolfe Tone, and the Catholic lawyer, Denys Scully (1773–1830). The use of the term 'emancipation' for the demanded removal of the disabilities remaining after 1793 evoked an implicit comparison with black slavery. The Protestant historian, W.E.H. Lecky (1838–1903), would repeat the denunciation of the discriminatory code with all the righteous judgementalism of the late nineteenth-century liberal intellectual. To this principled liberal outrage against religious tyranny was added a corpus of more visceral material drawing on popular memory and eventually historical research.[22] Thus, the penal laws assumed mythic status and became part of the armoury of politicised Catholicism, in the way that the 1641 massacre served the political purposes of Protestants.

The case for Catholic emancipation had an ideological basis that was irrefutable in terms of early nineteenth-century liberalism, but its achievement came in 1829 not through the triumph of an idea but through political pressure. The weight of that pressure was provided by a popular movement comprising ramified associations, mass meetings and demonstrations, popular subscriptions, public banquets, newspaper propaganda and the pressurisation of voters by the unfranchised, that was precocious by the standards of the day as an unarmed (and at least in that sense 'democratic') expression of a full-blown modern nationalism. Liberal Protestants supported emancipation on ideological grounds, but by the 1820s O'Connell was pitching the appeal in blatantly nationalist terms. 'The Catholic people of Ireland are a nation', he declared in 1826.[23] When in the early 1830s he went on to promote repeal of the Union, very few liberal Protestants followed, but he had potential allies in those Protestants, especially in Dublin

---

[22] For example, P.F. Moran, *Historical Sketch of the Persecutions Suffered by the Catholics of Ireland under the Rule of Cromwell and the Puritans* (Dublin, 1884); W.P. Burke, *Irish Priests in the Penal Times, 1660–1760* (Waterford, 1914).

[23] O. MacDonagh, *O'Connell: the Life of Daniel O'Connell, 1775–1847* (London, 1991), p. 231.

Corporation, who had never been reconciled to the loss of the Irish Parliament. However, co-operation proved impossible between the O'Connellites who sought in repeal a further expression of Catholic nationalism, and those who sought a return of the parliament that had upheld Protestant privilege.

At the passing of the Act of Union it was the intention of the Prime Minister, William Pitt, and the expectation of Catholics, that emancipation would follow speedily. While it is idle to speculate on how Irish politics might have developed in that event, it can be said that the failure to deliver emancipation provoked a campaign that created a modern nationalist movement in which Irish nationality was reinvented with Catholicism as its key identifier. Because it drew so many of the clergy into political activity, and because it raised dramatically the political stature of Catholicism, the emancipation campaign advanced by leagues the place of the Catholic hierarchy in public life. From the 1820s the bench of bishops begins to emerge as an institution of national scope. The existence at Maynooth from 1795 of a government-funded seminary designed to serve the entire country promoted within the Church itself the consciousness of a national mission. Shortly before his death, Lord John George de la Poer Beresford (1773–1862), a powerful ecclesiastical magnate who was old enough to recall pre-revolutionary times, remarked that when he was a boy 'the Irish people' meant the Protestants, whereas now it had come to mean the Roman Catholics.[24]

If the 1790s and subsequent decades witnessed a political transformation of the Irish Catholic collectivity, it saw concomitant changes in the political organisation of Irish Protestants. With the foundation of the Orange Order in 1795, counter-revolutionary Protestants had acquired a formidable mechanism for the promotion and defence of their interests. Temporarily suppressed in 1825, it was replaced in 1828 on an interim basis by the Brunswick Clubs, formed in response to the emancipation movement. Opposed to the Act of Union at the time of its passing, the Orangemen became staunch unionists in response to the rise of Catholic nationalism and its embrace of repeal. The Order would acquire a significant social function for Irish Protestants at home and abroad, and in the mobilisations against Home Rule in the period 1886–1914 it filled a role corresponding to that of the Catholic parish network and various cultural organisations on the other side. From the early 1830s, Protestant political sentiment found a purposeful outlet in the Conservative Party which for decades to come would punch above its weight on the Irish electoral scene. It was an alliance in which the landed gentry were a crucial element. Whether Whig or Tory, and irrespective of how they had felt about the Union in 1800, landlords had come to conclude by the 1830s that the maintenance of the social order as they understood it depended on the British connection.

---

[24] J.C. Beckett, *The Anglo-Irish Tradition* (London, 1976), p. 10.

The radical Presbyterian milieu of Belfast in which the Society of United Irishmen had flourished in the 1790s survived into the new century in however attenuated a form. It was a ready source of sympathy for Catholic emancipation but one so alienated by O'Connell's aggressive assertion of Catholic nationality that no enduring conjunction of forces was possible. Not only the menace of a mobilised Catholic majority but the conviction that the Union was serving their objectives better than any possible alternative reconciled liberal Presbyterians to government from Westminster. They would continue to oppose landed interests and vote Liberal until the polarisation on the issue of Home Rule, when they threw in their lot with the wider Protestant community. But radicalism, both political and religious, had been a minority element among Presbyterians from much earlier. In 1830, the now dominant advocates of subscription in the Ulster Synod saw their non-subscribing opponents depart to form the Remonstrant Synod before themselves uniting with the Seceders in 1840 as the General Assembly of the Presbyterian Church in Ireland. Given the minuscule numbers of Presbyterians outside of Ulster, the adoption of a national title is an interesting instance of the way in which things that are neither nationwide nor nationalist tend to be designated in national terms simply because the nation/country is there.

Confessional antagonism in Ireland in the first half of the nineteenth century cannot be explained solely in terms of conflict in the political arena. This was a period of intense ecclesiastical strife as established interests of various kinds looked to a revival of the Church and religion as a guarantee against the recrudescence of the revolutionary spirit. John Wesley visited Ireland several times from 1747 on, and Methodism secured an enduring place. The earlier Methodist missions in Ireland were supplemented from 1806 by the Hibernian Bible Society and from 1818 by the Irish Society for Promoting the Education of the Native Irish through their own Language. By the 1820s, the Established Church and the Presbyterians, fired by the evangelically derived fervour of this 'second reformation', had embarked on a more determined campaign than at any time in centuries for the conversion of Irish Catholics. The establishment of a large number of schools where literacy and Bible reading were combined provided a point of entry to many families eager for basic education. Support for the Catholic Association and its emancipation campaign was part of the response of the Catholic Church. There were many in the 1820s, including senior Anglican divines on the one hand and devotees of the Catholic Pastorini's prophecies concerning the destruction of Protestantism on the other, who fell into that recurring temptation of the confessionally minded, namely, envisaging the disappearance by conversion or otherwise of rival communions. There was significant government support in the 1820s for Protestant churchmen who held out the prospect of a new Ireland in which a population entirely converted to reformed religion would also be loyal British subjects.[25] The abandonment of that illusion was signalled in 1831 with the institution of a system of government-financed national schools designed to permit each of the denominations to provide religious instruction to the children of its own adherents. The state was declaring its neutrality.

Although disestablishment was some way off, the Church of Ireland had arrived at a watershed in its life, a fact further emphasised by the Church Temporalities (Ireland) Act of 1833 that peremptorily combined dioceses, suppressed ten bishoprics and reallocated revenues. For two centuries, and especially after 1660, it had woven a rich web of ritual and rhetoric around the supports of civil power, fulfilling with its memorial days, its anthems and its commemoration sermons the mission of the national Church. By 1833 it was clear that the state in Ireland was intent on abandoning the arrangement.[26]

Daniel O'Connell may on occasions have allowed himself to envisage the prospect of Protestantism in Ireland fading away when deprived of the supports of establishment, but he combined with his Catholic nationalism a fundamentally liberal view of political society, and one with a place for a minority. Following his term as the first Lord Mayor of Dublin after the 1840 municipal reforms, and the first Catholic in the office since 1689, he put in place an arrangement for rotation of the office that allowed it to be held every second year by a Conservative. In 1839, the Chancellor of Austria and unofficial policeman of the German Confederation, Metternich, dismayed at O'Connell's combination of Catholic politics and liberalism – he was then supporting a Whig/Liberal government at Westminster – proposed that a restoration of ecclesiastical property would pacify Irish Catholics. In fact, O'Connell, the consistent advocate of a free Church in a free state, was foremost among those diverting Irish Catholics away from the idea of replacing one religious establishment with another. However, O'Connell never permitted liberal principles to get in the way of emotive platform oratory. Even when he was campaigning for repeal of the Union and no longer for any specifically Catholic objective, O'Connell would on occasion appeal to the Catholic identity and prejudices of an audience. It seems unlikely that even in his own mind he had worked out a reconciliation between Catholic nationality and non-confessional citizenship.

Catholic nationality went hand in hand with the consolidation and flowering of institutionalised Catholicism. From beginnings made in the last quarter of the eighteenth century, the Catholic Church in Ireland developed by stages over several generations the physical and institutional structures that it had been largely denied under the penal laws – a well-articulated

---

[25] Stewart J. Brown, 'The new reformation movement in the Church of Ireland, 1801–29' in S.J. Brown and D.W. Miller (eds), *Piety and Power in Ireland, 1760–1960* (Belfast, 2000), pp. 180–208.

[26] See Jacqueline R. Hill, 'National festivals'.

parochial system, a rich variety of well-populated religious orders (male and female), convents, hospitals and schools, most of them funded by the state.[27] Paul Cullen (1803–78), Archbishop of Dublin from 1852, and from 1866 the first Irish-born cardinal, personifies the triumphs of nineteenth-century Irish Catholicism. He is of particular interest for this study as an instance of a key inventor of nationality who was simultaneously opposed to nationalist politics: experience of the Roman revolution of 1848–49 and of Irish politics in the early 1850s left him with the conviction that nothing but trouble would come from popular mobilisation.

Like Jonathan Swift, the Jacobite poets, O'Connell and Parnell, the cardinal railed fiercely against the English (Catholic and Protestant), while taking for granted that doing business with them was part of the order of things. His strategy was that of hard bargaining with the government to secure changes in Irish law and institutions that would benefit Catholicism. He believed that, in his time, providence had aligned the interests of the Catholic Church, his Irish Catholic collectivity and the British Empire. His animosity was great against the Fenians for threatening this alignment. When W.E. Gladstone made his only extended visit to Ireland in 1877 he stayed at Carton and Kilruddery and other houses of the aristocracy, but their owners were not part of the Ireland of his past and future overtures and neither were the liberal Presbyterians. Gladstone's Ireland in 1877, as it had been for a decade, was that of Cullen. Ten years later, Gladstone's Ireland would be that of Parnell, which is to say the same collectivity as Cullen's, but now less fully attuned to the Empire and much more accommodating of the Fenians.

Although the inter-Church competition for souls continued in ever more institutionalised form into the second half of the nineteenth century, it was generally conducted more sedately than before.[28] After 1870, the grievance of a Church establishment was gone. However, other causes of friction and grievance took on new importance. Competition for positions in the public service and in private business intensified and was conducted as a matter of course with reference to religion, Belfast and its shipyards providing the most notorious cockpits. The fierce inter-ethnic animosities that many emigrants encountered in the cities of Britain and the USA were recycled into Irish life. As Irish society was modernised, so was it confessionalised: the newer vertical division facilitated the religious segmentation of society even more than did the older horizontal one. By the final third of the nineteenth century, confessional segmentation was an undeniable feature of Irish society, with schools, hospitals and every aspect of associational life becoming increasingly denominationalised. A similar segmentation of Dutch society

---

27 See Kevin Whelan, 'The Catholic Church in County Tipperary, 1700–1900' in William Nolan and Thomas McGrath (eds), *Tipperary: History and Society* (Dublin, 1985), pp. 215–55.
28 See Jacinta Prunty, *Dublin Slums, 1800–1925: A Study in Urban Geography* (Dublin, 1998).

along confessional lines was transcended, and also entrenched, during the Great War with Catholics and Protestants, drawn together by the need to maintain the country's neutrality, arriving at an accommodation and a demarcation that lasted for generations. There was to be no Irish equivalent.

The great agrarian conflict sparked off in Ireland by the agricultural depression of the late 1870s, and which provided the primary propulsion for the Home Rule movement of the following thirty-five years, clearly had potential to cut across confessional lines. Tenants had a common interest irrespective of religion, and Presbyterian tenants in Ulster had a particularly notable record of assertiveness vis-à-vis their landlords. At the mid-century, in the first phase of politicised tenant agitation, incipient collaboration between Catholics in Leinster and Munster and Presbyterians in Ulster was such that one of the promoters could subsequently write, however hyperbolically, of a 'league of north and south'.[29] There was no repetition a generation later when the tenants in effect waged two separate campaigns, a generally peaceable but effective campaign by Presbyterian and Church of Ireland farmers in much of Ulster, and in the rest of the country the celebrated 'land war' promoted by the Land League under Parnell, Davitt and others who would form the elite of nationalist politics over the following decades. The polarisation was by no means complete – many Protestant farmers in Leinster and Munster were seen to support Land League demonstrations, and everywhere there were Catholics whose interests brought them into conflict with the League – but the land crisis did much more to reinforce than to transcend confessional divisions. Thus, the volunteer 'emergencymen' who came to the assistance of the ostracised Captain Boycott in Co. Mayo, and of numerous other 'boycotted' landlords and agents were frequently Orangemen rallying to the aid of beleaguered co-religionists. The small minority of landlords who were Catholics generally followed their class interests, having little choice, since in fact their tenants made no exception of them on the basis of their religion.

The polarisation occasioned by the land war set the pattern for the division over Home Rule that erupted in the mid-1880s. This in turn became the nationalist versus unionist dichotomy that was to be the main shaper of the Irish political scenario in the twentieth century. The basis of this division was never simply religious: it had a multiple basis in which, however, religion was the dominant element. There would always be Protestant supporters of Home Rule (many of them in positions of leadership) and there would always be Catholic unionists (very few of them politically prominent), but they would always be utterly unrepresentative of the generality of their co-religionists. In general, unionists were more willing to invoke religion as the basis of their political stance, typically expressing an old apprehension in a

---

[29] C.G. Duffy, *The League of North and South: An Episode of Irish History, 1850–54* (London, 1886).

newly popular aphorism: 'Home Rule is Rome rule'. Not all unionists were prepared to cite concern over religion, the historian Lecky being a case in point. He feared not Roman tyranny but the subversion of property rights and the social order, and undoubtedly many who did cite the 'Rome rule' fear also had other qualms. But when all due allowances have been made there is no denying that the two camps into which the Home Rule question divided Ireland were defined primarily by religious affiliation.

Throughout most of the nineteenth century, the Catholic Church success-fully promoted a modernising ethos that deeply influenced the lives, atti-tudes and mores of an increasing proportion of adherents. The priests and their lay collaborators were to the fore in the curbing of agrarian secret soci-eties, faction fighting, illicit distillation, and uncontrolled popular gather-ings of various kinds, including devotions at holy wells on saints' days. Schools, larger churches, convents, religious orders, Roman-approved devo-tions, and parish missions all had a place in setting new standards. Even if its theology and worship were Roman and its language, law and commerce mainly English, this newly structured way of life was subordinate rather than subservient to these hegemonic systems, distinctively Irish and in sev-eral senses undeniably national. More thorough instruction in the tenets of the faith meant that the generality of Catholics learned more about the doc-trinal issues that separated them from Protestants, thus deploying ideology where previously for many there may have been only instinctive group loy-alty. But if the markers of confessional difference were newly highlighted, the new Catholic ethos was to a great extent identical with the style and content of contemporary Protestantism. For Catholics and Protestants alike, puritanical mores ('Victorian values' as some would have it) provided the test by which lower-middle-class and working-class people attained the sta-tus of respectability. Developments in religiously based popular culture from about the 1820s onwards made the population of Ireland more homo-geneous, while at the same time rendering the signs of confessional division among them ever more ineluctable.

From the 1880s, with the burgeoning involvement of the lower-middle classes in associational life, the hold of a long-gestating respectable puri-tanism on public culture visibly strengthened, and it would not lose its potency over most of the island for eighty years or so. Among Catholics, an intensification of popular piety within approved channels was evidenced by phenomena such as the flourishing of devotion to the Sacred Heart of Jesus. And, as shown especially in the case of Patrick Pearse, the younger genera-tion of Catholics coming of age in the early twentieth century tended to dis-play religious devotion and personal piety to an extent not evident in nationalist activists of earlier times: communal recitation of the rosary was regular practice in rebel garrisons during the Easter Rising. Endorsement of Sinn Féin as the new political leaders of the nation in the period 1917–21 was greatly facilitated for the bishops by evidence of the pious Catholicity of the cadres. While Sinn Féin, like the Nationalist Party, adhered to the doctrine of non-confessional nationalism, both shared the ambiguity going back to O'Connell's time of combining that with the de facto Catholic definition and inspiration of the movement.

The puritanical mindset had the sanction of religion as represented by most of the hierarchs of the time, but neither its roots nor its scope were confined to any one confession or to the sphere of religion in general. Without taking account of it, one cannot understand twentieth-century developments in language policy, literature, sport, music or politics – as will be seen in later chapters. The mindset was puritanical as in modern usage, which does not imply close modelling on the Puritans of the seventeenth century. It was highly prescriptive and dogmatic, promoting the assumption that everything was either obligatory or forbidden, and so did not place a high value on individual freedom of choice. Intolerance was epitomised in a readiness to demonise dissidents and opponents and to brand people and institutions as untouchable, without concern for the human dignity or rights of individuals, including the right of reply. Such a censorious system depended on vigilantes ready to discover and, if necessary, to root out departures from prescribed behaviour or ideas. Not all the vigilantes were clerics, and not all clerics were vigilantes.

The Government of Ireland Act of 1920 prohibited the endowment of any religion or the enactment of any law discriminating on the basis of religious belief, strictures that were repeated in the constitution of the Irish Free State in 1922 and in the 1937 constitution. The latter, however, in a quite contradictory spirit, also included a statement recognising the special position of the Roman Catholic Church 'as the guardian of the faith professed by the great majority of [the state's] citizens' (article 44) and a prohibition on divorce (article 41). This, like legislation for film censorship in 1923, censorship of publications in 1929, and against contraception in 1935, reflected the absolutist position of the Catholic Church, rather than the more flexible, but certainly not permissive, attitudes of other Churches and communions.[30]

Through the first fifty years or so, the rulers of independent Ireland were susceptible to the nostrums of social philosophy and moral theology dispensed by Catholic churchmen, either collectively or as individual bishops or experts. To a considerable extent, what was being presented as the application of Catholic moral principle was rather a local version of a European-wide conservatism, gravely disturbed by the Great War's loosening of social controls and the subsequent impact on popular entertainment, especially in the forms of the cinema and jazz. From the 1940s, the no longer avoidable issues of the state's responsibility for social welfare provision and the fear of communist totalitarianism added to the concerns of paternalistic clerics and to their portfolios of injunctions. The reluctance of Irish governments down to the 1950s to extend the remit of the state might have been expected to

---

[30]   See J.H. Whyte, *Church and State in Modern Ireland, 1923–70* (Dublin, 1971).

disarm clerical concerns on that topic; instead, it simply fed them. In the 1950s there was a welter of episcopal strictures against the idea of government programming of the economy. The celebrated government White Paper of 1958, *Economic Development*, generally credited with initiating the state's first phase of economic achievement, flew in the face of these strictures. It was presumably by way of fireproofing that its author, Ken Whitaker, cited the views of the then Bishop of Clonfert, William Philbin, who was out of line with most of his colleagues in suggesting that the times called for active intervention in the economy.[31]

Prescriptions accorded the air of revealed truth, but that sometimes amounted to little more than an insular 'take' on the latest papal pronouncement, were interspersed with authentic, well worked out projects like Bishop Duignan's 1944 proposal for a scheme of national insurance. The politicians by no means always followed the guidance offered, especially if it cut across their political interests. Clerical victories were seldom as apparently clear-cut as that in 1951 when the Minister for Health, Dr Noël Browne, was forced into resignation following episcopal objections to his proposals for a mother and child scheme, but there were other than clerical interests that wished to see Browne out of office.

Interaction between the Catholic Church and a State left by partition with a ninety-three per cent population of professing Catholics was scarcely surprising, and need not be clinching evidence of a redefinition of the nation in the direction of identification with Catholicism. But this too happened, and again it is as might have been expected. De Valera, who was a paragon of circumspection in his choice of words, on several occasions declared Ireland to be a Catholic nation, while still maintaining that everyone on the island should belong to a thirty-two county nation state.[32] From the 1920s to the 1960s, a series of politicians from parties large and small publicly professed their fealty to the Church or the pope and affirmed that they were Catholics first and Irishmen or politicians second. De Valera made such a declaration, to applause, addressing a Fianna Fáil meeting in October 1931, just months before his first general election victory.[33] (There is an interesting contrast with another of Catholic Ireland's favourite twentieth-century politicians, President John F. Kennedy, who made himself electable in 1960 by affirming that he was an American first and a Catholic second.) Deference to Catholicism extended far across the political spectrum: in the late 1930s the Labour Party submitted its draft new (party) constitution for vetting by the Catholic hierarchy.[34]

---

[31] *Economic Development* (Dublin, 1958), p. 9.
[32] See, for example, *Irish Press*, 18 Mar. 1935 (St Patrick's Day address).
[33] *Irish Press*, 29 Oct. 1931.
[34] Fearghal McGarry, '"Catholics first and politicians afterwards": the Labour Party and the workers' republic, 1936–39' in *Saothar 25: Journal of the Irish Labour History Society* (2000), pp. 57–65.

Down to the 1970s, nobody hoping to draw substantial support, political or of any other kind, from the population of the twenty-six counties would have challenged the identification of Irish nationality with Catholicism. Nonetheless, neither de Valera nor the others attempted to give effective constitutional expression to this, along the lines, for example, of Salazar in Portugal: article 44 of the constitution was largely gesture without substance, if nonetheless significant for that. The principle of a free Church in a free state, a legacy of O'Connell, Gladstone and the Liberal non-conformists, was deeply rooted, and neither de Valera nor his opponents ventured to discard it in favour of Catholic *integralisme*. It was, then, scarcely at all through the constitution, only to a limited extent through the law, and mainly through wider cultural life and practice, that the Irish Free State and its preponderant majority completed the invention of the Irish nation as Catholic.

Beginning with the new police force, the Garda Síochána, in 1923, various state services were placed under the patronage of the Sacred Heart of Jesus or the Blessed Virgin Mary. In 1929, the centenary of Catholic Emancipation was marked by the issuing of a commemorative stamp and by the participation of large contingents of soldiers and Garda Síochána in an open-air religious ceremony in Dublin attended by an estimated quarter of a million people. This served as a trial run for the International Eucharistic Congress held in Dublin in June 1932. With a papal legate and numerous ecclesiastical dignitaries from around the world, an impeccable display by the forces of the state, and the sounding of the eighth-century bell of St Patrick at a mass in the Phoenix Park attended by an estimated one million people, where Count John McCormack sang 'Panis angelicus', this was possibly the most elaborate expression ever of Catholic nationalist triumph. Catholic Ireland's favourite Englishman, G.K. Chesterton, was at hand to write a book about it all,[35] reassuring evidence that *they* were taking notice. At the Eucharistic Congress, uniformed soldiers had participated in the formalities of the liturgy, as they would do over the years on numerous lesser occasions, sloping arms, sounding bugles and so on. If the state came to the Church, the Church also came to the state: over the following decades numerous official occasions were marked by Catholic services. To take an unlikely example, an annual festival launched by the Government in 1953 to promote tourism, *An Tóstal*, was opened in each of the early years with a mass in Dublin's Pro-Cathedral.[36] In other words, an observer might be mistaken for thinking that there was, indeed, an Established Church in the land.

For well over a century, Catholics had been able to place the stamp of their faith in the form of numerous highly visible church buildings on a

---

[35] *Christendom in Dublin* (London, 1932).
[36] Information supplied by Dr Irene Furlong.

landscape previously monopolised by Anglican structures and medieval ruins. From the 1920s, new public and wayside shrines began to appear in greater numbers, culminating in 1954 in the widespread replication of the grotto at Lourdes in connection with the centenary of the proclamation of the dogma of the Immaculate Conception. As in church building, so too in education, the Irish Catholic Church had made up in the second half of the nineteenth century for the deficit caused by its deprivation of temporalities in earlier ages. Its position in education was not under the slightest threat from an independent Irish government, and the non-interventionist policy gave the other Churches the same privileges. In the area of hospitals and other charitable institutions, the pre-independence achievements of the Catholic Church had been less complete, if nevertheless impressive. The decades following independence witnessed the filling of this gap after a fashion. Various services that had been at least partially the responsibility of public bodies before 1922, such as those for unmarried mothers, were handed over to religious congregations and not subsequently subjected to due support or inspection. More positively, in the 1940s and 1950s, Archbishop John Charles McQuaid of Dublin brought vigour and determination to the establishment of various new and badly needed social services. However, in other countries, the welfare state was already taking responsibility for such matters. McQuaid was the most formidable and successful episcopal proponent of the Catholicisation of public life, one of his triumphs in the field of symbolism being that he prevailed upon the national broadcasting services to carry the twice daily ringing of the angelus bell. But he had numerous more ephemeral successes to his credit, such as forcing the abandonment of the Dublin Theatre Festival in 1958 because he disapproved of two items on the programme, Sean O'Casey's *The Drums of Father Ned* and an adaptation from James Joyce's *Ulysses* by Hilton Edwards and Mícheál MacLiammóir.

Just as in the South majority religion was flaunted without any reference to the sensibilities of the small Protestant minority, so in Northern Ireland the motto of 'a Protestant parliament for a Protestant people' was freely invoked even though it excluded more than one third of the population. Indeed the large size of the minority served as a pretext for more effective discrimination: if they were not curbed they might soon take over! After Basil Brooke, a future Prime Minister at Stormont, had called in 1933 for Protestant employers to take on Protestant workers rather than Catholics, he responded to subsequent criticism by asserting that this was the only way to counteract increasing Catholic numbers and avoid being voted into the Free State. It was accepted on all sides that, a tiny few excepted, Protestant equalled Unionist and Catholic equalled Nationalist. The Government of Ireland Act under which the state had been established precluded discriminatory laws, but that was not a sufficient safeguard. Protestant schools became state schools, while Catholic schools, refusing to accept state control, had to make do with a lower level of support. Access to employment in the public service was weighted overwhelmingly in favour of Protestants, and the structures and functioning of local government were susceptible to similar bias. Political and economic considerations apart, there was a pre-occupation with curbing cultural manifestations of Catholic nationality. The imposition of Protestant mores was typified by the Sunday closing of playgrounds on the part of local authorities. The image of Northern Ireland officially promoted was either that of a part of (Protestant) Britain or that of 'Protestant Ulster'. As in the South, there was no sense of any obligation to honour the collective rituals of the minority.

North and South, the upholding of a confessional identity by the state became unsustainable in the 1960s, largely because of the impact of trends in western society and economy generally. The inability of government and population in Northern Ireland to accommodate the change was the prelude to the three decades of civil unrest and terror euphemistically known as 'the Troubles'. North and South, the decline in the hold of the prescriptive men-tality has reduced the extent of the influence of Churches. The Second Vatican Council (1962–65) provided the Roman Catholic Church with a preparation for the changes ahead, which opportunity, in the Irish case, was only partially utilised.[37]

The capacity of the Church to influence public culture in the South has been in decline since the 1960s, as has the readiness of opinion-formers to support the identification of religion and nationality. By the late 1990s it was possible for a senior politician to describe the South as a post-Catholic country. Certainly the level of Catholicisation of society had been much reduced, but the accuracy or otherwise of the statement is less interesting for present purposes than the fact that it provoked very little adverse reaction. However, the decline of religion as an acknowledged badge of nationality does not change its heuristic value for historical purposes or its relevance in Northern Ireland.

Silence over or denial of the role of religion (or, more exactly, confes-sional affiliation) in the political affairs of the country is a stock posture of politicians and commentators. Thus, the thirty years of northern Troubles at the end of the twentieth century have been reported largely in terms of unionism and nationalism, loyalism and republicanism, while everyone hears Protestant and Catholic. The formality is preserved in the Belfast Agreement that identifies the collectivities it is setting securely opposite one another as unionist and nationalist, with the right to be respectively British and Irish. In fairness to all concerned, it must be conceded that the conven-tional disavowal of religious labels is generally based not on any desire to dissimulate, but on a recognition that following on the revolutions of the late eighteenth century, religion has lost its status as a theoretical basis for

---

[37] See Louise Fuller, *Irish Catholicism since 1950: The Undoing of a Culture* (Dublin, 2002).

secular political institutions. And Northern Ireland is not the scene of a religious conflict in the sense that either side is proposing to convert the other to its views on transubstantiation or salvation by faith alone. Indeed, religion in Northern Ireland, as elsewhere, is in a phase in which such issues of doctrine matter little to most adherents. But there is more to religions and confessions than doctrine. They are communities of identity, and as such they are the key to much of Irish history for centuries past. They are the structure, while the settler/native myth is superstructure, not the other way around.

The Reformation and its consequences have left England, Wales, Scotland and Ireland each with very different confessional configurations that have done much to distinguish their respective nationalities. The most distinctive feature of the Irish case is not that the country is religiously divided – for so has each of the other three been for many centuries past – but that the division extends to the question of national identity. To argue, as some have done, that it is the adherence to Catholicism of the majority of the population that has prevented the assimilation of Ireland into a wider British state is to miss the point, for neither Scotland nor Wales has been assimilated. What Catholicism – together with British attitudes to Catholicism – did impede was an accommodation such as was achieved in the Scottish and Welsh cases. Social and economic trauma combined with the denial of full political and civil rights to alienate Irish Catholics from the link enforced by the Union. But that was not the end of the story: an amicable accommodation in the form of Home Rule – which might or might not have proved viable – was on the cards as late as the eve of the Great War in 1914. This was a different accommodation from those of Scotland and Wales, but it was nonetheless an accommodation. It was not the Catholics but the Protestants of Ireland who prevented its accomplishment. There were economic and social motivations behind the resistance to Home Rule, but the main thrust of unionism was the resistance of Protestants to being ruled by the representatives of the Catholic majority that had invented its own version of the nation. Unionist protestations of devotion to rule from Westminster for its own sake were shown to be so much window-dressing when in 1921 the Protestants of the newly carved out Northern Ireland readily accepted a Home Rule arrangement for the six county area in which they enjoyed a majority and where they could proceed with their own exercise in nation invention, while their co-religionists in the remainder of the country were left high and dry.

If there are places on earth where there is clarity and consistency on the matter of national identity and its bases, they do not include either Britain or Ireland. Inhabitants of Ireland may describe themselves as one or more of Irish, British, English, Northern Irish, Ulster folk, nationalist, republican, unionist or loyalist, but it still remains the case in Northern Ireland, as it was in the whole of Ireland until the 1920s or 1930s, that the best – though a far from infallible – indicator of anyone's wider political allegiance is their religion. That is because these allegiances were invented in the first instance mainly, although not exclusively, on the basis of religious affiliation.[38]

Nationalism is so important precisely because it has – like organised religion and charismatic leadership – the capacity to command collective allegiance of a kind that defies precise analysis. While nationalism can flourish without either religion or *duce*, as a prop, it is greatly strengthened by a combination with one or both, as is well instanced by the history of nationalism, leaders and religion in Modern Ireland.

---

[38] For a sensitive analysis of the issues see J. Liechty and C. Clegg, *Moving Beyond Sectarianism: Religion, Conflict and Reconciliation in Northern Ireland* (Dublin, 2001).

|4|

Language

By the seventh century AD Christian clerics had laid down in Ireland the foundations of a literary culture on the evidence of which the country enters the realms of recorded history. As elsewhere in the West, the language of Christian liturgy and learning was Latin, but a vernacular language, too, gained literary status at this unusually early time, adopting for this purpose the Roman alphabet of the Latinists. The two literatures became the charge of a learned elite, thoroughly Christian in its allegiance, but by no means narrow in its preoccupations. How many vernaculars were spoken in fifth-century Ireland is unknown, but the learned elite acknowledged only the dominant one, that of the Gaels. The stage of its evolution reached in the period from the seventh to the tenth centuries is designated in modern scholarship as Old Irish.[1] The language was the vital element in a distinctive culture that also embraced a political and legal system. Medieval Gaelic civilisation provides a striking example of the potential for a community of identity not dependent upon a centralised polity. The language was the hall-mark of the culture, but integral to it also was a multipolar, fissiparous, but shared, political system that evolved over the centuries. How a single language came to dominate such a polity to the extent that even place names in earlier languages vanished almost without trace is a great question to which there appears to be currently no full answer.

Eoin MacNeill had as little justification as any other nationalist, then or since, for asserting that medieval precedent is prescriptive for modern nationality, but he had exceptionally beguiling evidence, by his own lights, in what he found in early Christian Ireland. On the authority of his schol-arly expertise he could declare that:

---

[1]   The authoritative survey of the development of the language over the ages is K.R. McCone (ed.), *Stair na Gaeilge* (Maynooth, 1994).

Beginning with the sixth century chronicle, every Irish history is a history of Ireland – there is not one history of a tribal territory or of any grouping of tribal territories. Every Irish law book is a book of the laws of Ireland – there are no territorial laws and no provincial laws.[2]

What this does not acknowledge is that most of the annals have a distinctly provincial or regional bias and that it was only in the 1630s, in response to the early modern sense of nationality, that an annalistic compilation with a consciously national perspective was composed.[3] At any rate, the uniformity of the written language is remarkable, with the same standard being observed, mandarin style, wherever it is used, despite the fact that the spoken language must have been marked by considerable dialectic variation. Ancient Greece provides an example of a learned culture, based on language, flourishing in the absence of political unity, but even there the written language had its dialects. No doubt the devotion of the clerics to a uniform Latin set a headline for the vernacular in Ireland, but the Christianised Angles and Saxons of the neighbouring island wrote in their several dialects and did not arrive at a standard English until the tenth century. From early times, language provided a learned elite in Ireland with the basis for a sense of common identity, but MacNeill had too much historical perspective to be tempted into claiming that this sentiment was in medieval times 'fully formed in the popular mind'.[4]

The image-makers of the Gaels identified people and language, and, as we have seen in chapter two, they invented an eponymous ancestor, Gáedel Glas, who was credited with the invention of the language shortly following the fall of the Tower of Babel as recorded in the book of Genesis. This kind of exercise in linguistic chauvinism, extending to claims that the chosen tongue was that used in the Garden of Eden, would continue to flourish for over a thousand years in respect of Irish and many other languages. One elaboration in the Irish case, taken up by Geoffrey Keating, purported to show that the language devised by Gaedel Glas had been that of the earliest invaders of Ireland, and not only of the Milesians, thus intensifying its links with the country, but without ever giving it a name cognate with that of the country.

In fact, never in historical times has Gaelic been confined to the island of Ireland. By the middle of the first millennium AD invaders from Ireland had established it in Scotland, where it still survives under the designation of Scottish Gaelic. Again coming from Ireland, it found a foothold in the Isle of Man in early medieval times, surviving into the twentieth century as Manx, and there was a less enduring presence in parts of Wales and perhaps

2   E. MacNeill, *Phases of Irish History* (Dublin, 1919), p. 246.
3   J. O'Donovan, *Annála ríoghachta Éireann: Annals of the Kingdom of Ireland by the Four Masters* (Dublin, 6 vols, 1848–51).
4   As no. 2.

Cornwall. There are several layers of significance to the use of the term 'the Irish language' in place of 'Gaelic'. For outsiders over many centuries, 'Irish' simply designated the language spoken by those seen as the indigenous inhabitants of the country and, depending on the particular outsider's opinion of the latter, the overtones might range from neutral to fiercely derogatory. In eighteenth-century Scotland, Lowland detractors of the distinctive ways of the Highlands referred to the Gaelic used there as the Irish or Erse language, 'Erse' being a variant of 'Irish' used almost exclusively with reference to language, and found also in Ireland. This usage was sometimes neutral but scarcely ever complimentary. In twentieth-century Ireland, the insistence that (in speaking or writing English) the term 'Irish language' rather than 'Gaelic' should be used, was meant as an assertion that it, and it alone, was the national tongue. Included, too, was the largely unconscious abandonment of the Gaelic of Scotland to its own fate.

The concept and reality of a standard literary language held sway for the users of Gaelic at least until the sixteenth century, but the standard did change in two phases to reflect evolution of the language, as what we now call Old Irish gave way to Middle Irish and that in turn, around 1200, to Classical Early Modern Irish, the latter to retain its hold for four centuries. The twelfth-century ecclesiastical reformers were determined to set the relationship between religious life and scholarship on a clear footing, and in the Irish context that meant the ending of the symbiosis between ecclesiastical and secular learning in church schools and monasteries. The latter was reorganised in the bardic schools that emerged in the thirteenth century. These were the reserve of hereditary specialists in poetry, law, *senchas*, music, medicine, etc., who were inextricably linked with the structures of privilege and power in the Gaelic system. The relationship is epitomised by the period's rich deposit of bardic poems – routine compositions of great technical complexity by professional versifiers in praise of dynastic rulers, mighty and petty.

The disruption occasioned by twelfth-century ecclesiastical reform had been compounded by the Anglo-Norman invasion, which resulted in the displacement of Gaelic power in the east and south-east of the country. The vernacular of the new aristocracy was Norman French, while their followers and the bulk of the incoming settlers were linguistically Germanic and laid the foundations of a Hiberno-English dialect of Middle English that became the distinctive vernacular of the 'English nation' in Ireland. In parallel with developments in England, this demotic tongue displaced Norman French as the spoken language of the ruling elite around 1300. The latter, however, remained as a legal language alongside Latin far into the fifteenth century.[5]

---

[5] Alan Bliss and Joseph Long, 'Literature in Norman French and English to 1534' in Art Cosgrove (ed.), *Medieval Ireland, 1169–1534* (Oxford, 1987), pp. 708–15.

Norman French is the language of the statute enacted by a parliament meeting at Kilkenny in 1366 that sought to secure the fortunes of English as a vernacular and in other ways to shore up English culture in Ireland. By then the hybridisation of cultures was advancing apace and this the Kilkenny statutes endeavoured to halt. Not only was the speaking of Irish in the areas of English settlement prohibited under pain of forfeiture of land or liberty pending payment of sureties against further offence, but also forbidden to the English of Ireland were other occasions and consequences of hybridisation, including miscegenation, the Irish hairstyle, Irish naming practices, and the employment of Irish entertainers.[6] This legislation proved to be futile and the Gaelic system, and especially the language, continued to expand at the expense of a receding English lordship that was in practice confined to the towns and to parts of Leinster. In Connacht and Munster, the heirs of the Norman barons adopted Gaelic culture and the language on a large scale. Gerald FitzMaurice FitzGerald (1357–98), third Earl of Desmond, was well known as a Gaelic poet. He and other Gaelicised Norman rulers were patrons of the Gaelic learned classes. Within a few generations, the Lord of Kilkenny itself, James Butler, the fourth Earl of Ormond, was engaging scribes to make copies of Gaelic texts. While late medieval Ireland was far from being a homogeneous society, it did experience a strong wave of homogenisation arising not only from commingling within the island but also from the impact of secular change affecting it simply as part of the wider world.

In this process, the homogenising vernacular was Irish, and by the sixteenth century English (or, more exactly, Hiberno-English) was largely confined to the towns, to the baronies of Forth and Bargy in south Wexford, and to the district of Fingal, north of Dublin. Godfraidh Fionn Ó Dálaigh, a bardic poet of the fifteenth century, could write as follows:

> There are two kindreds for whom poetry is composed in Ireland . . . – the Gaels . . . and the English. In poetry for the English we promise that the Gael shall be banished from Ireland, while in poetry for the Gaels we promise that the English shall be hunted across the sea.[7]

In other words, a division between the 'nations' of Ireland was maintained for many on the basis of a myth of descent and not, as the statutes of Kilkenny and other expressions of official policy had intended, on the foundations of a division of language and culture. Nevertheless, there would always be those, particularly within the Pale, who made a virtue of being English speakers, even if in the sixteenth century most of them probably also had a knowledge of the spoken Irish that was rising all around them.

---

[6]   E. Curtis and R.B. McDowell (eds), *Irish Historical Documents, 1172–1922* (London, 1943), pp. 52–9.

[7]   Translation by Eleanor Knott quoted in A. Cosgrove (ed.), *Medieval Ireland, 1169–1534* (Oxford, 1987), p. 324.

English became the language of Irish legislation in the late fifteenth century at a time when its fortunes as a spoken language in Ireland were in decline. The Irish Parliament in 1537 passed an Act (28 Hen. VIII, c.15) enjoining that all the inhabitants of the island 'to the utmost of their power, cunning and knowledge' should learn and speak English, and also putting an obligation on every parish priest to establish an English school. The immediate practical impact was minimal, but the act is important in that it signalled – as had legislation of the previous year in respect of Wales – that the language of government in the emerging Tudor state would be English. However, in the Parliament of 1541 at which the medieval lordship was replaced by the kingdom of Ireland with Henry VIII being declared King, proceedings had to be explained in Irish. This reflected both the general advance of the language and the presence of several Gaelic lords who were then being newly drawn into the workings of the polity. In the event, the consolidation of the state – requiring as it did the dissolution of the territorial power of the local lords – was not achieved by conciliation but primarily by force, plantations and dispossessions. As key components in the Gaelic system of dispersed power, the language, and the professionals who were its elite custodians, came under attack. Hence the proscription at various times of 'rhymers', harpers and of the whole panoply of the learned classes. The influx of administrators, soldiers and planters that was so vital to the new political order bolstered the position of English, and well before 1600, a knowledge of English was seen to be a requirement for anyone aspiring to gain or retain a significant place in the Irish political firmament. Thus, even as Gaelic was apparently prevailing as a spoken language throughout the land, knowledge of the standard written English of England was becoming the norm for the chief men of leading families, and for churchmen, even in those parts of the country previously least touched by English culture. The spoken English of the dominant minority from the early seventeenth century onwards was the language of recent arrivals from England, which in due course developed into a distinct dialect of modern English.

Irish would remain the majority language for nearly two centuries more, but in the early seventeenth century it lost the elite dimension that it had possessed for so long. The dispossession of the Gaelic lordships is only part of the explanation, for the new political order brought also a new market-oriented economic order that undermined the ethos of lordly lavishness on which the Gaelic learned classes had depended. Seventeenth-century Ireland was the scene of enormous economic turmoil, and even the acquisitions of the supreme colonial speculator, Richard Boyle, Earl of Cork, were not immune from dramatic decline. In an environment in which even the pioneers of the new order were not economically secure, few established dynasties could cope. The principal leaders of the rebellion of 1641 in Ulster were not dispossessed Catholics, but Old Irish Catholics who had secured land at the Ulster plantation and had subsequently run into debt in operating a cash economy in which no amount of family status would meet the demands of a mortgagor.

By the 1640s, autonomous Gaelic political power was a thing of the past and Irish speakers of political significance were merely one element within a royalist and mainly religion-defined coalition – the Catholic Confederation – contending for control of Ireland. The crushing of that confederacy by the Commonwealth brought further destruction on what remained of a distinctive Gaelic culture. But even a victory for the Confederates would not have made Irish the language of power in the state: long since the 'natural' leaders of what remained of a Gaelic interest had adopted English as the language of political business. Later in the century, most politically conscious speakers of Irish were supporters of King James II, especially in his struggle with William of Orange, but, while a Jacobite victory might have improved their linguistic lot, it would scarcely have made of Irish the language of administration. The Jacobite Irish Parliament of 1689, predominantly Catholic as it was, operated in English as a matter of course. According to Louis Cullen, who has an unrivalled knowledge of the relevant sources, the last known case of a will completed in Irish would appear to date from 1675.[8]

Irish remained the language of a majority of the population, but in an *ancien régime* polity rulers and elites had little concern with the linguistic habits of non-elites. Jonathan Swift declared in 1729 that:

> it would be a noble achievement to abolish the Irish language in this kingdom, so far at least as to oblige all the natives to speak only English on every occasion of business, in shops, markets, fairs and other places of dealing.[9]

This should probably be read as a gush of enthusiasm for improving the condition of those outside the realm of elite civility rather than as evidence of any animus against the language in itself. The dean of St Patrick's Cathedral was apparently indifferent to the specifically pastoral consequences of language choice, but it was not always so for ecclesiastics, who might be an exception to elite unconcern, charged as they were with inculcating doctrine and morals in the masses. Their initiatives frequently had important consequences, both for the definition of national languages (the influence of Luther on the creation of a standard German being an outstanding case) and for the condition of non-official languages (such as Occitan in southern France).

---

8   Louis M. Cullen, 'Patrons, teachers and literacy in Irish' in Mary Daly and David Dickson (eds), *The Origins of Popular Literacy in Ireland: Language Change and Educational Development, 1700–1900* (Dublin, 1990), p. 30.
9   J. McMinn (ed.), *Swift's Irish Pamphlets* (Gerrard's Cross, 1991), p. 130.

An example from nearer home is more pertinent to Ireland. While the framework of the Irish state was refashioned in the second quarter of the sixteenth century with a distinct if subordinate existence, Wales ceased to have any constitutional existence in 1536 when, by the 'Act of Union', it was unilaterally incorporated on a unitary basis into the English state. As part of this absorption, the courts and the administration would henceforth be conducted in English, and all those hoping to participate in public business would have to become proficient in the official language of the kingdom. At the same time there was no official hostility to Welsh per se, and the principal exponents of the language were men of humanist outlook who were enthusiastic apologists for the new political order. The first books in Welsh were published in the 1540s and the hope that the Scriptures would be made available in what advocates described as the British language was soon being articulated. In an astute gesture, Elizabeth I consented by an Act of 1563 to the translation of the Bible and the Book of Common Prayer. The latter and the New Testament were published in Welsh four years later, and thereafter the divine service in the vernacular was available to most Welsh people, so that language and reformed religion helped one another to prosper. The Welsh Bible was the centrepiece of a popular literary culture that achieved formal self-celebration by the beginning of the eighteenth century and existed side by side with English as the language of state and of out-of-country business: some of the principal proponents of Welsh culture would be based in London.

The Welsh case is unusual insofar as Protestant churches in Europe generally required conformity to the official language of the state. Queen Elizabeth displayed a similar inclination to accommodate the Irish language: in 1567 as the Welsh New Testament and Prayer Book appeared, she provided funds for the production and printing of an Irish translation of the New Testament. There is evidence that the Queen had some personal interest in the language as had several of the English administrators and propagandists of the age.[10] Also in 1567, Gaelic appeared in print for the first time with the publication in Edinburgh of John Carswell's translation of John Knox's *Book of Common Order* as *Foirm na nUrrnuidheadh*.

As between Welsh and Irish, the different time scale in which results were produced speaks for itself. The resources provided by Elizabeth I were used to publish in 1571 a volume containing an introduction to the Irish alphabet and a catechism (*Aibidil Gaoidheilge & Caiticiosma*) translated by John Kearney, treasurer of St Patrick's Cathedral and a Cambridge graduate. But the Irish New Testament did not appear in print until 1602, following a complicated history of translation and printing, in which the dominant actor was the Kilkenny-born William Daniel. He was another Cambridge

---

[10]   See T. Crowley, *The Politics of Language in Ireland, 1366–1922: A Sourcebook* (London and New York, 2000), pp. 23–52.

graduate, and for a time in the mid-1590s a fellow of Trinity College, Dublin, and later became Archbishop of Tuam. With continuing government backing, Daniel published an Irish translation of the *Book of Common Prayer* in 1608. The translation of the Old Testament into Irish was achieved under the direction of William Bedell, an Englishman who was provost of Trinity College, Dublin (where he enforced the learning of Irish) from 1627 to 1630 and Archbishop of Kilmore from 1630 to 1642. Although the work of translation was finished by 1638, the complete Bible in Irish did not appear in print until 1685. In several countries, the first translation of the Bible into the vernacular is a celebrated point in the invention of the nation. In Ireland, the achievement of William Daniel and William Bedell has not been the subject of widespread acclaim, although Bedell, almost from the time of his death, has been the subject of a minor cult.

The availability of the Scriptures in Irish a century earlier would scarcely have affected the fortunes of the state religion, since the Church did not have the resources or personnel to reach the populace through either English or Irish. Besides, the language issue went to the heart of an ambivalence within the Church. For Bedell, evangelising in Irish reflected a pastoral imperative, but others were not so sure. All understood that religious conversion implied conformity to a 'civility' that was identified with the English language. Thus, while Bedell in Kilmore made outstanding efforts to fill parishes with clergy who could preach and minister though Irish, he also required them to set up English schools, as was expected of them by law. Consciously or not, the model was that of Wales: an anglophone state and Church, but with the gospel made available in their vernacular to those not schooled in the official tongue. But for many the inclusion of the majority seemed beyond contemplation, either from Calvinist theological principle, calculation of political and economic self-interest, or dismay at the prospect of the effort involved in attempting to win over a population within which, already by the 1590s, allegiance to the Church of the Counter-Reformation was deeply embedded. The rule adopted by the Church of Ireland in 1634, at Bedell's behest, that the New Testament and the Book of Common Prayer should be made available in Irish wherever the language was prevalent, was but poorly observed.[11] This ambivalence continued through the Cromwellian period when intense government hostility to Irish was juxtaposed with spasmodic provision of preachers in the language.[12] When in 1697 a bill to ban Irish was introduced (unsuccessfully) in the Irish House of Lords, its proponent was not a politician per se, but a sincere and exceptionally hard-working bishop motivated by pastoral concerns. Soon afterwards, the efforts of an

---

[11] T. McCaughey, *Dr Bedell and Mr King: The Making of the Irish Bible* (Dublin, 2002), pp. 22–3.

[12] T.C. Barnard, *Cromwellian Ireland: English Government and Reform in Ireland, 1649–60* (Oxford, 1975), pp. 175–81.

enthusiast taking the other view of the Church of Ireland's mission, Rev. John Richardson, produced a book of sermons in Irish in 1711 and an Irish catechism in 1712. Shortly thereafter, enthusiasm for evangelisation in either English or Irish fell almost entirely out of favour for several generations. But the handiwork of Daniel and Bedell never fell into complete disuse. The extent of any church's quotidian use of Irish over the centuries is quite irrecoverable, but even in the case of the Established Church casual evidence survives, such as that of daily sermons in Irish being preached in St Patrick's Cathedral, Dublin throughout Passion week in 1758.[13]

The Roman Catholic Church had its pastoral strategies clearly set out at the Council of Trent (1545–63). Since the liturgy was in Latin and there was little emphasis on access by the faithful to the Scriptures, the issue of the vernacular was less controversial than for Protestants, but it was nonetheless vital in respect of preaching, catechesis and hearing confessions. The implications of the Tridentine formula for the approach to users of non-elite languages was well exemplified in the case of France where, in the seventeenth and eighteenth centuries, the preponderance of publication and literary standardisation in Occitan and Breton was the work of the priests. Irish was similarly served, even if not to a comparable extent. The Limerick-born Richard Creagh, who became Bishop of Armagh in 1564, composed a catechism in Irish and English as well as a draft introduction to the study of Irish. These circulated in manuscript through clerical circles. Beginning in 1611 with Bonaventure O'Hussey's *An teagasc Críosdaidhe* (Antwerp), catechisms in Irish, books of sermons and dictionaries were printed mainly in those places on the continent where Irish Catholics enjoyed the facilities of scholarship. This pastoral material was intended for the use of priests who would communicate orally with their flocks. It did not constitute an attempt to promote the language, much less to inculcate popular literacy therein.

The Roman congregation that held responsibility for Ireland, De Propaganda Fide, decreed in 1650 that all students entering the continental colleges where priests for the Irish mission were educated should have a command of Irish, unless they came from the parts of Leinster where Irish was not the vernacular. This surely suggests concern that some priests were emerging from these colleges who were not equipped to minister in Irish. It can be assumed that in subsequent generations, especially in the eighteenth century, the exempt area was extended informally as Irish contracted. Litigation of 1764 involving the college at Lille threw up apparently contradictory evidence concerning the need for Irish for the ministry in Leinster as a whole.[14] However, acquiring knowledge of English, spoken and written,

---

13 F.R. Bolton, *The Caroline Tradition of the Church of Ireland* (London, 1958). See Pádraig Ó Snodaigh, *The Hidden Ulster: Protestants and the Irish Language* (Belfast, 1995) for an assemblage of evidence.

14 T.J. Walsh, *The Irish Continental College Movement: The Colleges at Bordeaux, Toulouse and Lille* (Dublin and Cork, 1973), pp. 150–61.

was taken for granted as a mark of the educated cleric. Like the state Church, the Roman Catholic Church, whether when giving its allegiance to the Stuarts or the Hanovers, regarded English as the public language of Ireland. This did not lessen the duty of preaching in their own language to Irish-speakers. The first generation or two of Irish Catholic publication on the continent witnessed a flowering of creative devotional composition in Irish. This subsequently petered out, leaving the field to the formulae of catechisms and standard sermons. Like their French counterparts in respect of that country's non-elite languages, the Irish bishops included in their number several devotees of Gaelic scholarship. In 1735, James Gallagher, Bishop of Kildare, published in Dublin a collection of sermons in Irish with facing English translation: *Sixteen Irish sermons in an Easy and Familiar Style on Useful and Necessary Subjects*. Bishop John O'Brien of Cloyne and Ross, the compiler of *Focaloir Gaoidhilge-Sax-Bhéarla* (Paris, 1768), was a considerable Gaelic scholar, as was John Carpenter, Archbishop of Dublin, 1770–86. An example of exceptional dedication is provided by John Murphy (1772–1847), who began study of the language following his appointment as Bishop of Cork in 1815, came to master it and assembled one of the great collections of manuscripts in Irish. Archbishop John MacHale (1791–1881), a native speaker of Irish, was exceptional in many respects, including his encouragement of the study of the language at his diocesan college, St Jarlath's, in Tuam, Co. Galway, and his published translations of classical and popular works, and eventually of the opening books of the Old Testament.

The enthusiasm of these four prelates was untypical and the extent to which the ideal of preaching and catechising in Irish was realised at different times and in different places can scarcely be recovered in any adequate fashion. This situation was scarcely changed dramatically by the impact of Maynooth College (founded in 1795), where the majority of Irish secular priests emerging in the nineteenth century would receive their training, except insofar as the number of dioceses in which it could be claimed that Irish was no longer required for pastoral purposes was increasing. In any case, a relative deficiency in Irish-language catechesis in some areas would seem to be the most likely explanation for the fact that the main successes of the 'second reformation' were in Irish-speaking areas in the west. The promotion of the study of Irish may have been MacHale's response, but many others undoubtedly saw the answer in a fuller Anglicisation. Throughout the nineteenth century students at Maynooth took Irish classes, of sorts, as required by their individual bishops, but the condition of the language in the college in the second and third quarters of the century reflected the general abandonment which was its fate in the country at large.[15]

From early in the seventeenth century there were significant numbers of

---

[15] P.J. Corish, *Maynooth College, 1795–1995* (Dublin, 1995), p. 213.

Irish speakers among both Episcopalians and Presbyterians in Ulster, some of these adherents being Irish-born and others Gaelic speakers among the recent planters from Scotland. Over subsequent centuries, ministry in Irish was a constant feature of Presbyterianism, and not only in Ulster: in 1719, the Synod of Ulster had to deal with a request to provide preachers for Scottish Gaelic and Irish speakers in Dublin. The Synod's interest in Irish was at its highest level in the period 1710–20 when, among other arrangements, provision was made for the publication of a catechism in Irish. If the Irish/Gaelic mission subsequently dropped out of the limelight for some generations, it remained important at ground level, and returned as a headline preoccupation with the 'second reformation'. Presbyterians were particularly active in the evangelical mission to Irish-speaking Catholics in the second quarter of the nineteenth century.

Archbishop MacHale expressed regret that circumstances had not permitted Geoffrey Keating to provide an Irish translation of the Bible instead of using his 'pure idiomatic style' to embellish 'trivial legends'.[16] This was to ignore the fact that Counter-Reformation Catholicism provided little incentive for vernacular translation of the Scriptures. Despite MacHale's own initiative and some unpublished endeavour of others, the piecemeal publication of what would be a complete version of the Bible in Irish under Catholic auspices began only in 1964, in time for incorporation of the vernacular in the post-Vatican II liturgy. The complete work appeared as *An Bíobla Naofa* (Maynooth, 1981) under the direction of Professor Pádraig Ó Fiannachta.

The ability to read Irish had always been a minority accomplishment among speakers of the language, and as the Irish populace acquired literacy it did so in English. The move to literacy and to English was well under way when eventually in the early 1800s the Irish Bible was released in vast quantities as part of the great evangelical campaign (see chapter three). This 'second reformation' led significant members of Protestant clergymen to acquire proficiency in Irish. St Columba's College was established in 1843, originally at Stackallen, Co. Meath at the initiative of prominent laymen, to provide young candidates for the Church of Ireland ministry with a thorough knowledge of Irish. At least in some parts, parochial ministers and missionaries were preaching in Irish until late into the nineteenth century.

Irish Bibles might be readily available, but the speakers of the language had to learn to read before making use of them. The evangelical societies endeavoured to promote this necessary literacy by paying people proficient in the language to give basic reading lessons to others. This strategy was largely undermined by the manifest determination of so many Irish speakers

---

[16] J. MacHale, *An Irish Translation of the Holy Bible from the Latin Vulgate with a Corresponding English Version Chiefly from the Douay* . . . vol. 1: Genesis to Josue (Tuam, 1861), preface, p. viii.

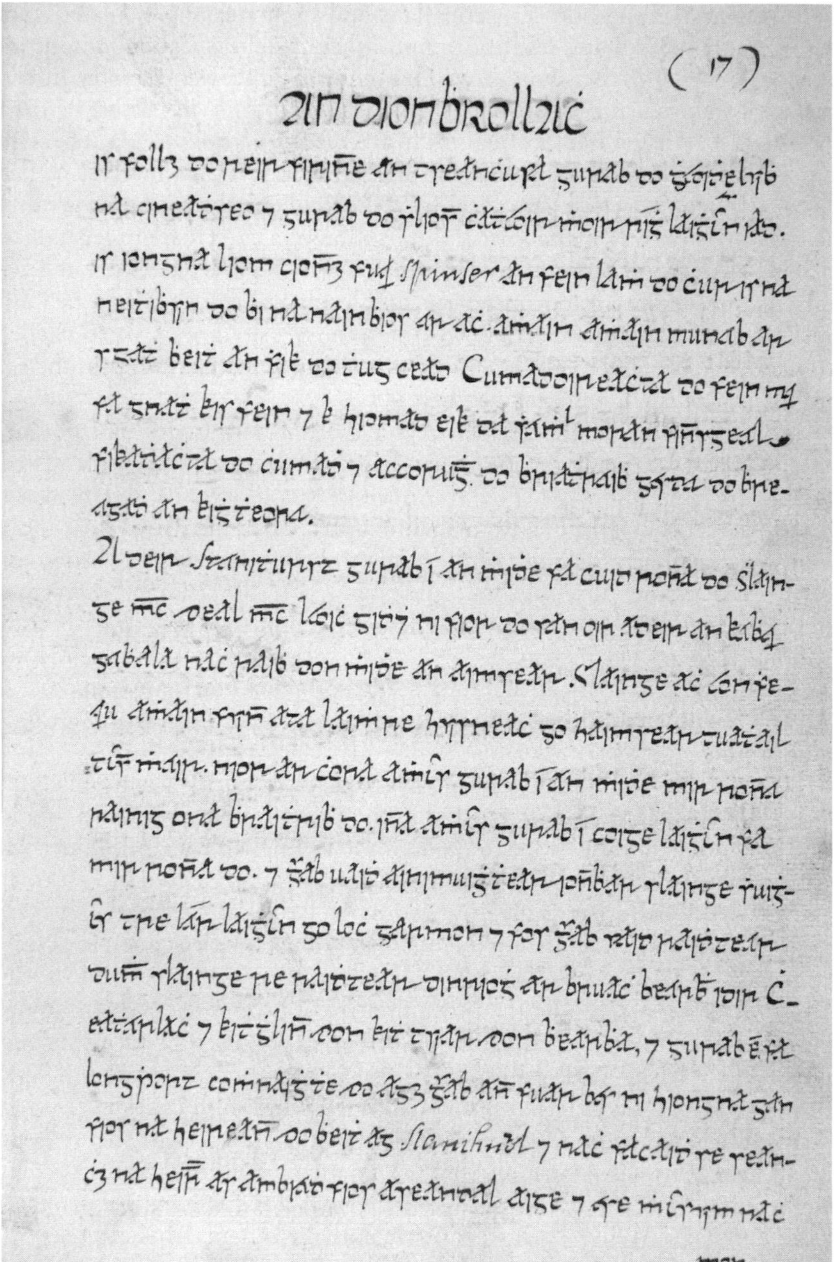

Figure 4.1 Page from an eighteenth-century manuscript of Geoffrey Keating, *Foras feasa ar Éirinn* (St Patrick's College, Maynooth: Murphy Manuscripts Collection, MS 102, p. 17; reproduced by permission of the Librarian, National University of Ireland, Maynooth).

that the first objective of formal instruction should be to achieve proficiency in English. Nevertheless, the 'Irish teacher' became a significant figure in many parts of the country in the first half of the nineteenth century. By way of reaction, some Catholic ecclesiastics undoubtedly adopted a more negative attitude to the use of the Irish language.

If the translation of the Bible into Irish did not have a major impact on the language, it did involve the invention of something that eventually became an emblem of Irish nationality, namely 'Gaelic' script. When the language first appeared in print with Carswell's translation of the *Book of Common Prayer* in 1567, ordinary Roman type was used. But the initiative taken by Queen Elizabeth in the same year led to the devising in Dublin of a script more reflective of the appearance of Gaelic manuscript, notably in mirroring the basic shape of the insular half uncial lettering used in Ireland from the sixth century onwards. When Catholic exiles in the Spanish Netherlands set up a printing press in 1611, they followed suit. Roman type was used subsequently for some religious and popular publications in Irish and has always been used for Gaelic in Scotland, but 'Gaelic' type (there were to be many variants) came to be seen as the norm for the printing of Irish. In a

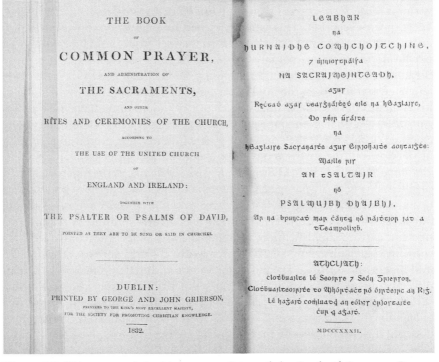

Figure 4.2 Title pages of dual-language edition of the *Book of Common Prayer*, printed in Dublin in 1832.

striking instance of the investment of the existential with imagined essential meaning, Gaelic lettering came to assume iconic status. In the nineteenth century, the practice grew of printing English wording in Gaelic script for formal settings, such as the title-pages of expensively-produced volumes with a 'national' flavour. Requiring as it did a separate typewriter, Gaelic script was an extreme inconvenience in the twenieth century, but its abandonment was stoutly resisted for decades. Brian Ó Cuív has cited one opponent of change as declaring: 'Tis very hard to bring the Irish out of the English [sic] letters', as if the 'Gaelic' variant on a common European tradition had some intrinsic quality over and above the variant in common use throughout the western world.[17] But there is no denying the reality of the powerful associations that the script had acquired – ranging from national transcendence for some to intimations for others of the terrors of dysfunctional schooling in the Ireland of the 1920s to the 1950s.

The emergence of a popular religious print culture in Irish would have been of potentially great significance for the language, as such a development in the eighteenth century was for Welsh. Its absence in the case of Ireland cannot be put down entirely to antagonistic political authority. Many of those, laity and clergy, who were literate in Irish in the seventeenth century displayed an elitist attitude carried over from the bardic era. Theobald Stapleton with his *Catechismus seu Doctrina Christiana Latino-Hibernica* (Brussels, 1639) is an exception. This work is valued by linguistic scholars as a pioneering attestation of popular usages (as distinct from the classical usage of bardic literature still perpetuated by his contemporaries) and it is so because the author intended, as a matter of policy, to facilitate access to the written language and to loosen the hold of the specialists. But in the eyes of some of his contemporaries, the strongest evidence of the iniquity of the new political order was that it encouraged the lower classes to become uppity, one example of this being the conceit of pipe-smoking. The pretensions of such upstarts are pilloried in the anonymous seventeenth-century satire, *Pairlement Chloinne Tomáis*. Dáibhí Ó Bruadair (*c.*1625–98), one of the most celebrated of all Irish poets, disparaged Cromwellian and other settlers precisely as upstarts. Subsequently, Irish learning was to reside in many a humble abode, but it remained the property of a minority. Greatly reduced in social prestige and artistic sophistication, attenuated in its scope and conflated in its contents, Gaelic learning survived as a living cultural activity down to the mid-nineteenth century. The old scribal mode endured and there was no significant transition to print until the early nineteenth century. Central to this survival were scribes who depended on the arbitrary patronage of individual landlords, clerics or strong farmers. Their manuscripts drew on the inheritance of the past but also on the oral culture of the Irish-speaking population.

---

[17] 'The changing form of the Irish language' in Brian Ó Cuív (ed.), *A View of the Irish Language* (Dublin, 1969), p. 25.

In the seventeenth century, apart from their utilisation of Irish for religious purposes, the Catholic exiles on the continent, and particularly at the Franciscan College in Louvain, pioneered the scholarly study of the Irish past, deploying both bardic learning and Renaissance scholarship. The outstanding products of their work include the so-called 'Annals of the Four Masters'[18] compiled by Michael O'Cleary and others, and John Colgan's Bollandist-style hagiographical works published in the 1640s. James Ussher (1581–1656), Dublin-born, professor of Divinity at Trinity College and in due course Bishop of Meath and Archbishop of Armagh, was one of the great humanist scholars of the age. His *A Discourse of the Religion Anciently Professed by the Irish and the British* (Dublin, 1631) drew extensively on Irish-language sources to argue the case for a historical precedent for independence from Rome. He readily shared source material with his confessional adversaries on the continent and published an amount of non-polemical Irish material. Another Dubliner and pillar of the establishment, Sir James Ware (1594–1666), a pioneer of Irish antiquarian studies, engaged the services of Dubhaltach Mac Fhir Bhisigh, one of the last of the professional Gaelic genealogists.[19] By the early eighteenth century, a few dozen of the leading professional Irish scribes and savants were eking out a living in Dublin city. For another century and a half they and their successors would be involved in a fruitful commerce with scholars and dilettantes interested in the language for a variety of reasons.

Demonstrating the existence of an ancient Irish civilisation had been a preoccupation of Keating, the Louvain Franciscans, and others in the early seventeenth century. In the eighteenth century, the same issue acquired some importance in the politics of the ruling classes (see chapter two). Several other factors contributed to a wider interest in Irish. Edward Lhuyd in his *Archaeologia Britannica* (1707) had launched the concept of Celtic languages, and made comparative linguistic study of Irish feasible. The sporadic rise during the later stages of the Enlightenment of interest in things exotic, including secondary languages, was given focus in the case of Gaelic by the 'Ossian' phenomenon. In 1760, a Scot, James Macpherson, published a version in high-flown English verse of tales from the *Fiannaíocht*, the Gaelic oral corpus featuring Oisín (Ossian) and his warrior companions (the *Fianna*).[20] Macpherson's work had a major impact on European sensibility. There was much Irish resentment of his appropriation of the *Fianna* for Scotland, especially as he simultaneously denigrated the historical culture of Ireland. Once again, a common inheritance was fuelling antipathy between

---

[18]   John O'Donovan, *Annála Ríogachta Éireann: Annals of the Kingdom of Ireland by the Four Masters* (Dublin, 6 vols, 1848–51).
[19]   Nollaig Ó Muraíle, *The Celebrated Antiquary Dubhaltach Mac Fhir Bhisigh (c.1600–1671): His Lineage, Life and Learning* (Maynooth, 1996).
[20]   *Fragments of Ancient Poetry, Collected in the Highlands of Scotland and Translated from the Gaelic or Erse Language.*

inventors of Scottish and Irish nationality. By way of reaction, the claims of ancient Irish civilisation were all the more assertively advanced. The Irish Academy, founded in 1785 (and known from 1786 as the Royal Irish Academy), gave institutional expression to the contemporary enthusiasm for Irish antiquities.

Such goodwill is also in evidence as a secondary feature of the ethos of the United Irishmen, the radical movement that pioneered the doctrine of Irish separatism. Their newspaper the *Northern Star* published, in 1795, *Bolg an tSolair or the Gaelic Magazine*, a substantial volume that included the essentials of a primer and a varied collection of sample readings. The emphasis is on access to a neglected treasure, a language of superb qualities and the key to the 'antiquities' of Ireland and Great Britain. The term 'national language' is used, but there is no concept of a nationality spiritually dependent on the language in the style of Herder: Irish is being promoted for its own sake, not out of any abstract principle.[21] (This is in contrast to the contemporary attitude of Bunting in respect of music: see chapter six.) Patrick Lynch had previously taught Irish in Belfast. Publicising his classes, the *Northern Star* adverted to two further benefits of a knowledge of Irish. The first was that merchants could do business in every part of the country. Secondly, it pointed out that:

> By our understanding and speaking of it we could more easily and effectively communicate our sentiments and instructions to all our countrymen, and thus materially improve and conciliate each other's affections.[22]

Thus were succinctly identified the practical and structural bases on which in country after country nineteenth-century national language would be invented. But the *Northern Star* posited no such superstructure. And in the event, commercialising and democratising elites did not need to learn Irish in order to gain access to a society that would come all the way to meet them.

In the early nineteenth century, the state joined the ranks of the patrons of Irish learning. The Irish Commissioners of Public Records, established in 1810, engaged Edward O'Reilly (1765–1830) to catalogue the Irish manuscripts in Trinity College. The townland survey of Ireland conducted by the Ordnance Survey, begun in 1825, was intended to map the country in minute detail, to define boundaries, and to standardise place names. (See chapter eight). The survey drew on the resources of Gaelic scholarship, employing first O'Reilly, and then John O'Donovan (1806–61) and Eugene O'Curry (1794–1862) to provide advice on place names. In addition to

---

[21] Brendan Clifford and Pat Muldowney, *Bolg an tSolair: A Reprint of the Gaelic Magazine of the United Irishmen Containing Poems, Songs, Dialogues in Irish and English and an Irish Grammar by Patrick Lynch, Charlotte Brooke and others, with a Profile of Patrick Lynch and Charlotte Brooke* (Belfast, 1999), pp. 9–11 (pp. 3–10 in original).

[22] Breandán Ó Buachalla, *I mBéal Feirste cois cuain* (Dublin, 1968), p. 30.

serving the purposes of the Ordnance Survey, the work of O'Donovan and O'Curry took on a life of its own. Through the contacts generated by their work for the survey they became the central figures in a stream of editing and publication that between 1840 and 1900 put in place many of the chief landmarks of modern scholarship in the Irish language. Some of this depended on individual initiative or was promoted by one or other of a number of antiquarian societies. Government support was significant, as in the funding of the Brehon Law Commission from 1852 and the inclusion of editions of several major Irish texts in the Rolls series. The state also supported the complementary process of acquisition and centralisation of manuscripts, particularly through funding of the Royal Irish Academy. The Queen's Colleges, established at Belfast, Cork and Galway under the 1845 Act, all had chairs of 'Celtic', bearing out the fact that the Gaelic literary and linguistic inheritance had come to be accepted – not least by the state – as part of the Irish national patrimony. When the Catholic University was opened in 1854 under the rectorship of J.H. Newman, Eugene O'Curry became Professor of Irish History and Antiquities. None of this is altered by the realisation that very few college students presented themselves to study the subject. The study of Old and Middle (i.e. pre-1200 AD) Irish was greatly facilitated by the publication of the *Grammatica Celtica* of Johann Kasper Zeuss in 1853. The status of Irish was further enhanced from the 1860s onwards with the cult of things Celtic promoted by Ernest Renan and Matthew Arnold. A knowledge of Irish was required for certain positions in the Public Record Office of Ireland established under an Act of 1867.

While the state might support scholarship in the Irish language, schooling was another matter. Here, the National Board of Education, which had been funding primary schools from 1831, followed for nearly half a century a policy of unmitigated Anglicisation. While this has been decried by later generations, much of whatever objection there was at the time seems to have centred on the likelihood that pupils with Irish as the home language would learn English more efficiently if their teachers were allowed to instruct them through Irish. Nationalists were more likely to complain about the lack of a distinctive national spirit in the curriculum than about the teaching of English. In their mission to bring literacy in English at the expense of Irish they were meeting the overwhelming wish of Irish public opinion through most of the nineteenth century.

Acceptance of the Gaelic inheritance as a worthy subject of study, as a distinctive mark of Irish nationality, or even as the manifestation of the Arnoldian Celtic mystique, were quite compatible with an acceptance, either fatalistic or utilitarian, that Irish would soon cease to exist as a spoken language. Of the Gaelic scholars of the nineteenth century and their backers, only a small proportion can be shown to have had either hope or concern for the future of spoken Irish. John O'Donovan's children were reared without a knowledge of the language. The most inexorable social

movement in modern Irish history has been that of native Irish speakers –
beginning in the east by the middle of the eighteenth century and spreading
through all classes and all provinces to a culmination about two hundred
years later – to acquire the use of English. Significant, too, but thus far much
less powerful, has been the counter-current promoting the use of the language, either independently of or in conjunction with scholarship. This, the
work of English speakers with varying levels of competence in Irish, had its
beginnings in the eighteenth century. Subsequently it was promoted by
Evangelicals, Irish and English, for their own specific ends, in the early and
middle decades of the nineteenth century. By the 1840s, the preservation of
the spoken language had been taken up as a cause by a scattered group of
middle-class people quite distinguishable from the Evangelicals, although
some had undoubtedly come under evangelical influence.

In 1842, a Romantic version of nationality of a kind flourishing on the
continent began to be promulgated in Ireland in a newly founded weekly,
the *Nation*. This was the work of a group of middle-class intellectuals who
would subsequently be known as Young Ireland. Their chief ideologue was
Thomas Davis who had imbibed an essentialist concept of nationhood, and
that concept owed much to German theorists for whom language was the
nation's soul. Indeed, the inhabitation was not only spiritual but had a physical basis: 'the language which grows up with a people is conformed to their
organs'. Language, like other features of the nation, was a manifestation of
race: 'How unnatural – how corrupting – 'tis for us, three-fourths of whom
are of Celtic blood, to speak a medley of Teutonic dialects.' The deduction
– that 'a people without a language of its own is only half a nation. A nation
should guard its barriers more than its territories'[23] was in logic the prelude
to an all-out campaign to make the revival of Irish the first item on the
nationalist agenda.

However, Davis matched passionately embraced ideology with a clear-
headed pragmatism. The *Nation* did indeed acquire a font of Irish type, but
used it sparingly. Thomas Swanton, a landed Protestant and language
enthusiast from West Cork, complained in December 1846 that 'Mr D[avis]
led me to expect some Irish in the *Nation*. I at last procured [it] last Saturday
when lo! not a word of Irish from beginning to end of it.'[24] Far from launching himself on a revivalist campaign, Davis reassured monoglot readers that
there was no intention of a language reversal: the most he asked was that the
upper classes would have Irish taught to their children in place of French or
German.[25]

The formation of a national community did indeed require a common
language, but, contrary to the assumptions of such as Herder and Mazzini,

---

[23] *Nation*, 1 Apr. 1843.
[24] Mairéad Nic Craith, *Malartú teanga: an Ghaeilge i gCorcaigh sa naoú haois déag* (Bremen,
       1993), p. 20.
[25] *Nation*, 30 Dec. 1843.

this did not have to be a distinctive language. Since the 1820s, Ireland had experienced a precocious popular national mobilisation focused on the leadership of Daniel O'Connell. While O'Connell had, on occasion, made use of Irish on the platform, the great bulk of his famous oratory had been in English, and – Ulster apart – there was a clear correlation between the mobilisation and the spread of English. Typically of a nation-inventing intellectual elite, the young men of the *Nation* went about the raising of national consciousness and the promotion of civic virtues by means of composing and disseminating uplifting popular ballads: and apart from an occasional transliterated Irish refrain, these were in the language of mobilisation – English. Thomas Davis had already been stopped in his tracks in 1843 by the dilemma that arises from trying to accommodate the English language to an essentialist view of the Irish nation. The dilemma was to recur. Meanwhile, several other Young Irelanders, including Charles Gavin Duffy and John Mitchell, were in the words of one authority, 'mildly contemptuous' in their attitude to linguistic revival.[26] Despite his labours for the language, and his position as an icon of Catholic nationalism, Archbishop John MacHale did not in his time establish either the concept of the language as an essential of nationality, or the notion of Irish as the bearer of any essential religious content.

John O'Daly (1800–78) is an interesting contrast to Davis, insofar as he was motivated by a devotion to the language for its own sake. He was employed by the evangelical Irish Society for some years before becoming a bookseller and then a publisher. He himself anthologised eighteenth-century Gaelic poetry but, writing to the weekly *Nation* of 31 May 1845, the benefit he proposed as following from a revival of the Irish language was that:

> The philosophical orations of our Burke – the fine essays of our Swift – the simple splendour of our Goldsmith – the magnificent orations of our Flood, Grattan, Sheridan, Curran, Plunkett, O'Connell, Shiel, etc. and other varied works of such minds should appear in native dress.

The language, he warned, would die, if the present generation did not bestir itself. O'Daly was prepared to use any and every argument he could lay hands on to win support for the language: its richness, its antiquity, its value as a key to other antiquities, its utility for merchants, clergymen and lawyers. By 1845 he was wielding the concept of the necessity for a national language. If repeal of the Union were to be carried, how was Ireland without its own language to measure up to the other nations of Europe?[27]

O'Daly was secretary of the Celtic Society, founded later in 1845, but it did not become the agent of language revival that he had hoped for. He was

---

[26] Richard Davis, *The Young Ireland Movement* (Dublin, 1987), p. 263.
[27] *Nation*, 31 May 1845.

in due course a guiding light of the Ossianic Society, founded in 1853. This body, by contrast with earlier societies of a comparable kind, directed its efforts towards the cultivation of the Irish language and not merely to Irish scholarship. It had a radically different membership, with a significant concentration of middle-class men from districts, especially in the south-west, that had seen a drastic decline of Irish speakers in the famine years. Its publications were exclusively editions (in Irish with facing translation in English) of episodes from the *Fiannaíocht*, until recently to be found in the folklore of Irish-speaking communities.[28]

The IRB, founded in 1858, and subsequently the epitome of militant nationalism, included a number of language activists among its prominent men. The founder of the American wing, the exiled John O'Mahony, was a Gaelic scholar and produced a translation of Keating's *Foras feasa ar Éirinn* that was published in New York in 1857. His naming in 1859 of the American wing as the Fenian Brotherhood, a clear evocation of the warrior *Fianna* of Gaelic legend, resulted in the entire movement becoming known as the Fenians. Another leading Fenian figure, Jeremiah O'Donovan Rossa, was a typical member – as a shopkeeper in Skibbereen, Co. Cork – of the Ossianic Society; so too was James O'Mahony, a locally prominent Fenian in Midleton, Co. Cork. There was, however, no Fenian policy on language, other than an implicit assumption that English was and would remain the language of power and politics in Ireland. The movement's newspaper, the *Irish People* (Dublin, 1863–65) had displayed very little explicit interest in any aspect of cultural nationalism, although the editor, John O'Leary, was later to claim credit for service to that cause by his ruthless exclusion of reams of bad patriotic verse submitted by readers. Again, in the highly important agrarian and nationalist mobilisations achieved by Parnell from 1879 onwards, there was no identification of the Irish language as an essential of nationality.

Meanwhile, people of all political and religious persuasions continued to promote the cause of Irish, or at least to sympathise with it. The formation of the Society for the Preservation of the Irish Language in 1876 marked a significant consolidation. The Gaelic Union followed in 1880. The politicians may have been otherwise distracted, but by the mid-1880s what to do about Irish was on the way to becoming an issue that could not be ignored. Political and cultural life was transformed in many European countries in the 1890s with the flourishing of autonomous lower-middle-class associational life. In various countries and in various ways socialism, nationalism and confessional religion were transformed. In Ireland, a generation of educated, bicycling young men and women developed a multi-faceted nationalist movement that found in the Gaelic League, formed in 1893, an

---

[28] D. Murray, *Romanticism, Nationalism and Irish Antiquarian Societies, 1840–80* (Maynooth, 2000).

overarching organisation. The preponderantly monoglot membership set about acquiring Irish in the social setting of the Gaelic League branches. This was the movement that changed the language from an optional to a mandatory component of Irish nationality. That achievement was confirmed in 1910 when the senate of the recently founded National University of Ireland voted to make Irish a compulsory matriculation subject, not because most senators thought that this was good policy, but because the activists of the Gaelic League had a sufficiently widespread and effective network to put irresistible political pressure on the university authorities. Henceforth, deference to Irish as the national language was required of nationalist politicians and of anyone else who needed to cultivate the undivided support of nationalists.

The ideological basis for the promotion of Irish by the Gaelic League comprehended earlier elements, notably the impulse to save a priceless treasure that had driven John O'Daly and others, and Thomas Davis' combination of nationalist theory and racialist assumption. To these was added a wave of devotion to Irish as evidence for the existence of an ancient culture and polity now being brought to new light by the endeavours of historians such as Eoin MacNeill, one of the founders of the Gaelic League. A golden-age Gaelic past provided Irish nationalism with a historicist legitimacy far more powerful, and more attuned to the expectations of the age, than the evocation of Grattan's parliament by O'Connell and Parnell. Douglas Hyde, first president of the Gaelic League, had declared in a famous manifesto of 1892, 'The necessity of de-Anglicising Ireland', that:

> The bulk of the Irish race really lived in the closest contact with the traditions of the past and the national life of nearly eighteen hundred years, until the beginning of this century.[29]

Implicit in Hyde's argument for de-Anglicisation was the perception of national culture as a self-contained, homogeneous entity with an enduring essence. This discounted variation over time and space, and the ever-changing character of all societies. It is a nice irony that, as L.P. Curtis has pointed out, this concept of cultural purity was an alien product, promoted a generation earlier in the same terms as Hyde's by the Anglo-Saxonist historians.[30]

Like Davis a half-century earlier, Hyde in 1892 did not follow through on the logic of his linguistic nationalism, demanding only that the self-governing state he assumed to be just around the corner ('[T]he Celtic race is presumably about to largely recover possession of its own country'[31]) would

---

29 Quoted in Tony Crowley, *The Politics of Language in Ireland 1366–1922: A Sourcebook* (London, 2000), p. 185.
30 L.P. Curtis, Jr, *Anglo-Saxons and Celts: A Study of Anti-Irish Prejudice in Victorian England* (Bridgeport, 1968), p. 113.
31 As no. 29 above.

provide Irish-speaking schoolteachers, local officials and magistrates in the Irish-speaking areas. As for the rest:

> It should not be very difficult, with the aid of the foremost foreign scholars, to bring about a train of thought which would make it disgraceful for an educated Irishman . . . to be ignorant of his own language.[32]

There is nothing here to demand a departure from the four-hundred-year-old assumption that English is the language of Irish public and commercial life. Lack of clarity about its precise objective was to be an enduring feature of the revival movement, but such ambiguity did not take from the status which Irish was to retain throughout the twentieth century as a mark of nationality.

Unlike the Gaelic Athletic Association, the Gaelic League was not from the beginning a sign of division between nationalist and unionist. As proselytising missionaries, as scholars, and as revivalists, Protestants had been strongly associated with the Irish language throughout the century. This long-standing interest was continued under the auspices of the Gaelic League: Hyde himself was a member of the Church of Ireland and the son of a minister. Indeed, the new movement spearheaded by the Gaelic League attracted many unionists because of its critique of the old political nationalism of the home rulers and its refreshing ethos of local co-operation and self-improvement. Up and down the country, from the Glens of Antrim to Westport to Kilkenny city, unionists participated in the public activities of the League well into the first decade of the new century. Not until 1915 did the Gaelic League declare itself to be in the nationalist political camp, whereupon Hyde resigned as president of the organisation because, although a nationalist himself, he was committed to the political neutrality of the League. Soon the language would be synonymous with Sinn Féin nationalism.

Already the relationship between the language movement and Catholicism had been transformed. Fr Eoghan Ó Gramhnaigh, Professor of Irish at Maynooth from 1891 to 1896, and his successor, Fr Michael O'Hickey, were both senior figures in the Gaelic League. For some years in the early 1900s, enthusiasm for Irish swept through at least part of the Maynooth student body. A religious justification was to hand for this clerical commitment. If Irish was the quintessence of the national, it was also the essence of pure religion. If Irish was the barrier against the encroachment of English culture in general, it was *ipso facto* a shield against the intrusion of secularism, free-thinking and disregard for clerical authority that some priests liked to denigrate globally as 'English paganism'.

Writing in 1890, Ó Gramhnaigh (then Eugene Growney), lamented the

---

[32]   Ibid.

paucity of Catholics in the field of Irish language and literary scholarship, which was dominated by Protestants, Irish and foreign. He quoted an unnamed Irish-American asserting that Irish language and literature was 'full of the spirit and the teachings of Irish Catholicity' but did not elaborate. Instead, the clearest argument for the study of Irish that he put to his co-religionists was that it would save them from being at a disadvantage in contending with Protestants about the Churches' respective claims to St Patrick.[33]

By 1898, a lay advocate of revival was advancing the claims of Irish on Catholicism at a much more elevated level. Irish should be venerated:

> ... by reason of its close and inseparable connection with holy faith, with which it has travelled hand in hand influencing and being influenced, through the long span of fourteen hundred years ... Irish is prominently the language of prayer and devotion.[34]

In 1901, Fr. John M. O'Reilly in a Gaelic League pamphlet declared that the survival of Irish was essential if 'the church of this nation' was to survive. The language enshrined a mind that 'has come down to us unstained by memories of revolt, unblemished by scoff or sarcasm against a solitary tittle of doctrine'.[35]

As a general rule, Gaelic League propagandists did not identify the language with the interests of confessional Catholicism. However, their promotion of Irish as a barrier against the troubling social and intellectual changes of the age – denigrated as manifestations of the corrupt civilisation of the neighbouring island – resonated particularly well with Catholic pastors. In any event, generations of strangeness had been wiped away in a few years, and for those who wished it, Irish language and Catholic religion were available as the basis of a composite ideology. Or, to look at the matter in another way, the danger had been obviated that a nationality redefined to incorporate the language as a quintessence might be impelled to question the place of the Roman Catholic Church. This accommodation was of crucial importance to all the interests concerned. This is not to say that the Church was about to subordinate its wider interests to the language movement, a point well illustrated by the dismissal of Michael O'Hickey from his chair at Maynooth in 1909 after he had appeared to be putting the politics of the language revival before the esteem of the hierarchy.

The ultimate absorption of the language issue into the wider politics of

---

[33] E. Growney, 'The national language' in *Irish Ecclesiastical Record*, 3rd ser., vol. xi (1890), pp. 982–92.
[34] Henry Morris, 'The loss of the Irish language and its influence on the Catholic religion in Ireland' in *Fáinne an lae*, I, no. 13 (1898).
[35] J.M. O'Reilly, *The Threatening Metempsychosis of a Nation* (Dublin, 1901) quoted in T. Crowley (ed.), pp. 199–202.

the period is typified by the conversion of many prominent Gaelic League Protestants to Roman Catholicism; for example, Aodh de Blacam, Roger Casement, Lord Ashbourne and others, though not Hyde. This development is not unrelated to the infusion of the language movement by the pervasive, puritanical ethos of the period, hostile to difference and pluralism. Hyde could be inspirational when he wrote of Irish and its speakers, but even his words could exude the tyrannical tone of prescriptive duty. Those who combined linguistic and religious correctness rose to the ultimate heights of judgmental self-righteousness in Catholic nationalist Ireland. In early 1916, with the Gaelic League in abeyance as its former modes of action were inhibited by wartime conditions, the language movement was directed down a new associational road with the institution of the *fáinne*. This small metal ring supplied from an office in Dublin (at two shillings and sixpence for the silver version, seven and sixpence for the gold) and worn on the lapel, became the emblem par excellence of cultural and spiritual nationalism. The *fáinne* was a declaration of ability to speak Irish and so an invitation to others similarly endowed to converse in the language. This created a household of the saved by contrast with the miscellaneous character of the early Gaelic League.

The October 1917 convention at which the new Sinn Féin was consolidated as a political party was dominated by the Gaelic League generation of nationalists. Following on the rhetoric of the revival, resolutions were proposed to the effect that Irish be the language of the Sinn Féin executive, that party communications not in Irish be banned, that only Irish speakers be nominated for parliamentary elections, and that Irish be made 'imperative' for all members.[36] These were turned down on the grounds of impracticality. But no such reservation was applied to the wider project, and the first meeting of Dáil Éireann in January 1919 was conducted in Irish. Subsequently, pragmatism reasserted itself, with business conducted in English but in the context of gestures such as the use of Irish versions of personal names. The Irish delegates signing the Anglo-Irish 'articles of agreement' on 6 December 1921 used Gaelic forms: 'Art Ó Gríofa' rather than 'Arthur Griffith', and so on. The institutions of the newly independent state would be clothed in Gaelic nomenclature that in many instances served to repackage British institutions as Irish ones and create the illusion of continuity with an ancient past. Parliament became the *oireachtas*, the Commons became the *dáil*, the head of government became the *taoiseach*. While 'Sinn Féin' ('ourselves') was a neologism derived from a modern political slogan, the two most successful political parties in independent Ireland – Fianna Fáil and Fine Gael – boasted names that were redolent of early Gaelic civilisation and the scholarship of Eoin MacNeill.

---

[36] Michael Laffan, *The Resurrection of Ireland: the Sinn Féin Party, 1916–23* (Cambridge, 1999), p. 237.

On several fronts, the government of the new Irish Free State cut earlier dreams down to realistic size. It provided no such leadership (or, depending on one's point of view, engaged in no comparable backsliding) on the language issue. The republic, the Sinn Féin courts and economic protectionism were abandoned in deference to *Realpolitik*, but the language remained in the realm of *Idealpolitik*, an untouchable piety in respect of which the Government would not surrender the high ground. Davis, Hyde and Pearse had in their time given assurances that the objective of the revival was bi-lingualism, but in the Irish Free State few dared set a boundary to the linguistic march of the nation. Rhetoric and gesture presaged advance to a universally, if not exclusively, Irish-speaking nationhood. (In retrospect we can see that this was unrealistic, but it was scarcely as utopian as the contemporary attempt to prohibit the production, sale and consumption of alcohol in the USA.) The 1922 Constitution decreed that 'the national language of the Irish Free State (Saorstát Éireann) is the Irish language, but the English language shall be equally recognised as an official language'. This was to be reformulated in the 1937 Constitution so as to emphasise the piety while retaining the pragmatism: 'The Irish language as the native language is the first official language. The English language is recognised as a second official language.'

The introduction of Irish into the schools on a compulsory basis had been Sinn Féin policy since 1917, and implementation at primary level began early in 1922 in advance of any opportunity to equip teachers for the change. By the end of the decade, the infant classes of over ninety per cent of primary schools were being instructed wholly or partially through Irish, a language most of them never heard in the home, by a teaching force many of whose members were but poorly equipped and supported for the task.[37] This was the basis of a structure that extended through the primary and secondary levels and (to a lesser extent) the third level. The burden of satisfying national honour was being placed on the shoulders of children and teachers: the principal ideologue behind the policy, the Jesuit Timothy Corcoran, Professor of Education at University College, Dublin, did not trouble to acquire the language himself. The schools' Irish policy was inefficient for its purpose, was damaging pedagogically to many children, and led to much *cur i gcéill* ('making a pretence'). Instead of reassessing objectives or looking out for a more efficient, humane and honest scheme, successive governments over decades ignored warnings and objections and treated the existing policy as a sacred cow. By the mid-1930s the Department of Education was advocating that standards in virtually every other subject at primary level, including mathematics and English, should be allowed to decline in order to prioritise the teaching of Irish. Rural science was made

---

[37] A. Kelly, *Compulsory Irish: Language and Education in Ireland, 1870s–1970s* (Dublin, 2002), p. 44.

optional, which effectively meant its abandonment.[38] Significantly, religious instruction was not put at risk in the same way as other subjects, the Catholic Church insisting that this always be provided in English where that was the language of the home.

The policy of compulsion in the national schools was informed by an awareness that these institutions had contributed greatly to the spread of English in the previous century and an assumption that they might now be used with equal effect to achieve a reversal. The analogy was flawed in that the level of parental pressure and societal enthusiasm for the change to English was not to be replicated in respect of a recovery of Irish.

The introduction of Irish language requirements for entry to the civil service, and subsequent promotion, was in itself scarcely an unreasonable measure, but here too *cur i gcéill* became the order of the day. While many civil servants were among the most proficient users of the language, for the establishment generally, Irish became a totemic exclusionary device. The attitudes with which an Irish-speaking future was anticipated by servants of the state is well illustrated in the case of the new police force, the Garda Síochána. The commissioner, Eoin O'Duffy, believing that rising generations would emerge as Irish speakers from the primary schools, expected his force to make ready for this. Realising by the later 1920s that his men, despite evident goodwill towards the language, were collectively making poor progress with Irish, he adopted a more interventionist approach. This included the purchase of a Linguaphone machine for every station, paid for by a 'voluntary' deduction from pay across the force. Soon O'Duffy had set a date – 31 December 1938 – after which members who had not acquired competence would be dismissed. Nothing came of this, the Linguaphones gathered dust, and an assessment in 1946 established that about twenty per cent of the force was proficient in Irish. That unimpressive level of Gaelicisation is put in perspective by a civil service memorandum of 1936 archly insisting that the force was 'considerably in advance of the general public regarding the Irish language' and adding that 'the minister is reluctant to assent to the expenditure of public money towards widening the gap between gardaí and the general public.'[39] It was an utterance that encapsulated both the factual truth about the level of popular fluency and the detachment – to put it no more strongly – of a large section of the establishment from an ideal that only a few openly questioned.

Alongside the attempted Gaelicisation of the country at large through the schools, the Irish state, at least since the mid-1920s, has endeavoured to prevent the decline in the number of native speakers in those areas, mainly along the western and southern seaboards, where they were in a majority – the *Gaeltacht*. At times, the linguistic policy has been difficult to tell apart

---

[38] Ibid., p. 46.
[39] Liam McNiffe, *A History of the Garda Síochána* (1977), pp. 127–30.

from economic support for what are in general disadvantaged areas. On this issue also there has been much *cur i gcéill*. Since 1956 there has been a separate government department of the Gaeltacht. The outcome of Gaeltacht policy is the subject of detailed research on the ground reported in Reg Hindley's book *The Death of the Irish Language: a Qualified Obituary* (London, 1990). The verdict of this authoritative examination is, as the title suggests, somewhat pessimistic. However, Hindley's work is preoccupied with native speakers and is much less appreciative of the function of those for whom Irish is a second language, the category on which the future of Irish depends.

Standardisation of the national language by state agency is one of the most basic functions of modern nation-building, and one for which conditions were ripe in newly independent Ireland. Two of three main dialects were competing for domination of the grammatical standard. The orthography was impeded with redundant graphemes derived from the seventeenth-century literary standard. While the Gaelic script was used in schools and the Roman script for the state's official publications, the government-run publishing house (*An Gúm*) produced books – mainly translations of English classics – in each. In contrast with its resolve in the matter of Irish in the school curriculum, the state was remarkably backward in respect of standardisation. The famous dictionary compiled by Father Dinneen (1860–1934), and published in 1904, provided a widely used standard of orthography, but one based on 'classical' practice and so bristling with redundant phonemes.[40] An official standard in spelling was not made available until 1945 and in grammar until 1958. In this as in other respects, the Irish state was an apparently reluctant shaper of the nation. That is not to minimise the impact of state Gaelicisation on the face of independent Ireland, ranging from bilingual roadsigns and street names to the names of semi-state bodies such as Aer Lingus, Bord Fáilte and Coras Iompair Éireann. However, the place of non-governmental and even individual initiative in the promotion of the language, so important before 1921, was to remain very significant after independence, and still remains so. As would be expected in a democratic society, a strong Irish-language interest group has flourished since the 1920s, both inside and outside the public service.

The mainstay of this Irish language lobby was the presumption in its favour supported by the ethos of prescriptive nationalism. The force of this mentality was displayed to the full in reaction to the appearance in the mid-1960s of the concerted campaign against 'compulsory' Irish, conducted by the Language Freedom Movement (which itself hosted some intolerant voices). This proved, however, to be the last virtuoso display of an outdated hegemonism as a permissive era dawned. By the 1970s full-scale compulsion in the schools and a strict language requirement for the public service were

---

[40] Pádraig Ó Duinnín, *Foclóir Gaedhilge agus Béarla: an Irish–English dictionary.*

no longer sustainable. They were replaced by a fudge. A series of official pronouncements from the mid-1960s to the early 1980s somewhat shame-facedly redefined the objective of government policy as a bilingual society in which English would continue to be the dominant language.[41] This has not dented the status of Irish as a national emblem. A recent state-funded adver-tising campaign promoted the language as 'part of what we are'. While the naivety, even the impropriety, of this slogan is patent in reference to the sen-sibilities of an age so properly conscious of ethnic diversity, at another level it conveys succinctly what is now approximately a century-old fact about invented Irish nationality. What is lacking is a realistic definition of target structures and institutions to secure the practical, as distinct from the notional, status of the national language. Experience shows that few avenues or positions are now closed to those without Irish, not even the office of cabinet minister with responsibility for the Gaeltacht. But there is still scope for grievance in arbitrary or uneven application of formal require-ments, mainly in the education sector. On the other hand, the official and symbolic status of Irish does not ensure that those who so wish can depend on being able to use the first official language in their official business with the state. The day when every police car will contain at least one fully bilin-gual garda síochána is a distant prospect. It remains to be seen if the state and those who recognise in the Gaelic language a precious inheritance can deal effectively with the century-old incubus of rhetoric and vested interests that weigh on the present-day language and so find for it realistic future prospects.

The peculiar position of Irish as a national language is well illustrated by its status in the European Union. While it is an official language of the Union, into which many EU treaties etc. are translated, neither at accession nor subsequently has any Irish Government displayed an overwhelming wish to have it officially designated as a working language. If it were, Irish ministers would be expected to use it (as the Greeks use Greek or the Danes use Danish), something most of them would find impossible, for want of competence. No other first official national language of an EU member country is in a similar position.

The strain of enthusiasm for Irish that was a feature of Belfast Presbyterian life from the late eighteenth century and well into the nine-teenth[42] had left sufficient momentum for the recently founded and Unionist-dominated Queen's University to create in 1909 a lectureship in Celtic. The Gaelic League had reached the city in 1895 and had, at least ini-tially, drawn the support of individual unionists. By the early 1920s the identification of the language with Sinn Féin politics was so complete that only hostility could be expected from the new northern state, unless it was

---

41   Seán Ó Riain, *Pleanáil teanga in Éirinn, 1919–85* (Dublin, 1994), pp. 12–21.
42   Ó Buachalla, *I mBéal Feirste cois cuain* (Dublin, 1968).

about to attend to the sensitivities of its nationalist minority. In the event, Irish was allowed in those schools that sought it as an optional subject, on the same basis as Latin and French. Otherwise, Irish was regarded as a badge of opposition to the state and for more than half a century was to have no place in official public life, including the broadcasts of BBC Northern Ireland. The peculiar experience of those language enthusiasts living in the northern state, combined with an apprehension that the Ulster dialect of Irish was being short-changed in the South, led in 1926 to the formation of Comhaltas Uladh ('the Ulster Association') which was in effect a breakaway from the Gaelic League. Thus, rather bizarrely, the Irish language movement mirrored the political partition of which it so thoroughly disapproved. Comhaltas Uladh conducted its separate promotional campaign in subsequent decades with considerable success, turning to the Donegal Gaeltacht as a source of the living language and a venue for summer schools. The enthusiasm of most Catholics in Northern Ireland was considerably cooler. Irish was offered in about twenty per cent of Catholic primary schools by the early 1930s. The funding for teaching it was withdrawn by government in 1933, at the behest of populist unionist MPs and against the advice of the civil service, but this had little impact on the numbers. In Catholic secondary schools the uptake was rather better, partly because of the language requirement for civil service jobs in the South.[43]

The revitalisation of nationalism in Northern Ireland during the Troubles, and especially in the 1980s, has included a resurgence of interest in, and promotion of, Irish. Various features of the movement's history in the South are evident, as if in a speeded-up replay. There is a small core of the dedicated who have mastered the language, speak it on all possible occasions, have set up Irish-medium schools and have even created a small exclusively Irish-speaking housing estate in west Belfast. Others have used the language as an exclusionary device, a badge of difference, or as a metaphysical justification for political extremism. For most nationalists in Northern Ireland, as in the South, Irish is now an emblem of their nationality, but not a language that they envisage themselves speaking. Its emblematic appearance in public places is a necessary feature of the reconciliation of nationalists to the prevailing order.

Despite all of this, a minority (admittedly tiny) of unionists is drawn to Irish. Government funding of the language – significant since the late 1980s – has had a bias towards representation of Irish as a common cultural inheritance in which unionists can share without betraying their political faith. This approach has had but limited success, and in the linguistic provisions of the Belfast Agreement of April 1998 it is modified by the 'parity of

---

[43] Prionsias Mac Aonghusa, *Ar son na Gaeilge: Conradh na Gaeilge, 1893–1993, stair sheanchais* (Dublin, 1993), pp. 221–7; M. McGrath, *The Catholic Church and Catholic Schools in Northern Ireland: the Price of Faith* (Dublin, 2000), pp. 100–5.

esteem' formula. So, an all-Ireland body is to promote Irish in both jurisdictions, but it is also to promote Ulster Scots, a 'derived variety' – in Ireland since the sixteenth century – of the language of lowland Scotland, itself a variety of English.[44] The intention would appear to be to provide unionism with a counterweight to Gaelic and thus to complete the symmetry of the Agreement's consociational structures. Thus may parity of contrariness be effected? Already, in the wake of the Agreement, multilingual job advertisements have appeared in Belfast – in English, Irish, Ulster-Scot and Cantonese. If there is to be a flourishing of Ulster-Scots, written and spoken, that will indeed be a surprise out-turn, but in a world context it will not constitute an exceptionally outlandish case of language reinvention for political purposes. National languages have been invented on the basis of less promising raw material.

The commercial calculations behind the collective move to acquire English that took off about the middle of the eighteenth century among the Irish-speaking populace are reaping rewards beyond the imagining of the Anglicising generations. American domination of a globalising world gives enormous potential advantage to native speakers of English. Their first-language competence in English forms part of the explanation for the successes of the servants of the Irish state in their dealings with the European Union, successes that have included the securing of huge transfers of European funds to Ireland under various programmes. And the success of Irish people as individuals in securing advancement within – and to the top of – the EU establishment is now provoking the kind of envious protest once directed against the Scots within the British Empire. Being an anglophone country gave Ireland a crucial advantage in attracting the foreign investment that supported the economic transformation of the country in the 1990s, making it by some criteria (though not in terms of public amenities or services) one of the wealthiest countries on earth. The investment in question, like other aspects of Irish advantage on the world stage, owes much to the identification of tens of millions of Americans (or more precisely a plutocratic handful from among them) with Ireland, and this is also the source of considerable potential for Irish influence in Washington. These are advantages that an Irish-speaking Ireland would never have enjoyed. For reasons that we need not explore here, it has become normal for citizens of the United States to combine primary loyalty to their country with a secondary loyalty to an ethnic identity from which they can draw various kinds of emotional draughts. Many of the millions of Americans who describe themselves as being of Irish ethnicity could have chosen to be something else had they so wished. Surveying her or his grandparents, an American could have two, three or even four ancestries from which to choose. If Irish is one of

---

[44]   J.J. Smith, 'Scots' in Glanville Price (ed.), *Languages in Britain and Ireland* (Oxford, 2000), pp. 159–70.

them, it has the enormous attraction, by comparison with Italian, German, Swedish, Greek, or a host of others, of being accessible in English. Arguably, its linguistic circumstances give modern Ireland the best of all worlds – full accessibility to the language of international business of all kinds and, simultaneously, the patina of exotic distinctiveness provided by a first official language with which neither inhabitant nor visitor is forced to engage.

The various anomalies that any fair assessment of the place of Irish in the invention of modern Ireland must point to should not detract from the fact that its identification with the nation has undoubtedly contributed greatly to the prospects of survival of the language, and has been perhaps the most important factor in its bearing substantial literary fruit in the twentieth century. A movement that has made possible the poetry of Máire Mhac an tSaoi and Seán Ó Ríordáin, to mention but two, has enriched the nation and the world. If, as some linguists predict, between fifty and ninety per cent of the world's languages are set to die in the twenty-first century, there is a very good chance that Irish will not be one of them. But it will probably not be surviving as a national language in the sense understood by Herder and Mazzini, that is, as the mother tongue and working vernacular of an entire political collectivity. Even in countries where this model applies, closer inspection will always discover a unique relationship between language and polity. The situation of Irish is closer to that of Welsh or Basque, national languages spoken by only a minority of the national population but with two important differences in Ireland: firstly, the number of native speakers is much smaller, and, secondly, the teaching of the language in the schools has patently been less effective.

Scottish Gaelic has developed along its own lines in recent centuries. Nevertheless, some Irish scholars have become specialists in its language and literature.[45] The differences are such as to provide a range of objections to the creation of a common standard, and the standardisation of Irish involved so much internal dialect politics that keeping more links with Scottish Gaelic open would have been a luxury.

Two trends have given shape to Ireland's distinctive experience of linguistic nationality. One, working itself out slowly, but apparently inexorably, over a quarter of a millennium, is the movement on the part of native speakers of Irish to acquire English. Its enduring motivation is the desire to find a place in the modern world. The second, in place for almost as long, is the attempt by speakers of English to save Irish. Behind this perhaps is a perception that the modern world, once reached, leaves something to be desired. The first movement, because it was so frequently accompanied by a desire to jettison Irish, or not to transmit it to the next generation, rather than to achieve bilingualism, involved irreparable cultural loss, and

---

[45] M. Ní Annracháin, *Aisling augus tóir: an slánú i bhfilíocht Shomhairle MhicGill-Gain* (Maynooth, 1992).

also meant that all the modernising processes that depend on a common popular language would occur in English. Thus the inventors of Irish nationalism were deprived of the opportunity – seized upon so eagerly by their counterparts elsewhere – to sanctify the language of modernisation as the distinctive national language. But the counter-movement ensured that the inventors were not deprived of a comparable alternative opportunity.

Recourse to secular trends may not, however, be sufficient by way of explanatory investigation of the failure of the independent Irish state in the 1920s and 1930s to establish Gaelic as the effective national language, especially as partition had left it with a population over ninety per cent of which was ostensibly nationalist. The desire was there on the part of those in government, and perhaps even the expectation, that Gaelicisation was inevitable. However, there was a reluctance to exercise state power – except over children in the classroom – and those most favourably disposed toward Irish included those, such as Eoin MacNeill and Eamon de Valera, who were least enamoured of the pretensions of the state, as distinct from the nation. But, when all is said and done, the explanation may lie in the relative difficulty of Irish as a language. Like any other tongue, Irish is available to anyone who is sufficiently motivated, but its difficulty sets the required motivation at a very high level indeed. If a language could be put on like a cloak, Rev. Professor Timothy Corcoran and most of the Irish Free State elite would have eagerly dressed themselves in Irish, and the populace would have followed suit with more or less enthusiasm.

5

Literature

The nation, and most of the polities and power systems with which the world in historical times has been endowed, would be inconceivable without literature in the wide sense of things written down and conserved for repeated consultation over time. Repeated consultation, not only over time but also in different places, is the hallmark of texts that link together the possessors of ideology, including nation-inventing ideology. Medieval Ireland provides an impressive instance of the emergence and development of a learned elite that brought the art and technology of the manuscript to the highest level of achievement and was linked together by literature in the vernacular and to a wider world by Latin.

The advent of printing in the fifteenth century began a process of widening of the circle of access that reached its culmination in most western countries in the nineteenth century with the availability to almost all citizens of master texts for their own perusal. In Ireland, as the previous chapter has explained, this process – the basis everywhere of modern nationalism – was worked out mainly in English, with Gaelic literature remaining largely in manuscript. Print for the masses has always been supplemented by visual illustrations, and, since the turn of the twentieth century, by film. The likelihood is that in time it will become clear that, in the second half of the twentieth century, visual media overtook print as the great connector of people, in a way that has affected not only the content but the form of nationality: later chapters identify new elements in the category of Irishness that would be impossible without the impact of film and television. But, whatever may be happening around us now, and whatever the future may hold, it remains the case that, historically, nationalism, and the conditions under which it emerged and developed are intrinsically linked to the world of print.

The current chapter is concerned mainly with literature in the restricted sense of formal fiction, poetry and drama. These works and their creators constitute a significant element in the nation invention of many countries, even if it is scarcely a significance that justifies the assertion of the English romantic, P.B. Shelley, that poets are 'the unacknowledged legislators of the world'.[1] The impact of literature on the invention of nations takes many forms. The *Lucíadas* of Camoën has provided Portugal from the sixteenth century onwards with a foundation epic and also with an object of collective pride. Dante wrote *The Divine Comedy* at the beginning of the fourteenth century in an idiom constructed from various dialects that he hoped would become the language of a large state.[2] When that came to pass in the nineteenth century, many of the citizens of the new kingdom of Italy practised their new national language by reading a novel, Manzoni's *I Promessi Sposi*. Several of Shakespeare's plays served to bolster the spirit of English national assertiveness in the late Elizabethan age. In recent centuries his works have provided England with the national cultural trophy par excellence. Apart from being instruments in the invention of the nation, or ornaments of national display, works of literature are regularly deployed in the discourse of essentialist nationality as expressing or representing national 'spirit' or character. The works of Camões, Dante, Manzoni and Shakespeare mentioned above are so used, as are Cervantes' *Don Quixote* for Spain, Goethe's *Faust* for Germany, Multatuli's *Max Havelaar* for the Netherlands or Mark Twain's *Huckleberry Finn* for the USA (in such contexts invariably referred to as America).

A corpus of literature in the national language, preferably including the works of at least one internationally acknowledged genius, is a standard feature in the panoply of a modern nation. In the case of Ireland, there are two languages, and two literatures, that in Irish with its admirers largely confined to an internal audience, and that in English occupying a place of considerable prominence in the eyes of the world. The relationship of the two and their relative claims to national status have constituted a recurrent conundrum in the invention of the modern nation and one particularly fraught for those who thought, or still think, about nationalism in essentialist terms. There are smaller bodies of medieval literature in Latin and Norman-French and a considerable corpus of neo-Latin writing.

For want of labourers in the vineyard, the full riches of early Irish saga literature have not yet been displayed to the world. However, at least one example is widely known, namely the *Táin Bó Cuailnge*, one of a number of stories in the so-called Ulster cycle. There has been much debate among the small number of those competent to pronounce on such matters about the relationship of these tales to putative oral precedents. The current consensus supports the view of the late James Carney that the sagas as we have them

---

1   Percy Bysshe Shelley, *A Defence of Poetry* (1821).
2   Tore Janson, *Speak: a Short History of Languages* (Oxford, 2002), pp. 118–22.

were composed by Christian literary men.[3] This was probably in the eighth century. The stories, however, purport to deal with an earlier, prehistoric period and contain antique elements and features that are of great interest. In particular, they depict a warrior culture reminiscent of some aspects of social institutions of the Gauls described by Julius Caesar and others, and they also contain themes of Indo-European provenance. If there is an extant literary reflection of the ancient Celts, this is it. The *Táin* is the source of the legends of Cú Chulainn, Queen Medb (Maeve), etc. that have had such an impact on Irish literature and related culture since being rendered in English in the later nineteenth century.

While the sagas are written in a combination of prose and verse, there is also an extensive corpus of poetry in Old Irish and Middle Irish, that is to say, for the period down to the twelfth century. There is even sufficient known about a handful of the poets for the emergence of a modest prosopography.[4] A number of anthologies are available, of which the best known is probably Gerard Murphy, *Early Irish Lyrics* (Oxford), first published in 1955, which has translations and, in addition, notes that are of value to those without a knowledge of the original language.

Even before the emergence of literacy in the vernacular, Latin, as the language of the Church, was flourishing in Ireland. *The Oxford Book of Medieval Latin Verse* (ed. by F.J.E. Raby, 1959) contains several Irish items, including 'Altus prosator' attributed to St Columcille (alias Columba, *c.*521–597), a work of religious piety, indicating acquaintance with the Latin version of the Bible in use before Jerome's Vulgate version. St Columbanus (d. 615) is represented by a poem addressed to a friend. There, too, are several religious pieces from the seventh century, including the hymn 'Sancti venite'. Also included, and dating from around AD 800, is a poem by an Irish monk on the continent, which, while it is mainly a personal reflection on life and its hazards, uses the phrase 'amor patriae' (love of country) in respect of the attitude of the friend to whom it is addressed, and who is returning to the land of the Scotti (Ireland).[5]

Norman-French was established in Ireland from the later twelfth century as the vernacular of the ruling elite among the Anglo-Normans. While it may not seem to have struck very deep roots, it has left two noteworthy literary relics. One, known as 'The song of Dermot and the earl' and assigned to the early thirteenth century, is a poem describing in some detail the story of how Dermot MacMurrough secured the services of Strongbow and brought him and his followers to Ireland. The other is a local poetic piece of about two hundred lines, celebrating the digging of a trench around the Anglo-Norman town of New Ross in 1365, and it has been taken as evi-

---

3   Tomás Ó Cathasaigh, 'Early Irish narrative literature' in K. McCone and Katharine Simms (eds), *Progress in Medieval Irish Studies* (Maynooth, 1996), p. 56.
4   Liam Breatnach, 'Poets and Poetry', ibid., p. 77.
5   pp. 59–68, 69–71, 80–1, 98–9.

dence that at least down to this date there was an audience for literature in Norman-French.[6] Outside of the ruling class, the language of the colony was English, and enough verse survives to show that down to the end of the fourteenth century it supported literary endeavour. The most substantial relic remaining is a fantasy piece satirising monastic luxury, *The Land of Cokaygne.*[7]

The Gaelic system readjusted sufficiently well to the Anglo-Norman invasion for the learned classes to secure a continued place as a privileged order whose ministrations were vital to the legitimation of political power. By the early thirteenth century a new literary standard had been adopted, that known as Classical Modern Irish. Now separated from the structures of ecclesiastical organisation, the learned classes organised their business in the bardic schools. They maintained the older forms of learning according to their lights: indeed, they were preoccupied with maintenance rather than innovation, and can be seen in some ways as an archaising, dogmatic caste. However, such generalisation runs the risk of excusing failure actually to inspect the evidence, and a cogent case has been made for the need to undo major neglect of the prose production of the period.[8] Somewhat better served is the dominant poetic genre of the period, bardic poetry. Formulaic praise poetry, composed item by item for individual patrons, its main interest is historical rather than aesthetic. Indeed, even in advance of the full availability of the corpus, its interpretation is already a matter of debate among historians of the early modern period.[9]

From the early seventeenth century onwards, and with the collapse of the Gaelic political system, Irish poets found themselves without the supports they had been accustomed to enjoy, and dependent on a public that was not trained in the complexities of bardic verse. The result was the emergence of poetry in a more popular idiom and generally in syllabic (as opposed to accentual) metre that survived in a manuscript culture until the early part of the nineteenth century. This was the vehicle for a substantial amount of political expression, of antagonism to the new order in society, and – especially in the form of the *aisling* or vision poem – of hope for a reversal of the political order by the restoration of the Stuarts. The convention of the *aisling* is that the poet meets a beautiful woman who tells a tale of distress and abandonment, and at the end identifies herself as Ireland waiting for rescue by help from over the seas. The Gaelic poetry of this epoch has been anthol-

---

[6] Alan Bliss and Joseph Long, 'Literature in Norman French and English to 1534' in Art Cosgrove (ed.), *Medieval Ireland, 1169–1534* (A New History of Ireland, iv) (Oxford, 1987), pp. 708–20.

[7] See Angela Lucas, *Anglo-Irish Poems of the Middle Ages* (Dublin, 1995).

[8] Caoimhín Breatnach, 'Early Modern Irish prose' in K. McCone and K. Simms, *Progress in Medieval Irish Studies*, pp. 189–206.

[9] Katharine Simms, 'Literary sources for the history of Gaelic Ireland in the post-Norman period', ibid., pp. 207–15.

ogised by Seán Ó Tuama, with English translations by Thomas Kinsella, as *An duanaire, 1600–1900: Poetry of the Dispossessed* (1981).

Of course, not all of the poetry was political. An amusing item by Aodh Mac Gabhráin, 'Pléaráca na Ruarcach', was rendered into English in 1720 (from a crib, not the original) by Jonathan Swift (1662–1745), Dean of St Patrick's Cathedral, Dublin, as 'O'Rorke's feast'. While the search for an Irish language source for some of the themes in *Gulliver's Travels* appears not to have yielded any positive results, 'O'Rorke's feast' is a reminder that the two languages and the people who produced their literatures were not set rigidly apart. Daithí Ó hÓgáin and others have noted that Swift (like Daniel O'Connell) is one of the archetypal heroes of later Gaelic folklore.

As early as 1754, Paul Hiffernan proposed the idea of a literature that was English in language but made distinctively Irish by drawing on Gaelic sources.[10] A beginning along these lines was made in 1760, but in Scotland rather than Ireland, with the publication of James Macpherson's *Fragments of Ancient Poetry Collected in the Highlands of Scotland and Translated from the Galic or Erse Language* (1760). The enormous appeal of Macpherson's work across Europe gave a great boost to the cult of things Celtic, which would in due course have manifold repercussions in Ireland. Published translation was advanced in Ireland with C.H. Wilson, *Poems Translated from the Irish Language* (c.1782), and reached a significant level of achievement and success with Charlotte Brooke, *Reliques of Irish Poetry* (1789). The publication in translation of Gaelic literature, especially poetry, was to exert a profound impact on letters in nineteenth-century Ireland. While many translations were no more than literal and functional, some acquired literary status in their own right, especially the efforts of J.J. Callanan, Samuel Ferguson, James Hardiman, James Clarence Mangan and Edward Walsh.

In addition to conventional poetry and song, the creative fare available to Irish speakers included accounts from the *Fiannaíocht*, the cycle of stories about the adventures of Fionn Mac Cumhaill and his band of warriors living an adventurous outdoor existence in the legendary times before the arrival of St Patrick. Since at least the twelfth century this material had been in play between oral and manuscript traditions. It had the additional strength of having been adapted in the various localities to the dinnseanchas – mainly etiological lore about physical features and place names.[11] It was the version of these stories extant among Gaelic speakers in Scotland that provided Macpherson with his raw material. But for all the wealth of what existed in their native language, Irish speakers suffered from the disadvan-

---

[10] J. Leersen, *Mere Irish and Fíor-Ghael: Studies in the Idea of Irish Nationality, its Development and Literary Expression Prior to the Nineteenth Century* (Cork, 2nd edn.; 1996), p. 352.

[11] Robert Welch (ed.), *The Oxford Companion to Irish Literature* (Oxford, 1996), pp. 193–4.

tage that it was not in print. The fact that well before the end of the eighteenth century literature in English geared towards the masses was available cheaply and in great quantities, while Irish language material was still almost entirely manuscript-bound, must have greatly encouraged and facilitated language change.[12]

Meanwhile Irish authors, at home and as emigrants in England, had been contributing significantly to literature in English at every level, none more magisterially than Swift, whose *Gulliver's Travels* first appeared in 1726. Oliver Goldsmith (1728–74), born in County Longford, was another of the luminaries of eighteenth-century literature in English with a novel, *The Vicar of Wakefield*, the elegaic poem, *The Deserted Village* (1770), and a play, *She Stoops to Conquer* (1773). Crowning a career of achievement in and out of the theatre, the Dublin-born Richard Brinsley Sheridan (1751–1816) published the stage classic, *A School for Scandal* in 1777. Novel writing in Ireland flourished from the middle of the eighteenth century, some of it reflecting political issues, including the patriot enthusiasm of the age. Ireland did not have a literary figure to match Sir Walter Scott's impact in Scotland but, in the early decades of the nineteenth century, novelists from a variety of backgrounds and a variety of viewpoints were presenting Irish life and Irish issues in the currently conventional literary form.

The English-born Maria Edgeworth (1767–1849) settled in Longford as the daughter of a progressive landlord, produced in 1800 what is regarded as the first regional novel in English, *Castle Rackrent*. Scott owned to its influence on his work.[13] Lady Morgan (*c*.1776–1859) was married into establishment circles but had recent Catholic and Gaelic-speaking antecedents; in her fiction – most notably *The Wild Irish Girl* (1806) – she was a pioneer of the Romantic depiction of Ireland, and advocated emancipation for Catholics and understanding between Ireland and Britain. Michael Banim (1796–1874) and John Banim (1798–1842), Kilkenny-born middle-class Catholic brothers, collaborated to produce *Tales of the O'Hara Family* (1825) and *Father Connell* (1842), in addition to authoring individual works. Of similar background was Gerald Griffin (1803–40), author of a substantial body of work, including *The Collegians* (1829). William Carleton (1794–1869) was a native speaker of Irish from County Tyrone who conformed to the Established Church and supported the Union. A prolific writer, he created – particularly in *Traits and Stories of the*

---

12   See Niall Ó Cíosáin, 'Printed popular literature in Irish, 1750–1850: presence and absence' in Mary Daly and David Dickson (eds), *The Origins of Popular Literacy in Ireland: Language Change and Educational Development, 1700–1920* (Dublin, 1990), pp. 45–58; Rolf Loeber and Magda Stouthamer-Loeber, 'Fiction available to and written for cottagers and their children' in Bernadette Cunningham and Máire Kennedy (eds), *The Experience of Reading: Irish Historical Perspectives* (Dublin, 1999), pp. 124–72.
13   Robert Welch, *Oxford Companion to Irish Literature* (1996), p. 168.

Irish Peasantry (1830–44) – a colourful record of the society from which he had emerged, using a distinctive and memorable prose style. Also prolific in his output of fiction was Charles Lever (1806–72), a Dubliner of middle-class Protestant background, whose novels include *Harry Lorrequer* (1839), *Charles O'Malley* (1841) and *Lord Kilgobbin* (1872).

Because of the interest generated by the brilliant and self-conscious literary movement of the late nineteenth and early twentieth centuries, the impression is sometimes created that much of the nineteenth century was a blank page as far as literary endeavour is concerned. That is very far from being the case. In his excellent work of reference, *Ireland in Fiction: A Guide to Irish Novels, Tales, Romances and Folklore,* published in a new edition in 1919, Stephen J. Brown lists more than seventeen hundred books. This work includes only books set in Ireland or dealing with Irish matters, and takes no account of other fiction written by Irish people. Even on its own terms, Brown's list is undoubtedly incomplete. Brown's succinct summaries show that in this literature every viewpoint on the Irish political spectrum is advocated: from rabid Orange bigotry by way of eirenic advocacy of 'coming together' to rabid Green bigotry, and from extreme anti-Popish venom by way of indifferentism to extreme anti-Protestant venom. Sometimes the viewpoints are combined in unexpected ways. Here is the description by Brown of *The Viceroy* (London, 3 vols, 2nd edn., 1841) by the Belfast-born John Fisher Murray:

> Written mainly to satirise Dublin Castle, its government and the ascendancy aristocracy. Incidentally it shows up the average Englishman's ignorance of things Irish. It also reveals the author as a lover of Ireland after his own fashion. Strong Protestant bias. Except in the case of a visit to O'Connell at Derrynane, which is well described, everything Catholic appears coarse and vulgar. Fr. Corrigan is a 'stage Irish' priest. Moves somewhat heavily as a story, but is full of clever pictures of the times. A satirical tone is adopted throughout.

In some instances, Brown has to speak severely, as with Thomas R.J. Polson, *The Fortune Teller's Intrigue* (Dublin, 3 vols, 1847):

> An unusually objectionable and absurd libel on the priests and people of Ireland. The latter are represented as slavishly submissive to the former, who are spoken of as 'walking divinities'. The priests attend their dupes at their execution for agrarian crimes, telling them that they are martyrs for the faith. The scene is Co. Clare.

M.T. Pender, *The Green Cockade* (Dublin, 1898) advances its prejudices more subtly:

> A love story, the scene of which is set in Ulster during the rebellion. Full of romantic adventures. Historical characters introduced: Lord Edward, Putnam

McCabe, and especially Henry Joy McCracken . . . No attempt at impartiality. The government side is painted in the darkest colours.

Others display no interest whatsoever in politics or religion. Take, for example, Marguerite A. Power, *Nelly Carew* (London, 2 vols, 1859):

> The heroine, daughter of an Irish landlord, is driven by the scheming of a crafty French stepmother (once her governess) into marriage with an Irish *roué* and leads a life of bitter humiliation. But her honour is stainless through it all and there is a happy ending. Characters are for the most part admirably drawn. The moral is good. The brogue is well done.

The representation of peasant speech is a frequent element, but the 'anthropological' interest is not confined to speech. The variety of actual *locales* described, either from observation or imagination, is astonishing. It is worth noting that the relative number of women appearing as authors in this collection is strikingly good by comparison with almost any other Irish forum of the age. Eminent among these female authors are Edith Somerville (1858–1949) and Violet Martin, alias Martin Ross, (1862–1915) who published jointly as Somerville and Ross and whose output included *The Real Charlotte* (1894) and *Some Experiences of an Irish R.M.* (1899).

Brown has only one entry each for Joseph Sheridan Le Fanu (1814–73) and Bram Stoker (1847–1911). In fact, Le Fanu's collected works fill fifty-two volumes and constitute a rich, varied and significant deposit, including *The House by the Churchyard* (1863) and *Uncle Silas* (1864).[14] Stoker's entry in Brown's catalogue is his only novel set in Ireland: *The Snake's Pass* (1891); but he is best remembered as the author of *Dracula* (1897). Omitted altogether, in accordance with the criteria, are two other authors of Dublin birth: Oscar Wilde (1854–1900) and George Bernard Shaw (1856–1950). Both moved to London in their twenties and won for themselves international stature as playwrights and literary giants. The post-1900 entries in Brown's guide include luminaries such as George Moore (1852–1933) and James Joyce (1882–1941), the latter receiving particularly ascerbic treatment. Brown was a Jesuit whose particular mission it was to promote Catholic literature, and he was instrumental in the establishment of a Catholic library in Dublin. This 'confessionalising' tendency was offset by the 'nationalising' impetus that led him to compile a comprehensive catalogue, with a commentary that is in general very fair-minded. The principal value of Brown's list of seventeen hundred of 'the good, the bad and the ugly' for present purposes is that it serves as a warning about the distortion that is involved when we focus on a small number of books or authors and proceed to pontificate about literature and nationality.

---

14 See William J. McCormack, *Sheridan Le Fanu and Victorian Ireland* (Oxford, 1980).

The interest of the United Irishmen of the 1790s in the nationalist uses of literature was real but limited.[15] Its main component was a concern with the effective use of popular song for propaganda purposes as epitomised by the anthology, *Paddy's Resource,* with its subtitle: *being a select collection of original and modern patriotic songs, toasts and sentiments compiled for the use of the people of Ireland* (Belfast and Dublin, 3 vols, 1795–98). However, a desire to use popular culture for nationalist political purposes is not the same as a wish to nationalise popular culture (although there was also a limited manifestation of that in the 1790s: see chapter six). While their newspaper, the *Northern Star,* displayed appreciation of the translation work of Charlotte Brooke, it is clear that the creation of national literature was not part of the organisation's core programme.

Half a century later, the endeavours of the Young Irelanders had much more ambitious literary objectives. They promoted national balladry, as the United Irishmen had done, hoping to provide an alternative to the frequently uncouth, sectarian or 'unmanly' fare available to the populace from the more demotic balladeers in city streets and country towns. Thomas Davis led the way in this as in so much else, turning out rousing verses for the *Nation* from its inception in 1842. So successful was the endeavour that an anthology, *The Spirit of the Nation,* was published the following year, taking definitive shape in 1845 and becoming an immensely popular volume reprinted copiously over the next one hundred years. A dozen or more of the ballads have secured a place in the general repertoire of Irish songs. Apart from Davis, the contributors included Charles Gavan Duffy, Charles P. Meehan, Michael Doheny, J.D. Frazer and M.J. Barry. Barry in his turn edited a selection, *The Songs of Ireland* (1845), drawing on material spread over the preceding half century, and like the *Spirit of the Nation,* published by James Duffy of 23 Anglesea St., Dublin. In the same year, the same publisher launched yet another anthology, Charles Gavan Duffy's *Ballad History of Ireland* which also was to be reprinted repeatedly in subsequent decades. Another, but less successful, collection followed in 1846: D.F. McCarthy's, *The Book of Irish Ballads.* James Duffy is a prime example of the nation-making print capitalist; without his entrepreneurial thrust, the impact of Davis's labours might have been much less.

While Davis attached prime importance to propagandist balladry, the *Nation* also nurtured verse of a wider scope, albeit generally with a flavour of nationality. Its pages hosted contributions by James Clarence Mangan, Denis F. McCarthy, Gerald Griffin and Edward Walsh. The *Nation* also noticed the work of authors who were not deemed to be on the repeal side in the political struggles of the day, such as Carleton, Lever and Sylvester

---

[15] M.H. Thuente, *The Harp Re-strung: the United Irishmen and the Rise of Irish Literary Nationalism* (Syracuse, 1994).

Mahony (alias Father Prout). For Davis what mattered most was that they were Irish, and so potential ornaments to the nation.

Young Ireland's programme of nation-building in the literary sphere is well manifested in the Library of Ireland, a somewhat heterogeneous collection published by James Duffy between 1845 and 1848 and subsequently reissued in twelve pocket-size volumes, with gilt harps and shamrocks on cover and spine. There is history, with an emphasis on episodes of Irish resurgence, notably: Thomas McNevin, *The History of the Volunteers of 1783* (1848); T.D. McGee, *A Memoir of the Life and Conquests of Art MacMurrough, King of Leinster from A.D. 1377 to A.D. 1417* (1847); and C.P. Meehan, *The Confederation of Kilkenny* (1848). Following Davis's untimely death in 1845, two volumes were devoted to collections of his poems and essays. The nation-inventing intent of the Library of Ireland is further signalled by the thrust towards anthologising national literature. *The Casket of Irish Pearls: A Selection of Prose and Verse from the Best Irish Writers* (1848) edited by Thornton MacMahon ranged widely but not in accordance with any evident plan. Much more significant was D.F. McCarthy's *The Poets and Dramatists of Ireland with an Introduction on the Early Religion and Literature of the Irish People* (1846). Here we find an attempt to survey the field and to define Irish literature.

In Young Ireland we see what was to be the closest identification between the leadership of a significant political movement and literary nationalism. While the Fenian *Irish People* (1863–65) was consciously modelled on the *Nation* of the 1840s and did gesture towards national literature and verse, it did not identify the movement it promoted with cultural nationalism. Charles Stewart Parnell seems to have had little interest in literary matters, although his sisters Anna and Fanny both wrote poetry. Individual proponents of Home Rule and Parnellites, like 'repealers' before them, might have strong and definite views on literature in its relationship to Irish nationality, but in that field they had no party line to follow.

Even if only as a commercial proposition, the promotion of 'national' literature lived on. James Duffy produced a series of magazines between the late 1840s and the mid-1860s, all with an emphasis on 'Irish' fare: the *Irish Catholic Magazine,* the *Fireside Magazine* and the *Hibernian Magazine.* Catholicism was part of Duffy's formula, but his list of contributors was not exclusivist in denominational terms. The same was true of the *Irish Monthly,* launched in 1873 by Matthew Russell, S.J. with the stated purpose of fostering Irish literature. Some of the better contributions in the first decade and a half came from a group of women writers, including Rosa Mulholland, Ellen O'Leary, Katharine Tynan, Rose Kavanagh and Dora Sigerson. In 1886 it carried a poem entitled 'The Stolen Child' by William Butler Yeats (1865–1939), Dublin-born, aged twenty-one, and already certain of his calling as a great literary man.

It is clear from the foregoing that through the eighteenth and nineteenth centuries there was an abundance of literature in English that was in one or more senses Irish: written by authors born or living in Irelamd; or dealing with Irish subjects; or engaging with Irish issues; or self-consciously intended as elaboration on a national inheritance (as with a series of the translators of Gaelic poetry); or (as with Davis and the publisher James Duffy) intended to edify the nation. Then, from the 1880s, the production and celebration of Irish literature in English *as distinctively Irish* was taken up, and with so much success that the work of the following period of thirty years or so has received worldwide recognition as the Irish literary revival, or renaissance.

Not untypically of pioneering manifestations of nationality, the first impulse was generated among exiles. By the early 1880s there had been added to the networks of Irish associational life in Britain a number of 'junior Irish literary clubs' designed to provide a new English-born generation with Sunday School classes in the culture of the homeland and 'to develop their now dim Celtic talents'.[16] Promotion was in the charge of a committee of middle-class women, including Frances Sullivan, the wife of A.M. Sullivan who had formerly been editor of the *Nation*, then an MP from 1874 and was at that time settling into his new career at the English bar. Particular success attached to the Southwark club, where the programme of history, song, story and legend was arranged and presented by Francis A. Fahy of Kinvara, Co. Galway, a young civil servant, and versifier, who was to write songs such as 'The Ould Plaid Shawl' and 'The Donovans'. Fahy took the lead in 1883 in the formation of the Southwark Irish Literary Club. Several years of lively activity followed, including 'original nights' – when members presented new work, mainly ballads and sketches – and there were lectures by members or invited guests. The range was wide. John Redmond MP spoke on 'Wexford in '98'. There was a paper on 'Pat in foreign parts'. Various deceased Irish poets and novelists were given individual treatment. Justin McCarthy MP held forth on 'The literature of '48'. Sophie Bryant lectured on 'The early races of Ireland'. D.J. O'Donoghue ruffled feathers when his talk on 'France and Ireland' turned into an attack on Gallic ingratitude for centuries of Irish support.[17]

The thrust of the Southwark society's interest was primarily, but by no means exclusively, literary. And the working definition of Irish literature employed was broad, embracing as it did some of the fugitive pieces of members, many of them talented working journalists with aspirations to produce something of more enduring interest than their daily or weekly copy. There were 'Gaelic nights', but as yet no sense of exclusive Gaelic claims. One project contemplated but not achieved was a selection of the poems of Charles J. Kickham. When Daniel Crilly MP lectured on Fanny

[16] W.P. Ryan, *The Irish Literary Revival: Its History, Pioneers and Possibilities*, p. 12.
[17] Ibid.

Parnell in March 1888, the audience included a first-time visitor, William Butler Yeats. He had already drawn momentum from somewhat similar societies in Dublin – the Contemporary Club and the Young Ireland Literary society. He now opportunistically canvassed the members of the Southwark society for subscriptions to his forthcoming book of verse, *The Wanderings of Oisin* (1886).[18]

The distinctive voice audible in *The Wanderings of Oisin* was the harbinger of a poetic career of genius, and that genius was to develop thanks to an enormous degree of self-belief and a willingness to promote his work through individual contacts and amenable groups. In this spirit, Yeats took the lead in 1891 in reconstituting the Southwark club as the Irish Literary Society, returning to Dublin in 1892 to found the National Literary Society there. The societies were intended to promote a revival of the Library of Ireland scheme of the 1840s. The sole surviving patriarch of Young Ireland, Charles Gavan Duffy, proprietor of the *Nation* from 1842 to 1855, had returned in 1880 from a successful second career in Australia, where he had risen to eminence as Prime Minister of Victoria and earned a knighthood. Duffy had devoted himself to writing up Young Ireland and he was a very desirable – and very willing – participant in the new library venture. Proving to be much more than the figurehead Yeats intended him to be, Duffy was largely instrumental in wresting control of the project from the ambitious young poet. In the event, the library idea proved to be outmoded and Yeats found other and better platforms.[19] It was not to be uniform bindings, but certain common sources of inspiration and reference, that would distinguish the Irish literary revival.

Drawing on the mythologies, themes and modes of the Gaelic inheritance for the purposes of a modern literature in English provided the core of the literary revival. This involved the putting aside of much that Thomas Davis and the original members of the Southwark group regarded as Irish literature. Samuel Ferguson (1810–86) is seen as a precursor of the literary revival because, as a Gaelic scholar with access to the old literature, he drew on its resources for the purposes of his own poetry in English. The cumulative efforts of scholars over several generations ensured that by the 1880s Gaelic sources were accessible, albeit in generally recondite formats. Standish James O'Grady served up this material in exciting, highly charged, and above all accessible form in works such as his *History of Ireland: the Heroic Period* (1878) and *History of Ireland: Cuchulain and his Contemporaries* (1880), based on the Ulster cycle. Thanks to O'Grady, others could draw on this material themselves and, equally importantly, they could depend on having an audience for whom it was a known currency of reference.

---

[18]　R.F. Foster, *W.B. Yeats: A Life; I: The Apprentice Mage* (Oxford, 1997), p. 82.
[19]　Ibid., pp. 118–22.

The other new referential matrix deployed by Yeats and other poets and artists of the renaissance is most conveniently described as folklore. The col-·lection of stories and accounts of popular beliefs from the lips of country people was a fashion already in the 1820s. Thomas Crofton Croker's influential *Fairy Legends and Traditions of the South of Ireland* was published in 1825.[20] Folklore collectors, like all other searchers for knowledge, tend to find information only in the categories that interest them. As the title of Crofton Croker's work indicates, he was fascinated by popular belief about the world of fairies. As in many other societies, there was widespread belief among Irish people – and not only the 'peasantry' – that the tangible world coincided with a universe of, mainly malevolent, actors invisible to humans, except perhaps for a few who paid a heavy price for their insight. The anti-rationalist Yeats was quite happy to make play with such ideas, and thus fancifully make contact with the wellsprings of popular being, just as he participated in spiritualist experiments and Madame Blavatsky's fashionable theosophy, and thereby cultivated the company of the *avant-garde*. Yeats compiled collections of folk material published as *Fairy and Folk Tales of the Irish Peasantry* (1888) and *The Celtic Twilight* (1893). In subsequent years he was to conduct his own researches among country people in Galway.[21]

Folklore can also mean popular song. Douglas Hyde collected and anthologised Gaelic verse and song, most famously in his *Love Songs of Connacht* (1893). Padraic Colum's 'She Moved through the Fair' is a literary man's brilliant take on popular song. A street ballad inspired Yeats's 'Down by the Sally Gardens', and several of his themes are coloured, as several of his poems are inspired, by similar material. To create a distinctive version of English for the new literature was one of the challenges which its advocates set themselves. In the early decades of the nineteenth century – for example, in the verse translations of J.J. Callanan such as 'The Outlaw of Loch Lene' and 'Gougane Barra' – the possibility had already been seized of rendering Gaelic material into an English form that would capture the peculiar metrical internal rhyming features of Gaelic poetry. Ferguson and Mangan had taken up the challenge, occasionally with remarkable success. In the period of the revival, Yeats, Austin Clarke, and others achieved innovative metrical developments that drew creatively on Gaelic models. In his translations Douglas Hyde perfected a diction intended to represent the spoken English of Irish country people. For about three hundred years, dramatists and prose writers had been representing the distinctive idioms and usages of Hiberno-English speech in print. This practice was given a strikingly fresh start, in different ways by different authors, in the period of the

---

[20] See Diarmuid Ó Giolláin, *Locating Irish Folklore: Tradition, Modernity, Identity* (Cork, 2000).
[21] See Mary Helen Thuente, *William B. Yeats and Irish Folklore* (Dublin, 1980).

literary revival. The term 'Kiltartanese' has been used to refer to the highly effective language devised by Lady Augusta Gregory (whose residence was in the barony of Kiltartan, Co. Galway), for her version of the Gaelic mythological corpus presented in *Cuchulain of Muirthemne* (1902) and *Gods and Fighting Men* (1904). A literary version of Hiberno-English speech was a requirement for a convincing contribution in drama to the revival. Lady Gregory, W.B. Yeats, John M. Synge, T.C. Murray and Sean O'Casey achieved this, with very different styles, in the creation, over a period of less than thirty years, of one of the classic repertoires of world theatre. Both Synge, in non-urban settings (*In the Shadow of the Glen, Riders to the Sea* and *The Playboy of the Western World*), and O'Casey (*Shadow of a Gunman, The Plough and the Stars* and *Juno and the Paycock*), in working-class Dublin settings, devised language that was not only fresh but has proved to have durability.

A recent book by Christopher Morash has placed the historical study of theatre in Ireland on an entirely new level of information and interpretation.[22] Morash documents and describes the extraordinarily intimate links between theatre, politics and government in Dublin from the early seventeenth century until the twentieth. Also from around 1600, Irish issues, Irish images, Irish playwrights and Irish actors feature on the London stage. In the 1780s there had been a short-lived 'National Theatre' in Dublin. By the second half of the nineteenth century, Dublin audiences had regular access to a complete range of stage productions, from Shakespeare all the way to performing animals. Historical plays with political overtones were constructed so as to balance the sensitivities of different interests, if necessary by negotiation. In this way, from the 1860s, Dion Boucicault with works like *The Colleen Bawn* and *The Shaughraun*, could play to popular nationalist sentiment and, at the same time, not be deemed a threat by others. In 1884, an enterprising Londoner, J.W. Whitbread, assisted by the Limerick-born Hubert O'Grady (1841–99), introduced as the staple of the Queen's Theatre a species of Irish political drama that celebrated nationalist attitudes uninhibitedly, and made no concessions to the feelings of others, with melodramas such as *The Eviction, Emigration, The Famine* and *The Fenian*. It seems reasonable to deduce that Yeats, Lady Gregory and Edward Martyn had in mind the vulgar nationalist fare of the Queen's Theatre, rather than the vulgar London or cosmopolitan fare of Dan Lowrey's Star of Erin Music Hall, when they set about providing a more highbrow alternative in the form of the Irish Literary Theatre.[23] This was launched in 1899, and in 1904 became the Abbey Theatre.

Funded by the state since 1924, the Abbey Theatre is one of the more dis-

---

[22] Christopher Morash, *A History of Irish Theatre, 1601–2001* (Cambridge, 2002); see also C.J. Wheatley, *Beneath Ierne's banner: Irish Protestant Drama of the Restoration and Eighteenth Century* (South Bend, IN, 1999).
[23] Morash, pp. 108–20.

tinctive Irish ventures into nation invention. It can be seen, very justifiably, as a tangible relic of the cultural revival movement. But it is also a reminder of something that 'revivalist' interpretation tends to ignore: the role of the Irish state over the past four hundred years in the invention of the Irish nation. The second quarter of the century in Ireland did not match the first for brilliant new dramatic creation, and the Abbey was not always to the forefront when a new era dawned, but it has sooner or later provided the seal of approval for all of the major Irish playwrights that have emerged in recent decades, including John B. Keane, Hugh Leonard, Tom Murphy, Brian Friel and Frank McGuinness.

Writing in 1919, Robert Lynd, a sympathetic but not blindly supportive observer of what had transpired over the preceding decades, declared that no movement had ever been more industriously 'written up' than the Irish literary revival in English.[24] He accorded pride of place in this marketing enterprise to Ernest Boyd's *Ireland's Literary Renaissance* (London, 1916), while also picking out from the 'whole library of books about it at the disposal of the historian' the published reminiscences of George Moore, Katharine Tynan Hinkson and Yeats. If the literature of the period just before and after the turn of the twentieth century is one of the ornaments of Irish nationality, that is in itself the result of invention: the awareness of a unity embracing diverse material highlighted from among a sea of less distinctive contemporary work came to pass because the concept was successfully promoted, in the first place, and most assiduously, by Yeats himself. That we see a movement rather than the work of individuals is a credit not only to Yeats's ambition but to his personality. The picture of WBY as a person that emerges from the first volume of Roy Foster's colossal and compelling biography is not entirely attractive, but one admirable trait that does shine out is a readiness to recognise and promote talent in others, something evidenced most strikingly in his treatment of James Joyce.[25]

For all its success at home and abroad, the right of the new literature to represent itself as Irish was not universally conceded. Indeed, three mutually incompatible definitions of Irish literature have been in use, and their advocates frequently in contention. 'Irish' literature in the most comprehensive definition could mean literature written by an Irish person, whether in Irish or English, or, defined in the narrowest term, it might connote only work in the Irish language. An intermediate position applied the term to all work written in Irish, and to writing in English that could be deemed to be Irish in character or inspiration. Closely linked to the contention about these different definitions was the disputed meaning and use of the term 'Anglo-Irish' as applied to literature.

The literary revival had run side by side with the language revival; they

---

[24] R. Lynd, *Ireland a Nation*, p. 169.
[25] R.F. Foster, *W.B. Yeats: A Life; I: The Apprentice Mage* (Oxford, 1997), pp. 275–8.

had drawn on many of the same enabling forces and on overlapping cadres of enthusiasts. It was in a presidential address to the National Literary Society that Douglas Hyde in November 1892 delivered the paper on 'The necessity of de-Anglicising Ireland' that is credited with inspiring the formation of the Gaelic League in the following year. Yeats, who was in the audience, detected in Hyde's declaration the implication that literature in English did not match up to the definition of Irish nationality now being set forth. He moved, with a newspaper article, to promote the definition that suited him: 'Irish literature could be written in English, but in a Gaelic mode'. In support of his case Yeats could – and did – cite the success of Hyde's own renditions of Irish material into English.[26] With the language revival under the auspices of the Gaelic League quickly embarking on a programme of Irish language composition and publication, many of its adherents, following the logic of Hyde's clarion call and the impulse of their own enthusiasm, came to see literature in Gaelic as the only worthwhile or valid Irish literature. In this spirit, the nineteen-year-old Patrick Pearse, in 1899, denounced the Irish Literary Theatre on the premise that 'literature written in English cannot be Irish', and drew the corollary that, 'if once we admit the Irish literature in English idea, then the language movement is a mistake'. He made clear that he would have no objection to Yeats ('a mere English poet of the third or fourth rank') conducting an enterprise described as 'the English Literary Theatre', or simply 'the Literary Theatre': 'but when he attempts to run an "Irish" Literary Theatre it is time for him to be crushed'.[27] Within a few years Pearse would adopt a more tolerant attitude towards Yeats's theatre, but the view that literature in English could not be truly Irish was to retain its dogmatic hold for many (though not for all) of more than one generation of Irish language activists.

Meanwhile, Peadar Ó Laoghaire, Pádraig Ó Conaire and others, not least Pearse, were founding a body of literature in modern Irish that would flourish through the twentieth century.[28] A momentous choice for those embarking on this enterprise in invention was whether to base their language on Irish as currently spoken, which did not have agreed standards, or indeed any literary standards, or to adopt a classical standard, which in practice would have meant that of Geoffrey Keating's *Foras feasa*. Pearse was among those who insisted, successfully, that a modern nation needed literature in a modern idiom.[29]

Douglas Hyde contributed the volume on Ireland to the Library of Literary History published by T. Fisher Unwin at the turn of the century. It

---

[26] Ibid., p. 126.
[27] *An Claidheamh Soluis*, 20 May 1899.
[28] Pilib Ó Laoire, *The Prose Literature of the Gaelic Revival, 1881–1921: Ideology and Innovation* (Pittsburgh, 1994).
[29] Ruth Dudley Edwards, *Pearse*, pp. 96–7.

deals exclusively – and magisterially – with literature in Irish. The rest is summarily dismissed in the opening paragraph of the preface:

> I have abstained altogether from any analysis or even mention of the works of Anglicised Irishmen of the last two centuries. Their books, as those of Farquhar, of Swift, of Goldsmith, of Burke find, and have always found, their true and natural place in every history of *English* literature that has been written, whether by Englishmen themselves, or by foreigners.[30]

That evaded addressing the position of those Irish people who wrote in English but on distinctively Irish topics and in what they, and the English, and foreigners, would see as distinctively Irish modes. And, of course, Hyde, like his antagonists in this terminological conflict, was in thrall to an essentialist concept of nationality that did not allow for the possibility that exclusive classification by nation would not always meet the complexity of life as lived.

That literature in the English language could express quintessentially Irish thoughts and feelings was the foundational axiom of the literary revival. Ernest Boyd put the matter succinctly when, in the preface to the first (1916) edition of *Ireland's Literary Renaissance*, he defined his subject matter as 'literature which, although not written in Gaelic, is none the less informed by the spirit of the race'.[31] Composing in June 1922 a preface to a new edition (published in 1923), Boyd clearly feared that the project he admired was under threat of being submerged or sidelined by the victorious Sinn Féin controllers of the emerging Free State. The leaders of that movement, he declared, had dismissed his authors as 'unnational because they used English as their medium'. As for the Sinn Féin rank and file, it had, he alleged:

> ... made a virtue of its ignorance of and contempt for the literature which has done more than anything else to draw the attention of the outside world to the separate national existence of Ireland. Synge was denounced as an un-Irish decadent by the leading Sinn Féiners of his time, and to this day the Irish [i.e. the Abbey] Theatre is regarded askance by the ultra-patriotic.[32]

In support of his own viewpoint, Boyd might have cited Thomas MacDonagh, one of the executed leaders of the Rising of Easter 1916, whose *Literature in Ireland* was published shortly after his death. A lecturer in English at University College, Dublin and a practising poet, MacDonagh wrestled with the challenge of justifying the national credentials of poetry in

---

[30] D. Hyde, *A Literary History of Ireland from the Earliest Times to the Present* (London, 1899), p. xi.
[31] Boyd, p. 9 of 1923 edition.
[32] Boyd, pp. 6–7 of 1923 edition.

English. He did show critical astuteness in this enterprise, but he was also capable of indulging in the chauvinism, so common among Irish Irelanders of all kinds at the time, which attributed superiority to Ireland and things and people Irish in all intellectual, moral and spiritual matters. Robert Lynd dealt succinctly with MacDonagh on this score:

> MacDonagh contends that while the Irish use words which are coins, the English merely use words which are counters. The truth is, in both countries the great mass of writers make use of the counters of convention.[33]

Boyd's definition of Irish literature was that of Yeats in his early and middle years, and it is one that has been associated (though of course not exclusively) with Protestants identifying with Irish nationality, be they unionist in politics, like Ferguson, or nationalist, like Yeats. In 1834, Ferguson had fiercely denounced James Hardiman's *Irish Minstrelsy, or Bardic Remains of Ireland* (Dublin, 2 vols, 1831) because, as he saw it, Hardiman represented Gaelic poetry as the property of Catholic nationalism, thus denying it as an inheritance to Irish Protestants. The dispute about the definition of 'Irish literature' at the beginning of the twentieth century has overtones of the same conflict, even if it has now to be expressed in different terminology. F.S.L. Lyons in *Culture and Anarchy in Ireland, 1890–1939* (1979) treats of a conflict between 'Irish Ireland' and 'Anglo-Irish Ireland'. It is something of a commonplace to represent Protestant interest in the literary revival, and in cultural revival generally, as an endeavour to compensate for the decline of political, landed and ecclesiastical privilege, and this point is sometimes put in accusatory tones, as though Protestants were not as entitled as anyone else to hitch their wagons to rising stars.

Boyd dismisses peremptorily any idea that Goldsmith or Sheridan, Wilde or Shaw can be admitted to his canon: they may be Irish-born but their work is not informed by the required spirit.[34] They are embraced, however, in a third definition – predating the formulations of the revival period and never quite displaced by them – that regards Irish literature simply as the work of any Irish-born author. For all of Davis's essentialist instincts, the Young Ireland view of national literature was comprehensive. In the Library of Ireland, *The Poets and Dramatists of Ireland with an Introduction on the Early Religion and Literature of the Irish People* (1846), edited by Denis F. McCarthy, includes Stanihurst, Roger Boyle, Swift, Farquhar and Richard Steele. McCarthy's volume was planned as the first part of a multi-volume opus (the others did not appear) and does not reach as far as the nineteenth century. One of the most successful of Irish anthologies has been *The Cabinet of Irish Literature: Selections from the Works of the Chief Poets,*

---

[33] Lynd, *Ireland a Nation* (1918), p. 169.
[34] Preface to first edition (p. 9 of 1923 edition).

Orators, and Prose Writers of Ireland (1880), originally the work of Charles A. Read and taking definitive shape in the four-volume 1906 edition prepared by Katharine Tynan Hinkson. Here, too, the test of Irishness is birth, and the effective chronological starting point is the early seventeenth century. Nor is Irish subject matter a criterion: G.B. Shaw is included (*Arms and the Man*) and Bram Stoker (*Dracula*). Similarly inclusive in range and even more extensive in its coverage was *Irish Literature* (Chicago, 1904), edited by Justin McCarthy and published in ten elegant volumes.

A robust defence of the older comprehensive approach – under double attack for forty years by the proponents of both the literary and the linguistic revivals – was made in 1926 by Hugh A. Law in his *Anglo-Irish Literature*:

> The older generation never doubted – poor, simple folk – that Molyneux and Swift, Berkeley, Burke, Grattan, Goldsmith, Sheridan were to be accounted Irishmen. Nowadays England's claim to these is seldom contested; nay, to contest it is to write oneself down un-Irish.

He points with a gentle ironic touch to the manner in which Yeats and his followers – having formerly denied Irish nationality to others – were now themselves subjects of denunciation, as in a recent newspaper article where they were dismissed as 'foreigners' imbued with 'rancorous enmity to the Irish people'[35]. In fact the later Yeats was to rework his own myth along lines that extended his literary ancestry back beyond Mangan and Ferguson to embrace the worthies of the eighteenth century.

The term 'Anglo-Irish' applied to literature (as in the title of Law's book) has itself been a bone of contention. In 1846, Denis F. McCarthy used it in the introduction to *The Poets and Dramatists of Ireland* to refer to Swift, Burke, Goldsmith and Sterne, all of whom he was about to claim for Ireland, while acknowledging that they were generally included in the English literary pantheon. 'Anglo-Irish' was adopted by D.P. Moran of the *Leader*, in 1900, to denote all 'literature concerning Ireland written in English', in a context in which this implied downgrading, literature in Gaelic being the one true kind of Irish literature in his 'Irish Ireland' perspective. Yeats responded testily, clearly unwilling to strengthen his opponent's hand by blackening a designation that Moran would then apply all the more eagerly, but making the point that some literature in English (he cited William Allingham's 'Farewell to Ballyshannon') was quintessentially Irish. And, he implied, an exclusivist concept of Irish literature based on language would also exclude the Latin writing of the early Irish Church.[36] Boyd in his *Ireland's Literary Renaissance* (1916) uses 'Anglo-Irish' and 'Irish'

---

[35] Hugh Law, *Anglo-Irish Literature* (Dublin, 1926), pp. 7–11.
[36] Text reproduced in Tony Crowley, *The Politics of Language in Ireland, 1366–1922: a Sourcebook* (London, 2000), pp. 190–2.

interchangeably, always taking the former to be confined to that work in English which has an essentially Irish character. St John D. Seymour's *Anglo-Irish Literature 1200–1585* (1929) makes convenient use of the term but has little bearing on the contested issues of modern literature. From the 1920s, Anglo-Irish literature has almost invariably been taken to comprehend the English-language work of all Irish authors (still leaving to the argumentative the question of *who* is Irish). This is how it was understood by Daniel Corkery when he published his *Synge and Anglo-Irish Literature* (1931) in which he reiterated his Irish Irelander's conviction that it was quintessentially flawed, and this notwithstanding the fact that he had himself made an enduring contribution to it, in particular with his novel, *The Threshold of Quiet* (1917). This can be seen as just inconsistency on Corkery's part, or as a manifestation of the contradiction that awaits all ideology. Those with a more positive view of the type of literature in question were also generally content with the term in its comprehensive usage: a highly successful scholarly organisation, established in 1968, was named the International Association for the Study of Anglo-Irish Literature.

For some, following Hyde, 'Irish literature' means literature in Irish. However, Seamus Deane's *A Short History of Irish Literature* (1986) is a study – apart from an opening chapter on the Gaelic background – of English-language literature. At the same time, he defines as 'Anglo-Irish' that literature 'written in the English language by people of Irish birth and connection' (although he specifies a few exceptions), in the period beginning in the 1690s, but with an unspecified *terminus ad quem*. The literatures of Ireland are covered without discrimination between languages in Robert Welch's *Oxford Companion to Irish Literature* (1996). This indispensable and generally excellent volume concludes that 'Anglo-Irish literature is a serviceable term to describe a tradition of Irish writing in English from the Norman invasion to the literary revival'. Apart from begging a question about 'tradition', this leaves several threads hanging, but it indicates accurately enough the current constraints on the usage. As he shows in *Irish Classics* (London, 2000), Declan Kiberd is able to dissolve the problem by treating of works in both languages with equal facility, but this solution is not available to many. In literature, as in other fields, problems of nomenclature signal the ongoing inventions and reinventions of the Irish nation. (In reference to political history, the term 'Anglo-Irish' has different but also fluid connotations: see chapter two.)

The representation of stock national characters in fiction can have an impact on nation invention. From around 1600, Irish stereotypes were appearing on the London stage thus launching the phenomenon of the 'stage Irishman', a term generally extended to include stereotypical figures in prose fiction. The stage Irishman was at different times over the centuries treacherous, deceitful, indolent, belligerent, truculent, loquacious, verbally blundering, unreasoning, droll, soft-hearted, sentimental, sociable and much more besides. Little of this was entirely complimentary and some of it was positively demeaning.[37] Not surprisingly, the stage Irishman became a *bête noire* in the eyes of many of the inventors of the nation. However, before resorting to a plaint about colonialism, it should be borne in mind that national stereotypes were part of the stock in trade of European fiction from early modern times, and indeed there are much earlier precedents ('All Cretans are liars.'). If London had stage Irishmen, it also had stage Welshmen and stage Scotsmen, and Paris had stage Greeks, stage Italians, stage Spaniards and stage Jews.

There were particular complications in the representation of Irish characters for an English audience. One was that Ireland had recurring political overtones, so that changing political circumstances affected the response to any evocation of the country. Another was that the speech of an Irish character could not be credibly represented, whether with negative, favourable or neutral intent, without endeavouring to render Hiberno-English accent and usage. This remained an issue even for those primarily addressing Irish audiences, either as dramatists or as novelists.

Charles J. Kickham (1828–82), in the widely popular *Knocknagow or the Homes of Tipperary* (1873), deals with the problem by giving standard English voices to characters over an implausibly wide range of social strata. However, the comic servant Barney Brodherick, alias 'Wattletoes', is endowed with a startling (if convincingly represented) 'brogue', a dwarfish physique in cast-off clothes, and a propensity to enunciate the kind of verbal gaffe known for generations as an 'Irish bull'. The stage Irishman was acceptable to the inheritors of the Irish earth provided that he was confined to the ranks of the perpetually dispossessed. In other ways, too, the repudiation of a set of national images deemed to be demeaning may have been less than complete. The actor Cyril Cusack and others may have reflected dominant attitudes in demonstrating successfully against the showing in Dublin in 1930 of the American film *Smiling Irish Eyes*, the hero of which was a character 'tenuously connected with [Samuel] Lover's [stage Irish] Rory O'Moore',[38] but at least one very prevalent self-image still owes much to a benign version of the stage Irishman (complete with the implications for gender roles): a great way with words (unlike others that could be mentioned) and universally liked, because so friendly, easygoing and ready for a song.

The literary revival has been given a place in political history that is the product of a number of inventions. The Irish Parliamentary Party was thrown into disarray by the fall of Parnell in 1890 and his unexpected death in 1891. By the end of the decade, the burgeoning of cultural and associational life, and in particular the literary revival, was already being explained

---

[37] See Joep Leersen, *Meere Irish and Fíor-Ghael* (Cork, 2nd edn., 1996), *passim*.
[38] *The Oxford Companion to Irish Literature*, p. 535.

as a response to the post-Parnell political vacuum. Subsequently, Yeats was to promote this idea assiduously and it has become something of a commonplace in historical surveys. In fact the literary, language and Gaelic sports movements all either had their beginnings or received crucial momentum during the years preceding the demise of Parnell. Indeed, it could be plausibly argued that it was the political successes of nationalists in the 1880s, rather than the political malaise of the 1890s, that inspired the development of culturally nationalist projects. None of this is to deny that some who were disgusted by politics in the 1890s turned to cultural matters for an alternative.

Writing towards the end of his life, as if in review of the moral responsibilities of the artist, Yeats was to ask:

> Did that play of mine send out
> Certain men the English shot?
> ('The man and the echo' in *Last Poems* (1936–39))

For much of the 1880s and 1890s Yeats had been a member of the IRB, albeit with no known commitments beyond the rhetorical and the convivial. This phase of his politics found its most memorable expression in the play *Cathleen Ni Houlihan*, which he co-authored with Lady Gregory in 1902. In the setting of the French landing at Killala in 1798, the play idealises sacrifice in the service of a personalised Ireland, an old woman rejuvenated at the end of the play as a girl 'with the walk of a queen', when her young men go forth to redeem her 'four green fields'. It received public performances in April 1902 with Maud Gonne in the title role and was praised ecstatically by advanced nationalists delighting in its celebration of revolution. It may be, indeed, that *Cathleen Ni Houlihan* then or later captured the imagination of some young men who, as a consequence, took a series of decisions which led to them being in arms against the Crown in 1916, but this would be very difficult to establish. A majority of the signatories of the proclamation of the Irish Republic on Easter Monday 1916 had been activists in the literary or language revivals, or both. The president of the provisional government of the Irish Republic, Patrick Pearse, had spun for himself and others a mystical ideology of revolution and sacrifice, drawing on Christian theology and on the Old Irish sagas. He had made of the legendary Cuchulainn a symbol of heroic self-sacrifice in battle.

Given the above, it is small wonder that the 1916 Rising and the subsequent emergence of the independent Irish state (in 1922) are frequently seen as having a causal connection with the cultural movements: there are enough misleading clues to lead the unwary into a straightforward case of the logical fallacy of *post hoc ergo propter hoc*. The political and strategic framework within which the Rising was planned and executed was in fact quite independent of literary or linguistic movements. Since early in the

nineteenth century it was clear to be seen that the only prospect of a separation of Ireland from Britain lay in taking advantage of British involvement
in a major war. England's difficulty would be Ireland's opportunity. The
Fenian organisation was formed in the late 1850s by men who had seen the
apparent opportunity of the Crimean War come to nothing and were determined not to be unprepared for the Anglo-French war which they expected
to follow shortly afterwards. For much of the 1860s they hoped that the
Civil War would give rise to an Anglo-American conflict and, with that
prospect fading, some of them attempted to precipitate matters by invading
Canada. Contrary to all that might have been predicted, Britain avoided
another war with a major power until 1914. The IRB had survived through
the interval, going through various transformations, and it was from within
the IRB that the Rising was mooted and planned. However, not even this
organisational survival was necessary: the opportunity created by the Great
War was an invitation to separatists, whether or not they had some generations of strategic thinking behind them. Tom Clarke, the oldest of the signatories, was a republican veteran with a record of nearly forty years, fifteen
of which he had spent in prison. His participation in the Rising owed nothing to the cultural nationalism of preceding decades. John Devoy, who
directed the crucial Irish-American input into the plan for an insurrection,
had been waiting for this opportunity for forty-five years. It is undoubtedly
the case that the cultural movements coloured the political revolution, but
the abandonment of Home Rule in favour of the demand for self-determination – like the revolution of October 1917 in Russia – came about as a
consequence of strategic and political upheavals, domestic and foreign.

Before 1916, Yeats, at least, had reached an accommodation with British
power. By 1910 his republican youth was so far behind him that he lobbied
for a civil list pension and was awarded £150 per annum.[39] *Cathleen Ni
Houlihan* may have struck a stridently irredentist note, and there may have
been a sensation about the failure to close for the death of King Edward VII
in May 1910, but the theatre was not seen as posing a threat of subversion.
Indeed its earliest pledge-givers included W.E.H. Lecky, historian and
Liberal Unionist MP for Trinity College Dublin, and John P. Mahaffy,
Fellow of Trinity College, and a sharp critic of the Irish-Ireland programme.
British army officers were among the most reliable patrons of the Abbey.
When, in the aftermath of the Rising, the long-serving chief secretary,
Augustine Birrell, was endeavouring to explain how he had been taken by
surprise, he cited his perception of the national theatre as a forum where the
'wild sentimental passion' tending towards revolution was being tamed.[40]

---

[39] Foster, *W.B. Yeats: A Life*, vol. 1, p. 428.
[40] Quoted in W.G. FitzGerald, *The Voice of Ireland: A Survey of the Race and Nation from
all Angles by the Foremost Leaders at Home and Abroad* (Dublin and London, n.d.
[1924]), p. 468.

The national and international stature of the output of the Irish literary revival is so great that unjustified conclusions can easily be drawn about its impact on the literary culture of its time in Ireland. The literary revival was concerned mainly with poetry and drama, but the mainstay of popular literature for all classes had for long been prose literature, either in magazine, or more particularly in book form. Moore, Corkery, James Stephens, Seamus O'Kelly and James Joyce account for most of the prose produced down to 1923 that can with any conviction be advanced as a product of the literary revival. Meanwhile the long-established genres of serious and popular fiction, the great bulk of Brown's seventeen hundred, continued to flourish.

A case in point is the continued popularity of Kickham's *Knocknagow*. This rambling story of rural life around the middle of the nineteenth century first appeared in book form in 1873, but only became widely popular after the publication of a third edition in 1887. Thereafter it continued to be reprinted regularly by Duffy and then Gill until the 1970s. It was also reprinted many times in an American edition by Benziger Brothers of New York. *The Field Day Anthology of Irish Writing* (1991) opines that it is the most frequently reprinted of all Irish novels, but does not deal with the implications of this significant fact, if fact it be.[41] Insofar as *Knocknagow* deals with politics it is warmly nationalist, but in a generalised way that displays very little of the particular ideology that might be expected in the work of a leading Fenian who had spent over three years in gaol for his politics. The excerpt presented in the *Field Day Anthology* is unrepresentative in featuring the views of a minor and untypical character, Phil Morris, a somewhat cantankerous veteran (possibly) of 1798, arguing the case for 'physical force'. Insofar as *Knocknagow* has a dominant plot it concerns the fortunes of tenant farmers at the mercy of an unscrupulous agent and of an inattentive (but well-meaning) landlord. Far from ringing any Celtic note or campaigning for de-Anglicisation, *Knocknagow* happily depicts a society eagerly adopting the manners and modes of Victorian respectability. Brown's summary is worth quoting:

> One of the greatest, if not the greatest of all Irish novels. Yet it is not so much a novel as a series of pictures of life in a Tipperary village. We are introduced to every one of its inhabitants and learn to love them nearly all before the end. Everything in the book has been not merely seen from without but *lived* by the author. It is full of exquisite little humorous and pathetic traits. The description of the details of peasant life is quite photographic in fidelity, yet not wearisome. There is the closest observation of human nature and of individual peculiarities. It is realism of the best kind. The incidents related and some of the discussions throw much light on the land question. The author does not, however, lecture or

---

[41] Vol. 2, p. 248.

rant on the subject. Occasionally there are tracts of middle class conversation that would, I believe, be dull for most readers.

Unlike Joyce, Kickham does not describe bodily functions, and unlike Yeats he does not treat of fairies. Such reticences were part of the appeal of *Knocknagow* for a society anxious to assure itself and the world of its respectability, and to be allowed to suppress its embarrassments – a point well caught by Terry Eagleton.[42] (Brown castigated Moore and Joyce for their 'entire absence of reticence'.) In 1895 at Ballyvadlea, within a few miles of the location of the fictional Knocknagow, the real Bridget Cleary was burned to death by her husband before a group of neighbours and relations when his application of folk antidotes to a suspected fairy intervention went disastrously wrong.[43]

As a literary achievement, *Knocknagow* is scarcely even in the second division. But while it thus may have little place as an enduring ornament to the nation, it is in another respect a key document in the invention of one particular time-bound version of the nation. It reflected, and in turn burnished, as no other work did, the self-image of the 'peasant proprietors' whose ethos dominated most of the island from Parnell to Lemass. It can be asserted with some confidence that *Knocknagow* was ten times better known to 'the boys who fought the Black and Tans' than either Cú Chulainn or Cathleen, the daughter of Houlihan. And neither novel nor play is likely on its own to have sent out anyone to shoot or to be shot.

The case of *Knocknagow* shows that in literature as elsewhere the reception of 'de-Anglicisation' was a complex and incomplete business. In this respect, the popular uses of literacy deserve some attention. *Ireland's Own*, a magazine specialising in historical adventure tales, quizzes and yarns of ghostly happenings in ruined castles, flourished from 1902 onwards. This was the epitome of fireside reading for the multitudes. The frame of reference was Irish and the tone was sufficiently national to appeal to collective loyalties, without being so specific as to risk alienating any significant body of customers. For communal entertainment around the fireside or in the parish hall, the recitation had come into its own by the late nineteenth century. Texts could be lifted from school books, cut from newspapers and magazines or located in dedicated volumes. *The Reciter's Treasury of Irish Verse and Prose* (1915), edited by Alfred Percival Graves, was a deluxe anthology. The genre was close to one segment of the popular song repertoire to which Graves had contributed the light-hearted 'Father O'Flynn'. There was nationality here, but without political specificity, and without the linguistic purity or literary pretensions of the revivalists. The hold of such material, and the circulation of *Ireland's Own,* was dented, not by the stric-

---

[42] Terry Eagleton, *Heathcliff and the Great Hunger* (London, 1995), p. 153.
[43] Angela Bourke, *The Burning of Bridget Cleary: A True Story* (London, 1999).

tures of language and literary revivalists, but by later social and technologi-
cal changes such as the proliferation of the cinema and television. These
same changes were to render futile the campaigns of purists of all kinds
against the instruments and forces of Anglicisation and vulgarity. D.P.
Moran put the challenge in typically colourful wording at the very beginning of the twentieth century when referring to the material on which the
Gaelic League had to work:

> Observe it in the music halls yelling inanely at low jokes and indecent songs;
> watch it coming from a patriotic meeting roaring "The boys of Wexford"
> between the "half-way" houses; see it in petticoats in its thousands filing into the
> circulating libraries and the penny novelette shops for reams of twaddle about
> Guy and Belinda.[44]

Just as the tone of *Ireland's Own* demonstrates the popularity of nationalist
sentiment, so the demand for 'penny novelettes' and for the despised low-
brow English newspapers shows its limitations.

If a great Irish novel did not emerge in the nineteenth century, amends
were certainly made in the twentieth. James Joyce's *Ulysses* (1922) is the
national literary showpiece beyond compare: worldwide, James Joyce now
rivals Shakespeare as a subject of proliferating scholarly studies. The ornament has been but belatedly put on display. The dominant ideology of the
Irish Free State provided little scope for the celebration of literature in
English; on the contrary, it encouraged a spirit of vigilantism with respect to
books, so that self-appointed or ecclesiastically sanctioned guardians of
morality felt entitled, and even obliged, to prevent others from reading anything that they themselves found objectionable. With the Censorship of
Publications Act of 1929, the state forestalled the vigilantes by establishing
a censorship board that proceeded to ban books in great numbers. Any
explicit treatment of sexual matters was sufficient to have a work of fiction
banned (and the same applied to books providing information on contraception). Thousands of books by foreign authors were proscribed and
almost every major Irish writer and many lesser ones had works similarly
affected. Whatever else newly independent Ireland wished to cultivate for
adornment, it was not modernist literature in English. The legal situation
was not modified until 1967. *Ulysses* was never banned, for the simple reason that its reputation was so notorious that before the 1960s nobody
would have invited inevitable trouble by openly importing or selling it. A
few bookshops stocked it, but only under the counter. It can be safely
asserted that not before the 1970s did the Irish readership of *Ulysses* exceed
that of *Knocknagow*. With the subsequent eclipse of the censoring mind-set,
the way was clear for the adoption of Joyce as a national asset. In recent

---

[44]   D.P. Moran, *The Philosophy of Irish Ireland* (Dublin, 1905), p. 80.

decades, the celebration of 16 June (the Bloomsday of *Ulysses*) has become the subject of public recognition and commercial promotion.

Joyce had fled the encroaching nets long before 1922, and Samuel Beckett (1906–89) was settled permanently in Paris by the late 1930s. Partially in reaction to the repressive ethos of the new Ireland, the main literary figures of the period from the 1920s to the 1950s still in the country, such as Yeats, Sean Ó Faoláin, Frank O'Connor and Austin Clarke were engaged in a critique of the prevailing order, something that bolstered a concept of literary folk as prophetic commentators on the law and the polity, if not exactly Shelleyan legislators. If some poets, playwrights and novelists have maintained nation-forming ambitions, they have been outdone in this by a section of academic interpreters. By the 1980s, aesthetics was falling out of fashion in university departments of literature: as a token of this the term literature itself was repudiated in favour of 'writings'. As a new principle of organisation, the discipline (or, to be more exact, dominant segments of it) embraced political critique. This was particularly the case in the United States of America, where most English literature departments (unlike most history departments) regard Ireland as prime matter for study.

The major work of nation invention in the realm of Irish literature in the last quarter of the twentieth century was the *Field Day Anthology of Irish Writing*, edited by Seamus Deane, in three volumes (1991). This was undertaken under the auspices of Field Day, a company which had played an innovative role in the cultural politics of the preceding decade, beginning as a theatrical group and expanding its scope to include publication of a variety of mainly polemical pamphlets. The use of 'writings' rather than 'literature' in the title of the *Field Day Anthology*, implies a refusal to 'privilege' the aesthetic over the rhetorical. Accordingly, political manifestos and programmatic statements from various areas of activity are included. Interestingly, this follows the precedent of the first edition (1880) of the *Cabinet of Irish Literature*: only for the second edition (1906) was the more exclusive understanding of literature employed. Field Day emulates the *Cabinet of Irish Literature* and Justin McCarthy's *Irish Literature* (1904) in its inclusion of Irish-born authors without distinction of language, and goes further in giving appropriate coverage to the deposit of Irish writing in Latin and Norman-French. Having dealt thus resolutely with the issues of the earlier twentieth century, the editor came under criticism for not having attended to concerns of more recent vintage, specifically for inadequate recognition of the place and contribution of women. Two volumes of writings by and about women appeared in 2003.[45]

Historians in Ireland acquired in the 1930s a set of conventions allowing them, by and large, to tolerate one another's political allegiances. These

---

[45] Angela Bourke et al. (eds), *Irish Women's Writings and Traditions (Field Day Anthology 4 and 5)* (Cork, 2003).

arrangements, for all their faults, have survived several heavy squalls, and may or may not be set to endure into the future. That such accommodation is more elusive in the field of Irish/Anglo-Irish literature/'writing' studies seems evident from editorial attitudes in the *Field Day Anthology* and from other sources.[46] The influence on this situation of a pervasive insurgency in literature departments in American universities merits exploration. However worthy battling the imperialists may be in US academe, in Ireland fighting the British about literature, or anything else, quickly involves contending with inhabitants of Ireland in the persons of Northern unionists. Field Day has yet to find a solution to this conundrum.

Indeed, Field Day conveys a sense of being a service not simply to the nation but to an assertive variety of nationalism in search of a substitute for an abandoned but sorely missed essentialism. (The answer may lie, deflatingly, in football rather than in the written word.) Thus, when the *Anthology* embraces Swift and Burke there is a sense that they are being wrested from the English as part of a zero-sum game against the old enemy. Whatever the intent, the essays of 'political turn' literary scholars in comprehension of nation, politics or society on the basis of canonical texts and without recourse to the range of sources utilised in other disciplines, *ipso facto* abandon openness. The ostensible scope of Declan Kiberd's celebrated *Inventing Ireland* (1995) is very creditably – restricted in the subtitle: *the literature of the modern nation.*

If the *Field Day Anthology* (vols 1–3) comes to be seen as the expression of a time-bound and unsustainable ideological take on Irish literature, it will still stand as a monumental achievement, to be plundered by the architects of smaller, if more viable, projects. As for benchmarks in Irish cultural history, of enduring significance are the surveys by Roger McHugh and Maurice Harmon of Irish literature in English as it was viewed around 1980, on the eve of critical meltdown.[47]

Literature in English provides Irish nationality with some of its most acclaimed ornaments. The pantheon includes Swift, Goldsmith, Burke, Wilde, Shaw, O'Casey, Yeats, Joyce and Beckett, to mention only the dead. Three of these – Yeats (1923), Shaw (1925) and Beckett (1969) – and Seamus Heaney (1995) have won the ultimate accolade of a Nobel prize. Almost all spent large portions of their lives outside of Ireland and six of them also feature in the literary halls of fame of Britain or France. Genius does not worry about passports or zero-sum games, and neither does the audience for national icons.

---

[46] See Edna Longley, *The Living Stream: Literature and Revisionism in Ireland* (Newcastle-upon-Tyne, 1994).

[47] M. Harmon, *Select Bibliography for the Study of Anglo-Irish Literature and its Background* (Dublin, 1977); R. McHugh and M. Harmon, *A Short History of Anglo-Irish Literature from its Origins to the Present Day* (Dublin, 1982).

|6|

Music, song and dance

Irishness has particularly rich and complex connotations in the realm of music, a situation epitomised by the role of the harp over centuries as a national symbol. It so happens that more than half the Bronze Age horns known to have survived from antiquity in Europe and the Middle East have been discovered in Ireland.[1] As this fascinating fact comes to be more fully appreciated, it will undoubtedly provide fuel for the Irish music myth. Indeed, already there have been recreations on screen in which the ancient horns feature alongside the popular twentieth-century percussion instrument, the bodhrán. Throughout almost all of its millennium and a half of recorded history, which begins more than a thousand years after the period of the Bronze Age horns, Ireland has had a reputation for music. Even Giraldus Cambrensis could write:

> It is only in the case of musical instruments that I find any commendable diligence in the people. They seem to me to be incomparably more skilled in these than any other people I have seen.[2]

That Giraldus, so disparaging of the inhabitants in other respects, praises their music-making in this way can be taken as telling evidence, but what it proves principally is the force of the myth. Neither empirical investigation nor original insight was a strong suit with Giraldus, and it seems likely that no amount of accomplishment on the part of Irish musicians would have won his approbation if praising Irish music had not been a well-established trope. The sources for hard information on the characteristics of music in

---

1 P.F. Wallace, *A Guide to the National Museum of Ireland* (Dublin, 2000), p. 25.
2 Gerald of Wales, *The History and Topography of Ireland* (Harmondsworth, 1982) translated by J.J. O'Meara, p. 103.

Ireland in medieval times are not scarce but they are difficult of access and the process of interpreting them has a long way to go.[3]

The pre-eminence and longevity of the harp is one of the few apparent certainties. The harp was in use in antiquity throughout Europe and the Middle East. A distinctive version of the instrument featuring wire strings came to prominence around AD 1000 in Ireland, and over subsequent centuries this flourished also throughout Britain and elsewhere in northern Europe. Like the Bronze Age horns, the wire-strung harp represented the technology of a particular epoch, even if it did prove to be particularly long-lived. Reflection on the date of its emergence should be enough to dispel any notion of its being part of an ancient, misty 'Celtic' inheritance. From as early as the thirteenth century, the harp (in gold and on a blue field) had been identified as a heraldic emblem of Ireland. But the decisive development in the installation of the harp as a national symbol was its depiction on the Irish coinage issued by Henry VIII in 1534. This is another reminder that the invention of national symbols is not a monopoly of nationalists. Installed as ruler of the entirety of the two islands, in 1603 King James I adopted a royal coat of arms in which Ireland was, and still is, represented by the harp. Almost every subsequent regime in Ireland has used a version of the harp, with or without the crown, as a state symbol. Successive patriotic and nationalist movements have sought not to displace the harp but to possess it for themselves. The harp featured on the seal and coinage of the Catholic Confederation in the 1640s and on a green flag hoisted by the Confederate General, Owen Roe O'Neill. Elements within the Volunteer movement in the later eighteenth century used the harp as an emblem and the United Irishmen made extensive symbolic and metaphorical use of it. (Set beneath the image of a harp, they used the motto: 'It is new strung and shall be heard'). In the mid-nineteenth century, the Guinness firm (strong supporters of the Union) astutely adopted the harp as a trademark on the way to making their famous product into the 'national beverage'.[4]

Meanwhile, what of the instrument itself and its practitioners? Having served over many centuries as privileged, professional retainers with a well-defined function within the Gaelic socio-political system, harpers found their world turned upside down in the decades around 1600. Frequently tar-

[3]   Ann Buckley, '"and his voice trembled like a terrible thunderstorm . . .": music as symbolic sound in Medieval Irish society' in Gerard Gillen and Harry White (eds), *Music and Irish Cultural History* (Dublin, 1995) (Irish Musical Studies, 3), pp. 13–76; see Brian Boydell, 'Music before 1700' in T.W. Moody and W.E. Vaughan (eds), *Eighteenth-century Ireland, 1691–1800* (Oxford, 1986) (A New History of Ireland, vol. iv), pp. 542–67.

[4]   Barra Boydell, 'The iconography of the Irish harp as a national symbol' in P.F. Devine and Harry White (eds), *The Maynooth International Musicological Conference, 1995: Selected Proceedings, part two* (Dublin, 1996) (Irish Musical Studies, 5), pp. 131–45; idem, 'The United Irishmen, music, harps, and national identity' in *Eighteenth-century Ireland: Iris and dá chultúr* , xiii (1998), pp. 44–51; G.A. Hayes-McCoy, *A History of Irish Flags from Earliest Times* (Dublin, 1979).

geted for collective repression or annihilation while still part of that system, once detached from it they might sink or swim as individuals in the new order. The destruction of harps, as of church organs, was an aspect of the iconoclasm of the Commonwealth period. Before and after the 1650s some harpers were lionised by the lords of the new dispensation. In fact, many responded successfully to the changed patterns of patronage. Through the seventeenth and into the eighteenth century they were purveyors of a wide range of music. This included exquisite airs of undoubted but unmeasurable antiquity. Also included was material of more recent origin: the most celebrated of all harpers, Turlough Carolan (1670–1738), was a prolific composer of tunes, some of them influenced by the work of continental contemporaries such as Arcangelo Corelli (1653–1713).[5] By the 1790s, practitioners of the harp were few and aged. Their instrument, together with much of its associated store of music, had been superseded by the violin and union (or uileann) pipes, with repertoires that only partially coincided with that of the harp. Even the establishment of harp schools in Belfast and Dublin in the early 1800s did not reverse the decline of the old craft. The new century witnessed the production in Dublin by John Egan of a new variety of harp, gut-stringed, with modern mechanics, modelled on European exemplars and geared to the needs of the middle-class drawing room and the concert hall. This, effectively a different instrument, quickly became the dominant style of harp in Ireland as elsewhere.[6]

When John Milton in 'Lycidas' referred to the 'old bards, the famous Druids', he contributed to the concept of the bard as a talismanic figure of the older insular societies. This notion conflated various functions, real and imagined, and in the cases of Wales and Ireland its main accoutrement was the harp, although in fact the medieval Irish bard was of secondary status within the learned classes and was a practitioner of verbal composition and not of music.[7] The cult of things antiquarian and 'Celtic' in the eighteenth century endowed the harp with a semi-sacral status, apart altogether from its political symbolism in Ireland. The identification of the harp with the emerging antiquarian patriotism of the age was well exemplified in Joseph Cooper Walker's *Historical Memoirs of the Irish Bards* published by the Royal Irish Academy in 1786.

In Ireland, as elsewhere, the eighteenth century witnessed a rising interest in popular music on the part of cultural elites. Anthologies of popular airs identified as Irish began to appear in the 1720s. The popular tunes that were the distinguishing innovation of John Gay's *Beggar's Opera*, produced with such enormous success in London in 1728, included several that were iden-

---

5   Donal O'Sullivan, *Carolan: The Life, Times and Music of an Irish Harper* (Dublin, new edn., 2001).

6   Fintan Vallely (ed.), *The Companion to Irish Traditional Music* (Cork, 1999), pp. 169ff.

7   See Kenneth Nicholls, *Gaelic and Gaelicised Ireland in The Later Middle Ages* (Dublin, 1972), pp. 82–3.

tified with Ireland, and this was even more pronounced in subsequent works on the 'ballad opera' model produced to acclaim in London and Dublin over a period of decades. Harp music and airs such as 'Eileen Aroon' had a place alongside the works of internationally celebrated composers at Dublin's fashionable concerts at least from the 1740s.[8]

Not surprisingly, it was the inheritance of the harp, at once lionised and endangered, rather than any other area of this musical life that attracted the attention of antiquarians. Bardic conventions, initiated primarily by exiles living in London, were a well-established feature of cultural life in Wales. But it was apparently the example of Scottish nation-inventors organising bagpipes festivals that inspired John Dungan, a merchant resident in Denmark, to sponsor a competitive assembly of harpers in his native Granard, Co. Longford. This convened in 1781 and in a number of subsequent years, attracting no more than nine practitioners on any occasion. Ten harpers, all of them very elderly, attended the more famous Belfast harp festival of July 1792. The organisers of this event were functioning in the milieu in which the Society of United Irishmen – with the harp as its emblem – was flourishing. They declared themselves to be motivated by concern for the honour of the country, being solicitous 'to preserve from oblivion the few fragments which have been permitted to remain as monuments to the refined taste and genius of their ancestors'. They provided that scholars would be present to make a record of the presentations of the harpers.[9]

Irish music had been written down and published for generations previously for its own sake or for its commercial potential. In July 1792 it was to be transcribed and preserved as an inheritance of the nation. The canonisation of Irish music was under way. When Edward Bunting, the transcriber at the Belfast Harp Festival, declared in 1796 that it was 'a debt which every man owes to his country . . . to render permanent the fleeting products of every species of genius'[10], he was giving expression to one of the most characteristic impulses of the nation inventor, and was showing that within a few decades of the publication of Herder's *Abhandlung ueber den Ursprung der Sprache* ('Treatise on the Origin of Language', 1772), the sensibility that it represented was touching progressive Presbyterian Belfast. Typical of the nation invention process was the election of one element of the available corpus of music as the bearer of the stamp of authentic nationality. The harp was accorded privilege because of assumptions, founded on the bardic myth, about the antiquity of its repertoires. This equation of presumed antiquity with authenticity made no allowance for the great bulk of the music played and sung by contemporaries. In the event, Bunting did not

---

[8]   Nicholas Carolan, *'The Most Celebrated Irish Tunes': The Publishing of Irish Music in the Eighteenth Century* (Cork, 1990); Brian Boydell, *A Dublin Musical Calendar, 1700–60* (Dublin, 1988).

[9]   Charlotte M. Fox, *Annals of the Irish Harpers* (London, 1911), pp. 97–8.

[10] Quoted in Breandán Breathnach, *Ceol rince na hEireann* (Dublin, 1976), p. 103.

confine himself to the repertoire of the harpers in compiling his three volumes of the 'ancient music of Ireland', all with arrangements for the
pianoforte, published in 1796, 1809 and 1840 respectively. Edward Bunting
(1773–1843) did not initiate the collection of Irish music for publication,
but he is the anchor figure in the great endeavour of music collecting as service to the nation that runs from the late eighteenth century to the late twentieth. A native of Armagh and a music teacher and church organist by
profession, Bunting resided in Belfast for many years with the family of
Henry Joy McCracken, who was executed for his part in the 1798 Rising in
Antrim. He followed up his transcription work at the Belfast harp festival
with fieldwork in various parts of Ulster and Connacht. The music he published represents but a small fraction of what he amassed. The piano provided a new and international dimension to the market, and Irish
entrepreneurs were not slow to respond. Bunting may have delighted in
recording the inheritance of the harpers for antiquarian and patriotic reasons, but he published the music in arrangements for the piano, an agent of
international diffusion and commercial exploitation. There would have
been little point in publishing it otherwise, but the transposition, like any
translation, could not convey the original intact (which is not to suggest that
there was a pure Platonic form of the tunes at any stage).

George Petrie (1790–1866) was the leading light of the next generation of
collectors. An artist by profession, Petrie stands as one of the giants of scholarly exploration of the Irish past. It was he who in 1833 made the decisive,
if not immediately triumphant, judgement on the controverted question of
the origins of round towers. He made visual and written records of vast
quantities of architectural and archaeological remains; he worked with John
O'Donovan and Eugene O'Curry on the Ordnance Survey; he rescued and
studied a large number of artefacts; and he published several books. In 1851
he was founder and first president of the Society for the Preservation and
Publication of the Melodies of Ireland, which four years later published *The
Petrie Collection of the Ancient Music of Ireland*. Petrie succeeded in proving, if proof were needed, that the population of Ireland possessed a treasure
trove of enchanting airs, but he failed to vindicate his Herderian notions
about a well-spring of pure native music. In fact, his published collection is
quite an eclectic mixture.[11]

Like Petrie, Patrick Weston Joyce (1827–1914) delved into a wide range
of Irish scholarship, publishing not only on music but also on grammar, literature, phonology, ancient and general history and place names. A native
of County Limerick, he was brought to Dublin in 1856 as one of a hand-
picked group of outstanding national school teachers. He graduated from
Trinity College in 1861 and was principal of Marlborough Street Training

---

[11] George Petrie, *The Petrie Collection of the Ancient Music of Ireland*, edited by David
Cooper with Irish modernised and edited by Lillis Ó Laoire (Cork, 2002).

College from 1874 to 1893. He was a member of the Society for the Preservation and Publication of the Melodies of Ireland, publishing his first collection, *Ancient Irish Music*, in 1873, and his main one, *Old Irish Folk Music and Songs*, in 1909. Joyce had contributed to Petrie's collection, and Petrie to Bunting's, and all three had drawn on the published and unpublished work of other enthusiasts.

Perhaps the most uncharacteristic of the great collectors was Francis O'Neill (1848–1936), chief of police in Chicago from 1901 to 1905. A native of south-west County Cork, O'Neill lived in Chicago from the age of twenty-five. There he found numerous other Irish people who, like himself, had brought with them an attachment to the music of home. In a classic instance of national homogenisation, O'Neill devised a system of transcribing tunes because he found that immigrants from one part of Ireland were unacquainted with tunes from another part.[12] He published *The Music of Ireland* in 1903 and *The Dance Music of Ireland – 1001 Gems* in 1907. This remained the standard work until the advent of Breandán Breathnach's *Ceol rince na hÉireann*, more than half a century later.[13] Working on his own initiative, for the Department of Education, and finally with the Irish Folklore Commission, Breathnach (1912–85) systematically processed and supplemented existing collections and made himself the leading twentieth-century authority on Irish music, estimating that it contained over seven thousand dance tunes. As an exercise in music-historical scholarship, the ultimate affirmation of a national canon is Aloys Fleischmann's massive *Sources of Irish Traditional Music, c.1600–1855* (1998). The establishment in Dublin in 1987 of the state-funded Irish Traditional Music Archive marked the institutional recognition of the place of popular music in the creation of an Irish nationality. The progress of study and reflection on what was not until recently a very fashionable subject of academic notice is epitomised by Fintan Vallely's invaluable compilation, *The Companion to Irish Traditional Music* (Cork, 1999).

As a historical phenomenon, popular song, like popular music, is much more complex than the canonical approach can represent. The diversity of popular song in early modern Ireland was enhanced by the introduction, with English and Scottish settlers, of the 'old' ballad, a European genre that would be altered in a variety of ways by local influences and the passage of time. Meanwhile, songs in Irish and in English were being sung to tunes, some of which were common to Ireland, England and Scotland, while others were to be found only in Ireland; and anything found only in Ireland was unlikely to be found throughout Ireland. As elsewhere in western Europe from the seventeenth century, songs of all kinds were circulated in cheap printed form as single-page broadsheets sold by street 'ballad singers', a cus-

12   Liz Doherty in *Companion to Irish Traditional Music*, p. 285.
13   Vol. 1, 1963; vol. 2, 1976; vol. 3, 1985; vol. 4, 1997.

tom that survived at cattle fairs and hurling matches past the middle of the twentieth century. There was constant interaction between processes of written and oral transmission, although Irish-language song remained largely in the oral mode, and, when committed to paper, was more likely to be in manuscript than in print. The composition of new songs to existing airs was the concern of oral practitioners, of amateur pen-pushers and of commercially minded professionals. Occasionally, newly written or newly discovered airs were added to the repertoire. In any case, airs were constantly being modified to accommodate changing tastes and the evolving technology of musical instruments.

While politics and its conflicts did not dominate the area of popular song, they did provide a significant input to the corpus. Following the example of the Volunteers in the 1780s, the United Irishmen in the 1790s made use of the song culture of the day to promote their cause, producing in 1795 the songbook, *Paddy's Resource*. The colossus of Irish songwriting, Thomas Moore (1779–1852), combined United Ireland inspiration with the personal preoccupations of a Romantic poet. As a student in Trinity College from 1794, Moore encountered and embraced the ideas of the United Irishmen: his closest friends were Robert Emmet and William Hudson, both activists, but Moore himself was never a man for the front line. His political outlook and his musical talent drew Moore to Edward Bunting's collection of airs. By 1799 Moore was in London, intending to study for the bar. Instead he became a celebrity, thanks to the outstanding attractiveness of his personality, his eloquent conversation and the publication of a book of verse – a translation of the odes of the Ancient Greek poet, Anacreon. Down on his luck in 1806 and back in Dublin, Moore was introduced to John and William Power, two enterprising musical publishers. For them he agreed to provide melodies – new songs set to old airs that could hopefully emulate the success of various Scottish anthologies. The result was the famous series of 'Moore's Melodies', 124 in all, published in ten parts from 1808 to 1834. The melodies were well geared to the taste of the age and enjoyed enormous success in Britain and on the continent of Europe. Moore ranked with his friend Lord Byron and Sir Walter Scott as an icon of English-language Romanticism in the eyes of European contemporaries. Clearly the attraction lay to some extent in the astute selection of airs, but the key factor was the quality of the songs and in particular the exquisite matching of air and song.

The melodies obviously chimed in with the cultivated sensibility of the age, even if their sentimentalising of fellowship, parting and loss would appear tedious and cloying to later generations. About one third of the melodies have an Irish political content, and it is one redolent of the rhetoric of the United Irishmen. The expression is sufficiently stylised to avoid censorship, or worse. Moore, in the introduction to the fourth number (1811), adverted to a rumour 'which had been circulated industriously in Dublin' that the delay in its appearance was owing to government interference. He dismisses the possibility as an anachronism ('ballads have long lost their revolutionary powers'), but he makes no apology for the politics of his lyrics.[14] Moore infused an awareness of Ireland as 'the sweet sad island of sorrows' into the sensibility of his own and subsequent ages. He sought to convey not simply that Ireland had a wondrous store of 'national' music (as Burns had previously done for Scotland), but that the music possessed an exquisite character that was the product of centuries of suffering under tyranny.

Through most of the nineteenth century Moore was hailed as Ireland's national poet. Even beyond mid-century some of his verses were being reproduced in broadsheet form, having made the dramatic leap from drawing-room songbook.[15] Nevertheless, Thomas Davis, who praised the melodies profusely, feared that they were too refined to be accessible to the masses. And what was currently accessible to the masses, Davis considered to be almost entirely unworthy of the nation he envisaged. Printers in Dublin, Cork, Belfast and Drogheda were able to make a living from the production of great quantities of broadside songs ('ballads' in an extended sense) of poor quality and deplorable content, an irredeemable mass, in Davis's words, of 'threadbare jests, ribaldry, mock sentiment from the heathen mythology, low thoughts and barbarous misuse of the metres and rhymes of the language'.[16] He found some Irish-language broadsheet songs recently printed in Cork to be no more uplifting than the equivalent in English. Davis was well aware that there existed a vast quantity of popular song in Irish that had never been in print, but this too he considered to be – apart from a small, older element – unworthy:

> Most . . . were composed during the last century and, therefore, their structure is irregular, their grief slavish and despairing, their joy reckless and bombastic, their religion bitter and sectarian, their politics Jacobite and concealed by extravagant and tiresome allegory.[17]

In fact the popular Irish language songs of the period bristled with terminology deriving from the seventeenth century in which Protestants were 'the foreign litter of Calvin', 'English-speaking brutes', and worse. Much of this carried over to broadsides in English. Whatever else constituted the legacy of 1798, it was not the abandonment of prejudice based on religion and pre-

---

[14] Thomas Moore, *Moore's Poetical Works Complete in One Volume* (London, 1875), pp. 220–1.

[15] Georges-Denis Zimmermann, *Songs of Rebellion: Political Street Ballads and Rebel Songs, 1780–1900* (Dublin, 1967), p. 75.

[16] Thomas Davis, 'Essay on Irish songs' in J.M. Barry (ed.), *The Songs of Ireland* (Dublin, 1845), p. 32.

[17] Ibid., p. 33.

sumed origins desired by Wolfe Tone, and which Davis in his turn hoped to achieve.[18] In both tongues, the language could be blood-curdling, as for instance in the following excerpts from a broadside occasioned by the massacre of a tithe proctor and twelve policemen at Carrickshock, County Kilkenny in 1831:

> Who could desire to see better sport,
> To see them groping among the loughs,
> Their skulls all fractured, their eyeballs broken,
> Their great long noses and ears cut off?[19]

Davis was dismissive (not altogether fairly) of *Paddy's Resource* and of the songwriting efforts of the Volunteers and the United Irishmen, and perceived that his generation had the obligation of providing, in both English and Irish, a 'ballad' literature that would elevate both popular taste and popular political attitudes. Cleaning up both the vulgarities and the atavisms of popular song, and thereby, he believed, of popular attitudes, was central to his programme. He believed that Scotland already possessed such a repertoire of popular song and that the poet Beranger had recently provided France with the same.

One of Davis's own contributions to this worthy project, 'A nation once again', utilises evangelical language and imagery and implicitly equates with sin, crude emotions and prejudices such, no doubt, as those conjured up by Carrickshock; for Davis, an 'angel voice' was speaking, and:

> It whispered, too, that 'freedom's ark
> And service high and holy
> Would be profaned by feelings dark
> And passions vain or lowly:
> For freedom comes from God's right hand
> And needs a godly train
> And righteous men must make our land
> A nation once again.

But with balladry as with so much else in his programme, Davis had no answer to the problem that assertion of nationalism required antagonism towards the imperial power, and that much of the population antagonism to England was not separable from antagonism towards Irish Protestants. A century and a half after its composition, this sober song in which Davis

---

[18] See Tom Dunne, ' "Tá Gaedhil bhocht cráidhte": memory, tradition and the politics of the poor' in Laurence M. Geary (ed.), *Rebellion and Remembrance in Modern Ireland* (Dublin, 2001), pp. 93–111; Maura Cronin, 'Memory, story and balladry: 1798 and its place in popular memory in pre-famine Ireland', ibid., pp. 112–33.

[19] Cited in Georges-Denis Zimmermann, *Songs of Irish Rebellion: Political Street Ballads and Rebel Songs, 1780–1900* (Dublin, 1967), p. 206.

identified the winning of freedom with a 'godly train' (or at least one version of this song) became synonymous with the expression of uninhibited political passions, usually in settings that Davis would certainly have regarded as bacchanalian. It is rather as if English football supporters of the less circumspect type were to adopt William Blake's 'Jerusalem' as an anthem.

In addition to what Davis and others contributed in the pages of the *Nation*, numerous individuals in subsequent decades added to the store of Irish nationalist balladry in English, for example, the dramatist Dion Boucicault (1820–90) with the best-known version of the 'The wearing of the green' in 1850, the young Fenian writer John Keegan Casey (1846–70) with 'The rising of the moon' and the journalist T.D. Sullivan (1827–1914) with 'God save Ireland' in 1867. P.J. McCall (1861–1919) was the poet laureate of the 1798 centenary, composing 'Kelly the boy from Kilann' and reworking earlier material as 'Boolavogue'. In the first decade of the twentieth century, Arthur Griffith devoted considerable time to political 'ballads' and was himself the composer of at least one successful example, 'Twenty men from Dublin town'. Even where the nationalism was uninhibited, the form and style came to conform to the norms of respectability that Davis advocated.

These political songs took their place as a substantial but minority element in a repertoire of popular song in English (from a variety of sources) that flourished through the nineteenth century and far beyond, at weddings, fairs and races, in drawing rooms, music halls and concert rooms. Charles J. Kickham (who made his own contributions to the genre of the patriotic ballad, particularly with 'Patrick Sheehan') provides, scattered throughout the pages of *Knocknagow*, a mosaic of music and song in a rural South Tipperary setting around mid-century. A band of six fifes and a large drum processes to church on Christmas morning. An expensively dressed and accoutred uileann piper circulates between the houses of nobility, gentry and Catholic clergy. Less favoured pipers and fiddlers play at country weddings. Dilettantes experiment with the concert harp and guitar, and translate songs from Irish. The daughters of wealthy farmers play the piano, particularly Moore's melodies, some of which are also rendered on the clarinet by a medical student. The piano also serves to accompany patriotic ballads from the *Nation*. As for airs, the 'Coulin' is a general favourite, but although such Irish airs are venerated, many Scottish tunes are also popular, usually sung to locally composed verses. The self-effacing hero, Mat the Thresher, excels not only at a range of sporting and agricultural skills, but also as a singer who can bring a tear to every eye in the house. His songs come to him mainly by way of broadsides purchased from itinerant sellers, and they are mostly rendered to well-known Irish airs. However, the one most popular with Mat's audiences has 'the sentimentalist of sentimental lyrics' by the contemporary Englishman, Haynes Bayley, and is entitled 'Oh, no, we never mention her'.[20] Kickham is non-judgemental about this favourite of the popular London stage and even pokes a little fun at the musically chauvinist Fr. Kearney for mistakenly taking the air to be Irish. Little trace remained, it would seem, of the practice of Irish language singing in an area which after 1798 produced one of the great examples, 'Sliabh na mBan' (not to be confused with Kickham's own 'Slievenamon').

No doubt there was a rough end to the song-making spectrum that lay beyond the reaches of Kickham's reportage, but we have in *Knocknagow* a depiction, so patently undesigning as to carry much conviction, of the emergence in rural Ireland of the broad features of the eclectic popular music and song culture of the Victorian era and beyond. While the earlier broadsides may have been ostracised for their crudity, this was in other respects an inclusivist repertoire, open to contributions from many quarters. The political section could be ignored by those who disliked it. Irish Protestant contributors included one of the most prolific of all, Percy French (1854–1920) ('The mountains of Mourne', 'Come back, Paddy Reilly, to Ballyjamesduff', etc., etc.) and Alfred Perceval Graves (1846–1931) ('Father O'Flynn').[21] Many of the songs of the American Stephen Foster were firmly established favourites in Ireland in the second half of the century. The Irish in America and in Britain participated in this national repertoire, with Irish America making a particularly strong contribution around the turn of the century ('When Irish eyes are smiling', 'Mother Machree', 'The old bog road', etc.), but also creating its own distinctive collection that did not travel particularly well across the Atlantic.[22] Over and above this collection of countrywide scope, each district adopted its own set of songs dealing with local events, places and personalities of note. Kickham's 'Slievenamon' is a prime example of this genre.

The Irish song repertoire of his time was celebrated in various ways by James Joyce, and perhaps is best known to the world at large now from the rendition of 'The lass of Aughrim' by Frank Patterson in John Houston's film *The Dead*, a version of Joyce's short story of the same name. The song itself is a particularly arresting instance of the potential complexity of Irishness being derived from the 'old' ballad genre. The most famous practitioner of the English-language popular Irish repertoire was John McCormack (1884–1945). When he made his mark at Covent Garden in 1907, McCormack became the first Irishman for a century to reach the heights of international operatic fame. He subsequently embarked on a concert career featuring operatic arias and Irish parlour songs. He became one of the world's first celebrity recording artists, thanks in large measure to the following he obtained in the USA for his Irish material. While he never

---

[20] p. 155.
[21] See Colm Ó Lochlainn, *Songwriters of Ireland in the English Tongue* (Dublin, 1967) for a fascinating survey.
[22] Mick Moloney, *Irish Music on the American Stage* (Cork, 1993).

blended with the politics of his age, the impact of his fame on Irish national self-esteem in the second, third and fourth decades of the century is inestimable.

McCormack had launched his career with victory in the solo tenor class at the Feis Cheoil of 1903 in Dublin. The Feis Cheoil was instituted in 1897, from within the same milieu that produced the Gaelic League, with the purpose to 'promote the general cultivation of music in Ireland, with particular reference to Irish music', but eventually lost its original emphasis on self-consciously Irish music, and came by the 1920s to be devoted to what, for want of any fully satisfactory terminology, we may call 'art' music – the repertoires and practices of the formal European inheritance, sometimes referred to as 'classical' music.[23] The Feis Cheoil has flourished since then with that remit, a reminder that many Irish people expend much time and effort on music that is national only in the sense of having some nationwide structures, and that is Irish, not in the sense of having a distinctive accent, but in the sense of being practised in Ireland by Irish people. Music and song that are Irish in the prescriptive sense (and on which other Irish people, and some of the same Irish people, expend much time and effort) are catered for by the Oireachtas, an annual gathering, also instituted in 1897, directly under the auspices of the Gaelic League.

Dancing as a widespread popular pastime is attested in Ireland from the seventeenth century. Forms and styles varied locally and regionally within a wider culture that extended to most corners of Britain and Ireland, and perhaps to continental Europe also. As dominant tune types emerged in the eighteenth century, the jig was associated with Ireland, the reel with Scotland, and the hornpipe with England. In any case, all three came to flourish throughout the two islands. The development and diffusion of dance forms was the work of the itinerant dancing master. Originally employed by the upper classes, he became in the course of the eighteenth century a regular feature of popular social life, teaching a greatly prized skill and giving the localities access to ever-changing trends and fashions.[24] Throughout most of Britain and Ireland dancing masters established many different types of step dance, particularly those for jigs, reels and hornpipes. Step dance as a mode of solo performance needed to be complemented by group dances to extend participation in social functions and to maximise the clientele of the dancing master. Movements for these group dances came to be drawn from a series of French models whose popularity swept across Britain and Ireland at various times in the eighteenth and early nineteenth centuries in the form of minuets, coutillons and quadrilles. That the army may have been an agent of diffusion is suggested by the fact that one of the

---

[23] Fintan Vallelly (ed.), *The Companion to Irish Traditional Music* (Cork, 1999), pp. 121–2;
      see also Joseph Ryan, 'Nationalism and Music in Ireland' (Ph.D. thesis, National University
      of Ireland (Maynooth), 1991).
[24] Breathnach, *Ceol rince na hÉireann*, pp. 43, 49–54.

most enduring of the 'set' dances was named the 'lancer'. Different combinations ('sets') of tune types and dance steps were adapted to the new movements in different regions and districts.[25] The rich variety of popular dancing in Ireland in the nineteenth century was further enhanced by the arrival and absorption of continental European dances such as the waltz and the polka. In *Knocknagow*, Mat Donovan's sister, Nellie, is unimpressed by the polka, the new dance craze holding sway in the big farmer's parlour, declaring that 'they'd soon get tired uv it – on'y for the ketchin'.'[26]

The Gaelic League quickly developed a social dimension in the years after its foundation in 1893. The prescriptive nationalist mindset dictated that the social activity, like the language, should bear the stamp of nationality. The London branch of the League held an evening of social dance on 30 October 1897 in Bloomsbury Hall, adopting the designation 'céilí' for the event, a usage borrowed from Scots Gaelic but previously unknown in Ireland. Thus was an institution born. Exclusion of less decorous songs such as 'Phil the Fluter's ball' served the sense of respectability which was also essential to the new ethos, but the available repertoires still lacked the impact of native authenticity required by the purist mentality.

A purified corpus of dances was devised by drawing on the resources of Patrick D. Reidy, a former dancing master in the Kerry and west Limerick area, then resident in Hackney. Reidy was engaged to teach a selected group of dances from his regional repertoire, excluding 'sets' and other obviously hybrid items. A troupe of his students travelled to Dublin for the Gaelic League's Oireachtas in 1901. Their display made a strong impression, and its main elements, four-hand and eight-hand reels, were soon being taught as 'céilí dances' in conjunction with the League's language classes. However, the invention of a pure Irish dance proved to be a business fraught with controversy. The cry was soon raised that four and eight-hand reels were no more authentically Irish than 'sets' and 'lancers'. The controversy that ensued in the pages of the League's newspaper, *An Claidheamh Soluis*, and elsewhere, was a classic example of cultural elitists vying for the power that comes from successfully imposing one's particular version of purity. A commission of enquiry set up by the League in 1903, and conducted with the formality of a parliamentary equivalent, served only to pour oil on the fire. With no end to the controversy in sight – and with women being pressurised to refuse invitations to take the floor for un-national dances – a stalwart of the League, Einrí Ó Muirgheasa, attempted to bring a fresh perspective:

> I will go back to fundamental principles and ask, why bother about Irish dancing at all? We find English dances spread all over the country, danced by all classes, popular and easy. Why then disturb this condition of things? What justification

---

[25] *Companion to Irish Traditional Music*, p. 346.
[26] p. 229.

is there for upsetting all this and introducing what are in most places new dances?[27]

Again in early 1906, Eoghan Brioscú intervened in a similar vein:

> Is a Frenchman the less French because he dances a waltz, a *pas de quatre*, or an Irish jig? No, certainly not. Then an Irishman is not the less Irish because he waltzes or joins in a set of lancers.[28]

But if prescription and purism were in order in the field of linguistics, what right did Ó Muirgheasa and Brioscú have to exclude them from dance? Eventually, the Gaelic League passed its control of the forms and structure of céilí dancing to a specialised offshoot, the Irish Dancing Commission (An Coimisiún le Rincí Gaelacha), and the work of canon foundation was crowned with the publication in 1939 of *Ár rincí fóirne*, effectively the code of céilí dancing. Here is a classic instance of the invention of a national tradition. By an act of will, one element is taken from an existing national and international matrix, is reshaped in line with an imagined earlier pure state and is declared to be not only essentially national but to have a monopoly of nationality in its sphere.

Like other prescriptions for living nationally, céilí dance was treated in independent Ireland with lip service from almost all, and with enthusiastic support from some, while most took it with with a grain of salt. The designated dances were widely learned and were performed at numerous céilís, grand and small. Concern about easy mixing of the sexes had made guardians of propriety wary of dancing, and most of the movers of the Gaelic League were keen guardians of propriety, not a few of them possessing the puritanical streak that goes with being a propagator of cultural imperatives. In that context, céilí dancing was invested with an aura of constraint and decorum that supposedly distinguished it from other, morally hazardous, dances. So it could be promoted where other dances might be opposed. In the event, it not infrequently functioned as a Trojan horse, for unless under firm management, the céilí could easily find room for dances of an unapproved kind. Those under firm control included the numerous *feiseanna* (plural of *feis*) at which local branches of the Gaelic League convened to promote the cause and to enjoy themselves in so doing.

Céilí bands emerged in the 1920s to serve the needs of the céilí. They typically had eight to fifteen members playing any one of a nearly infinite combination of instruments, but almost invariably including fiddle, accordion and drum. The popularity of the céilí bands was greatly boosted by the exposure they received on the national radio station, 2RN (later Raidió

---

[27]   *An Claidheamh Soluis*, 24 Feb. 1906, cited in Helen Brennan, *The Story of Irish Dance* (Dingle, 1999), p. 35.
[28]   *An Claidheamh Soluis*, 10 Mar. 1906, cited in Brennan, p. 36.

Éireann), from its inception in 1926. Off air, some of the more commer-cially minded of the céilí bands catered for a wider range of tastes, going beyond the mandatory reels, jigs, hornpipes and marches to include waltzes and polkas. In fact, alongside céilí dancing other forms continued to flour-ish. A participant in strict céilí on one night might within the week be danc-ing 'sets' at a crossroads platform, or accomplishing the foxtrot in the hotel ballroom of the nearest big town. The cheap bicycle had been transforming social life since the turn of the century and that, together with the impact of the internal combustion engine in the 1920s and 1930s, facilitated the devel-opment of something like a craze for social dancing occasions. Hunt balls and similar events were patronised by a broad spectrum of middle-class society. In the 1920s and 1930s, formal dinner dances for charitable pur-poses formed an important part of the social life of the Garda Síochána.[29] Set dancing in its numerous local variants had not lost its hold despite the strictures of the Gaelic League. At the same time, the gramophone was offering exposure to other music. And after small-town cinemas in 1929 had shown the first talking movie, *The Jazz Singer* with Al Jolson, things would never be the same again, even if the full impact was to be delayed for a generation. Soon Gaelic League branches felt it necessary to have in place a system of summary expulsion for members discovered infiltrating jazz steps into the céilí. A wide range of political and ecclesiastical worthies had already put on record their abhorrence of the new craze.

The exuberant dance culture of the 1920s and 1930s was typified by all-night events in a variety of venues from private homes to commercial halls. In several places throughout the country, private speculators, some of them 'returned Yanks' with un-deferential attitudes to conventional authority, had established dance halls. This was of obvious interest to the arbiters of morality. In other ways, too, the authorities in Church and state were alarmed: at various times, republicans and blueshirts ran their own dances and were able to add the proceeds to their funds. Roman Catholic bishops and the editor of the still confessionally Protestant *Irish Times* had been making their concern known long before the passing of the 1935 Dance Halls Act which introduced state licensing and so an element of police con-trol. The general impact was to move dancing from private houses and crossroads into clerically controlled parish halls and privately owned com-mercial establishments. The larger spaces increased the need for céilí bands, as distinct from the smaller and less formal groupings of performers appro-priate to houses and platforms.

One consequence of the general escape from the tyranny of cultural pre-scription in the 1960s and after was the re-emergence of set dancing from the state of disgrace to which it had been relegated by the Gaelic League. In a nice illustration of the arbitrariness of cultural national designations, by

---

[29]   Liam McNiffe, *A History of the Garda Síochána* (Dublin, 1997), p. 121.

the 1980s 'set' dancing, now promoted by the Gaelic Athletic Association and other agents of national culture, had assumed the role of the quintessential Irish social pastime. It was also nationalised in the sense of being standardised at national level, to the loss of various regional variants. So overwhelming was the surge to set dancing that by the late 1990s a movement to revive céilí dancing was in train.[30]

Side by side with its interventions in the area of group dancing, the Gaelic League had reinvented Irish solo step-dancing. As with the group dances, this was done by selecting a small portion of a varied country-wide inheritance shared with the neighbouring island and then impressing on it a certain character. The essential consideration was to arrive at a form that could be reduced to written description and bureaucratic management. Decorum was another requirement. Popular step-dancing had been a vigorous, sweaty pursuit with scope for individual expression. 'Irish' step-dancing was to be marked by the rigid back, hands by the side, head up and eyes to the front, with all movement confined to the lower half of the body. It proved to be a winning formula, so much so that the older forms of step-dancing passed from use, except for some local survivals such as the *sean-nós* (old style) of Connemara, rehabilitated towards the end of the twentieth century.

An Coimisiún le Rincí Gaelacha, to which the Gaelic League has consigned responsibility for step-dancing since 1929, manages a system of registration of schools (which have flourished since the 1920s), teachers and students. Rules for performance and competition are controlled as in a codified sport. So is dress, and the result has been one of the more serious attempts to invent a national costume. Like everything else, the permitted variation in uniforms is closely regulated. After an initial experiment with knee breeches, in the style of Douglas Hyde, the kilt was borrowed from Scotland for males. Decoratively, the dominant note was a reflection of the Celtic revival. For bureaucratic refinement, this system, whose creators and operators have remained unsung, might have been the envy of the Ministry of Education in the French Third Republic. It also proved to be capable of extension overseas and, in due course, céilí step-dancing has been established in Britain, North America, Australia, New Zealand, Kenya, South Africa and parts of continental Europe. The United States has proved to be a particular stronghold, with parents seeing in step-dancing a means of fastening their offspring to Irish ethnicity. More recently, branches in the United States of America, in the spirit of lifelong learning, have been to the fore in the creation of an adult-entry category. Since 1969, annual world championships with up to 2,000 competitors have been held in Ireland. For several generations of parents seeking an accomplishment with which to endow their children – at the price of fees, outfit, transport to lessons, monitoring of practice – Irish step-dancing has been an alternative to piano, vio-

---

[30] Letter to editor, *Irish Times*, 29 Nov. 1996.

lin and swimming. The entire scheme clearly depends on the willingness of parents and guardians of the young to part with fees and otherwise make sacrifice.

The stage show *Riverdance* (1994) and its derivatives are a direct, if unlikely, product of céilí step-dancing. The expertise of the principals and of the members of the dancing troupes comes from training since childhood in the distinctive forms approved by the Coimisiún le Rincí Gaelacha. Where, before, the only possible career reward for accomplishment in the art was to be in turn a teacher of others, employment with *Riverdance* or a derivative is now a possibility. What has been constructed from and around this expertise is, however, very far removed from the ethos of the Coimisiún, the Gaelic League and the feiseanna. While *Riverdance* is a product of modern Ireland and Irish America, the links with the ancient Irish past suggested by the programmatic storylines are pure invention. By any objective analysis, the show has little more to do with ancient Ireland than with ancient Japan. What's here is a late twentieth-century invention based on an early twentieth-century invention, and one that meets the requirement of contemporary entertainment for a level of eroticisation such as the earlier era could not contemplate and the earlier invention decisively precluded. As an ostensibly Irish cultural product, *Riverdance* has had an international impact comparable with that of Moore's melodies, although the durability of that impact in the case of the show has yet to be tested.[31] The projects also have in common that both have been brought to the world as commercial speculations and have proved immensely profitable for all concerned.

Like Irish dancing, singing in Irish was affected by the Gaelic League. In the 1780s, Robert Owenson (1744–1812) had an audience in Dublin for renditions of Irish-language songs in the original and in English translation.[32] Edward Bunting arranged for an Irish-speaking colleague, Patrick Lynch, to visit Connacht in search of the Irish words for airs collected from the harpers. However, Bunting's published volumes provide English words exclusively. Putting English words, either original or translations, to airs collected from Irish speakers became a regular practice over generations.[33] A small part of the work of Patrick Weston Joyce was pioneering the publication of song airs together with words in Irish. His *Irish Music and Song* (1887) has been described as 'the first collection of Irish [language] songs to have the words set syllable by syllable under the appropriate notes'.[34]

Songs in Irish became a staple of the primary school curriculum in the South after 1922. For most members of the first few generations of school children in the newly independent state, music in school meant exposure to

[31] See Fintan O'Toole, *The (ex)isle of Erin* (Dublin, 1996), pp. 143–56.

[32] Mary Helen Thuente, *The Harp Re-strung: the United Irishmen and the Rise of Irish Literary Nationalism* (New York, 1994), pp. 52–3.

[33] See ch. 5, 'Literature'.

[34] Breathnach, *Ceol rince na hÉireann*, p. 112.

songs in Irish, ranging from the sublime to the trivial.[35] As with the language itself, the response in the main was characterised by deference to a national piety rather than by enthusiasm. The national standing of the English-language repertoire going back to Moore and beyond was implicitly downgraded. Thus John McCormack's programme did not match up to strict nationalist requirements. He was, however, fireproofed against criticism by his Catholic credentials, which were underscored when in 1928 he was created a papal count. Significantly, his records were played on air by 2RN.

In any case, the school songs in Irish were in their own way as much a contrivance as Moore's melodies, set to conform, as they were, to the requirements of conventional formal music. In this, as in other respects, the revivalist nationalism of the early twentieth century was dedicated to standardisation. Song in Irish as performed by native speakers (in the sean-nós) was utterly different, and was incapable of being adapted to the needs of serried school ranks. Sean-nós was cultivated as a national treasure by the Gaelic League and others, but not as a mark of nationality for wider acquisition. From the 1950s, less prescriptive notions of what constituted acceptable decorum removed some lingering concerns about the respectability of sean-nós singing, as of much else.

The music to accompany popular dancing in Ireland, like the dancing itself, was 'nationalised' in a variety of ways in the course of the twentieth century. This development was underpinned by the music's designation as 'traditional', a term with strong Herderian connotations in this context, suggestive of an innately distinctive 'folk' culture expressing the personality of the nation. Only the music of the 'céilí' dances – jigs, reels and hornpipes – was deemed to be traditional, polka airs being marginalised and waltz tunes similarly outlawed. Céilí music was accorded the status of essential national expression by 2RN. Broadcasting promoted standardisation, something also encouraged by early commercial recordings for gramophone, especially in the USA in the 1920s. It was as in fulfilment of its national remit that Radio Éireann in 1947 acquired a mobile recording unit and subsequently engaged Ciarán Mac Mathúna and others to resume, with the aid of the latest technology, the venerable practice of saving Irish music for posterity. The fruits of this professional work, conducted as it was without a nod to either Herder or Chauvin, demonstrate the wealth and endless variety of popular music-making in Ireland – on fiddle, melodeon, accordion, flute, tin whistle, concertina, banjo and several instruments besides – before the impact of developments in the 1960s and after.

A voluntary organisation, Comhaltas Ceoltóirí Éireann (literally, 'the society of musicians of Ireland'), launched under this name in 1952 on earlier foundations, instituted a structure that would promote and manage

---

[35] Marie McCarthy, 'Music education in the emergent nation state' in Richard Pine (ed.), *Music in Ireland, 1848–1998* (Dublin, 1998), pp. 67–9.

'traditional' Irish music. Despite inclusivist professions, CCÉ soon acquired a managerial elite practised in the rhetoric of a revivalist piety, which it was able to maintain, while at the same time proving extraordinarily adept at coming to terms with, and even exploiting, the world, the flesh and the devil, in the shape of moral revolution and commercial opportunity. There is a close parallel here with the Gaelic Athletic Association (GAA) in the example of an organisational elite providing an ideological superstructure with prescriptive nationalist features, while the rank and file of participants in the fetishised activity have a political and ideological profile indistinguishable from that of the population at large. The annual festivals, rotating between provincial towns, that CCÉ instituted in the 1950s under the title of the *fleadh cheoil* ('festival of music') constituted a revival of large, unstructured popular gatherings for the purposes of entertainment and drinking, such as Church and state had largely suppressed for the best part of a century. By the 1960s it was one of the highlights of the annual calendar of festivals – including the Kilkenny Beer Festival, long since superseded in that upmarket city – that marked the reversal of a century and more of rigid social control. The fleadh cheoil banished for many the association of traditional music with didactic pieties.

Similarly, the playing of music in public houses, which had been frowned upon for generations, acquired new status in the 1960s in another example of loosening constraints. From the late nineteenth century, publicans had accommodated long-standing and widespread antipathy to their trade by adhering to strict government licensing laws and to a largely self-imposed code for the conduct of business in a demure and orderly fashion. In the first half of the twentieth century, singing and music in public houses were frowned upon. The customers stood at the bar or sat on hard high stools. In a well-run establishment, to raise a voice in either song or anger was to risk ejection. Over most of the country, women were excluded by conventional mores from public houses, apart from a few lounge bars developed in Dublin in the 1930s in imitation of the movies, or the closed-off areas ('snugs') in some premises, where approved persons might be admitted at the discretion of the proprietor. In the economic boom of the 1960s, publicans could afford to build lounges with comfortable seating, tables and carpets. The style was generally eclectic. An easing of formerly strict notions of respectability reduced ambivalence about the public house and, in particular, allowed women to drink in public. It was in these circumstances that music and song were readmitted to the pubs. Thus was born the version of the Irish pub that is now thought of the world over as the quintessential manifestation of Irish national culture. Wherever on earth the consumption of alcohol is officially tolerated, the economy generates private disposable income and society is open to foreign influences, the designer-style Irish pub is to be found and a particular myth of Irish national character, newly reinvented in the 1960s, is perpetuated. If live music and song are not

Figure 6.1 Eimear Quinn, winner of the Eurovision Song Contest, Oslo, 1996 (Peter Harding, Radio Telefís Éireann stills collection).

always available, they are always part of the myth. Like *Riverdance*, the Irish pub is particularly interesting as an exercise in the invention of nationality driven from start to finish by commercial interests interacting with changing social demands.

Changes in ambience went hand in hand with changes in forms and performance, such as swept through popular music in the English-speaking world generally in the late 1950s and early 1960s. The readiness of the Irish market for a change of style was already evident in the late 1950s with the commercial success in live performance and on record of the solo ballad singer Bridie Gallagher. It was, however, in the more modish form of the 'group' that the transformation would come. The breakthrough was made in the early 1960s by four exiles, the three Clancy brothers from Carrick-on-Suir, Co. Tipperary and Tommy Makem, from Keady, Co. Armagh, operating in the milieu of Greenwich Village (New York) and in the context of the American 'folk revival'. They drew selectively on the English-language Irish song repertoire with which they had grown up and also not a little on the contemporary English folk movement personified by Ewan MacColl. However, purists could not prevent their presentation and acceptance as a quintessentially Irish act, and in that guise they led a revolution in Irish popular entertainment, setting off what could be described as a ballad craze.[36] Appearances were crucial, a point highlighted when, in January 1961, the Clancy Brothers and Tommy Makem were fitted out in Aran sweaters for the Ed Sullivan Show. This touch of marketing genius completed the appeal of the group, and there followed nearly a decade of highly successful touring and recording, and a permanent place in the gallery of inventors of Irish nationality. The Dubliners and a host of other groups followed suit. They brought to Irish singing an air of unstuffy informality and an element of stage performance that appealed to many of the same instincts as the contemporary pop groups. They also shared with the latter the ubiquitous new musical prop of the age, the guitar.

To the dismay of many, rock bands began in the early 1970s to try their hand with traditional Irish music, the lead being taken by Thin Lizzy and Horslips, original exponents of 'Celtic rock'. Horslips raised the stakes by gesturing to ancient Ireland with an album entitled *The Book of Invasions – a Celtic Symphony*, thereby invoking a link that was as imaginary in respect of the traditional music as of rock. Celtic rock paved the way for the presentation of traditional music in a completely new style. In line with the trend affecting other forms since the 1960s, so with 'traditional' Irish music, solo performance now gave way to 'session' playing for amateurs, and, in the case of professional performance, the seated formalities of the céilí bands gave way to stand-up 'groups', sometimes referred to as 'bands', but most decidedly not as 'céilí bands'. These 'bands', including among their

---

[36] See Mick Moloney in *The Companion to Irish Traditional Music*, p. 20.

number such accomplished acts as the Bothy Band and De Danann, both formed in 1974, soon came to form with the ballad groups a single 'Irish music' business.

The céilí bands had introduced a strong percussive element into the music, normally in the form of the big drum. In the 1960s and after, the bodhrán, a tambourine-style frame drum, was incorporated into Irish music-playing in a striking instance of the 'invention of tradition'. The use of the bodhrán before this had been localised and largely confined, in terms of the calendar, to the customary hunting of the wren on 26 December.[37] Not only was the instrument a novelty, but the rhythmic beat it provided was, as the cultural censors of an earlier generation might have pronounced, 'alien'. Yet, by the mid-1970s, the bodhrán had become synonymous with Irish traditional music, and it is now as widely associated with Ireland as the shamrock (the identification of the latter with Ireland being, of course, a piece of early modern invention), if not yet the harp. There is a parallel here with the movement of the bouzouki in the twentieth century from the seedier margins of Greek society to the status – at least in the eyes of tourists – of national icon. A sure indication of the successful invention of a tradition is when it is incorporated into artistic representations of earlier times. The film *Titanic*, released in 1997, makes anachronistic reference to the bodhrán, depicting it as in use as part of general music-making in 1912. Mythic connotations have been heightened by John B. Keane's novel, *The Bodhrán Makers* (1986) in which the instrument symbolises resistance to moral oppression.

Much of the importance of the Irish music phenomenon launched in the 1960s and 1970s lies in its international reach. The attachment of those in Britain and the USA identifying themselves as Irish was to be expected, but they were joined by many compatriots who did not claim any Irish connections. Not only that, but the interest spread to significant numbers of people outside the countries of English vernacular. Irish music and song, as redefined by the groups of the 1960s and their successors, are not only listened to in countries around the world but have been taken up by enthusiastic practitioners in many places, with significant concentrations in continental Europe and Scandinavia. In Germany and several other countries, the cult of the 'folkish' has been tarnished by the excesses of twentieth-century nationalism, so that the resort to the folk idiom of another country which just happens to be small and unthreatening has obvious attractions. The fact that this package of music and song presented itself (almost entirely) in English, just as the educated youth of continental Europe were about to embrace that language, was a very important factor. Like watching *Dallas* un-dubbed on TV, listening to a Dubliners record could help one prepare for the serious things of life.

---

[37] Eric Cunningham in *The Companion to Irish Traditional Music*, pp. 28–32.

In assessing the connotation of Irishness in the area of music and song, it may be useful to have recourse to the metaphor of language (or idiom), with accent and dialect respectively signifying minor and major distinctiveness. In these terms, the popular dance music of the past two or three hundred years is an international idiom. In the eighteenth and nineteenth centuries, reels, jigs and hornpipes were as much part of life in England as in Ireland. Among his many accomplishments, the novelist Thomas Hardy (1840–1828) played such music, for a quantity of which he possessed manuscript notation. The language was known throughout Britain and Ireland and everywhere in the world where emigrants from these islands had settled. There were numerous regional and local accents, of which Ireland possessed not one but many. In the first half of the twentieth century, an Irish dialect (subsequently recognised as 'traditional Irish music') of this international language, was developed as part of a process of nation invention. It still had a very close resemblance to the Scottish version, also to a considerable extent homogenised as 'national', while in England this language never achieved national status and may have almost disappeared, to be partially compensated for by infusions from Ireland and Scotland. The Irish dialect of the first half of the twentieth century was modified in the 1970s, and in this modified form (and still referred to as 'traditional Irish music') it has acquired an international clientele. It should be noted, too, that the unmodified form, with seldom a bodhrán in earshot, and involving self-professed céilí bands, is still in a healthy state, at least in parts of the country, and can be heard several times weekly on RTÉ Radio. The success and development of the dance music has not necessarily fostered the slow airs that are so striking a part of the inheritance.[38] These airs, one or two traceable to the late sixteenth century and many of them of exquisite beauty, are obviously remnants of an earlier language (in the metaphorical sense), but here, too, conclusions concerning national origins should be carefully phrased. George-Denis Zimmermann, author of a magisterial study of a segment of the English language song repertoire in Ireland, has this to say about the national origins of airs:

> It would be unwise, however, to dogmatise about the nationality of the tunes, or even of some of their stylistic features. There has been a constant interchange of melodies between Ireland and Great Britain, more particularly since the end of the sixteenth century ... All we can hope to determine in many cases is whether a tune has been in Ireland for a long time or not.[39]

Certainly airs such as 'The Coolin' ('An Cúilin'), 'Dónal Óg', 'Úna Bán' and 'Eamonn an Chnoic' have been in Ireland for a long time, and there is no

---

[38] Ríonach Uí Ógáin, 'Traditional music and Irish cultural history' in Gerard Gillen and Harry White (eds), *Music and Irish Cultural History* (Dublin, 1995) (Irish Musical Studies, 3), p. 96.
[39] Zimmermann, p. 110.

reason to doubt that they were composed there, but little seems to be established for certain about the geographical scope of the language to which they belong.

Marching music made by drum and flute (or other wind instrument) is a very old idiom and one widespread in Europe. It is attested in New Ross, County Wexford in 1265.[40] Music bands were a notable feature of the Volunteer movement of the 1770s and 1780s. Amateur brass and reed bands flourished widely from the early nineteenth century. They were an integral part of Fr. Theobald Matthew's mobilisation on behalf of temperance that began in 1838, and, unlike other forms of demonstration, could scarcely have been conjured entirely from thin air. Trade associations in Dublin and other cities had their own bands, and bands seem to have been common in many localities in the second half of the century. They constituted a prominent aspect of various mobilisations, especially the land war. Notwithstanding their function in nationalist movements, the bands did not have an exclusively nationalist repertoire: both Thomas Davis in the 1840s and Douglas Hyde in the 1890s indicated concern about them. The Scottish development of the pipe band was emulated on a large scale in Ireland in the later nineteenth century. The marching band idiom with a very definite Irish accent is at the heart of the celebratory practices of the Orange Order, particularly the annual parades and demonstrations of 12 July.

The twentieth century has produced several popular languages in music and song that are either unalterably American or inexorably cosmopolitan, and so allow for little local accent. This need not inhibit national exploitation of the fame of celebrated practitioners. Jimmy Kennedy (1902–84), a native of Omagh, County Tyrone was one of the outstandingly successful songwriters of the century with compositions like 'Red sails in the sunset', 'South of the border', 'The teddy bears' picnic' and numerous others to his credit. His achievement is occasionally acknowledged, but 'Red sails in the sunset' is not deemed to participate in any way in essential Irishness. Even in the case of U2, four Dubliners who make up one of the most successful of all rock bands, and whose achievement is a source of much notice, prejudice about what constitutes 'Irish' music means that national pride is invested in their success rather than in the music on which that success is based, because it is not deemed to be of Irish essence.

While ballads and traditional music were taking off in the Ireland of the 1960s, this was also the era of the showbands. These were a streamlined development of the 'ballroom' orchestra, geared to covering the latest pop music and song and some older standard pieces for the clientele of large dance halls. Although the showbands were enormously successful and were an indigenous response to the conditions of the 1960s, they are not recog-

---

[40] Alan Bliss and Joseph Long, 'Literature in Norman French and English' in Art Cosgrove (ed.), *Medieval Ireland, 1169–1534* (Oxford, 1987) (A New History of Ireland, ii), p. 718.

nised as a manifestation of the national essence. Country and Western is an American musical language of which a distinct Irish dialect has developed, that for some at least has the credentials of nationality. However, it is the 'traditional' music and ballad movements, taken together, that are viewed, at home and abroad, as the essence of Irish music.

Unlike sport, music provides relatively few set-piece opportunities for testing national prowess in international competition. The best known of what opportunities there are is the annual Eurovision Song Contest for new compositions. Winning this on six occasions, the first in 1970, has been seen as reassuring evidence of national competence in the international arena. The musical language of Eurovision is generally pop of the blandest type, but several of the Irish entries have been in a national idiom.

The premier international language of music and song is the art music of elite European culture with the associated ecclesiastical and operatic repertoires. Several aspects of this were securely established in Ireland by the early part of the eighteenth century with the choirs of the two Dublin cathedrals as the mainstay. Their members made possible the first ever performance of Handel's *Messiah* in the Music Hall, Fishamble Street, Dublin on 13 April 1742, with the composer himself directing. This stellar event and Handel's nine months of residence in the city, highlight, as admittedly they flatter, the place of Dublin in the cosmopolitan world of art music. But there is strong supporting, if more humdrum, evidence, in that a significant number of continental musicians worked in the Irish capital during the eighteenth century for shorter or longer periods. The famous Italian composer Francesco Geminani lived in Ireland for a total of ten years, dying in Dublin in 1762. The traffic was not all one-way. Among his other feats on the continent and in London, the Dublin-born tenor Michael Kelly (1764–1826) sang in the first performance of Mozart's *Marriage of Figaro* at Vienna in 1781. The pianist, John Field (1782–1837), also from Dublin, had an international career that extended to St Petersburg. He is recognised as the pioneer of the nocturne. The background to such excellence was a critical mass of ordinary practitioners, most of them amateurs and some of them aristocrats, such as the Earl of Mornington (1735–81), father of the Duke of Wellington and professor of music at Trinity College, Dublin from 1764 to 1774. More than sixty firms selling sheet music have been recorded for Dublin in the period 1780–1830, and various provincial centres followed suit on a smaller scale.[41]

Aristocratic patronage was significant and, with its decline by the second quarter of the nineteenth century, the middle class in Ireland proved less effective than in some other countries at taking up the slack. An Irish Philharmonic Society was formed in 1826 and maintained a high standard over four decades, but no *Musikverein* emerged to sustain the more formal

---

[41] Ita M. Hogan, *Anglo-Irish Music, 1780–1830* (Cork, 1966), p. 101.

professional orchestra that might have permitted a fuller participation in the developments of the age. However, amateur musicality and choral work flourished. Particular favourites were *The Bohemian Girl* (1843) by Michael Balfe (1808–70) and *Maritana* (1845) by William Vincent Wallace (1812–65); these Irishmen were among the most successful opera composers of their generation outside of Italy. *The Bohemian Girl* and *Maritana*, together with Julius Benedict's *The Lily of Killarney* (1862), are sometimes referred to as the Irish 'Ring', but unlike Wagner's works they do not have a distinctive national accent.

The establishment in 1848 of the Royal Irish Academy of Music, dedicated to providing structure, control and measurement in instrumental teaching and learning, represents acknowledgement of the place of European art music in the cultural life of the country and the institutionalisation of its infrastructure on a country-wide basis, as modern society demands. The direction taken by the Feis Cheoil in the early twentieth century underlined the firm place of art music in Irish life. A question given some attention recently is that of why art music in Ireland did not take on a distinctive national accent as happened in other countries, in other words, why there has been no Irish Smetana or Kodály. Harry White, the chief exponent of the question, along with Joseph Ryan, has formulated the issue as follows:

> Why could not Ireland achieve what Poland achieved in the nineteenth century and Hungary in the twentieth: art music of international currency underwritten by a tangible corpus of ethnic melody?[42]

There is, of course, no law of nature decreeing that all nations have to match the same benchmarks. But, in fact, numerous composers in the nineteenth and twentieth centuries have worked with airs from the Irish popular or 'traditional' repertoire. The issue can be addressed concretely by examining the case of Charles Villiers Stanford (1852–1924), the leading instance of a major composer who engaged with Irish popular music. Born in Dublin and trained there and in Cambridge, London, Leipzig and Berlin, after Elgar the leading musical figure in Britain (as composer, academic and teacher) for thirty years before World War I, Stanford always saw himself as an Irishman. A significant amount of the material in his vast output has Irish reference: an *Irish Symphony* (no. 3) (1887); an opera, *The Veiled Prophet* (1877), based on Thomas Moore's epic poem *Lalla Rookh*; another opera, *Shamus O'Brien* (1896); six 'Irish rhapsodies' (1901–23); an edition of

[42] Harry White, *The Keeper's Recital: Music and Cultural History in Ireland, 1770–1970* (Cork, 1998), p. 69; and see Joseph Ryan, 'Nationalism and Irish music' in Gillen and White (eds), *Music and Irish Cultural History*, pp. 101–15.
[43] Thomas Moore's *Irish Melodies Restored, or, Songs of Ireland* (1895); *The Complete Collection of Irish Music as Noted by George Petrie* (3 vols, 1902–5).

Moore's melodies and of Petrie's collection.[43] He also composed settings for numerous Irish songs.[44] Orchestral and choral works of Stanford's featured very prominently on the programme of the Feis Cheoil in the early years, while it was still attempting to focus on a specifically Irish agenda.[45] Here was more than enough to support national status for Stanford, if conditions were otherwise conducive to this. One obstacle was that Stanford held strongly unionist political views, so that nationalists were not likely to give him credit for his nationality. The fact is that in the early twentieth century, as part of the wider movement towards an essentialist definition of Irish culture, art music was deemed to lack proper national credentials. Thus, in Henry Grattan Flood's *History of Irish Music* (1905), a distinction is made between 'Celtic-Irish' and 'Anglo-Irish' music, the latter encompassing art music. Being replete with chauvinist assertions and assumptions and learned (but unreferenced) gobbets illustrative of Irish precocity from pre-Patrician times, Grattan Flood's book had much appeal in the early twentieth century. And its massive, if frequently tendentious, erudition still commands respect. Grattan Flood exhibits not the slightest antipathy towards 'Anglo-Irish' music, revelling, as he did, in anything that could minister to Irish pride, but, in the early decades of the century, the designation carried, in music as in other spheres, an ineluctable charge of alien-ness.

The equation of art music with Anglo-Irish music has been taken to substantiate a 'hidden Ireland' view in musical historiography, still reflected in quite recent work, according to which the country's music was strictly segregated along ethnic lines. But even Grattan Flood's volume is awash with details that make nonsense of such a dichotomy. Thus, for instance, the most distinguished of the harpers at the Belfast festival of 1792, Denis Hempson – the last to use the old style of harp playing and to pluck the strings with long, hardened nails rather than with the tips of the fingers– had as patron, not the scion of some surviving Catholic landed family, nor even some enlightened Belfast merchant, but the Rev. W. Hervey Bruce, who in 1804 became a baronet of the United Kingdom.[46] Carolan's patrons were predominantly Catholic, but they were not exclusively so, and both he and his music were well known to Protestants in Dublin and among the country gentry.[47] The fact is that, when allowances are made for socio-economic class, there is no basis for believing that for any substantial period of time Catholics and Protestants in Ireland, or, for that matter, inhabitants of Ireland and Britain, have lived in radically different musical worlds. True, the classes that could indulge themselves with art music were predominantly Protestant until well into the nineteenth century, but Catholics at an early

[44] Jeremy Dibble, 'Stanford, Charles Villiers' in *The New Grove Dictionay of Music Online*, ed. L. Macy (accessed 17 Feb. 2003) <http://www.grovemusic.com>
[45] Axel Klein, *Die Musik Irlands im 20 Jahrhundert* (Hildesheim, 1996), p. 38.
[46] p. 250.
[47] O'Sullivan, *Carolan*, pp. 56–7, 227–86.

opportunity installed their own universalising church music, and entered
secular art music circles in Dublin and elsewhere. Most misleading of all is
the implication that Protestants, or English speakers, or town-dwellers, or
some other category of Irish residents, were cut off over generations from a
musical repertoire confined to some mythic native constituency. Of course,
the words of Irish songs were lost on those who did not know the language,
but that did not prevent them from sharing the tunes. What seems more
plausible is that the music available in early modern and modern times to
most people, most of the time, throughout Ireland and Britain, has come
largely from the same repertoire or set of repertoires.

The designation of art music as 'Anglo-Irish' in cultural revivalist ideology left composers for orchestra who would serve the national ideal with a
mountain to climb, as the following quotation from one of them, Eamonn
Ó Gallchobhair (1906–82), writing for publication in 1936, underlines:

> The Irish idiom expresses deep things that have not been expressed by Beethoven,
> Bach, Brahms, Elgar or Sibelius ... and ... where the vehicle used for the pre-
> sentation of the Irish idiom is the vehicle of any of these men or their schools ...
> then the Irishman is conscious of a clash of values ... and he rejects the presen-
> tation as 'wrong'. And so I say that in no Irish art as much as in music does the
> Irish mind hold fast to the set of values fundamentally its own.[48]

Believing that one had to go deeper than Beethoven and Bach was indeed a
heavy burden to bear, and more comparative work than has been accomplished to date may be needed – comparisons with the other arts in Ireland,
which were not similarly afflicted, and comparisons with the history of
music in other small countries – before an adequate explanation for the self-
infliction of this incubus can be found.

This, in any event, is the background against which to view the career of
Seán Ó Riada (1931–71). Fully equipped and on his way as a composer of
art music, in his thirties, Ó Riada switched most of his energy into work
with Irish traditional music and soon acquired what might be described as
national bardic status. His score for a celebratory film marking the fiftieth
anniversary of the Easter Rising, *Mise Éire* (1966), utilising the old air associated with the song 'Róisín Dubh', is the high point of the musical roman-
ticisation of Irish nationalism. Beginning in 1961, Ó Riada, with an
ensemble of individually and collectively brilliant musicians, Ceoltóirí
Cualann, and playing himself on harpsichord, produced renditions of dance
tunes and other airs for a path-breaking series of programmes on RTÉ
Radio. The formula was subsequently transferred to television and the concert hall stage. Here, in the words of Harry White, was 'traditional music,

---

[48] Quoted in Ryan, 'Nationalism and Irish music', p. 109. See Ryan, 'Assertions of
Distinction: the modal debate in Irish music' in Gillen and White (eds), *Music and the
Church*, pp. 62–77.

literally, in evening dress'.[49] White's words reflect dismay at the realisation that Ó Riada had achieved public and official acclaim (President de Valera was among those who came to listen) and the status of ultimate national music-maker, while abandoning the challenge of orchestral composition, and that this was made possible, perhaps inevitable, by revivalist ideology.

The liberties that Ó Riada took in the 1960s with Irish music, with céilí band convention, and with the concert format, would have been unthinkable in earlier decades, and presaged changes in the 1970s of which he could have scarcely conceived. His achievement was a paradox, innovative and at the same time geared to saluting old, but crumbling, pieties. The contradiction could not be sustained. Ó Riada disbanded Ceoltóirí Cualann in 1969 and died two years later in his prime, leaving behind an air of enigma. A group based on Ceoltóirí Cualann – the Chieftains – subsequently brought their highly polished versions of 'traditional' Irish music to a world audience and thereafter became pioneers of the Esperanto that now allows nation to talk to nation in the rich tones of a globalising 'world music'. This is at a far remove from the preoccupations that lay, or ostensibly lay, behind Ó Riada's Gaelicism.

Of course, there were Irish composers active in the first half of the twentieth century who were not inhibited by the imperatives of the revival, such as Hamilton Harty (1879–1941) and Arthur Duff (1899–1945). And by the 1960s, in music as in so many other areas, prescriptive attitudes were losing their hold. This meant that Irish composers no longer needed to feel compelled to engage in a search for the Celtic soul. While 'traditional' music and balladry retained an aura of national being, it became possible for the nation to take pride in other musical idioms. So it has become acceptable to salute Balfe and Wallace, Jimmy Kennedy and U2, and even Stanford, without fear of the charge of cultural treason. There is a parallel here with developments in sport (see chapter seven), particularly with the way in which soccer has become a vehicle for national pride and achievement, without acquiring the aura of national essence associated with hurling and Gaelic football.

None of this is to suggest that the writing of music with a distinctive Irish accent has been abandoned. Successful attempts to serve new purposes while drawing on an Irish musical inheritance include Shaun Davey's scores for television, film and stage (and the especially acclaimed *The Brendan Voyage*), Bill Whelan's music for *Riverdance* and Brendan Graham's popular songs. A particularly wistful style achieved by the Donegal-born singer, Enya, as composer and performer has placed her among the most successful individual artists on the planet.

Nothing in official, Gaelicising, or popular attitudes moved independent Irish governments to invest seriously in music. In 1921, Grattan Flood had

---

[49] White, *The Keeper's Recital*, p. 144.

predicted that self-government would lead to 'a national school of music such as the world has never seen'.[50] He could scarcely have imagined that there would be a sixty-year wait for a national concert hall. Since its arrival in 1981 it has provided a home for the National Symphony Orchestra, which is a responsibility of RTÉ. The governmental support that has enabled opera to maintain a precarious existence in Dublin has not extended to the provision of a dedicated venue. Primarily owing to the determination and enthusiasm of one individual, Dr Thomas Walsh (1911–88), the Wexford Opera Festival established in 1951 has won for itself a niche in the international operatic calendar. It is an example of an outstanding national ornament that has no claim to be essentially national.

There is little reason to believe that, when class differences are allowed for, Irish Protestants are less inclined than Catholics to sing and dance. The set dancing, the dance music, the slow airs and the song repertoire in English were common possessions, and to some extent still are. Nevertheless, in music as in other areas (most notably that of the Irish language), the appropriation of the 'traditional' for nationalism inevitably affected unionist perceptions. One response is to reject the Irish inheritance outright, a strategy fitting with the 'civic unionist' stance that represented unionism as a rejection of regionalism and ethnicity in favour of metropolitan citizenship. In this vein, one prominent unionist politician identified 'not dancing jigs' as one of the marks of unionist Britishness. But for other unionists, the lack of political validation did not negate the function of the music and dance. Thus, the official celebrations held at Balmoral showgrounds on 11 May 1935 for the jubilee of King George V included 'a display of Irish country dancing' by eighty-four Girl Guides from three counties. The dance to be performed was officially named as the 'Fairy reel' and described as 'a traditional Irish dance for six people', the music to be supplied by the Royal Ulster Constabulary band.[51] Over two centuries the Orange Order has developed a distinctive culture of music (especially for marching) and song associated with its annual commemorations of the Battle of the Boyne. And some at least of its halls were also venues of step-dancing and set dancing far into the twentieth century.[52] However, when the BBC Northern Ireland Orchestra broadcast a highly successful series of dance music arrangements by David Curry in the 1940s and 1950s, sections of unionist opinion and of the political establishment were uneasy about it.[53] The use of the term 'céilí' was particularly suspect, being associated with Catholic social events and self-conscious Catholic identity.

---

[50] W.H.C. Flood, *Introductory Sketch of Irish Musical History*, p. 99.
[51] Gillian McIntosh, *The Force of Culture: Unionist Identities in Twentieth-century Ireland* (Cork, 1999), p. 48.
[52] Gary Hastings in *Companion to Irish Traditional Music*, p. 288.
[53] John Moulden in *Companion to Irish Traditional Music*, p. 98; McIntosh, *The Force of Culture*, pp. 80–1.

The Counties Antrim and Derry Country Fiddlers' Association was established in 1953 to promote the interests of what it calls 'folk' music and of fiddle playing in particular. It illustrates all that needs to be said about notions of music and dance as markers of cultural difference:

> Drawing its membership from both religious traditions, it gave performances in aid of charity in Catholic and Protestant church halls and in Hibernian and Orange halls. It is still in existence but due to the troubles meets now [1999] in the Tullymore House Hotel.[54]

---

[54] John Moulden in *Companion to Irish Traditional Music*, p. 8.

|7|

Sport

In contemporary society, so prominent is the role assumed by sport, particularly the televised spectaculars served up on a regular basis throughout the entire year, that Juvenal's satirical jibe about the imperial Roman populace held in thrall by 'bread and circuses' has acquired an eerie resonance. Globally and nationally, televised sport, and particularly football, is now in the same bracket as politics and religion in terms of ability to attract public interest and allegiance and to project icons on the collective consciousness. Following the 2000 Olympic Games in Sydney, Dáil Éireann allocated time to questions about the disappointing performance of the Irish competitors, the implication being that sporting success not only matters to the nation but is a concern of the State. While the social aspect of sport in Ireland, past and present, is little studied, rather more attention has been paid to the relationship between sport and nationality. It is not that the scholarly literature on this is very extensive, but at least the role of Gaelic games in the invention of Irish nationality is well acknowledged. And the success of the Irish national soccer team around the turn of the 1990s set off a wave of celebration and reflection, and some academic work, and indeed creative writing, on the topic of sport and Irish identity.

The period between 1850 and World War I is the most critical episode in the general history of sport. From being regulated by regional custom, haphazardly organised and locally focused, various games and pastimes were changed to become codified, centrally administered and organised on a national basis. Many factors in social and economic life contributed to this revolution, such as improving communications and a rise in the disposable incomes of wage-earners. The outcome has been summarised thus: 'Sport, in its modern, organised, commercialised and extensive form, was truly an "invention" of the Victorian and Edwardian age.'[1] Sport, in its turn, has

---

[1] Neil Tranter, *Sport, Economy and Society in Britain, 1750–1914* (Cambridge, 1998), p. 16.

played a significant part in the invention of nationality, in Ireland and else-where. A familiar paradigm can be observed: sport has an existence onto-logically prior to nationality; as it is put on a modern basis, its organisational structures become coterminous with the state and it becomes in that sense national; once visibly national it is available to be invested with meaning and significance by nation inventors.

In England the formation of soccer clubs began in the late 1850s, and the need of clubs for a network resulted in the emergence of the Football Association in 1863. Various regional associations also flourished for a time, and several decades were to pass before the writ of the Football Association would run throughout the land. Acceptance of the idea that the country, and not a geographical region or some ad hoc division, pro-vided the proper and obvious organisational boundaries for a voluntary associational activity typifies the way in which the nation, simply by its availability as a conceptual framework, passively appropriates facets of life on which it has no intrinsic claim. With the development of soccer in Scotland paralleling that in England, it was possible to stage a formal international between the two countries as early as 1872. By 1888, an inter-associational soccer body linked the four countries of the United Kingdom, and in 1904, FIFA, an international body with worldwide pre-tensions emerged. The same paradigm was to be applied to numerous other sports, and in many cases the full paraphernalia were in place before 1914. The capstone of the process took the guise of a restoration of the Olympic Games of Ancient Greece, beginning at Athens in 1896 and developing over subsequent games.

The dominant template for modern sporting organisations was now in place. Sports would be played in accordance with universal rules, but under national authorities and on a national basis. The individual or the team, as the case might be, could compete in the wider world only on the nomination of a national authority and as a flag-bearer for the nation. This constitutes one of the most widespread and successful aspects of nation invention: glory in the prowess of the individual is appropriated to the imagined community, whereas objectively assessed it might more convincingly be confined to a smaller group. The benefits are not necessarily all on one side. In many sports, the national association provides facilities and other supports not otherwise available to the competitor. With sport, and especially the Olympic Games, providing a non-military forum for competition between nations, governments have been drawn into funding the national sporting effort, with varying impact on the independence of national sporting bodies. State intervention in Olympic sport has come in a multiplicity of modes from the sinister (most notably Hitler's use of the 1936 games in Berlin), by way of the dubious, to the benign.

International sporting competition has contributed to the promotion of Irish nationality, but with complications. Territorial partition of the island has produced disputes and confusion about the extent of the competing nation: twenty-six counties or thirty-two? And Ireland, like the USA and Australia, has acquired its own distinct games that are not shared with other countries and so cannot provide a forum in which to vie with the rest of the world. But games confined to one country have other ways of serving nationality, particularly by acquiring designation as native and an expression of the Herderian national soul, a phenomenon of particular interest in the Irish case. There are few twists or turns to the definition of the national that are not exemplified by Irish sport.

Cricket was standardised in the late eighteenth century, and in the 1820s it was the first of the codified field sports to gain a footing in Ireland. At first, the main agents of diffusion were the military (the Duke of Wellington had ordered that every barracks have a pitch), and young men returning from public school or university in England. Despite climatic contraindications, the game was well established at many locations in Ireland, especially in the south and east, by the 1860s. Hitherto unpublished local research in Co. Tipperary shows that cricket clubs proliferated there in the 1870s to an extent that cannot be explained on the basis of upper-class promotion. Indeed, one leader-writer in a local newspaper, revelling in the development, hailed cricket as a republican sport.[2]

In England, immemorial and locally varied ball games played with the foot or with a stick made the transition to modern codified sports – soccer, rugby, hockey – by way of the old universities and the public schools. Tolerated on a regular basis from the early nineteenth century, and appreciated merely as a means of dissipating youthful energy, games came by mid-century to be revered as an essential element in the pedagogy of character formation, and were reformulated in accordance with the demands of discipline, safety and confined spaces. In the second half of the nineteenth century, team sports became in England the quintessential masculine expression of nationality and/or imperialism. The young scholars and graduates spread these reformulated and respectable sports far and wide, and their instrument of diffusion was the club.

Past students of Rugby School, bringing home the version of football named after their Alma Mater, were responsible for the emergence of Ireland's first rugby football club in 1854. By 1879, when the Irish Rugby Football Union was established, there were seventy-seven clubs. The other version of football codified by the early Victorians, soccer or association football, found its earliest Irish foothold in the north-east, and when the Irish Football Association was formed in 1880 its headquarters were in Belfast.[3] While the codified games might be occasions of violence and drinking, they

2   I am indebted to Mr Patrick Bracken, BA for this information.
3   Neil Garnham, 'Football and identity in pre-Great War Ireland' in *Irish Economic and Social History*, xxviii (2001), pp. 13–31.

were the acme of decorum by comparison with the unregulated form of football that was a feature of earlier times, and which had virtually disappeared from Ireland after the famine as police, priests and landlords clamped down on disorderly or undisciplined collective practices of all kinds.

A game in which a ball is struck with a crooked stick (the *camán* or hurley) is attested from an early stage in the recorded history of Ireland, and this is usually rendered in English as 'hurling'. Astounding deeds of hurling prowess feature among the accomplishments attributed to Cuchulainn, hero of the ancient Ulster cycle of Gaelic mythology. This is evidence of the state of things when the stories in question were composed or redacted in the early and central medieval periods. However, so underdeveloped has been the scholarly study of the history of Irish sport that some quite recent purportedly factual works cite accounts of the legendary Battle of Moytura as evidence for the existence of hurling in 1272 BC! What can be said is that games of stick and ball are to be found in many ancient and later cultures, and that a number of modern codified forms have evolved, including cricket, hockey, shinty and hurling, to mention only team games.

The forms that hurling took in Ireland during earlier centuries are not easy to deduce, but Liam Ó Caithnia[4] has demonstrated that, by 1700, hurling matches and associated rituals had become well-established features of Irish life (rather like cricket in England). His account of hurling through the next hundred years, drawn to a considerable extent from contemporary newspaper files, is a most effective rebuttal of the 'hidden Ireland' concept that depicts a native culture cowering in the fastnesses and uncontaminated by the touch of a rampant alien ascendancy. While a correlation with political developments is missing from his survey, Ó Caithnia does show that, in the eighteenth century, hurling matches were played openly throughout the length and breadth of Ireland, and, it would seem, by the Irish in England, or at least in London; a newspaper notice from 1747 reads as follows:

> Hurling match at the Artillery Ground. Munster v. Leinster. This is the last match of the season, and as it is not attended with so much charge as cricket, to oblige the town the door will be only 3d.[5]

Hurling was not simply tolerated: it was supported and patronised by the gentry. Indeed, it was precisely because of this upper-class promotion that hurling prospered. Games were normally played for a wager. By the mid-eighteenth century the amounts at stake on an inter-county contest could reach one hundred guineas, a sum indicative of the involvement of people of considerable wealth. The near-universality of hurling throughout the island

---

4   Liam P. Ó Caithnia, *Scéal na h-iomána: ó thosach ama to 1884* (Dublin, 1980).
5   *Daily Advertiser*, 28 Sept. 1747, quoted in L. Ó Caithnia, *Scéal na h-iomána: ó thosach ama go 1884*, p. 18.

does not imply a single universal form of the game, or uniformity in the shape of the stick or the constitution of the ball. Although the evidence is far from clear, it may be that hurling in Ulster was distinctive in its form and patronage.[6] And in addition to the matches with limited numbers of players on pitches with defined boundaries, there was a version involving indefinite numbers on the road.

The political polarisation of the 1790s adversely affected hurling as so much else in public life, and by the beginning of the nineteenth century elite engagement with popular pastimes, including hurling, was drastically reduced. Particular Irish conditions apart, there was a general European trend towards class segregation of pastimes. *The Field Book: or Sports and Pastimes of the United Kingdom*, published in 1833, described hurling as the 'national game' of Ireland,[7] but at that stage it was in rapid decline in its vernacular form. The Catholic clergy and prominent merchants, who in other respects came to replace at least partially the landed gentry in public affairs, had little interest in promoting a communal pursuit that they were not equipped to control. Hurling lost prestige and in due course came to be associated with disturbance, and in some instances with resistance to the socio-political order, as when on occasions in Kilkenny and Tipperary in the early 1830s crowds assembling to protest against the tithe system carried hurleys, a practice soon discontinued, but not before the term 'hurlers' had become for some a synonym for agrarian menace. The famine was the final blow for hurling in many districts. By the 1850s, the forces of order represented by constabulary, parish priest and landlord were moving with enhanced effectiveness against all forms of uncontrolled popular assembly and pastime, so that hurling as an endemic sport came to be even more seriously confined.

In parallel with developments in England, a codified form of hurling (under the designation 'hurley') was established in Trinity College, Dublin by the 1830s. The first known rules for hurling were those composed in 1870 for the Dublin University Hurley Club. Following the typical pattern, the Irish Hurley Union was formed in 1879. Concomitantly, the game came to flourish in Protestant secondary schools. Thomas Davis, for whom both cricket and hurling together constituted a less appealing feature of his schooling, launched no great crusade for national games. The *Celt* (1857–59), a kind of shoestring version of the early *Nation*, carried an article on 3 October 1857 deploring the decline of football and hurling before quoits and cricket, but without conveying a conviction that nationality was at stake. In writing under the heading 'National sports' in the *Irish People* of 15 October 1864, Charles J. Kickham's concern was with suppression by

---

6   Ó Caithnia, *Scéal na h-iomána*, pp. 246–7.
7   Cited in L. Ó Caithnia, *Báirí cos in Éirinn roimh bhunú na gcumann eagraithe* (Dublin, 1984), p. 22.

the police of gatherings of young people for entertainment such as hurling, football and dancing, not with the national credentials of the pastimes themselves.[8]

In Britain and Ireland, the emergence of codified sport went hand in hand with the rise of competitive athletics as a popular entertainment, for athletics too were moving in the railway age from the parochial to the national arena. A meeting held in Trinity College park in 1857 is claimed to have been the first example in Ireland of the new style of athletics meeting.[9] Over the following twenty years such meetings became enormously popular throughout the land, as part of a wider international fashion. Even before the predictable emergence of national organisations, athletics provided a forum for international emulation when individual Irishmen went to compete at English meetings. By the 1870s, the Davin brothers from Carrick-on-Suir and other prominent athletes were heroes country-wide.

The structures of confessional and class division influenced sport, as for example in the case of the spread of hurley from Trinity College, Dublin to Protestant but not to Catholic schools. It was not, however, until the 1880s that sport in Ireland was politicised, in the sense that the individual's choice of sport and of sporting organisation was made to appear as a political or confessional act. This was brought about by the invention of Gaelic sports. The key figure in the process of invention was Michael Cusack (1847–1906). In the persona of the Citizen in Joyce's *Ulysses*, he is now almost as famous as Falstaff, a chauvinist, bragging in his case about national rather than individual heroics.

However, developments in Irish sport in the 1880s cannot be understood in terms of individual initiatives divorced from political and ideological pressures. Of first importance was the political chasm created by the land war in 1879 and the following years. The conflicting landlord and tenant interests were arrayed along lines dictated by religious denomination, economic interest and relationship to the state establishment. The identification of the tenants' cause with self-government for Ireland increased the stakes considerably. Sport was among the aspects of social life adversely affected, as Cusack acknowledged in a newspaper article in 1881. At this stage he was making valiant efforts to save Irish sport from permanent division along the lines of the solidifying political cleavage; he was, in his own words, 'trying to keep the platform of sport clear of the party spirit'.[10] By 1884 he had given up the effort and was setting about the formation of a separate sporting regime for 'Home Rule' Irishmen. His efforts resulted in November of that year in the foundation of the Gaelic Athletic Association (GAA).

---

[8] *Irish People*, 15 Oct. 1864.
[9] T. West, 'Elizabethans and Victorians: the origins of Trinity's senior sports clubs' in C.H. Holland (ed.), *Trinity College Dublin and the Idea of a University* (Dublin, 1991), p. 132.
[10] M. de Búrca, *Michael Cusack and the G.A.A.* (Dublin, 1989), p. 52.

Separation resolved in the Irish context certain problems that had affected sport inside and outside the country. Strict Protestantism interpreted the sanctity of the Lord's Day as debarring sporting activity. An act of the Irish parliament in 1695 provided for the enforcement of this conviction by the civil law and so the hurling contests advertised in the eighteenth-century press were scheduled for weekdays. No doubt hurling was also played on Sundays, but to advertise a Sunday match would have been provocative. In the second half of the nineteenth century, the evangelical spirit was sufficiently strong for many Protestants to find participation in Sunday sports impossible on conscientious grounds. While the Irish Catholic clergy were second to none in their concern about the social implications of sport, Catholic theology confined the demands of Sunday observance to attendance at mass and avoidance of 'servile work'. Mass having been attended, there was no canonical prohibition on lawful pastimes (although, as we have seen, the clergy might use their influence to prevent gatherings in the interest of social control). While Cusack's organisation was always to have some Protestant members and supporters, by providing sports and games on Sundays it effected a very significant liberation of Catholics and at the same time excluded the main body of Protestants.

The institutionalisation of sport occurred within a society constructed along lines of entrenched social classes. The young men emerging from public schools and universities in the nineteenth century saw their place in the world in terms of class. A historian of sport has the following salient points to make with respect to Britain:

> For most of the social elite sport was an opportunity for differentiation not conciliation, and was used to restrict rather than expand contact with social inferiors ... The first code of rules for athletics drawn up by the Amateur Athletic Club in 1866–67 specifically excluded mechanics, artisans and labourers from participation in an attempt to divorce amateur athletics from professional pedestrianism and preserve the former exclusively for the upper and middle classes.[11]

Having settled in Dublin in 1877 as a teacher with a keen enthusiasm for playing and organising sport – he was involved in athletics, hurling and rugby – Cusack had experienced the potentially limiting effects of such social exclusiveness. By creating his own organisation in the particular circumstances that applied, he discarded the incubus of middle-class elitism and contributed handsomely to the democratisation of Irish life. But the ending of horizontal division was achieved at the price of entrenching vertical division.

---

[11] N. Tranter, *Sport, Economy and Society in Britain, 1750–1914* (Cambridge, 1998), pp. 41–2.

The abandonment of formal exclusion is no guarantee of the achievement of inclusiveness, and the disappearance of horizontal division within Cusack's organisation was to take time. 'We practising and ye playing the matches' summed up the frustration of a rural labourer in the 1940s, looking at his parish team taking the field with what he perceived to be an unfair proportion of farmers' sons selected.[12] Indeed, like most manifestations of democratic advance in Ireland, Cusack's initiative was marked by a great anxiety to show that it could not be faulted for any want of respectability. Hence a strident insistence on amateur status: indeed, one of Cusack's main pretexts for withdrawing from the existing sporting set-up in the country was that it was not sufficiently efficient in curbing gambling and participation for award. He was offering to be an even more faithful upholder of the gentlemanly ideal of amateurism.

Neil Tranter quotes the following from a Scottish newspaper commenting in 1855 on the Highland Games:

> Never was there a time when the ancient renown of Scotland needed to be more celebrated and maintained ... Unless something is done to revive the popular spirit of the Highlands, its games and exercises, the sound of the Gaelic language and the pibroch will soon disappear from the northern glens.

Surprisingly, in light of later developments, such representation of sporting innovation as revival was remarkably slow to take hold in Ireland. However, it constituted an obvious line of rhetoric for Cusack to pursue, particularly as he was already active in the Irish language revival. His initiative would be formulated not as the new start it actually was but as a return to the past. The full name of the new body was the Gaelic Athletic Association for the Preservation and Cultivation of National Pastimes. Replying to an invitation to accept designation as one of the patrons of the association (the others were C.S. Parnell and Michael Davitt), Archbishop Thomas Croke of Cashel responded to the revivalist cue, deploring the widespread abandonment of 'our own grand national sports' and attempting a rather untidy list:

> Ball playing, hurling, football kicking according to Irish rules, 'casting', leaping in various ways, wrestling, handy-grips, top-pegging, leap-frog, rounders, tip-in-the-hat, and all such favourite exercises and amusements amongst men and boys, may now be said to be not only dead and buried, but in several localities to be entirely forgotten and unknown.

Croke continues his reminiscent list-making on a decidedly ambivalent note:

---

[12]   Attributed to John Marshall of Grangemockler, Co. Tipperary in oral sources.

No doubt there is something rather pleasing to the eye in the 'get up' of a modern young man who, arrayed in light attire, with parti-coloured cap on and racket in hand, is making his way, with or without companion, to the tennis-ground. But for my part I should vastly prefer to behold, or think of, the youthful athletes whom I used to see in my early days at fair and pattern, bereft of shoes and coat . . .

It is doubtful if either Cusack or Croke wished to reinstate the barefoot youth. If Croke thus, however unintentionally, uncovered the inadequacy of revivalism as applied to sport, he struck a note with much more powerful resonance in evoking the concept of the 'foreign' game: he instanced lawn-tennis, polo, croquet and cricket. These were depicted as imports from England and for that reason undesirable, like other influences from England, such as 'her fashions, her accent, her vicious literature, her music, her dances, and her manifold mannerisms'.[13]

It is important to observe the process of invention at work here. Tennis and cricket were no more foreign than tea-drinking, train engines, rosary beads, the Italianate glory of Croke's cathedral in Thurles, or numerous other things that the archbishop felt no need to renounce. Definition of the nation by selective rejection is one of the key ways in which nationalists (as also their opponents) contribute to nation invention. In due course, tennis was silently dropped from the 'foreign' list, and games to which Croke made no reference – soccer and rugby – were added. Other devices to take note of are Croke's successful identification of Britishness and foreignness, and the use of 'foreign' as a derogatory and emotive concept. Douglas Hyde would make more powerful use of these devices in 1892 in support of the language revival. Criteria of nationality advanced by nationalists are frequently directed not against the outside world but against internal opponents. Thus, Croke insisted not only that 'foreign' games were alien but that so too were most of 'the men and women who first imported and continue to patronise them'.[14] The archbishop was later to row back on the designation of 'foreign' games, but his letter of 18 December 1884 is frequently cited as the informal charter of the GAA.

In due course, the GAA has come to be identified principally with hurling and Gaelic football, but initially its main concern was with athletics. The Amateur Athletics Association (AAA) had been formed in Britain in 1879 with a view to standardising the many sports that it covered, all or most of which would be contested at a typical athletics meeting. Cusack now depicted the adoption of its standards by Irish clubs and at meetings in Ireland as intolerable foreign interference. The GAA demanded allegiance on the basis of 'Home Rule' for Irish athletics. Adopting a tactic well established in the practice of competing English sporting bodies, early in 1885 the

---

[13] Croke to Cusack, 18 Dec. 1884, quoted in *United Ireland*, 27 Dec. 1884.
[14] Ibid.

GAA declared that from 17 March any athlete competing at meetings other than those under its own auspices could not subsequently participate in GAA meetings. With the support of nationalist political organisations and interests, the GAA made a highly successful start in 1885 as an athletics authority, organising many meetings and annexing the allegiance of others already planned under other auspices. Not much adaptation was required since the GAA's rules differed very little from those of the AAA. The new order was most effectively represented by the GAA's insistence on the employment of its own appointed handicapper. Faced with the GAA's coup, leaders of clubs and associations which were determined, for one reason or another, not to be absorbed by the new body, came together and hurriedly formed the Irish Amateur Athletics Association (IAAA) in February 1885. The IAAA in its turn placed restrictions on participation by GAA athletes. Within a year, the line of division between the two was fairly clearly established, following as it did the country's wider politico-religious cleavage. In 1895, mutual restrictions were dropped and a duopoly arrangement agreed, under which every competitive athlete in the country had to join one or other association. This working compromise lasted until 1906.[15] Despite this conflict, several Irish athletes attained international success and heroic status at home during this period, such as Tom Conneffe from Clane, Co. Kildare and Tom ('Champion') Kiely from Ballyneale, Co. Tipperary.

Thus the GAA had staked its claim for 'Home Rule' athletics on the basis of maximising its share of control of a common code. By contrast, in field games it was to serve the nationalist interest by inventing distinctive codes. As its name implies, the GAA originally envisaged athletics as its primary concern but with two field games, hurling and Gaelic football, as supplementary pastimes. In the event, the field games were to dominate the future of the association. Dr Joe Lennon, in his authoritative study of the rules of GAA games, asserts that they are 'designer games'.[16] The purpose was to have codes to which all who wished to be adherents of the association would have to conform, relinquishing existing codes and the attachments they involved. 'Gaelic' football was not in the 1880s the expression of some distinctive Irish inheritance. Its rules were drawn up with a variety of precedents in mind – Australian football, soccer, rugby – and the main purpose was that they would be sufficiently different from other codes to create a barrier that could not be ignored. The challenge was intended in particular for rugby, a game which Cusack had played and promoted until shortly before his démarche. Rugby clubs were plentiful in town and countryside, particularly in Munster. They generally catered for both Catholics and Protestants, typically in an ethos of some deference to the gentry and the higher professions. The GAA, in effect, challenged these clubs to adopt its

---

[15] *Oxford Companion to Irish History*, pp. 275–6.
[16] J. Lennon, *Towards a Philosophy for Legislation in Gaelic Games* (Dublin, 2000), p. 17.

rules and its ethos or accept exclusion from the ranks of the Gaels. Some rugby clubs, such as Arravale Rovers in Co. Tipperary simply conformed. Elsewhere the rugby club continued side by side with the new popular code.

In the case of hurling, it was imperative that the rules should establish its distinctiveness from hurley and from hockey: Cusack had been at work along these lines since 1882. The game that emerged may be closer than hurley to hurling as Cusack, when a youth, saw it played in his native County Clare. However, there is no basis for the implication that hurley was less 'Irish' than the GAA game, unless having been practised mainly by Protestants is deemed to make it so. In fact, there is evidence that in the surviving pockets of pre-codified hurling in Clare, the GAA version met with initial resistance on the grounds that, like hurley, it too was a departure from demotic forms.[17] Generations of acquaintance with the codified forms of hurling and Gaelic football have created for Irish people mental associations redolent of tradition and immemorial usage. In fact, not only were most of those forms non-existent before 1884, but many of them did not take their classic shape until several years later. The two games are now played on an identical pitch with identical markings: in the early years, the hurling pitch was three times as large as that for football. At one stage in the 1880s, the scoring area was sixty-three feet wide, the central goal having point-scoring sections at each side in the manner of Australian football: the now familiar, indeed iconic, goal – tall uprights with crossbar – was legislated for only in 1910.[18] For a time, points affected the result only if there was an equality of goals; it took some years for the number of players on a team to be set at fifteen. As late as 1903, a GAA convention gave lengthy consideration to a motion that would have abolished catching the ball in football. If the original rules were designed to be distinctive rather than an encapsulation of tradition, they were reworked, not in the light of any striving to replicate an inheritance, but with a view to maximising their practicability and safety for the players, and their entertainment value for onlookers. These objectives were realised to an impressive extent, particularly in the case of hurling. It has to be borne in mind that a political or 'national' agenda would not of itself have secured and retained the enormous popularity of the games – especially in the open market place of recent decades – if they were not highly enjoyable to play and to watch. The continuing adaptation of the rules, astute central management and the growing professionalism of the (still unpaid) players had produced by the late twentieth century two sports with all the skills and attractions that the most demanding could require.

The Catholic parish as a political entity was called into the light by the O'Connellite mobilisations for emancipation and repeal in the period

---

[17]   Lennon, p. 16, footnote 17.
[18]   Lennon, p. 662.

1825–45, but it came into its own in the 1880s when Parnell's National League acknowledged without question its place as the basic unit of nationalist organisation. The land war at the beginning of the decade had dented the social influence of landlords in the countryside, at the same time strengthening the capacity of priests, shopkeepers and prominent farmers to mobilise parochial society. Almost from the beginning, the GAA moved to identify with the parish, even if the process would take decades to be completed. In rural Ireland, the GAA club would be the Catholic parish at play, and in contention for 'the credit of the little village'.[19] In this way, the association latched on to the structures of influence at the heart of political mobilisation.

Within the parish setting, the priest, whose functions defined the parochial collectivity, enjoyed an institutionalised advantage; this provoked, especially in cities and towns, the resentment of men with a sense of secular autonomy, and/or with ambitions to be leaders themselves, who almost invariably emerge under the designation of Fenians, or members of the Irish Republican Brotherhood. The IRB won control of the central organisation of the GAA in the late 1880s: at Parnell's funeral in 1891, which the priests ignored, the IRB provided a guard of honour of young men shouldering hurling sticks. Antagonism on the part of many bishops and priests, together with the friction between Parnellites and anti-Parnellites, seriously weakened the GAA for a decade or more. Whatever young activists might wish, clerical influence mattered greatly in the long run. When in 1913, the association acquired a national stadium, it was named in honour, not of the Fenian John O'Leary, a patron from 1886, or Parnell or Michael Davitt, patrons from the foundation, but of the other founding patron, Archbishop Croke. As part of the general Catholicisation of popular culture in independent Ireland from the late 1920s, the formalities surrounding major championship matches at Croke Park came to include the honouring of the incumbent Archbishop of Cashel (who was allowed to start the game by throwing in the ball) and the rendering of 'Faith of our fathers', a hymn of triumph over 'dungeon, fire and sword', actually written with reference to Roman Catholicism in England, but taken to refer to the Irish case. Such displays were discontinued in the 1960s in line with the new sensitivity to confessionalism.

For most of its history, the GAA has maintained one or more forms of exclusionary rule (or 'ban'), something of interest for this study because of the definition of nationality implied in such exclusions. Three types of ban can be identified: firstly, against individuals who play 'foreign' games, eventually extended to all 'patrons' of such games; secondly, against members of Crown forces; thirdly, a prohibition in the use of GAA pitches for 'foreign'

---

[19] Words of Mat Donovan as he musters his strength for a triumphant throw of the hammer in C.J. Kickham, *Knocknagow or the homes of Tipperary* (popular edition), p. 453.

games. Bans first appeared in the 1880s in the context of a socio-political struggle, (the land war, and its aftermath) in which ostracisation was so prominent a part that a new synonym was then coined for it – boycotting. In the late 1890s, a much-weakened GAA abolished all bans, but they were renewed in the early 1900s. Exclusionary practices sanctified by invocation of the true and the native fitted well with a particular kind of nationalism and a particular mode of religion that promoted the identification of 'taboos', of classes of persons who are untouchable, of books that must not be read, and of places that must not be entered. In this spirit, the political leaders of independent Ireland on 14 July 1949 stood outside the doors of St Patrick's Cathedral rather than enter while the obsequies of Douglas Hyde, first president of Ireland, were taking place inside. However, the *reductio ad absurdum* of this mentality had already been reached over a decade earlier when Hyde, co-founder of the Gaelic League, avatar of Irish Ireland, and a patron of the GAA since early in the century, fell foul of the ban on foreign games. In his capacity as president of Ireland, and accompanied by the Taoiseach, Eamon de Valera, he had attended an international soccer match between Ireland and Poland on 13 November 1938. Meeting the following month, the Central Council of the GAA effectively removed Hyde from the position of patron, although the technical act was a verdict that he had removed himself. Interestingly, there was explicit acceptance that Hyde's attendance at the match was an official duty.[20] As generally transpires with such forms of puritanism, the ban on participation in or attendance at foreign games occasioned much casuistry, hypocrisy and cynicism. Those appointed to police the ban were themselves permitted to attend foreign games in order to spy out transgressors. Particularly in provincial towns with thriving local soccer competition, appointment as an invigilator was much sought after as a licence to enjoy forbidden fruit.

The confidence which had enabled the GAA to part so casually with the services of the head of state as patron was based on the status it had achieved in the new political order. While the participation of GAA members and of the association itself in the push for independence over the period 1916–21 was as mixed and patchy as that of the nationalist collectivity in general, the British authorities looked on it as a visible manifestation of militant nationalism. On 21 November 1920, following the morning's assassination of fourteen undercover government intelligence agents in Dublin, a detachment of Black and Tans fired murderously on the crowd and players attending a football match at Croke Park, leaving twelve dead, including the captain of the Tipperary football team, Michael Hogan. This 'bloody Sunday' made of Croke Park a place of martyrdom and a locus of piety. Over the next half century, the failure of the state to develop any single national day of commemoration led to the emergence of All-Ireland

---

[20] *Irish Times*, 19 Dec. 1938.

final days at Croke Park as the nearest Irish equivalent to Bastille Day in France or Remembrance Sunday in Britain – the occasions when head of state and party leaders feel it incumbent upon them to attend and participate in ritual. Indeed, the links of the GAA with the independent state were close and significant from the beginning.

Next to the GAA itself, Ireland's most significant contribution to nationalist invention in the area of sport was the Tailteann Games, inspired by the *Oenach Tailten* of early medieval times, in which it was possible to see an Irish counterpart to the Olympic Games. From early in 1922, the Free State authorities devoted resources to the Tailteann Games project, and from the beginning the GAA was closely involved, not least insofar as Croke Park was the chosen venue. Substantial sums of money were forthcoming from the State and, even if they did not leave a profit, they set up a close relationship. The first Tailteann Games went ahead in 1924. Marcus de Búrca has summarised the offerings (in addition to hurling, football and athletics) as follows:

> Spread over a sixteen-day period in August, the games took in not only most popular pastimes but also literature, sculpture, music, several forms of aquatic and equine sport, chess, dancing, golf, tennis, billiards and even air racing.[21]

With contestants from around the world participating – they had to be of Irish birth or descent – this was an impressive display. The Games were held again in 1928 and 1932, after which they were discontinued. It is a commonplace that newly independent Ireland sought to develop justifying distinctiveness in the areas of language and religion. Sport should be added to that list, if account is to be taken of the promotion of the Tailteann Games and the concession of a 'special position' to the GAA. The ideological basis of the Association's status was the supposedly essential Irishness of Gaelic games. As with religion and language, the persuasiveness of the ideology owed much to the presence of a well-placed supporting interest group.

The wide range of sports celebrated at the Tailteann Games did not include certain games played by large numbers of Irish people, namely, soccer, rugby and hockey. Thus, the state came to adopt the GAA's concept and definition of 'foreign' games. It was not an automatic endorsement: the government and most pro-Treaty officials of the GAA were eager to have the ban lifted in 1922 as a sign that Ireland was now free, but anti-Treatyites within the organisation blocked the way, not wishing to concede that the new order represented a sufficiently large change. They had an ally on the other side of the political divide in General Eoin O'Duffy, commissioner of the Garda Síochána from 1922, who promoted Gaelic games, athletics and

---

21 M. de Búrca, *The G.A.A.: a history* (Dublin, 2nd edn., 1999), p. 132; see also W.F. Mandle, *The Gaelic Athletic Association and Irish Nationalist Politics, 1884–1924* (Dublin, 1987), pp. 216–19.

boxing within the security forces.[22] Indeed O'Duffy is the classic example of a politician who worked his way to public prominence through involvement in the organisational activities of the GAA.

O'Duffy lobbied his friends in government in support of the GAA's campaign for special taxation status, something that was conceded in 1927: the Association had been less than fully compliant since 1916, the intervening change to native government not having affected its attitude to fiscal matters. The 1927 concession speaks volumes about the place of the GAA in the power structure and ideology of the new state. Determined to display its superiority in national piety, the new Fianna Fáil government in 1932 copperfastened the GAA's tax advantages and at the same time withdrew from rugby and soccer organisations lesser concessions they had enjoyed since 1927.[23]

While the new Fianna Fáil party was deeply entrenched within the GAA, it also had useful links with 'foreign' games. Eamon De Valera, as a former student of Rockwell College, Co. Tipperary, was a lifelong devotee of rugby, and no doubt this was a matter of some reassurance for the upper-middle classes when it became expedient to repose trust in him in the 1930s. Reflecting the popular culture of his Dublin city background, the Fianna Fáil TD Oscar Traynor was prominent in soccer organisation. In 1943, as Minister for Defence, he ended the exclusion of 'foreign games' from the official pastimes of members of the national army. This was subsequently described by the General Secretary of the GAA, in a deliberate and formal address, as 'a national betrayal and a nullification of the natural order'.[24] In Co. Donegal, strong links with Scotland meant that soccer was a widely popular sport. The north Donegal TD, Neil Blaney, one of the most irredentist of Irish politicians of the second half of the twentieth century, was a leading figurehead of organised soccer.

In one of the several ironies that characterise the history of sport in twentieth-century Ireland, the soccer body patronised by Blaney (and of which he, following Traynor, became president), the Football Association of Ireland, is a twenty-six-county organisation. It had broken away in the early 1920s from the thirty-two-county Irish Football Association with headquarters in Belfast, which subsequently but only very belatedly accepted that it should confine itself to north of the border and call its international team Northern Ireland rather than Ireland. Soccer had established itself throughout the country before 1914, but the IFA had not achieved a strong national profile.[25] The FAI's international team was at first called the Irish Free State and then from 1936, Ireland and, from 1949, the Republic of

[22] Liam McNiffe, *Garda Síochána*.
[23] Marcus Bourke, *The G.A.A.: a history*, pp. 138–9.
[24] B. MacLua, *The Steadfast Rule: A History of the G.A.A. Ban* (Dublin, 1967), p. 85.
[25] Garnham, 'Football and national identity'.

Ireland. The story of Irish soccer since the 1920s is of particular interest because of the way in which it exemplifies the vagaries of the nationalist paradigm.

That soccer was played by the 'townies' who had joined the British Army for the Great War, rugby by the upper-middle classes, unionist and Redmondite, and Gaelic games by the 'boys' who won Ireland's freedom, is a flawed but not entirely baseless formula, and it was one that served to advance the claims of the GAA to a special status in independent Ireland. It is, as is usual with such formulae, a simplification. The 1924 semi-official celebratory volume, *The Voice of Ireland*, opens its section on sport, predictably enough, with a piece entitled 'Gaelic sports and the national revival'. In this, the GAA is asserted to have been in the van at every stage of 'the struggle' since 1884. But alongside the bombast, there are significant unforced admissions: that the oath of allegiance to the Crown imposed in 1919 on civil servants, including national school teachers, 'nearly wrecked the GAA' – presumably because so many members were prepared to take it and be expelled from the Association rather then forfeit their jobs; and that 'many Rugby and Association [i.e. soccer] teams ... supplied men for the [IRA] fighting line'.[26] Other articles covered hunting (Edith Somerville being the author), fishing and yachting, but there were none dedicated to rugby or soccer. Bloody Sunday enabled the GAA to create a myth about its role in the fight for freedom.

From 1926, national radio both boosted Gaelic games and helped to maintain their separateness. The spirit of the ban was upheld for decades as the reporting voices of Gaelic games were kept free from any taint of association with 'foreign' codes. Michael O'Hehir, whose inspired broadcast commentaries on hurling and football matches became a national institution, might also commentate on horse racing and might indulge his enthusiasm for other sports such as boxing, greyhound racing, American football and baseball on commercially sponsored programmes, but the faithful would not hear the magical voice polluted with mention of 'foreign' games. Even now (2003), Radio Éireann carries a Sunday night results programme devoted exclusively to Gaelic games. Like the broadcast Angelus on the same station, it is a treasured reminder of the way things used to be.

If radio facilitated the privileging of Gaelic games, television was to have the effect in sport, as in other areas of Irish life, of creating an open market. The accessibility of BBC television, initially on the eastern side of the country from the 1950s, brought English and Scottish soccer to the heart of Irish life. There was little point to a ban on attending soccer matches if Gaelic footballers and hurlers could watch the 'foreign' code in the privacy of their own homes, where only a Stasi-style vigilantism could have been effective. Logic on its own might not have led to the abandonment of this particular

---

[26] P. de Búrca, 'Gaelic sports and the national revival' in W.G. Fitzgerald (ed.), *The Voice of Ireland: A Survey of the Race and Nation from all Angles* (Dublin, [1924]), p. 581.

ban by the GAA (which happened in 1971) if the discrediting of authoritarian culture generally in the 1960s had not rendered it so hopelessly indefensible.

Meanwhile, the attraction of professional football on the neighbouring island was giving a new dimension to popular sporting culture in Ireland, frequently in the form of fan-style attachment to individual English or Scottish clubs. The basis of attachment could be some Irish link: Glasgow Celtic and Rangers had for generations given sporting expression to Irish confessional antagonism, and many young Irish people became fans of clubs patronised by friends or family in Britain. Equally, the choice of club might owe nothing to Irish connections. From the perspective of the prescriptive nationalism typified by the GAA ban, the sight of the masses of Irish youth going to work, to play, and even to pray, proudly attired in the most recently cut colours of Manchester United, Leeds United, Arsenal or Everton, is an abomination. In reality, this is just another instance of a shared field of culture common to both islands such as, for example, the somewhat earlier emergence of a popular taste for fish and chips. To see one as subversive of nationality and the other as not, is simply a matter of arbitrary choice.

Ironically, in the Irish case, professional soccer had become, before the end of the twentieth century, the occasion of levels of nationalistic enthusiasm beyond the dreams of chauvinism. There was a wider background pattern. From the early eighties it was evident that televised soccer was inducing unprecedented levels of popular international rivalry, for example between England and Scotland and between The Netherlands and Germany. In Ireland, a victory over England at the European Nations Cup finals in Stuttgart in August 1988 evoked a nationwide response transcending any previous social or regional limitations on support for soccer. In progressing through the necessary qualification stages and reaching the final stages of the World Cup in 1990 (held in Italy) and 1994 (held in the USA), and performing more than creditably at both, the soccer team established itself as the single most potent focus of national feeling for the Irish at home and abroad, particularly for those who had emigrated in the 1980s. The 'foreign' code had assumed a role that was beyond the reach of 'native' games, as a vehicle of triumph in the international arena. The stone rejected by the builder had become the cornerstone. These developments had deep significance. For those born after about 1960, the old authoritarian, prescriptive account of nationalism never carried any conviction or even meaning. They found, in support for the national soccer team, not a new nationalism but a new experienced meaning for nationalism. Irishness had been reinvented for a new generation.

By the early 1990s, Irish nationalism was enjoying the best of both worlds in the matter of team sports. Gaelic games provided cause for pride in national uniqueness, while soccer (and on occasion rugby) was demonstrating a national capacity to shine in the world arena. Awareness both in Ireland and Australia of the disadvantages of a country-specific code is evidenced by the ingenious arrangements ('compromise rules') that permit regular games between Gaelic and Australian Rules football teams.

The composition of international soccer teams has highlighted some of the ambiguities of national identity. Almost without exception, the Irish squad of recent decades has consisted of players in English clubs, since Irish clubs cannot afford the level of salary that players of international class can command. Some were born in Ireland, but many in England. The regulations governing international football allow a player to opt for any country of which he has citizenship. Irish citizenship is available to anyone with a parent or grandparent born in the country, a category that covers a large proportion of the population of England, including several prime ministers in recent decades. Some come from families who identify themselves as Irish, and an elite footballer emerging from this background would tend to see himself as an Irish footballer. Where the identity is not so keenly felt, there are calculations to be made about which country to opt for, along the lines of the big fish/small pond or small fish/big pond conundrum. Scouts are on the watch for promising young players in England who may have Irish eligibility of which they are themselves unaware. These footballers provide an exceptionally obvious example of individuals choosing a national identity for themselves without having to change anything, except possibly their passports. Many aspects of national identity are similarly arbitrary, but the choices are usually made in a less obvious way.

Nationalists in Northern Ireland identified fully with the triumphant Ireland football teams. Unionists were less likely to join in the frenzy of tricolour-waving and, in any case, they could look back to the glory days of Northern Ireland at the World Cup in 1982 and 1986. Within Northern Ireland, soccer is the only major sport shared by both sides of the religious-political divide. Although few club teams have been religiously homogeneous, several have been identified with one side or other, and sectarian conflict has suffused much of the competition between clubs.

While nationalists in Northern Ireland play soccer within the framework of a six-county association, they have had little to do with rugby, although it is organised on a thirty-two county basis. North and South, rugby retains a strong connection with the middle and professional classes, reaching just a few pockets of more popular participation, notably in Limerick city. Perhaps helped by its relatively limited social base, rugby, unlike soccer, has been able to cope with the formalisation of divided political allegiances in twentieth-century Ireland. The compromise achieved required unionists to accept use of the symbols of the Irish state (its tricolour and the national anthem) in connection with international matches, but this is no doubt balanced at a more subtle level by the satisfaction of having citizens of that state legitimate a sport that nationalist ideology has decreed to be

'British'.[27] Under a more recent refinement, the song 'Ireland's call' is used in place of the Irish national anthem at away internationals. Rugby scarcely has the same potential as soccer for mobilisation of mass enthusiasm, but international rugby matches do bring their own level of mesmerisation to daily life, North and South. For the purposes of this study, the difference between the sets of meanings attaching to two teams – soccer and rugby – playing under the national flag, illustrates nicely the contingent and invented character of national identity.

If nationalists in Northern Ireland shared soccer and had little to do with rugby, they had Gaelic games largely to themselves. While the GAA's irredentist principles may have had limited power to enthuse thwarted nationalists in the decades after partition, its games at least retained the advantage for Catholics of being played on Sundays, not unimportant under a regime which at local level frequently made an issue of Sunday observance in places of public recreation. With the mobilisation of the Catholic collectivity from the late 1960s, initially under the banner of civil rights and then under that of nationalism, the GAA assumed a very important function as a locus of autonomous social activity in an unambiguously nationalist setting. The GAA's credentials were highlighted by its generations-old regulations excluding members of the constabulary and other Crown forces from membership of the organisation and participation in its games. The political views of players and members covered the full range of the nationalist spectrum, with republicans on occasion seeming to have hijacked the organisation for its propaganda purposes. Predictably, there was conflict between the association and the state, typified by the commandeering of GAA grounds in Belfast and Crossmaglen, ostensibly because they were essential for security purposes. But it would be misleading to paint a picture of unrelieved confrontation. The authorities were well aware of the stabilising influence of the GAA, and the Association, in its turn, has been ready to accept public money for sporting and recreational purposes from the northern as well as the southern states.

The Northern Ireland Troubles have helped to perpetuate the role of the GAA as a nationalist oracle. Every large-scale sporting movement develops a directing and administrative hierarchy with interests and concerns that are differently balanced from those of the typical player or spectator. In the case of the GAA, the official cadres have for long assumed the role of guardians of national orthodoxy. For decades following independence they were, after elected politicians and clerics, among those most likely to be heard pronouncing on national rights and wrongs. Office-holding within the GAA provided a form of alternative to advancement within Church or political party. The great prize was the presidency of the Association, an office with an aura

[27] J. Sugden and A. Bairner (eds), *Sport, Sectarianism and Society in a Divided Ireland* (Leicester, 1993), p. 61.

comparable to that of a bishopric or a cabinet ministry. Despite the ideological preoccupations of the officer class, there is no reason to believe that
either players or followers of Gaelic games have been more attached to national
pieties or nationalist politics than any other cross-section of Irish Catholics.

The codification and institutionalisation of sport in the late nineteenth
century created a definite, if severely circumscribed, arena for women in
sport, particularly with tennis and hockey. In his oft-cited letter of
November 1884, Archbishop Croke identified female participation as a feature of the alien new sports displacing the old pastimes that he treasured.[28]
Promoting female autonomy was not a concern of the early GAA, and there
was little initial enthusiasm from within that body when in the early 1900s
nationally minded women enjoying enhanced social and political roles
began to play a version of hurling that was given the designation 'camogie'.
Governed by its own ruling body, the game has waxed and waned over the
decades, as has its relationship with the GAA. Camogie was much weakened in the 1930s and 1940s by internal conflict about the adoption of a
GAA-style ban against players of women's hockey.[29]

If the different team sports each managed, in its own way, to find a working solution to the problems created by political division and territorial partition, athletics was less fortunate. The crucial difference was that, whereas
in team sports Ireland, England, Scotland and Wales had always competed
separately, the new controlling body of the International Amateur Athletics
Federation that emerged following the 1912 Olympics decided that, for its
purposes, the United Kingdom of Great Britain and Ireland would be a single entity. This followed the pattern already established at the Olympic
Games. Securing recognition on the international scene as an independent
country was a major preoccupation of the Irish Free State. The ink was
scarcely dry on the Anglo-Irish treaty before moves were afoot to establish
a single athletics body. With an alacrity that can only have been a response
to strong political pressure, the two bodies that formerly had agreed to
divide Irish athletics along the political/confessional cleavage, the GAA and
the IAAA, surrendered their respective interests and supported the establishment of the National Athletics and Cycling Association (NACA) in May
1922. Its standing committee included prominent members of both parent
organisations. However, various clubs in the Belfast area withheld their
consent to joining in the new arrangements. In the subsequent negotiations,
NACA dispensed with its GAA-style ban on participation by members of
the Crown forces and agreed to have annual championships held on
Saturdays and Sundays in alternate years, clear evidence of a desire to
accommodate all confessions.[30] These concessions simply delayed the break
that was formalised in 1925 with the establishment of the Northern Ireland

---

[28] See note 13 above.
[29] See *Oxford Companion to Irish History*, pp. 70–1.
[30] P. Griffin, *The Politics of Irish Athletics, 1850–1990* (Ballinamore, 1990), p. 73.

Amateur Athletics, Cycling and Cross Country Association. It is by no means certain that unionist politics was the sole driving force behind this move. In fact much of the impetus had come from Belfast Celtic – a name synonymous with soccer-playing Catholics – which resented NACA's objections to some of the activities it liked to mix into athletics meetings, such as whippet racing, pony trotting and opportunities for betting.

Meanwhile NACA had sent the first Irish team, one representing the entire island, to the 1924 Olympic Games in Paris. Jack B. Yeats won a silver medal for painting and Oliver St. John Gogarty bronze for poetry, and, although the athletes were unsuccessful, this was the sporting equivalent of admission to the League of Nations. The 1928 Games in Amsterdam brought striking athletic success when Dr Pat O'Callaghan won the gold medal at hammer throwing. It was, however, the Los Angeles Olympic Games of 1932 that produced a mass popular mobilisation to celebrate national sporting triumph. The occasion was the homecoming of the team that had won two of the mere twenty-one gold medals on offer in athletics with Bob Tisdall's victory in the 400 metres hurdles and Pat O'Callaghan's retention of the hammer title. In the last days of August, just over two months after the Eucharistic Congress, they were feted in Dublin and elsewhere: one estimate claimed that a quarter of a million assembled to greet them in the capital. At the banquet in their honour in the Gresham Hotel, the recently elected head of government, Eamon de Valera, was joined by his predecessor, William T. Cosgrave. The messages of congratulation included one from the Prime Minister of Northern Ireland, Lord Craigavon, who had obviously been invited, and, while indicating that he could not be present, offered fulsome congratulations to Tisdall and O'Callaghan.

Hogging the limelight with the two medal winners, and not without justification, was the president of NACA and Irish team manager at Los Angeles, Garda Commissioner Eoin O'Duffy. It was the high point of the work as sports organiser that predated and outlasted his career as revolutionary, soldier, police chief and would-be Irish Mussolini. Displaying his confident grasp of the national sporting scene and the extent of his own ambition, O'Duffy informed his listeners at the Gresham Hotel banquet that he had made an informal bid to obtain the 1940 Olympic Games for Dublin. He observed that the Los Angeles stadium had cost one and a half million pounds, but suggested that Dublin could be provided with the necessary facilities for one third of that sum. By early 1933, O'Duffy was proposing a National Stadium for the Phoenix Park, the cost to be met by means of sweepstakes. His plans for hosting the Olympics in Dublin were to be overtaken by events, not least his dismissal from the office of Garda commissioner by De Valera in February 1933, but up to the time of his death in 1944 he was still advancing the cause of the stadium.[31]

---

[31] Griffin, pp. 110–16, 152.

Long before this, Ireland's Olympic status had been mired in contention. Some of the northern clubs, cut off from international competition when they left NACA in 1925, had sought recognition from the Amateur Athletics Association in Britain. The response was sympathetic, but constrained by the fact that NACA was the recognised body for the whole of Ireland. The situation was changed dramatically in August 1934 when the IAAF reworded its regulations to make explicit reference to political boundaries, with the Irish case clearly in mind. Instead of cutting its losses and making the most of the twenty-six-county remit now assigned to it by the international ruling body, NACA refused to withdraw its claim to control athletics in Northern Ireland. Considerations of political nationalism weighed heavily on the case. Accepting confinement to the South would mean abandoning those northern clubs that had remained loyal to NACA, and they made no secret of their inclination to stir up southern opinion. Since 1925, the implications of partition had sunk in more deeply, the economic war was now exacerbating Anglo-Irish relations, and the politics of athletics became identified with the politics of the constitution. From this perspective, to accept the IAAF ruling would be to condone partition. For refusing to abandon its claim to represent Northern Ireland, NACA, after several formal warnings, was suspended from membership of IAAF, with the result that its athletes were excluded from international competition. As a consequence, there was no Irish team at the 1936 Olympics and Pat O'Callaghan missed the opportunity of winning a third gold medal, although he was still the world's best at the hammer: in Fermoy on 22 August 1937 he broke the world record in place since 1913.[32] Another casualty was the Tailteann Games, not held again after 1932. Athletes from abroad competing at a meeting conducted by NACA would have faced suspension from all competition outside of Ireland and that was a sacrifice they could not be expected to make. Irish athletics in the mid-1930s provides a notable instance of an inflexible nationalism thwarting the interests of nationality. Though not uncommon, this is rarely so visible.

As early as 1937, a few clubs, mainly in Dublin, withdrew from NACA, showing that they saw no point in remaining within a system that excluded their best athletes from international competition. This was seen as treason by the clubs remaining with NACA and much bitterness ensued. Emotions were further heightened when the departed clubs formed a new association and sought, successfully, to be recognised by IAAF as the representative body for athletics in the twenty-six counties. Under the designation of Amateur Athletics Union, Éire (or AAUE), it soon established friendly contact with the Northern Ireland branch of the AAA. This was particularly necessary because international competitions involving Ireland, England, Scotland and Wales (the 'home' countries, as they were referred to) and also

---

[32] Griffin, p. 143.

France and Belgium, were a key feature of the athletics calendar, and it had become necessary to devise a formula for selecting a single Irish team drawn from two associations. Outside of Dublin, NACA retained the loyalty of all but a handful of southern clubs, and it was supported in its intransigent stance by the vigilantes of nationalist orthodoxy. Over a period of two decades, various attempts to effect an accommodation merely resulted in fresh rounds of vituperation.[33]

To complicate matters, the Olympic Council of Ireland was firmly in the control of NACA supporters. The result was confusion and contention about athletics representation at the Games in London (1948) and Helsinki (1952), and unseemly confrontations between members of the Irish delegations on both occasions. It was a measure of the parlous state to which internal division had reduced Irish athletics that lack of funding could be cited as having prevented the AAUE from sending Brendan O'Reilly, a promising high-jumper already qualified and selected, to the 1956 Olympic Games in Melbourne. Apart from all the normal obstacles in the way of success, a young athlete aspiring to Olympic status had to join the AAUE, and in so doing face down the opprobrium of breaking ranks on the national question. If selected to compete by the AAUE (thereby meeting the requirements of the IAAF), the athlete then faced the challenge of obtaining the endorsement of the Irish Olympic authorities, who supported the NACA view of the athletics controversy. The latter stage of the ordeal was eased in 1956 when the Olympic Council of Ireland agreed to treat AAUE nominations as applications from individuals. Against this unhelpful background, Ronnie Delaney secured a place at the Melbourne Games in 1956 and won the 1,500 metres, the blue riband of athletics. The welcome he received on his return, while enthusiastic, was not universal. A prominent NACA official is reported to have commented in the following terms: 'All honour to anyone who wins a gold medal, but nobody has won a gold medal for Ireland this year.'[34] No national politicians greeted Delaney on his return, and his triumph was limited to a civic reception by the Lord Mayor, Robert Briscoe, at the Mansion House, with the inevitable presentation of Waterford Glass.[35]

When the unification of the NACA and AAUE was eventually achieved in 1967 it came as the result of tortuous negotiations, with numerous false starts, extending over many years and involving a large cast of characters, including Jack Lynch TD and Lord Killanin. The amalgamation into a new body, Bord Lúthchleas na hÉireann (BLE), was achieved at the price of estrangement from the NIAAA, and of the emergence of a splinter group, the NACAI. A rapprochement with the NIAAA (achieved by stages down to

[33]   Griffin, pp. 82–138.
[34]   Griffin, p. 203.
[35]   *Irish Press*, 20 Dec. 1956.

1978) was based on two key points, one being provision for competition between NIAAA clubs and clubs in Northern Ireland affiliated to BLE, and the other the acceptance of Northern Ireland as a 'free zone'. This means that athletes resident in Northern Ireland have the choice of identifying themselves, for the purposes of international competition, with either Ireland or the United Kingdom. This was a foreshadowing of the flexibilities in the constitutional domain that characterise the Belfast Agreement of two decades later. The athletics solution defuses conflict but also segments support. To maximise his following, the Monaghan-born professional boxer of the 1980s, Barry McGuigan, whose main stomping ground was the King's Hall in Belfast, adopted a blue flag in place of either tricolour or union jack and used 'Danny Boy' in place of a national anthem.

While almost all sports are organised on a national basis, nationality looms large for some and not so for others. Included in the latter category are golf, tennis, hare-coursing and horse-racing, all common to the cultures of Ireland and Britain. Even here outstanding performers are seized upon as national champions. An early example was the greyhound Master McGrath, owned by Lord Lurgan, and three-times winner (in 1868, 1869 and 1871) of the Waterloo Cup, the blue riband of coursing, run annually at Altcar in Lancashire. His achievements were celebrated in balladry which still endures and are commemorated by a roadside monument near his place of origin, Colligan Lodge, Co. Waterford. Throughout the twentieth century a long series of equine champions (and their human handlers) have flattered Irish national sentiment. The non-politicisation of the category of sport being looked at here is well exemplified by the survival of upper-class Protestant influence in the controlling bodies of horse-racing for more than half a century after independence. Of the seventeen men who at various times held office as stewards of the Irish Turf Club in the period 1914–45 all were 'peers, officers in the British army or former landlords or their representatives', and subsequent dilution was slow.[36]

From Gaelic games to horse-racing, almost every sport played by Irish people has been touched by nationality, and they have in their turn contributed, if in very different ways, to the invention of the Irish nation.[37]

---

[36] T. Dooley, *The Decline of the Big House in Ireland: A Study of Irish Landed Families, 1860–1960* (Dublin, 2001), p. 266.

[37] Treatment of some of the issues discussed in this chapter can be found in M. Cronin, *Sport and Nationalism in Ireland: Gaelic Games, Soccer and Irish Identity since 1884* (Dublin, 1999).

|8|

Artefacts

Of the durable objects and structures produced by human endeavour, there have always been those invested with iconic status and used to support a cult of one kind or another, religious or political, or both. As with the basic referent of the term 'icon' – a depiction of Christ or one of the saints placed in an Orthodox Christian church – many artefacts are designed from the beginning for the purposes of a cult. The pyramids of Egypt are very spectacular structures of great antiquity constructed in the interests of dynasties combining divinity and tyranny. In Ireland, the great passage tombs, of which that at Newgrange, County Meath is the most celebrated (see illustration p. 16), are of comparable antiquity and of similar function. In each case, a modern nationality has adopted these ancient monuments for its own purposes. The Book of Kells (*c.* AD 800) is possibly the most striking Irish instance of an object created for an earlier cult – that of religion in an early medieval monastery – now used to boost the self-esteem of a modern nationality. In addition to borrowing, modern nationalists also create their own iconic artefacts in abundance, public statuary being a prime instance. Perhaps even more interesting is the manner in which nationalism appropriates artefacts, both old and new, that were created without any cultic purpose, ranging in the Irish case from personal ornaments of the Bronze Age to modern paintings. In Ireland, as in most European countries, the identification and collection of antiquities has been conducted largely in the framework of a modern nation and generally as a form of service to the nation. The main repositories of works of art in many countries are institutions that are 'national', usually in the sense both of being created by the state and serving as showcases of the nation's achievements. Practitioners of the modern archaeology that has developed from the 'antiquarianism' of earlier centuries have in recent times begun to look closely at the ways in which their discipline has been

influenced by nationalist assumptions, and Irish archaeologists are contributing significantly to this self-assessment.[1]

Sir James Ware (1594–1666) may be regarded as the pioneer of interest in
Irish antiquities. As a protégé and collaborator of James Ussher, Ware was
concerned primarily with the assembling and processing of Latin and Gaelic
manuscript sources for Irish history, but he extended his interest to inscriptions and monuments. According to one authority, the collecting of 'curios
and antiquities' began in Ireland towards the end of the seventeenth century.[2] Antiquarian activity gathered pace in Ireland, as elsewhere, in the
course of the following century, in due course attracting the interest of an
element among the 'improvers' who constituted the (Royal) Dublin Society.
In 1785, nationally minded antiquarianism acquired its own dedicated association with the formation of the Irish Academy (from 1786 the Royal Irish
Academy), Sylvester O'Halloran and Charles Vallancey being prominent
among the founders. The antiquities assembled by the RDS and the RIA,
augmented at various stages by private collections, purchased or donated,
constitute – along with the illuminated manuscripts in the RIA and Trinity
College, Dublin – what has come to be perceived as the nation's chest of
heirlooms. That a modern nation feels responsibility for such treasures is
very much to be applauded, even if the implausibility of the present-day
population taking credit for the achievements of those who lived in earlier
millennia cannot be overlooked. Of the metal objects, two sets stand out for
excellence: personal gold ornaments from the Bronze Age, and ecclesiastical
paraphernalia and brooches from the early Christian period.[3] The latter set,
including as it does such exquisite items as the Ardagh chalice (see illustration p. 86) and the Tara brooch, has come to be taken as proof and symbol
of the ancient Christian foundation of the modern Irish nation. The occurrence of similar decoration (ultimate insular La Tène) in the Book of Kells
and on the slightly later carved high crosses of the same era serves to consolidate the sense of a coherent civilisation imagined to be 'Celtic'. Mention
of high crosses is a reminder that the concerns of the antiquarians extended
beyond portable objects to structures, many of them in ruins, but some in a
more or less integral state, including not only high ('Celtic') crosses but also
the ninety or so distinctive round towers with which the island is endowed.
The question of the origin of the round towers proved highly divisive
because it would determine whether the golden age of the Irish national

---

1   Gabriel Cooney, 'Building the future on the past: archaeology and the construction of the
    national identity of Ireland' in Margarita Díaz-Andreu and Timothy Champion (eds),
    Nationalism and Archaeology in Europe (London, 1996), pp. 146–63; see also John
    Hutchinson, 'Archaeology and the Irish rediscovery of the Celtic past' in *Nations and
    Nationalism*, vol. vii, no. 4 (2001), pp. 505–19.
2   Máire de Paor, 'Irish antiquarian artists' in Adele M. Dalsimer (ed.), *Visualising Ireland:
    National Identity and the Pictorial Tradition* (Boston and London, 1993), p. 121.
3   P.F. Wallace, *A Guide to the National Museum of Ireland* (Dublin, 2000).

myth was to be located in pagan or Christian times.[4] With the general acceptance from the 1840s that the round towers were indeed ecclesiastical bell-
towers, rather than temples of some elder pagan faith, the identification of
the nation with the Celtic and the Christian was secured, although a group
of convinced 'paganists' would hold out against the evidence for years to
come. Be that as it may, while the patrimony is perceived as Celtic and
Christian, it also has assimilated to it in popular perception all that is
ancient in the land, including the Bronze Age gold and the Neolithic monuments such as passage graves, cairns and dolmens.

The place of artefacts in nation invention depends greatly on their reproduction in image. Indeed it might be argued, following Benedict Anderson's
point about the vital role of print capitalism, that modern nationalism is
inseparable from the circulation of iconic images in multiplicate. The drawing of Irish antiquities with a view to reproduction began in the later seventeenth century and flourished from the later eighteenth. By 1800, or shortly
thereafter, a set of stock emblems of Ireland (in such contexts now increasingly referred to as 'Erin') was in place. There was the harp, the shamrock,
the Celtic cross and the round tower; the wolfhound was added as a consequence of the prominence of that animal in the Ossianic stories. Subsequent
decades witnessed not only the widespread employment of these emblems,
but a burgeoning market for lithographic reproductions of views of venerated sites, especially ruined ecclesiastical complexes such as Clonmacnoise,
Glendalough and the Rock of Cashel (each of these, as it happens, endowed
with a round tower). Much of the demand came in the first instance from
tourists seeking travel books with useful and attractive illustrations, but a
consequence was that the literate public, and those who looked at books for
the pictures, gained access to visual evocations of a glorious past, thereby
receiving a crucial boost to their sense of nationality. By the 1840s, cheap
engravings were accessible even in homes which did not have any books.

Similarly replicated in numerous lithographs, places identified as being of
particular natural beauty, such as the Lakes of Killarney, the Vale of Avoca,
and the Giant's Causeway, were to the fore in underscoring another dimension of the nation as invented, namely possession of an abundant endowment of nature's gems. Moore in his melodies had done much to establish
this romantic idea as, for example, in singing the praises of the Vale of Avoca:

> There is not in this wide world a valley so sweet
> As that vale in whose bosom the bright waters meet
>   ('The meeting of the waters' in *Melodies* (1808))

Thus, enduring visual images were being created and diffused, at home and
abroad. The romantic delight in landscape inherited from the eighteenth

---

[4]   See chapter two.

Figure 8.1 View of Cashel, steel engraving by Charles Cousen in J. Stirling Coyne, *The scenery and antiquities of Ireland, illustrated from drawings by W.H. Bartlett* (London, 2 vols, [1840]), vol. 1.

century was widely 'nationalised' in the nineteenth century, so that in
Ireland, as elsewhere, the natural environment came to be appropriated to
the nation. Thomas Davis, in a didactic and celebratory piece entitled 'Irish
scenery', aimed particularly at encouraging the holidaying classes to 'see
Ireland first', made his climactic point by means of a quotation from a travel
writer identifying a scene for another lithograph:

> We have had descents of the Danube, and descents of the Rhine, and the Rhone,
> and of many other rivers; but we have not in print, as far as I know, any descent
> of the Blackwater; and yet, with all these descents of foreign rivers in my recol-
> lection, I think the descent of the Blackwater not surpassed by any of them. A
> detail of all that is seen in gliding down the Blackwater from Cappoquin to
> Youghal would fill a long chapter. There is every combination that can be pro-
> duced by the elements that enter into the picturesque: rocks, verdant slopes, with
> the triumphs of art superadded, and made visible in magnificent houses and beau-
> tiful villas, with their decorated lawns and pleasure-grounds.[5]

While celebration of the country's natural splendour and of its evocative
ruins are the stuff of nation invention, this does not necessarily imply a commitment to political independence. Those who indulged in it came from all
points on the political compass. It was the same with the cult of Irish symbols in the decorative arts. Shamrock, harps, wolfhounds, round towers and
high crosses proliferate as motifs in decoration of all kinds in the second half
of the century. Publication of decorations inspired by the elaborate tracery
in the thousand-year old Book of Kells,[6] and eventually of reproductions
from the book, further enhanced this sense of a supreme artistic achievement now identified as belonging to the Irish nation. Irish motifs were
widely used in furniture carving. Here and in other woodwork the utilisation of the hardened black timber of tree trunks dug up from peat deposits
– bog oak – became another mark of Irishness. Commercial printing of
images and copying of objects both exploited and promoted the sense of a
national inheritance that can do so much to ground modern nationalism.
But a cult of national heritage does not necessarily imply a commitment to
the political objectives of nationalists, and the correlation between the possession of replica national icons and political activism is not necessarily
high. Certainly the most ardent advocates – and inventors – of Irish nationality in the nineteenth century included many who were alienated from the
Irish nationalist movement of the age. And one of the keenest customers for
replicas of the Tara brooch was Queen Victoria.[7]

---

[5]   T. Davis, *Literary and Historical Essays*, p. 215.
[6]   A striking example, the title page of Samuel Ferguson, *The Cromlech on Howth* (Dublin,
      1861) is reproduced in Jeanne Sheehy, *The Rediscovery of Ireland's Past: The Celtic
      Revival, 1830–1930* (London, 1980), p. 25.
[7]   Ibid., p. 71.

In architecture, the nineteenth century witnessed an eclectic recourse to the styles of past ages and other cultures, as industrialising society sought a veneer of tradition for its unprecedented obtrusion of buildings and objects on the face of the earth. In Ireland, the contribution to be derived for these purposes from the country's 'Celtic' past was limited. Apart from the round towers, Irish pre-Romanesque structures in stone (as distinct from those in timber, which had left no traces other than postholes unrecognised until the twentieth century) consisted mainly of small, single-chamber churches making little pretension to ornamentation. However, the country's scattered examples of Romanesque could also be seen as ancient Irish, on the basis of predating the Anglo-Norman invasion. The prime example of this, Cormac's chapel, located on the Rock of Cashel (see illustration p. 239) and dating from 1127, is rich in continental-style decoration and motif, while retaining some distinctive Irish features such as smallness of scale and stone roofing. In subsequent decades, the application of Romanesque motifs in Irish churches was widespread. The Anglo-Norman invasion coincided with the arrival of Gothic.

In 1844, Daniel O'Connell had a private chapel built as an attachment to his house at Derrynane, Co. Kerry. Reflecting a sensibility that O'Connell would not have experienced throughout most of his career, the chapel was designed to reflect the shape and minimal features discernible in the ruined early medieval church on nearby Abbey Island, where various ancestors were buried. In 1847, at the height of the famine, a church was built by and for Irish-speaking converts to the Established Church at Toormore on the Mizen peninsula in south-west Co. Cork; the presiding minister, Rev. W.A. Fisher, made a point of the fact that it was designed 'after the pattern of the old Irish churches'.[8] The 'Celtic' revival (or 'Hiberno-Romanesque' revival, as it is generally designated with reference to church building) was under way. Over the following century, and especially from the 1860s onwards and in the early twentieth century, Catholics and Protestants constructed several more ambitious structures based on early Irish models, including St Patrick's at Jordanstown, Co. Antrim and the Honan Chapel at University College, Cork. Such ventures account for only a tiny fraction of the thousands of churches built or reconstructed in Ireland over this period. Most new churches of whatever denomination, insofar as they went beyond generally sound vernacular adaptation, were beholden to one or other international style, Baroque, Neo-classical or, predominantly, that of the Gothic revival preached by A.W.N. Pugin (1812–52).[9] The Celtic theme did make a substantial mark on funerary artefacts. O'Connell's grave in Glasnevin cemetery is marked by a round tower, and there are many examples at

---

8 Quoted in Patrick Hickey, *Famine in West Cork: the Mizen Peninsula, Land and People, 1800–52* (Cork, 2002), p. 237.
9 Alistair Rowan, 'Irish Victorian churches: denominational distinctions' in Brian P. Kennedy and Raymond Gillespie (eds), *Ireland: Art into History* (Dublin, 1994), pp. 207–30.

Glasnevin as elsewhere of mortuary chapels, mausoleums and headstones decorated with Celtic motifs. Most strikingly, the Celtic cross became, by the final quarter of the nineteenth century, virtually the standard form of the headstone in Ireland.

As we have seen above, Thomas Davis seemed content that the nation should glory in the country's stock of 'magnificent houses and beautiful villas, with their decorated lawns and pleasure-grounds'. Certainly, their occupants did glory in them, but as family rather than national ornaments. Widespread acceptance of the great houses of the gentry, in town or country, as part of the national patrimony, in the way that Davis assumed, was to be delayed until far into the twentieth century. Indeed, by the 1880s the 'big house' had become an oppositional symbol for most nationalists.[10] Civic pride in the architectural glory of late eighteenth-century Dublin had provided a market for the celebrated series of views of the city drawn by James Malton in 1791,[11] but the nationalists of the nineteenth and twentieth centuries generally identified Georgian Dublin with foreign domination. However, the Irish Free State did rebuild both the Custom House and the Four Courts following their near destruction in 1921–22, even if the restoration was not up to the highest standards of fidelity to the originals.

Considering more generally the attitude to fixed structures of historical significance that would in time be identified as national monuments, Davis again showed himself to be a thinker of rare perspicacity. He endeavoured to raise an alarm about the pillaging of ancient sites:

> Daily are more and more of our crosses broken, of our tombs effaced, of our abbeys shattered, of our castles torn down, of our cairns sacrilegiously pierced, of our urns broken up and our coins melted down. All classes, creeds and politics are to blame in this. The peasant lugs down a pillar for his sty, the farmer for his gate, the priest for his chapel, the minister for his glebe.

His remarks on a proposal in the 1840s to construct a road through the site of Newgrange have uncanny resonance a century and a half later:

> What then will be the reader's surprise and anger to hear that some people, having legal power or corrupt influence in Meath, are getting or have got a presentment for a road to run right through the temple of Grange! We do not know their names, nor, if the design be at once given up, as in deference to public opinion it must finally be, shall we take the trouble to find them out. But if they persist in this brutal outrage against so precious a landmark of Irish history and civilisation, then we frankly say that if the law will not reach them public opinion shall, and they shall bitterly repent the desecration. [They] may be Liberals or Tories,

---

[10] T.A. Dooley, *The Decline of the Big House in Ireland* (Dublin, 2001).
[11] Edward McParland, 'Malton's views of Dublin: too good to be true?' in Kennedy and Gillespie, pp. 15–26.

Protestants or Catholics, but beyond a doubt they are tasteless blockheads – poor devils without reverence or education . . . All over Europe the governments, the aristocracies and the people have been combining to discover, gain, and guard every monument of what their dead countrymen had done or been.

Irreparable losses would have been avoided if at any time in the following one hundred and fifty years it had proved possible to implement on any large scale his practical proposals:

> Is it extravagant to speculate on the possibility of the Episcopalian, Catholic, and Presbyterian clergy joining in an antiquarian society to preserve our ecclesiastical remains – our churches, our abbeys, our crosses and our fathers' tombs from fellows like the Meath road-makers? It would be a politic and a noble emulation of the sects, restoring the temples wherein their sires worshipped for their children to pray in. There's hardly a barony wherein we could not find an old parish or abbey church capable of being restored to its former beauty and convenience at a less expense than some beastly barn is run up, as if to prove the fact that we have little art, learning, or imagination. Nor do we see why some of these hundreds of half-spoiled buildings might not be used for civil purposes – as almshouses, schools, lecture-rooms, town halls. It would always add another grace to an institution to have its home venerable with age and restored to beauty.[12]

The Ordnance Survey provided a crucial service to monumental remains through the workings of its place names and antiquities section. Henceforth, all identifiable sites of archaeological interest were captured as consistently as was possible on a country-wide map series, and many of them were covered in the epistolary record of John O'Donovan's field surveys. This, however, did little to counteract the depredations of time and the lithic-asset strippers identified by Davis. A major factor in the problem of neglected antiquities, as Davis well understood, was the fact that all ancient ecclesiastical sites were deemed to be in the possession of the Established Church, and that any change in this arrangement involved highly charged constitutional principles. When these principles were indeed drastically revised by the Irish Church Act of 1869 which disestablished the Church, historic sites not required by the Church of Ireland for its ministry were declared to be national monuments and were placed under the care of the Commissioners of Public Works. The list of national monuments has been greatly extended since then, but they remain in the charge of a department of state in each of the two jurisdictions on the island. As was the case two centuries ago, the needs of tourism, now vastly more extensive and more important, remain a crucial driving force in the interpretation and presentation of national monuments.

The slow emergence of a national museum to hold those portable arte-

---

[12] Thomas Davis, *Literary and Historical Essays* (Dublin, 1845), pp. 42, 47, 51.

facts deemed to be the heirlooms of the nation might be thought to reflect the conflict about whether, in nineteenth-century Ireland, the nation was Ireland or the United Kingdom, but more to the point was the aspiration of London bureaucrats to exercise control over government-funded scientific institutions. From an early stage it was the decided stance of a coterie of devotees of antiquities in Dublin that the Royal Irish Academy collection (with that of the Royal Dublin Society) was indeed a national deposit that ought to be recognised as worthy of location in a national museum. Such people included George Petrie, who progressed from drawing and painting monumental sites to their study and analysis. When Petrie fell behind in his plan to catalogue the RIA collection, the task was taken on by a medical doctor and polymath, William Wilde, the founding figure of Irish archaeology, who completed the task in three volumes by 1862. Another supporter of the national museum proposal was Rev. J.H. Todd of Trinity College. Indeed, the campaign can be seen as a striking example of individuals of Protestant faith and unionist political outlook evincing the strongest sense of Irish national identity. Officially recognised or not, the RIA collection was becoming a de facto national institution. It was in receipt of government funding for purchases, and from the 1850s it was taking on loan the antiquities of the RDS. A royal commission in 1868 gave all concerned the opportunity to make a formal case and heard Wilde demanding to see 'our great national collection of antiquities properly housed, safely guarded, scientifically arranged and displayed as a great Celtic museum'. With his collaborators he also wished to see it under Irish control.[13] In the event, these ambitions were thwarted by the designs of the Department of Science and Art, South Kensington, and what eventually emerged under legislation of 1877 was a Dublin Science and Art Museum in which the antiquities from the RIA would be accommodated alongside various scientific and geological collections. The purse strings would be controlled from South Kensington.[14]

If there was not yet to be a national museum by name, the 1877 Act had provided for the institution of the National Library of Ireland, an indication that the creation of an explicitly national institution was not itself a problem. The National Library's core collection was to come by purchase from the RDS, which body would nominate eight of the twelve trustees. Here is a striking example of an early eighteenth-century patriotic 'improving' society providing the basis, at the behest of the state, for a late nineteenth-century national institution. To take another angle, the emergence of the National Library, in principle open to all citizens, from the 'members only' facilities

---

[13] Elizabeth Crooke, *Politics, Archaeology and the Creation of a National Museum in Dublin: An Expression of National Life* (Dublin, 2000), pp. 113–14.

[14] Richard A. Jarrell, 'The department of Science and Art and the control of Irish science, 1853–1905' in *Irish Historical Studies*, xxiii, no. 2 (Nov. 1983), pp. 330–47; Dublin Science and Museum Act, 1877 (40 & 41 Vict., c. 234).

of the RDS, exemplifies the type of civic modernisation that is the stuff of nationalism. Twenty years earlier, the society had made another of its collections available to the public in the form of the Natural History Museum.

In the event, library and museum were housed in the purlieus of Leinster House in matching new buildings constructed during the second half of the 1880s. The museum still had some way to go before achieving formal national denomination. The British Museum had a vision of itself as possessing universal scope, not to mention a remit for the Empire and for the entire United Kingdom. After it acquired by purchase a very significant Bronze Age hoard discovered at Broighter, Co. Londonderry in 1896, there ensued a long-drawn-out test of the relative status of the British Museum and the Dublin Museum of Science and Art with respect to Ireland. Nationalist politicians did not miss the opportunity to make political hay at what was easily represented as an insult to Irish nationality. At this stage, polarisation was so far advanced, precisely on the issue of Ireland's status in the United Kingdom, that unionists might have been expected to support the claims of the imperial institution. In fact, many unionists joined in the demands for the repatriation of the hoard and it eventually was transferred to Dublin in 1906. Two years later the Dublin Museum of Science and Art, now with Count George Noble Plunket as director, was renamed the National Museum of Ireland. Since 1900 it had been under the control of the Dublin-based Department of Agriculture and Technical Instruction.[15] In latter times, the museum has acquired additional premises for an enhanced range of collections, but its core location is still on Kildare Street, where almost under one roof with the seat of government, the antiquities are displayed that constitute the mythic heirlooms of the nation. There, too, though not comparably lustrous, is a collection of memorabilia of the War of Independence (1916–21), the empowering myth of those who have ruled from Kildare Street since 1922.

Despite the folkloric aspects of the revival, the folk and popular cultural inheritance never achieved as central a role in Irish nationalism as was the case in other small European states, in particular the Nordic countries. Nation inventors in Northern Ireland not only saw the potential of a myth that was an alternative to divisive and inconclusive political issues, but they also received public funding at a level exceeding anything available in the South. The result was the creation of the Ulster Folk Museum (now the Ulster Folk and Transport Museum) opened in 1964 at Cultra, outside Belfast. The main feature of this impressive project is the reassembling in one location of examples of various vernacular building types translated from around the Province in the years when structures of the older types were fast disappearing. Like most good national museums it is at once a

---

[15] P.F. Wallace, 'The Museum: origins, collections and buildings' in P.F. Wallace and R. Ó Floinn (eds), *Treasures of the National Museum of Ireland: Irish Antiquities* (Dublin, 2002), p. 9.

political statement about nationality (in this case an assertion of the distinctiveness of Ulster), an ornament to the polity and a source of fascinating knowledge for the curious visitor.

In the South, vernacular buildings received no comparable attention and the curious have to look closely in the countryside to find surviving older farmhouses. However, the National Museum did form a collection of portable 'folklife' artefacts and these now form the nucleus of the Museum of Country Life at Turlough Park near Castlebar, Co. Mayo. This is a recent development: official interest in the South was directed over the decades less towards material 'folklife' and more towards oral folklore, which the Irish Folklore Commission was established in 1935, on earlier foundations, to collect and study. Its collection, assembled with some Nordic inspiration, is one of the largest of its kind in the world and is a monument to a team of dedicated and talented people, but in particular to a nation inventor of gigantic energy and vision, Séamus Ó Duilearga (1899–1980).[16] The commission's concentration on the Irish language and its native speakers was justified in objective terms, insofar as the concern was to capture the fragments of a disappearing way of life, but that scarcely justifies the Herderian notions about nationality that were involved. Whether the language on balance benefited from identification with the rescue of the past is another matter. The chances are that in time to come, the collection of the Irish Folklore Commission will yield up things beyond the imagining of its compilers. Here surely is an outstanding example of a national treasure that in fact has but limited bearing on nationality, but that would not exist but for the desire to edify the nation. In 1971 the commission became the Department of Irish Folklore at University College, Dublin.

As with the national museum, so too in the case of a national gallery of art, the time gap between initial impulse and achievement was considerable. In the heady years of the 1780s in Dublin, a proposal for a national gallery and an academy had been seriously considered, but had come to nothing. Subsequently, in 1823, the Royal Hibernian Academy was chartered: its fortunes suggest that in Dublin there was much interest in pictures, but too few clients willing and able to make purchases.

Fittingly, the individual principally identified with the successful effort to make art available to the public was the leading Irish railway entrepreneur, William Dargan. When an exhibition was held in Dublin from May to September 1853 in emulation of London's Great Exhibition of 1851, Dargan provided a subsidy which ensured that one third of the floor space was given over to painting and sculpture, and this arrangement was perceived to have contributed much to the success of the exhibition as a crowd-puller. A number of those associated with the committee that assembled the

---

[16] See Diarmuid Ó Giolláin, *Locating Irish Folklore: Tradition, Modernity, Identity* (Cork, 2000), pp. 114–41.

paintings and sculptures for the exhibition came together before the end of 1853 and set in place an association named the Irish Institution devoted to 'the formation of a permanent exhibition in Dublin and eventually of an Irish National Gallery'.[17] The librarian of the Royal Hibernian Academy, George Mulvany, was prominent in this group. The main articulator of the case seems to have been John Edward Pigot (1822–71), a lawyer and Trinity College graduate. A friend of Thomas Davis, he had been one of the most prolific writers of Young Ireland, and, as son of the chief baron, he had been the member of the group closest to the Irish establishment. Almost inevitably, George Petrie was drawn in. The others now emerging as members of this group pressing for a typical piece of nation invention included: the Irish lord chancellor, Maziere Brady; the chief baron, David Pigot; the Earl of Meath; and several other members of the nobility. An act providing for the establishment of a National Gallery was passed in 1854, and in 1855 parliament voted a contribution of six thousand pounds towards the cost of a building, which was eventually opened in 1864.

In 1908, Dublin was endowed with a gallery of modern art at the behest of Sir Hugh Lane (1875–1915), a brilliantly successful art dealer turned Maecenas, who wished the public to have access to his collection of thirty-nine Impressionist and post-Impressionist masterpieces and other recent works. Following a dispute with Dublin Corporation about permanent premises, Lane withdrew the pictures and altered his will so as to bequeath them to the National Gallery in London, before encountering similar problems there and redirecting his favour towards Dublin. However, the codicil recording the latter change of heart was not properly witnessed, so that, when he was lost with the other victims of the *Lusitania* disaster, the London gallery became the legal inheritor of the Lane collection. Needless to say, the London trustees could not easily alienate their fortuitous windfall, even if they had been so disposed. On the basis that moral right superseded legal right, Irish interests campaigned for the return of the Lane pictures, and the question slipped easily into the paradigm of Irish grievance and English perfidy. A happy resolution was achieved in 1960 when it was agreed that the pictures would rotate between London and Dublin.

The National Gallery of Ireland and the Hugh Lane Gallery of Modern Art (as it is now called) have in common the fact that they were founded to make available to the Irish public some of the best of international art, and that they came in due course to serve also as showcases for Irish art. As with national museums, visitors have come to expect a display of national achievement from national galleries. As elsewhere, the National Gallery of Ireland deals with the matter by arranging its exhibits according to national 'schools', of which the Irish is one. The self-esteem of the nation is thus served in two different ways: firstly, its own artistic achievement is dis-

---

[17]   Catherine de Courcy, *The Foundation of the National Gallery of Ireland* (Dublin, 1985).

played; and, secondly, its possession of a share of an internationally presti-
gious currency – the treasures of world art – is advertised. Needless to say,
the individual visitor generally goes to a gallery of any kind for aesthetic and
educational purposes, but we would scarcely have national galleries if they
did not also serve national ends.

In the 1840s Thomas Davis declared that 'to the picture-hunter we can
offer little, though Vandyke's finest portrait is in Kilkenny, and there is no
county without some collection', thereby showing that his phenomenal
knowledge of the country was not infallible, for the 'magnificent houses and
beautiful villas' were in his time endowed not only with 'decorated lawns
and pleasure grounds' that might be glimpsed from outside the walls, but
with treasures hidden from the eyes of the outsider, including an impressive
store of old masters. The passing of such treasures from private possession
to public repository is the very stuff of nation building. However, the agricultural recession of the late 1870s, followed by the land war and its political consequences, ended the prosperity of the Irish landed class abruptly
and, as it proved, definitively. Under the Settled Land Act of 1882 owners of
entailed property were enabled to dispose of house contents. Any attempt to
acquire these, whether pictures or other furnishings, for the public, was not
conceivable in the prevailing political climate. Thus Rembrandts and Cuyps,
El Grecos and Tintorettos made their way to new English and American
owners. So, the particular form that the overthrow of landlord power
assumed in Ireland impoverished a class (that could not in any case have
retained its position indefinitely in a democratising age) without achieving a
concomitant enrichment of the nation.[18]

Despite unpropitious circumstances, the National Gallery's holdings
expanded surely if unspectacularly throughout the second half of the nineteenth century. A boon was forthcoming in the early twentieth century with
the unaccustomed accession of a large and significant bequest from a landlord's estate, that of the Earl of Milltown. At the same time, Hugh Lane, as
a trustee from 1904 and director from 1914 to his death, was moving the
Gallery up several notches by international standards with a series of astute
and generous donations (not to be confused with his collection of nineteenth-century French works which became the subject of the controversy
mentioned above). For forty years or so following independence, governments displayed little appreciation of the Gallery as an instrument of
national self-advertisement or anything else. The rise from semi-obscurity
began only in the 1960s with the arrival of money from the residue of the
estate of George Bernard Shaw. Coincidentally, 1964 saw the appointment
of a new director, James White, whose qualifications included an entrepreneurial flair for engagement with the public not previously associated with

---

[18] Davis, *Essays*, p. 213; T.A. Dooley, *The Decline of the Big House in Ireland* (Dublin,
2001), pp. 21–2 and 107–11.

the position. In the 1960s, the numbers visiting the Gallery were lower than in the 1860s: by 1980, the year of White's retirement, the figure had increased tenfold. One factor in the change was undoubtedly the decline of the puritanism that had exercised hegemony over the outlook of lower-middle-class and middle-class people. Art has overtones of luxury and indulgence that make puritans of all persuasions uncomfortable, even if they are not consciously rejecting it. A moderation of politico-historical attitudes to the so-called 'ascendancy' was also coming into play.

Ironically, the developments that had largely precluded landlord benevolence towards the National Gallery had also rendered the Gallery and everything to do with 'pictures' suspect to the dominant mentality of the emerging nation. So, the same political divisions that had distracted the classes also alienated the masses, and hampered the National Gallery's ability to minister to national sentiment by the presentation of an acceptable narrative of national artistic achievement. The anti-landlord animus of Irish nationalism from the early 1880s was such that the inescapable dominance of aristocratic culture in eighteenth-century art rendered the latter unacceptable as part of a narrative of national achievement. And, as the scarcity of surviving Irish painting from before the eighteenth century was most conveniently (if not comprehensively) explicable by reference to 'wars and invasions' (the landlords again!), there was no healing in the story. As James White set about attracting the public, and the tourists, into the National Gallery, he faced the problem that, unlike the National Museum with the Ardagh chalice, and Trinity College Library with the Book of Kells, his displays did not provide a link with the ancient Irish past.[19] Under those circumstances, the Gallery found the commercial offer of some fragmentary frescoes supposedly from an eleventh-century church near Lyons to be irresistible, precisely because they depicted Irish-style animal symbols for the evangelists, as used in the Book of Kells, and so offered a link to the Golden Age, all the more alluring because it validated the sense of Irish glory in Europe. Having been acquired by the National Gallery and prominently displayed for several years, the frescoes have been withdrawn from public view for some time past. Whether or not the gallery was deceived by a hoax, what is of interest for present purposes is the compulsion to establish a link with ancient tradition in order to compete with rival traders in the national past. The episode might have provided Shaw with an intriguing plot. In any event, the royalties from what GBS did write continue to propel the fortunes of the National Gallery, and it marked the advent of the new millennium with a major extension that keeps it abreast of its international competitors. In terms of its facilities and its holdings of European paintings, the National Gallery is an outstanding ornament to the country.

The National Gallery is the main repository of extant Irish painting from

---

[19] Interview rebroadcast on 'Bowman on Saturday', RTÉ Radio One, 19 Jan. 2002.

the eighteenth century to about the middle of the twentieth. Under the rubric of 'eighteenth- and nineteenth-century Irish art', the material is arranged in six rooms, predominantly following a single chronological sequence with a minimum of interpretative intervention. Thus, wisely, once contentious issues such as what is 'Irish' and what 'Anglo-Irish', or otherwise alien, are not raised. 'Modern Irish art' (approximately 1900–60) is located nearby but apart, and treated rather differently: there is a much more didactic tone, with opinionated commentary, suggesting that controversy concerning stylistic taxonomy is manageable in a way that issues of nationality are not. All this means that the Gallery provides material, rather than answers, for the discussion of the implications of Irish art for Irish nationality. An even more open approach is adopted by Anne Crookshank and the Knight of Glin in *Ireland's Painters, 1600–1940* (New Haven and London, 2002), the standard published guide to the subject. While there is no replacing the impact of a gallery display, this book does have the advantage of a chapter on the seventeenth century and is particularly valuable for its access to items in private possession, many of which it reproduces in colour. Like Walter G. Strickland's *Dictionary of Irish Artists* (Dublin, 2 vols, 1913), this is the kind of work which creates a national canon, one of the classic modes of nation invention.

In the early 1840s, with his incisive grasp of nationality, and in his assumed role of nation inventor, Thomas Davis addressed himself to the question of creating a national school of art. He observed that Ireland had produced many painters, at least a few of whom had achieved a high reputation, including James Barry (1741–1806). Of living artists, Davis selected the painters Daniel Maclise (1806–70) and William Mulready (1786–1863) and the sculptor John Hogan (1800–57) as 'high names'. Intimating one role of a national gallery, Davis declared that the best work of Irish artists past and present should be assembled in Ireland and made known to the public: 'This is essential to our reputation and renown.'[20] While Davis referred approvingly to the Royal Hibernian Academy, he knew that it was in difficulty for lack of patronage, and he encouraged alternative forms of support, including the art union in which individuals of moderate means clubbed together to buy a painting which would then be raffled between them, and of which all might obtain an engraving. The rising generation of artists should be trained and rewarded: from the ensuing pool of excellence there might arise a 'great spirit'. Yet, Davis was thinking of national 'reputation and renown' being vindicated by excellence in common international modes. His presuppositions were decidedly classicist: advocating a society to provide Dublin with a set of casts to match those already available to students in Cork, he cited as models 'all the greatest works of Greece, Egypt, Etruria, Ancient Rome and Europe in the middle ages'. Such models were all

---

[20] Davis, *Essays*, p. 155.

the more necessary for the budding Irish artist because of the current defi-
ciencies of the population:

> [H]e has about him here an indifferently-made, ordinary, not very clean, nor pic-
> turesquely-clad people; though, doubtless, if they had the feeding, the dress and
> the education (for mind beautifies the body) of the Greeks, they would not be
> inferior, for the Irish structure is of the noblest order.[21]

But if the style was to be cosmopolitan, classical European, the results
would still be national by reason of the subject matter. Davis, in his typically
programmatic manner, passed on with approbation a list of suitable subjects, many accompanied by suggested reading, either scholarly or inspirational: Moore's *Melodies* is the single item most frequently cited. As far
back as 1790 Joseph Cooper Walker had produced such a list. The subjects
on Davis's adopted catalogue range from the mythical ('The landing of the
Milesians') to the hypothetical and optimistic ('The lifting of the Irish flags
of a national fleet and army'). Other suggestions include 'Nial and his nine
hostages', 'The first landing of the Danes' and 'Crowning of Edward
Bruce'.[22]

In the event a 'national art' in the sense of depiction of significant historical and mythological subjects was to have but a fitful existence. Instead, the
connotation of Irishness in art has been extraordinarily varied. True, the
Cork-born James Barry, so admired by Davis, is generally regarded as having pioneered Irish historical painting with his 1763 piece on the legendary
baptism of the king of Cashel by St Patrick. Although he subsequently
appears to have spent little time on Irish subjects while making a career in
London, apart from revisiting the Cashel episode around 1800, significant
Irish patriotic meanings have been discovered in his great European histori-
cal/mythological works.[23] Another Cork-born artist working at the top of
his profession in London, Daniel Maclise, turned his hand to the marriage
at Waterford in 1170 of Strongbow and Aoife, daughter of Dermot
McMurrough. The resulting canvas was exhibited in 1854 and is now in the
National Gallery of Ireland. The nuptials as depicted by Maclise are heavy
with symbolic doom at the triumph of the groom's Norman cohorts over
the bride's ancestral Gaelic order. A comprehensive list of Irish historical
paintings is scarcely feasible at this stage, but what is clear is that such subjects account for a small proportion of the painterly effort of Irish artists.[24]
On the other hand, popular history books, especially from the 1860s, are

---

[21] Davis, *Essays*, p. 160.

[22] Davis, *Essays*, pp. 169–72.

[23] Luke Gibbons, '"A shadowy narrator": history, art and romantic nationalism in Ireland,
1750–1850' in Ciaran Brady (ed.), *Ideology and the Historians* (Dublin, 1991),
pp. 99–127.

[24] See Fintan Cullen, *Visual Politics: The Representation of Ireland, 1750–1930* (Cork, 1997),
pp. 50–80 ('The roles of history painting').

often well provided with imaginative drawn illustrations, the quality inevitably varying from book to book.[25] In other words, there is a difference with respect to interest in nation-specific subjects between painting on the one hand and mass-produced representation on the other.

Treatment of contemporary politics parallels that of history. The great demonstration in support of the demand for free trade held by the Volunteers at College Green on 4 November 1779 was recorded, predictably with some licence, by Francis Wheatley on a huge canvas completed the following year and now in the National Gallery of Ireland (see illustration, p. 104).[26] This, however, proved to be a false dawn as far as painterly reportage was concerned, for few of the great political events of the following century and a half were to be similarly recorded. There was, of course, portraiture of political leaders.[27] And Irish political developments were visually depicted and trenchantly characterised in pamphlets, and especially from the 1840s in illustrated newspapers and journals, most notoriously in *Punch*. But painters in general stayed clear of political subjects. Only a surprisingly small number of extant paintings deal directly with the famine or the land war, whereas both were subjects of more substantial illustration in the press. This is not to miss the point that ostensibly non-political works can convey conscious and unconscious political stances and that silence can be eloquent in its own way.

The case of Aloysius O'Kelly (1853–c.1941) may serve to illustrate some of the points at issue here. Born in Dublin, O'Kelly was immersed in nationalist politics. His brother, James (1845–1916), a prominent young Fenian in the 1860s, became a noted journalist with the New York *Herald* and was a key figure in the rapprochement with Parnell in the late 1870s, becoming Parnellite MP for North Roscommon in 1880 and an Irish Parliamentary stalwart down to 1918. The younger brother made an unsuccessful attempt to win a seat for the South Roscommon constituency in 1897 and provided politically charged illustrations for the *Illustrated London News*. However, his portfolio of paintings signals little of his political commitments: many of his subjects are taken from Egypt, Brittany or the USA, while his several Irish titles include *Feeding Hens, West of Ireland* and the recently rediscovered *Mass in a Connemara Cabin*, and none of them is overtly political.[28] At the same time, it is not unreasonable to read some political preoccupations into his Irish paintings. Far from depicting his west of Ireland subjects as

---

25   See, for example, Martin Haverty, *The History of Ireland Ancient and Modern* (New York, 1867) with a frontispiece entitled 'High chamber of Tara: convention of the national assembly of Ireland' and many similar items following.

26   James Kelly, 'Francis Wheatley: his Irish paintings, 1779–83' in Dalsimer, *Visualising Ireland*, pp. 145–65.

27   Especially of O'Connell: see Fergus O'Ferrall, 'Daniel O'Connell, the "Liberator", 1775–1847: changing images' in Gillespie and Kennedy (eds), *Ireland: Art into History*, pp. 91–102.

28   Crookshank and the Knight of Glin, *Ireland's Painters*, pp. 258–60.

impoverished victims of either circumstances or repression, O'Kelly presents pictures of well-fed, well-shod sufficiency. Instead of being located in the kind of one-room hovel suggested by the term 'Connemara cabin', the station is taking place in what, if it had a larger window, might be the kitchen of a comfortable farmhouse in Kilkenny or Wexford. O'Kelly wants to trade on the exotic connotations of the western seaboard, but it is crucial to his wider political concerns to depict his specimens of the Irish populace as respectable and comfortable.

In the era of self-conscious cultural revivalism at the turn of the century, the question of a distinctively Irish art raised its head as it had in the 1840s.[29] An Irish version of the arts and crafts movements emerged, and in areas such as stained glass, embroidery and book production, the influence of 'Celtic' themes was adapted with some success. The arts and crafts movement brought into temporary focus the question of national costume, an area of nation invention in which Ireland was to remain significantly backward by comparison with the United Kingdom's standard setter, Scotland. His donning of the kilt was the symbolic high point of King George IV's visit to Scotland in 1821: he had no comparable gesture to make on his visit to Ireland the same year. Subsequently, the researches of Eugene O'Curry gave credence to the idea that the kilt might also be the 'native' dress of Ireland. The shape of garment apart, there was the question of what particular cloth was distinctively Irish. In the early years of the twentieth century, revivalists took to wearing kilts for special occasions, or to dressing in rather distinctive tweed suits. Others, including Douglas Hyde, affected outfits with knee breeches.[30] But, in general, the women of Ireland seem to have spurned Hyde's exhortation of 1892 that they should turn their hands to spinning 'comfortable frieze suits of their own wool' for the men of Ireland, rather than having them wear mass-produced English cloth.[31] Outside of the area of Irish dancing, no costume achieved the status of acknowledged expression of nationality. The most enduring legacy of the arts and crafts movement is in the outstanding stained-glass windows produced over half a century by three world-class artists: Michael Healy (1873–1941), Harry Clarke (1889–1931) and Evie Hone (1894–1955).

However, as far as painting was concerned, there was little attempt to rediscover an Irish tone or to take any lead from either the Gaelic sources or the folklore that were being utilised by the literary revivalists. The main impact of the new linguistic and literary cultures on painting was to intensify the identification of the west of Ireland (and particularly the Aran Islands) as the location of quintessential Irishness. At least since the 1820s,

[29] AE (George Russell), 'Nationality and cosmopolitanism in art', in *Some Irish Essays* (Dublin, 1906).
[30] Sheehy, *Rediscovery of Ireland's Past*, p. 148. Mary Colum, *The Life and the Dream* (Dublin, 1966), pp. 92–4.
[31] See note 29, p. 141 above.

certain painters, some of them such as George Petrie with cultural preoccupations, had been captivated by one aspect or another of the western seaboard. Jack B. Yeats (1871–1957), brother of the poet, had painted his *Man from Aranmore* in 1905. Around 1910, the Belfast-born Paul Henry (1877–1958) came from London to Achill at the behest of a literary friend, Robert Lynd, and stayed for seven years to create a series of inspirational landscapes that soon became emblems of the nation, highly acceptable to the newly independent state. One commentator has written that Henry:

> ... created or established a stereotype of the west of Ireland landscape, compounded of looming mountains, sudden, almost apparitional small lakes, peatbogs and thatched cottages, a kind of God's own country untouched by mechanisation, capitalism, urbanisation or materialism.[32]

This is to say that he was a very successful contributor to nation invention. In 1912, a native of Limerick city recently established as an art student in Dublin came to Inisheer, the smallest of the Aran Islands. This was Seán Keating (1889–1977) who began to depict, rather than landscape, people of exotic location and character who nevertheless were seen as the quintessence of the Irish race: one of his paintings is entitled *Race of the Gael*.

In the period immediately before and after the coming of political independence, established painters provided a modicum of art with explicit political reference. Jack B. Yeats painted several pictures between 1915 and 1924 on political subjects. During a long and celebrated career, Sir John Lavery (1856–1941) had painted politicians and churchmen from all sides before recording the funeral of Michael Collins in August 1922. Shortly afterwards, he contributed to a celebration of the new state a canvas, *Blessing the Colours*, depicting a mitred prelate, right hand aloft, standing dominantly over a kneeling Free State army officer holding the tricolour. A portrait of his American-born second wife, Hazel, was incorporated into the design of the new Irish currency notes that appeared in 1928. In the Revolutionary period, Seán Keating produced group portraits of IRA activists. As a supporter of the treaty, Keating set himself the task of recording on canvas the hoped-for emergence of a modern economy and society in the Irish Free State. His greatest opportunity in this respect was provided by the construction of the Shannon scheme between 1925 and 1929, and his most discussed painting, a quarter century after his death, is *Night Candles Are Burnt Out*, an allegory on the triumph of the new electrically powered order in the land. This was a remarkable transition from the cult of the primitive to the cult of progress, and one which state and society would make much more slowly than Keating. A number of others, such as Maurice McGonigal (1900–79), saw a role for themselves as artists in the celebration of the newly emergent polity, but state patronage was never sufficient to

---

[32] Brian Fallon, *Irish Art, 1830–1990* (Belfast, 1994), pp. 98–9.

make the option overly attractive, and the stylistic realism that went with the depiction of state-building, in Ireland as elsewhere in Europe, was increasingly unfashionable. Long before the middle of the century the greater part of Irish artistic endeavour was being invested elsewhere.[33]

Even if art is seldom entirely innocent of political implications, in a modern capitalist society artists have a strong incentive to keep their work clear of obvious partisan statement. This is well exemplified in the case of Ireland, where so many aspects of cultural life were denominationalised in the nineteenth century, but not to any significant extent artistic institutions.[34] At various times, schools, hospitals, newspapers, stagecoaches and even hotels have had their clients allocating themselves on a denominational basis, but not art galleries. This is not to say that people did not notice whom they rubbed shoulders with in coaches or viewing rooms or that confessional tensions did not exist in the Irish art world. Such tensions were part of the background to disputes such as those within the Royal Hibernian Academy in the 1930s in which one of Seán Keating's trump cards was his claim to be a 'national painter'.[35]

Probably none of the areas of cultural life examined in this book illustrates more fully than does art just how straightforward, and at the same time how multifaceted, nationality can be. Tackling the theoretical issue of Irish art in the early twentieth century, Thomas Bodkin made the point that post-Renaissance art is like a universal language.[36] It is indeed one in which, since the seventeenth century, Irish people have been expressing themselves. In general usage, Irish art comprehends the work of any Irish-born artist or of any artist born elsewhere working in Ireland. Futility follows any attempt to define Irish art in exclusive terms, for example by reference to the presumed ancestry or religion of the practitioner. To remain with the language analogy, various distinctive accents may have been developed in Ireland, but their speakers have no more claim on Irishness that those Irish-born people speaking accents developed in other countries, or using standard pronunciation, or people of non-Irish origin who have come to Ireland to express themselves in whatever tones. Thus, Francis Wheatley's *Volunteers* is Irish art, even though the artist was an Englishman who spent only a short period in Ireland. But the same canvas could surely be exhibited in an English gallery as an example of English art. In fact zero-sum notions of national affiliation are especially inadequate in the field of art. Much Irish art is also English art, Italian art or French art, because very many Irish-born artists

[33] See S.B. Kennedy, *Irish Art and Modernism, 1880–1950* (Belfast, 1991).
[34] See Cyril Barrett, 'Irish nationalism and art' in *Studies* (Winter 1975), pp. 393–410.
[35] Andy Bielenberg, 'Seán Keating, the Shannon scheme and the art of state-building' in *idem*, (ed.), *The Shannon Scheme and the Electrification of the Irish Free State* (Dublin, 2002), pp. 114–37.
[36] Thomas Bodkin, *Four Irish Landscape Painters* (Dublin, 1920), pp. x–xi, cited by S.B. Kennedy, 'An Irish school of art?: depictions of the landscape in a critical period, 1880–1930' in Carla King (ed.), *Famine, Land and Culture in Ireland* (Dublin, 2000), pp. 153–68.

spent some or all of their careers abroad. Dublin-born Hugh Douglas
Hamilton (1739/40–1808) received his artistic training in the schools of the
Dublin Society before spreading a distinguished career over periods in
London, Rome, Naples, and again Dublin. He was only one of at least ten
Irish people prominent in the arts or antiquities known to have been resi-
dent in Rome in the second half of the eighteenth century. Another was
Thomas Hickey (1741–1824), whose career as a painter took him from
Dublin to London, Bath, Rome, Lisbon, Calcutta, China (with Macartney's
expedition) and Madras.[37] London was the main destination of migratory
Irish artists in the first half of the nineteenth century, and from the 1850s to
the Great War, Irish-born painters, like those from all over northern
Europe, participated in droves in the fashion of going to perfect their craft
in northern France or Belgium.[38] They included such eminent names as
Frank O'Meara (1853–88), Walter Osborne (1859–1903), Roderick
O'Conor (1860–1940), Paul Henry (1876–1958), William John Leech
(1881–1968), Mary Swanzy (1882–1978) and Mainie Jellett (1897–1944).
An exception was William Orpen (1878–1931), who trained in London.[39]
From the early years of the twentieth century, the annual Oireachtas, under
the auspices of the Gaelic League, included an art exhibition. Unlike every
other area of cultural life covered by the Oireachtas, there was no expectation of a distinctive national tone in painting.

If national or local accents counted for little in the language of painting,
they could sometimes matter more in sculpture. Because so much sculpture
can betimes be commissioned for a public or semi-public location, rather
than made for the market, the preferences of patrons have to be served, and
if the patronage is adequate, the artist who is so inclined can even afford to
identify with these preferences, whether political or ideological. Nation
inventors have been prominent among the patrons of sculpture. Politically
charged public sculpture was ensconced in Dublin with the unveiling on
College Green in July 1701, on the eleventh anniversary of the Battle of the
Boyne, of an equestrian statue of King William III that bore a striking
resemblance to the famous antique Roman statue of the emperor Marcus
Aurelius located on the Campidoglio. The statue, by Grinling Gibbons, certainly made a powerful political statement about the outcome of the Irish
war of a decade before. Dublin Corporation was the source of funding, and
three centuries later, local authorities are again among the principal patrons
of public sculpture. However, since the 1970s, this is very seldom of a political or even broadly didactic character, but seeks to enrich the visual environment, often with abstract forms, in ways that delight the eye and surprise
the viewer. Thus, the public function of sculpture has come to be largely

[37] Crookshank and the Knight of Glin, *Ireland's Painters*, pp. 103–13, 129–42.
[38] Julian Campbell, *The Irish Impressionists: Irish Artists in France and Belgium, 1850–1914*
     (Dublin, 1984).
[39] Bruce Arnold, *Orpen: Mirror to an Age* (London, 1981).

assimilated to that of painting, as a form intended for a mixed audience and devised so as not, in a pluralist society, to presume to advocate any doctrine or offend any political sensibility – whatever about occasionally outraging some aesthetic tastes. Previously, there had been centuries of public sculpture as solemn statement, much of it intent on reinforcing or developing national sentiments.[40]

The sentiment behind Irish Protestant memorialising of William and his successors crystallised with the passage of time into patriotism and this, in its turn, represented Ireland in sculpture as an idealised woman, a device widely used elsewhere also and identified in the case of Ireland as Hibernia. When in 1809, Dublin acquired the famous pillar as a memorial to Admiral Nelson, much of the energy behind the scheme came from Dublin Protestants (there were also Catholic merchants involved) who wanted to make an assertion of Irish identity within the Empire, whose war effort against the French they supported so enthusiastically.[41] Thus, resentment of the Act of Union was a driving sentiment behind the construction of Nelson's pillar, a point that would lose its meaning in later political configurations. The first sculptor to emerge as an exponent of Catholic nationalism was John Hogan (1800–58). Trained initially in Cork, he went to Rome in 1824 and from there fulfilled numerous Irish commissions before settling in Dublin in 1849. Functioning within the neo-classical mode and predominantly with marble, Hogan created statues of O'Connell, Davis and numerous prominent churchmen and laity, mainly but not exclusively Catholics. He executed many religious and funerary pieces.[42] Hogan's commemorative monument to the famous Bishop James Warren Doyle of Kildare and Leighlin shows the prelate as protector of a dejected Hibernia and conveys a clear message about the role of the Catholic Church in Irish public life. One of his few works to have explicit Irish historical reference is *Hibernia and Brian Boroimhe [Boru]*. Dating from 1855, this represents Brian, the symbol in nationalist discourse of successful resistance to foreign rule, as a boy carrying a short sword and under the care of a crowned Hibernia.

A nationality broader than that represented by Hogan or O'Connell was vindicated in the late 1850s and the 1860s when statues of Thomas Moore (1853), Oliver Goldsmith (1864) and Edmund Burke (1868) were put in place, the latter two before the façade of Trinity College and the former on nearby College Street. This carried no implications of cultural, much less political, separateness – all three had spent most of their careers in England – but what it did suggest was the considerable momentum behind the idea

[40] Judith Hill, *Irish Public Sculpture: A History* (Dublin, 1998).

[41] Jacqueline R. Hill, *From Patriots to Unionists: Dublin Civic Politics and Irish Protestant Patriotism, 1660–1840* (Oxford, 1997), pp. 276–7.

[42] John Turpin, *John Hogan, Irish Neo-classical Sculptor in Rome, 1800–58: A Biography and Catalogue Raisonné* (Dublin, 1982).

of Ireland as a nation that should make a display of its famous offspring. The 1850s and 1860s marked an era of public statue provision at the core of the capital city that was nation-making without being politically charged. The Goldsmith and Moore statues were the work of John Henry Foley (1818–74), an Irishman who spent a brilliant career in London, much of it on commissions that paraded the glories of empire. He was also the creator of Dublin's monuments to two major figures in the nationalist political pantheon, Henry Grattan (College Green, 1876) and Daniel O'Connell (Sackville St., later O'Connell St., 1882). Both projects were nearly two decades in train and each involved a complex of political interests that changed over time. Like Foley, the Dublin-born John Hughes (1865–1941) accepted commissions from all sides. His bronze statue of Charles J. Kickham in Tipperary town (1898) was followed a decade later by the Queen Victoria memorial in the grounds of Leinster House. His subsequent Gladstone memorial intended for Dublin was not ready before the establishment of the Irish Free State and was diverted to Gladstone's former residence at Hawarden.[43]

Oliver Sheppard (1865–1941) and all the sculptors mentioned above worked in the recognised international styles of their periods. However, Sheppard was able, within the norms of the new Romantic-realist style he had learned in France, to incorporate themes suggested by the literary revival. Influenced like so many others by Standish O'Grady's history, he was already by the mid-1890s, while living in London, producing work on subjects derived from the world of ancient Irish legend.[44] Encouraged by W.B. Yeats, he returned to Dublin. In 1914 he exhibited in plaster *The Death of Cuchulainn,* derived from O'Grady's and Lady Gregory's accounts of the demise in battle of the hero of the *Táin.* As part of his plans to wrest the inheritance of Easter Week from the control of republican dissidents, de Valera chose to install *The Death of Cuchulainn* in the General Post Office as the official commemoration piece of the Rising. It was cast in bronze and its official inauguration in April 1935 was the centrepiece of an extended ceremony that also included an army parade: de Valera presided, with a large contingent of veterans and relatives of the executed signatories lined up to validate by their presence his claim to the mantle of 1916.

Notwithstanding his personal attachment to the ethos of the Irish revival and his success in translating it into plastic art, Sheppard was not identified with a single political outlook. For example, he was offered, and accepted, commissions from unionists and from the supporters of the old Parliamentary Party. The role of leading professedly nationalist sculptor in this period belonged to Albert G. Power (1881–1945), who

---

[43] John Turpin, 'Nationalist and unionist ideology in the sculpture of Oliver Sheppard and John Hughes, 1895–1939' in *Irish Review*, no. 20 (Winter/Spring 1997), pp. 62–75.
[44] John Turpin, *Oliver Sheppard (1865–1941), Symbolist Sculptor of the Irish Cultural Revival* (Dublin, 2000).

acquired a kind of quasi-official position with the governments of independent Ireland by reason of his participation in 1920 in a Sinn Féin plan
to obtain a likeness of the dying hunger striker Terence MacSwiney in
Brixton prison.[45] Subsequently, he enjoyed an amount of government
patronage, a situation that did not change when Fianna Fáil acceded to
office. One of his best known works is the 1935 statue of the Gaelic
author, Pádraig Ó Conaire (1935) in Eyre Square, Galway. Sheppard and
Power are both identified with the profusion of nationalist monuments
throughout provincial Ireland that began in the early twentieth century.
One of the best is Sheppard's 1798 pikeman memorial of 1905 in
Wexford.[46] The period 1914–23 provided numerous communities, North
and South, with cause for local memorialisation, whether it was the
exploits and fates of IRA men or the memory of the fallen in the Great
War. In the decades that followed, significant sculptors such as Seamus
Murphy (1907–75) and Yann Goulet (1914–99) contributed to the stock
of War of Independence memorials, but most examples were the work of
less gifted creators.

Perhaps the most elaborate and substantial memorial built in Ireland
since Neolithic times is the National War Memorial commemorating the
victims of World War I at Islandbridge to the west of Dublin city. Designed
by Lutyens and constructed at government expense in the 1930s, it enjoyed
government support under both W.T. Cosgrave and Eamon de Valera. This
could be evidence of the broadmindedness of these two veterans of Easter
Week. It may also say something about the electoral weight, especially in
Dublin, of those former Parliamentary Party and unionist supporters,
including ex-servicemen of all social classes, who were prepared to accept
the new order but not to disown their own recent past. But the site of the
memorial – actually chosen by Cosgrave – is redolent of marginalisation.
The location originally proposed by the advocates of the project was
Merrion Square, near government buldings, but the cabinet prevented this:
only the hegemonic cause could be celebrated in the 'monumental city'.[47]
When eventually, in 1966, the Garden of Remembrance was created as the
nation's tribute to those who fell in the approved national cause, it was
much less grand than and not so extensive as the National War Memorial.
But it was located in town, on Parnell Square, at the head of the unofficial
national ceremonial way which leads down by the Rotundo, thence past the
Parnell memorial (by Augustus St. Gaudens, 1911) and through O'Connell
St., past the General Post Office and statues of the temperance organiser
Father Matthew (1891), the trade unionist Jim Larkin (1979), the

[45] Sighle Bhreatnach-Lynch, 'The art of Arthur G. Power, 1881–1945: a sculptural legacy of
Irish-Ireland' in Gillespie and Kennedy, *Ireland: Art into History*, pp. 118–31.
[46] Gary Owens, 'Nationalist monuments in Ireland, *c*.1870–1914: symbolism and ritual' in
Gillespie and Kennedy, *Ireland: Art into History*, pp. 103–17.
[47] Hill, *Irish Public Sculpture*, pp. 160–1.

O'Connellite and town improver, Sir John Gray (1879) and the Young Irelander, William Smith O'Brien (1870), to the O'Connell monument, and across O'Connell Bridge to the focal point of College Green, with the option of going by way of Dawson Street and the Mansion House, or Kildare St. and Leinster House, to St Stephen's Green with its own diffuse outdoor gallery of poets and patriots. It is a route used more for public demonstrations than for displays of state power.

The delay in instituting the Garden of Remembrance typifies the laissez-faire (and penny-pinching) approach of the Government to the provision of nationalist memorials. A similarly reactive attitude was evident in its approach to existing monuments that clashed with the nationalist ethos. The statue of Queen Victoria continued to preside over deputies as they entered and left Leinster House, until it was eventually removed in 1948. Other centrally located monuments offensive to hegemonic nationalist sentiment remained in place until picked off one after another by republican activists, whereupon the Government either finished the job or just cleared the debris and accepted the fait accompli. The statue of William III went in 1929, after the last in a series of attacks going back nearly a century. Explosive attacks removed George II from St Stephen's Green in 1937 and Lord Nelson from O'Connell St. in 1966. In 1945, in connection with the centenary of Thomas Davis's death, it was decided that he would have a permanent memorial on the former site of the statue of William of Orange, something that came to pass only in 1966. Since independence, there had been endless discussion of putting an effigy more in line with dominant pieties in place of Nelson atop the well-loved pillar. The Blessed Virgin, the Sacred Heart, St Patrick, Brian Boru, Wolfe Tone and Patrick Pearse were among the more strongly supported contenders. At no time was it likely that public authority in independent Ireland would intervene to demote the admiral, even though on his perch he overshadowed the precincts of the General Post Office hallowed by the events of Easter Week, 1916. Praiseworthy though this reticence in the imposition of hegemony may have been in some respects, it provided less circumspect nation inventors with a pretext to destroy both statue and pillar. In January 2003, the site, the focal point of the capital city, was given over to a steel spire one hundred and twenty metres high. Like the pillar it is a visually pleasing landmark out of scale with its surroundings, an up-to-the-minute gimmick and an assertion of both civic and national pride by the Dublin city authorities. But unlike its predecessor by two centuries it exalts no hero and bears no text.

The attitude of the governments of independent Ireland to imperial statuary paralleled their attitude to public demonstrations of pre-independence loyalties, particularly Armistice Day parades, which was one of great tolerance somewhat vitiated by an unwillingness to face down self-appointed upholders of the republican ethos who frequently behaved most intolerantly.[48] Similarly, the authorities were ineffectual in dealing with the Trinity College students who in the 1920s took advantage of the College's strategic location to sally forth on 11 November and endeavour to enforce observance of Armistice Day. In the context of conflict between ex-servicemen and republicans, in which a factor was the wide popularity among the population of wearing the British Legion poppy, a republican counterpart was invented in the early 1920s – the Easter lily.[49]

In Northern Ireland, imperial war commemoration focusing on the poppy and the Armistice Day ceremonies was an official cult, with numerous local war memorials erected as its shrines, the counterparts of the multiplying War of Independence memorials in the South. (There were also several local monuments in the South to the dead of the Great War.) Along with the memorials went versions of the cult of the cemetery. For those who commemorated the Great War, the war cemeteries in France and Belgium became places of piety. Nationalist Ireland already possessed its outdoor pantheon, Prospect Cemetery, Glasnevin. The Cemetery is in the first instance a product of the liberal aspect of the O'Connellite inheritance, even its name being suggestive of non-denominational vision. Set up in the early 1830s by a subsidiary of the Catholic Association to provide for those who resented having to defer to ministers of the Established Church when burying their dead in the old city churchyards, it accommodated those who could afford to pay a substantial fee for more attractive surroundings and rationally organised facilities. Contrary to the intentions of others of the initiators, O'Connell insisted that the Cemetery would be open to those of all denominations. O'Connell's own interment there in 1847 gave Glasnevin national status. When Irish-American activists brought the remains of the Young Irelander, Terence Bellew MacManus, home for burial in 1861 they envisaged interment alongside Wolfe Tone at Bodenstown, but their Irish collaborators secured a grave in Glasnevin instead. The burial of Parnell there in 1891 confirmed its status. In August 1922, Arthur Griffith and Michael Collins were interred at Glasnevin with all the solemnity that the new regime could muster.

If Glasnevin was the resting place of the more recently fallen, Bodenstown was the holiest place of republican pilgrimage. As in so much else, the impetus came from Davis, although the tussle between rival factions which came to mark the annual Wolfe Tone commemoration was less reminiscent of his philosophy than was the tolerant ethos of Prospect Cemetery.[50] The cult and

---

48 F. McGarry, '"Too damned tolerant?" Republicans and Imperialism in the Irish Free State' in *idem, Republicanism in Modern Ireland* (Dublin, 2003), pp. 61–85; Jane Leonard, 'The twinge of memory: Armistice Day and Remembrance Sunday in Dublin since 1919' in Richard English and Graham Walker (eds), *Unionism in Modern Ireland: New Perspectives on Politics and Culture* (Dublin, 1996), pp. 99–114.
49 Ann Matthews, unpublished paper.
50 C.J. Woods, 'Tone's grave at Bodenstown: memorials and commemorations, 1798–1913' in Dorothea Siegmund-Schultze (ed.), *Irland: Gesellschaft und Kultur VI* (Halle, 1989), pp. 138–48.

care of 'patriot' (that is to say, republican) graves at Glasnevin and elsewhere throughout the land was taken in hand by the National Graves Association, a voluntary body founded in 1926 with the same sense of mission as the associations that did similar work in respect of the dead of either side in the American Civil War. Soon a 'republican plot' came to mean not a threat of coup d'état but a well-tended green corner in a cemetery. At a time when attractive presentation of public spaces was not a major preoccupation of those in authority, the NGA set the headline for an instance of a wider patriotism. The canonising function of the NGA is best exemplified in its 1932 publication, *The Last Post*, which set out to list for the Dublin area the resting places of the known patriot dead of the period 1916–23. In subsequent editions, the spatial scope became nationwide and the temporal limits were pushed back to include the United Irishmen. In its unquestioning assumption about the propriety of commemorating 'our own' to the exclusion of others, the NGA was no more chauvinistic than similar associations in the USA, France or the United Kingdom.

A subsidiary preoccupation of the NGA was the renaming of public places in honour of nationalist/republican heroes. For in this, as in other areas, independence brought but a limited level of erasure of the inheritance of the imperial past. The street on the north side of Trinity College happened to be the birthplace of Patrick Pearse and had its name changed from Great Brunswick Street to Pearse Street, but outside the south wall, Nassau Street with its Williamite connotation retained its title. Existing law requiring ratepayers and residents to be balloted on a proposed change of street name put a brake on the ambitions of prescriptive nationalisers. Altered or not, all street names and all destinations on signposts were now displayed in Irish and English. Thus Victoria Villas remained as such but was also henceforward known officially as Bailtíní Buadha. There could be interesting variations on the general pattern. In Listowel, County Kerry, a town where the proprietor, the Earl of Listowel, retained substantial influence, the nationally minded town council combined the existing names in English with a set of changed names in Irish, so that, for example, William Street remained William Street but became simultaneously Sráid an Phiarsaigh (Pearse Street). As with changing what was already named, so in naming new developments, independent Ireland paid its respects to ideology but only up to a point. Typically, public authority estates would be named after Emmet, Pearse or Tone, or another mythic figure of national politics or culture, while most of the councillors who did this naming lived themselves, like other middle-class people, in developments with bland names that would sit comfortably in any American suburb. As with paintings, so too with houses, identification with any obtrusive expression of nationality can be detrimental to value in the market place. Approaching the end of a book like this, it is good to be reminded that, while nationalism may seem to be all-pervasive, there are limits to the areas of life over which it holds sway.

Variations on the relationship between nation and artefact are exemplified in the cases of Eileen Gray (1878–1976) and Alfred Chester Beatty (1875–1968). Born in Co. Wexford and trained in London, Gray became one of the most celebrated of modern designers during a long career, spent mainly in France, of which her homeland was largely oblivious. Recently the National Museum has acquired her archive and effectively 'reclaimed' her for Ireland. From a global perspective, the jewel among Irish cultural institutions is the Chester Beatty Library, the presence of which in the country is largely fortuitous, the American-born collector having moved to Ireland from Britain after the turn to socialism there in 1945, and having subsequently been assiduously courted by politicians. The collection includes some of the most significant manuscripts and miniature paintings from each of the great religions and literary cultures of the Near East and Asia. Here is a great Irish institution with no pretensions to essential Irishness.

The Sinn Féin movement from 1916 onwards marked its difference from the incumbent nationalist elite by adopting some changes in symbols. The green flag was replaced as the preferred standard of nationalism by the tricolour of green, white and orange that had previously been adopted briefly in 1848 and now became the flag of independent Ireland. For sung expression at high moments, Sinn Féiners set themselves apart by the use of 'The soldier's song' composed in 1907 by Peadar Kearney. This was distinctive only in the sense that it was chosen as a badge by a distinct group. Apart from a few stock phrases in Irish, there is little about it stylistically to distinguish it from T.D. Sullivan's 'God save Ireland' composed in 1867 and generally used as an anthem by the supporters of the Irish Parliamentary Party, nor indeed from Thomas Davis's 'A nation once again'. In terms of diction and sentiment all are derivative of Moore's *Melodies*. In 'The soldier's song' the 'despot' rules over the 'slave' in an 'Ireland' that rhymes with 'sireland'. Republican attachment to this anthem suggests caution with respect to the surmise that the revolutionaries were imbued with the sensibility and spirit of the literary revival. Its eventual adoption as the national anthem in 1926 may have been somewhat reluctant: before that the Free State had been using 'God save Ireland', but republican enforcers were intimidating cinema managers into playing the music of their preferred anthem at the conclusion of performances. At this point, a translation into Irish was adopted, and that is now almost invariably used in preference to the original words.

As far as visual icons of Irishness were concerned there was a noticeable reaction in the Free State against the hackneyed. The determination to avoid kitsch and also to steer clear of historical personages and historic settings led to the adoption for the new currency of a series of animal and bird figures. But 'Celtic' design remained in official favour, especially for prestige printing projects. While round towers, wolfhounds and shamrocks fell somewhat foul of official taste as arbitrated by such as Thomas Bodkin and

Figure 8.2 Engraved frontispiece of *O'Connell Centenary Record, 1875* (Dublin, 1878). This is a remarkable confection of images of Irish nationality, including round tower, 'Celtic' cross, wolfhound, maid of Erin with harp, 'Celtic' decoration of capitals and the use of Gaelic-style lettering for English words. The crown is a study in layered ambiguity. Is it intended for O'Connell's head, or not? In design it incorporates the serrated rim of the legendary 'Milesian' crown – associated with assertions of Irish independence since the eighteenth century – and the domed structure of the British crown. The surrounding sunburst effect is reminiscent of [American-based] Fenian iconography of the late 1860s.

W.B.Yeats, the harp, now without the crown, retained its venerable standing as an emblem of the state when, in late 1922, it was adopted for the
great seal of the Irish Free State.[51] Depicted in classic modern lines on the
obverse of the new coinage, its acceptability was never questioned. Used
since 2001 on the Irish minting of the euro coinage, it is possibly the most
visually effective of all the national symbols so employed. Adopted and
adapted for the logos of various enterprises, the harp is in the realm of artefacts what St Patrick is in the realm of historical personages, an almost universally recognised and unthreatening icon of Irish nationality.

Appropriately, however, the iconography of the harp as pre-eminent
national symbol replicates some of the dominant paradigms of all nation
invention. When it was first depicted on coinage in the sixteenth century, the
minting was done in London by people who had a general conception of the
harp but no knowledge of the particular characteristics of the Irish harp.
'Thus', Barra Boydell has written, 'the first widespread use of the harp as the
symbol of Ireland depicted the instrument, not as it was known in Ireland,
but according to the preconceptions of outsiders.'[52] It might have been an
omen. In subsequent centuries every conceivable artistic licence was taken in
the depiction of the Irish harp by those who did and those who did not have
an awareness of its specific features. In the search for authenticity, the
authorities of the Irish Free State decided that their image of the Irish harp
should be drawn from the oldest surviving example, a late medieval artefact
at Trinity College. The outcome of the new Irish government's initiative has
been summarised as follows:

> This design is modelled on the Trinity College harp but is more slender than the
> instrument appears today: when the Trinity College harp first came to antiquar-
> ian notice two hundred years ago it was in a damaged condition; shortly after
> 1840 the harp was poorly restored, resulting in the more slender shape that it
> retained until its expert restoration by the British Museum in 1961. Thus the
> model for the modern state's official symbol is in fact a poor nineteenth-century
> restoration.[53]

Here, surely, is an appropriate metaphor for nation invention, and not only
in Ireland.

---

[51] David Fitzpatrick, *The Two Irelands, 1912–39* (Oxford, 1998), p. 138.
[52] Barra Boydell, 'The iconography of the Irish harp as a national symbol' in P.F. Devine and
       Harry White (eds), *The Maynooth International Musicological Conference, 1995: Selected
       Proceedings, part two* (Dublin, 1996) (Irish Musical Studies, 5), pp. 131–45, at p. 133.
[53] Ibid, p. 145.

Conclusion

Jimmy O'Dea (1899–1965), the leading Dublin stage comedian of his era (and, incidentally, a long-time acquaintance of Seán Lemass) is generally credited with a quip about the harp being the appropriate symbol of Ireland because of its being an instrument operated by pulling strings. This witticism can serve as a useful reminder of things too easily overlooked in the study of ideology and culture, particularly the fact that manoeuvring for survival and advancement of self and family through access to material resources and socio-political advantage is the great constant of history. In this, Ireland is no different from anywhere else, so that any account of the country, past or present, runs the risk of abstraction if it loses sight of the struggle for land, and jobs, and places to live, or of the need to win friends and influence people in society. This is as applicable to the Ireland of the early Christian 'golden age' as to all of the less idealised ages that followed. The development of nationality and of nationalism is bound up with such gross concerns – specifically in Ireland the struggle for land – to an extent that the study of ideology tends to minimise.

Culture describes the particular patterned modes in which people address the perpetual material challenge as well as those in which they expend surplus time and resources. (There is no clear dividing line between the two.) Thus, culture is ontologically and temporally prior to nationality: there is culture – high, low and in-between – before there is national culture. But, of the various types of collective formation that shape the ebb and flow of human endeavours, the nation is now almost universal in its global occurrence and, within most societies, its reach is deep and wide, although never exclusive. One of the principal concerns of this book has been to explore the ways in which, in the case of Ireland, large tracts of cultural life have become 'national', frequently through appropriation of segments of universal phenomena that happen to fall within the island, but also by way of initiatives intended to create culture as 'national'. For either process, or when, as so often happens, they are inextricably linked, the appropriate description is invention.

Essentialist concepts of the nation support a Platonic notion of national culture. From that perspective many of the items in the category of nationality, that are, in fact, contingent and accidental, are deemed to be emanations of a supposed national spirit. Herderian theory follows on with assertions about 'national character' and 'the genius of the people'. Thus is the ground laid for difference between nationalities to be rationalised in the essentialising terms of heredity and race. Even if they eschew the latter step of the argument, some of those discoursing on the 'Irishness', 'Irish culture' and 'Irish identity' questions, even until quite late in the twentieth century, seem to work from assumptions about national essences and indefeasible culture. One sure indicator of this mind-set is a tendency to ascribe agency to 'the Irish people', and to write history or cultural criticism in the first person plural, as if there were some immanent 'general will' at work throughout the land.

This book has attempted to explore nationality on a very different basis. Acknowledging the antiquity of the national category in respect of Ireland, as in many other cases, it presents the contents of this category as having no essential common character, but suggests that they are, rather, the contingent and ever-changing products of time, place, opportunity and 'construction'. In this scheme of things the music of William Vincent Wallace, or U2, is as Irish as that of Seán Ó Riada; the Irish hockey team and what they play are as Irish as the Galway Gaelic football team and what they play; 'Castle Dawson' is as Irish a placename as 'Dún Chaoin'; Hillsborough Castle is as Irish a venue as Pearse's cottage in Rosmuc; and a baby born yesterday in the Rotunda Hospital to a Nigerian asylum-seeker is no less Irish than the oldest native speaker in Connemara. Such a perspective is of little use for the purposes of chauvinist nationalism or intransigent unionism. But it is, arguably, a better key to understanding the fascinating wealth, the ever-changing complexity, the infinite variety and the endless contradictions of a long-existing nationality such as Ireland's. One book cannot explore more than a small selection of these riches.

Further reading and reference

General surveys

Publication of the most comprehensive survey of the history of Ireland yet attempted is nearing completion. This is 'A New History of Ireland', published by Oxford University Press. It provides narrative coverage and also treatment of various aspects of social and cultural history.

Ó Cróinín, Dáibhí (ed.), *i: Prehistoric and Early Ireland*, Oxford, due 2003.
Cosgrove, Art (ed.), *ii: Medieval Ireland, 1169–1534*, Oxford, 1987.
Moody, T.W., Martin, F.X. and Byrne, F.J. (eds), *iii: Early Modern Ireland, 1534–1691*, Oxford, 1976.
Moody, T.W. and Vaughan, W.E. (eds.), *iv: Eighteenth-century Ireland, 1691–1800*, Oxford, 1986.
Vaughan, W.E. (ed.), *v: Ireland Under the Union i, 1801–1870*, Oxford, 1989.
Vaughan, W.E. (ed.), *vi: Ireland Under the Union ii, 1870–1921*, Oxford, 1996.
Hill, J.R. (ed.), *vii: Ireland, 1921–1984*, Oxford, due 2003.

The following is a selection of standard works:

Bardon, Jonathan, *A History of Ulster*, Belfast, 1992.
Barnard, T.C., *Cromwellian Ireland: English Government and Reform in Ireland 1649–60*, Oxford, 1975.
Bartlett, Thomas, *The Rise and Fall of the Irish Nation: the Catholic Question, 1690–1830*, Dublin, 1992.
Beckett, J.C., *The Making of Modern Ireland, 1603–1923*, London, 1966.

Boyce, D.G., *Nationalism in Ireland*, London, 1982.

Boyce, D.G., *Nineteenth-century Ireland: The Search for Stability*, Dublin, 1990.

Brady, C. and R. Gillespie, *Natives and Newcomers: Essays on the Making of Irish Colonial Culture*, Dublin, 1986.

Brown, Terence, *Ireland: A Social and Cultural History, 1922–85*, Dublin, new edn., 1985.

Buckland, Patrick, *A History of Northern Ireland*, Dublin, 1981.

Canny, Nicholas, *From Reformation to Restoration: Ireland, 1534–1660*, Dublin, 1987.

Canny, Nicholas, *Making Ireland British, 1580–1650*, Oxford, 2001.

Connolly, S.J., *Religion, Law and Power: the Making of Protestant Ireland, 1660–1760*, Oxford, 1992.

Corish, Patrick J., *The Irish Catholic Experience: a Historical Survey*, Dublin, 1986.

Cullen, L.M., *The Emergence of Modern Ireland, 1600–1900*, London, 1981.

Curtis, Edmund, *A History of Ireland*, London, 1950.

Daly, Mary, *Social and Economic History of Ireland Since 1800*, Dublin, 1981.

Dickson, David, *New Foundations: Ireland, 1660–1800*, Dublin, 1987.

Duffy, Seán, *The Concise History of Ireland*, Dublin, 2000.

Elliott, Marianne, *The Catholics of Ulster: a History*, London, 2000.

Ellis, S.G., *Ireland in the Age of the Tudors, 1447–1603: English Expansion and the End of Gaelic Rule*, London, 1998.

Fanning, Ronan, *Independent Ireland*, Dublin, 1983.

Fitzpatrick, David, *The Two Irelands, 1912–39*, Oxford, 1998.

Flanagan, M.T., *Irish society, Anglo-Norman Settlers, Angevin Kingship: Interactions in Ireland in the Late Twelfth Century*, Oxford, 1989.

Foster, R.F. (ed.), *The Oxford Illustrated History of Ireland*, Oxford, 2000.

Foster, R.F., *Modern Ireland, 1600–1972*, London, 1988.

Frame, Robin, *Colonial Ireland, 1169–1369*, Dublin, 1981.

Harkness, David, *Northern Ireland Since 1920*, Dublin, 1983.

Hoppen, K.T., *Ireland Since 1800: Conflict and Conformity*, London, 1989.

Jackson, Alvin, *Ireland, 1798–1998: Politics and War*, Oxford, 1999.

Kee, Robert, *The Green Flag: A History of Irish Nationalism*, London, 1972.

Keogh, Dermot, *Twentieth-century Ireland: Nation and State*, Dublin, 1994.

Kelly, James, *Prelude to Union: Anglo-Irish Politics in the 1780s*, Cork, 1992.

Lee, J.J., *The Modernisation of Irish Society, 1848–1918*, Dublin, 1973.

Lee, J.J., *Ireland, 1912–1985: Politics and Society*, Cambridge, 1989.

Leighton, C.D.A., *Catholics in a Protestant Kingdom: a Study of the Irish Ancien Régime*, Basingstoke, 1994.

Lennon, Colm, *Sixteenth-century Ireland: The Incomplete Conquest*, Dublin, 1994.

Lydon, J.F., *Ireland in the Later Middle Ages*, Dublin, 1973.

Lydon, James, *The Making of Ireland: From Ancient Times to the Present*, London, 1998.

Lyons, F.S.L., *Ireland Since the Famine*, London, 1971.

Mac Niocaill, Gearóid, *Ireland Before the Vikings*, Dublin, 1972.

Moody, T.W. and Martin, F.X. (eds), *The Course of Irish History*, Cork, 1984.

Murphy, J.A., *Ireland in the Twentieth Century*, Dublin, 1975.

Murphy, James H., *Abject Loyalty: Nationalism and Monarchy in Ireland During the Reign of Queen Victoria*, Cork, 2001.

Nicholls, K.W., *Gaelic and Gaelicized Ireland in the Later Middle Ages*, Dublin, 1972.

O'Beirne Ranelagh, John, *A Short History of Ireland*, Cambridge, 1983.

O'Brien, Máire and Conor Cruise, *A Concise History of Ireland*, London, 1972.

Ó Corráin, Donnchadh, *Ireland Before the Normans*, Dublin, 1972.

Ó Gráda, Cormac, *A New Economic History of Ireland, 1780–1939*, Oxford, 1994.

Ó Gráda, Cormac, *A Rocky Road: The Irish Economy Since the 1920s*, Manchester, 1997.

Ó Tuathaigh, Gearóid, *Ireland Before the Famine, 1798–1848*, Dublin, 1972.

O'Farrell, Patrick, *England and Ireland Since 1800*, London, 1975.

O'Farrell, Patrick, *Ireland's English Question: Anglo-Irish Relations, 1534–1970*, London, 1971.

Stewart, A.T.Q., *The Narrow Ground: Aspects of Ulster, 1609–1969*, London, 1977.

Townshend, Charles, *Political Violence in Ireland: Government and Resistance Since 1848*, Oxford, 1983.

Travers, Pauric, *Settlements and Divisions: Ireland, 1870–1922*, Dublin, 1989.

Works of reference and documentation

Volumes viii and ix of *A New History of Ireland* are major works of reference. The ancillary volumes to the series are also essential reference words.

Moody, T.W., Martin, F.X. and Byrne, F.J., *A New History of Ireland, viii: A Chronology of Irish History to 1976*, Oxford, 1982.

Moody, T.W., Martin, F.X. and Byrne, F.J., *A New History of Ireland, ix: Maps, Genealogies, Lists*, Oxford, 1984.

Vaughan, W.E. and Fitzpatrick, A.J. (eds), *Irish Historical Statistics: Population, 1821–1971*, Dublin, 1978.

Walker, B.M., *Parliamentary Election Results in Ireland, 1801–1922*, Dublin, 1978.

Walker, B.M., *Parliamentary Election Results in Ireland, 1918–92*, Dublin, 1992.

The Dictionary of National Biography provides very substantial coverage of Irish subjects. A *Dictionary of Irish Biography* is in preparation under the editorship of Mr James Maguire and is due for publication by Cambridge University Press in 2006.

The following is a selection of key items:

Boylan, Henry, *A Dictionary of Irish Biography*, Dublin, revised edn., 1998.

Breathnach, D. and M. Ní Mhurchú (ed.), *Beathaisnéis*, 6 vols, Dublin, 1986–2003.

Buckland, Patrick, *Irish Unionism, 1885–1923: A Documentary History*, Belfast, 1973.

Connolly, S.J. (ed.), *The Oxford Companion to Irish History*, Oxford, 1998.

Crookshank, Ann and the Knight of Glin, *Ireland's Painters*, New Haven, 2002.

Crowley, Tony (ed.), *The Politics of Language in Ireland, 1366–1922*, London, 2000.

Curtis, Edmund and McDowell, R.B. (eds), *Irish Historical Documents, 1172–1922*, London, 1943.

Fanning, Ronan, et al., *Documents on Irish Foreign Policy, vol. 1: 1919–22*, Dublin, 1998.

Field Day Anthology, 5 vols, Cork, 1991–2003.

Hepburn, A.C., *Ireland, 1905–25, vol. 2: Documents and Analysis*, Newtownards, 1998.

Mac Gréil, Mícheál, *Prejudice and Tolerance in Ireland*, Dublin, 1977.

Mac Gréil, Mícheál, *Prejudice in Ireland Revisited*, Maynooth, 1996.

Mahr, A. and Raftery, J. (eds), *Christian Art in Ancient Ireland*, 2 vols, Dublin, 1932–41.

Mitchell, Arthur and Ó Snodaigh, Pádraig (eds), *Irish Political Documents, 1869–1916*, Dublin, 1989.

Mitchell, Arthur and Ó Snodaigh, Pádraig (eds), *Irish Political Documents, 1916–1949*, Dublin, 1985.

O'Day, Alan and Stevenson, J., *Irish Historical Documents Since 1800*, Dublin, 1992.

Vallely, Fintan (ed.), *The Companion to Irish Traditional Music*, Cork, 1999.
Welch, Robert, *The Oxford Companion to Irish Literature*, Oxford, 1996.

Since 1938 *Irish Historical Studies* has provided comprehensive coverage of new publications in an annual (latterly biennial) listing entitled 'Writings on Irish History'. *Irish Economic and Social History* has published an annual 'Select bibliography of writings on Irish economic and social history' since 1974.

With funding from the Irish Research Council for the Humanities and Social Sciences, a committee led by Professor Jacqueline Hill at NUI, Maynooth will, over the period 2003–6, make 'Writings on Irish History' available in online searchable database format free to users. Some material will become accessible by stages via www.historians.ie from summer 2005 onwards.

Index